500
Delicious
dinners

500
Delicious dinners

One Pots, Pasta, Slow cooker, Casseroles, Roasts & more

This edition published by Parragon Books Ltd in 2014
LOVE FOOD is an imprint of Parragon Books Ltd

Parragon Books Ltd
Chartist House
15–17 Trim Street
Bath BA1 1HA, UK
www.parragon.com/lovefood

ISBN: 978-1-4723-5130-2

Printed in China

Project Managed by Kerry Starr
Cover and Internal Design by Beth Kalynka
Cover Photography by Ian Garlick
New Internal Photography by Mike Cooper
New Internal Home Economy by Lincoln Jefferson
New Recipes by Christine France and Robin Donovan
Introduction text by Anne Sheasby
Edited by Fiona Biggs

Notes for the Reader
This book uses both metric and imperial measurements. Follow the same units of measurement
throughout; do not mix metric and imperial. All spoon measurements are level: teaspoons are
assumed to be 5 ml, and tablespoons are assumed to be 15 ml. Unless otherwise stated, milk is
assumed to be full fat, eggs and individual vegetables are medium, and pepper is freshly ground
black pepper. Unless otherwise stated, all root vegetables should be peeled prior to using.

Garnishes, decorations and serving suggestions are all optional and not necessarily included in the
recipe ingredients or method. The times given are an approximate guide only. Preparation times
differ according to the techniques used by different people and the cooking times may also vary
from those given. Optional ingredients, variations or serving suggestions have not been included
in the time calculations.

The publisher would like to thank iStock for the use of images on chapter openers.

Contents

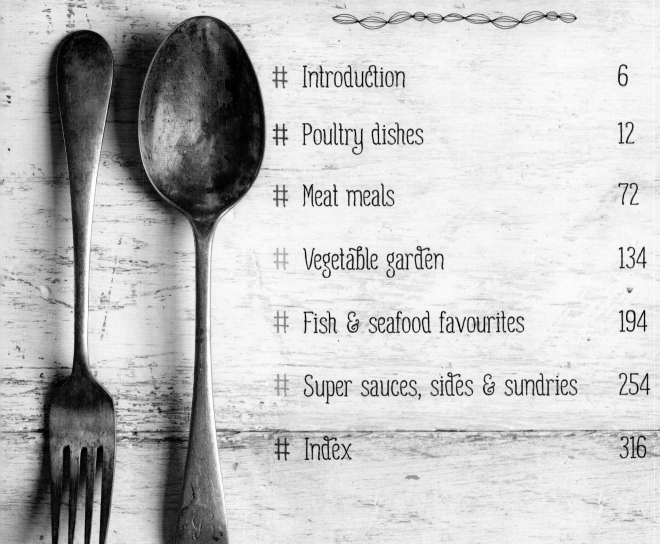

Introduction

This beautiful cookbook encompasses a choice collection of delicious dinners, offering a multitude of marvellous meals. You'll find everything from family-friendly meals to dishes ideal for informal entertaining. Whatever the occasion, there is something to suit all tastes.

We begin with a comprehensive collection of popular poultry dinners featuring some classic hearty soups, salads and stir-fries. Or, choose from choice dishes like lasagne, cannelloni, curry and fajitas, not forgetting the ever-popular roasts and rice dishes.

Next up is a magnificent selection of meat meals, including steaks, braises, hot pots, ribs, roasts, racks and stews. Family favourites include burgers, bolognese, sausages and chilli.

A further inspiring section encompasses some wonderful vegetable-based dinners. Choose from mighty main course salads and soups, popular pasta and pizzas, tempting tarts and pies, or warming cobblers, stews and gratins.

Fish and seafood favourites features family-friendly meals, such as fish cakes, pancakes, tacos, burritos, goujons, one-pots and pies, as well as those ideal for sharing with friends like casseroles, tagines, risottos and kebabs.

A final chapter is dedicated to some sauces, sides and sundries. It includes everything from home-made tomato ketchup, relishes, dips and coleslaw to hand-cut chips, roast potatoes and home-made bread.

So, choose your favourites from this superb selection of truly delicious dinners and get creative in the kitchen!

Back to basics

Be thrifty!

Shop wisely and effectively. Plan your meals for the week ahead, write a shopping list and stick to it.

It's a false economy to buy something on offer or in bulk, especially perishable goods, if you can't use it before it goes off.

Instead of using canned beans, buy dried beans, soak and cook them yourself. It takes more time, but will save on your spending.

Stock up on frozen vegetables; use them in cooking – they are economical, nutritious and tasty.

Waste not, want not!

Plan your menu carefully; make use of leftovers. If you cook a roast, use up any leftover cold meat in a hearty salad, curry, soup or tacos the next day. Use leftover roast meat bones to make delicious stock for soups, sauces and risottos.

Make more magnificent meals from other leftovers. Cooked vegetables are perfect for dishes like bubble and squeak, frittata, soup, and so on.

Chop leftover fresh herbs; freeze them in ice cube trays with a little water. Add the frozen cubes to casseroles, soups and sauces.

Freeze leftover fresh chillies for use another time.

Add chopped leftover fresh herb stems to soups, sauces, stocks and stews for added flavour.

Get canny in the kitchen – clever cooking on a budget

Buy in season
Get to know your local fruit and vegetable market. You can often pick up bargains, especially towards the end of the day – a great way to make savings. If you have a small garden or patio, grow your own fruit and vegetables – you'll be amazed what you can grow in a small patch of ground or in pots outside!

Use cheaper cuts of meat
Cut down on the number of meat- or fish-based meals you serve each week. Opt for cheaper vegetable-, pulse- or grain-based ones instead. Make meat dishes go further; add additional vegetables, canned beans or grains.
Cheaper cuts of meat are ideal for budget cooking. Many bargain cuts lend themselves to long, slow cooking methods, so are perfect for creating flavour-packed dinners like casseroles and stews. Packs of meat or fish off-cuts (bacon bits, smoked salmon trimmings) are often good quality and great value too.

Switch to own-brand products
Many own-brand products in supermarkets are as good as similar branded products, especially basic/economy ranges like canned tomatoes and sweetcorn, canned fish, fresh and frozen fruit and vegetables, dried herbs, curry pastes, and so on.

Batch cooking
Batch cooking and freezing dishes like soups, stews and lasagnes is ideal for saving overall cooking time in the kitchen, plus you create a home-made meal to enjoy when time is tight.

Buy a whole chicken and joint it yourself
Fresh (and frozen) chicken joints, especially breast and thigh fillets, can be pricey; make savings by buying a whole chicken and joint it yourself. Use any bones and bits you don't need to make a tasty stock (ideal for freezing).

Benefits of home cooking versus ready meals

Ready-meals may seem relatively economical and tempting to buy, but in reality they are usually not. With a little careful planning and effort, making your own delicious dinners will far outweigh any perceived benefits of buying ready-meals. There are health benefits too, as many ready-meals contain hidden fats, sugar and salt.

So, ditch the ready-meals and give creative cooking a go! You'll soon be a dab hand at dishing up delicious dinners and you'll make some sensible savings too!

Healthy eating

A balanced diet is one that provides the right amount of energy and nutrients your body needs. You are what you eat and your diet will be reflected in your general health. Combined with regular exercise, eating a healthy, balanced diet will help you to generally feel fit and maintain a healthy weight. It will also help to reduce the risk of developing illnesses such as heart disease, some cancers, stroke and diabetes. Eating the correct amount and right types of food is essential for everyone. Prudent portion control is also important.

Essential Kitchen Kit

Kitchen scales
A good-quality set of kitchen scales is essential for accurately measuring ingredients. Digital scales are the most accurate but spring or balance scales are just as good if used correctly.

Measuring spoons
Useful for accurately measuring small quantities of dry and liquid ingredients. They come in handy sets of 4, 5 or 6 spoons (and will measure out between ¼ teaspoon and 1 tablespoon).

Measuring jugs
A heatproof glass jug or transparent, hardwearing plastic jug with clear markings on the side and a good pouring lip makes easy work of measuring liquids.

Knives
Buy good-quality knives in several sizes/types to suit your needs. Choose well-balanced knives that are comfortable and not too heavy to hold. Wash knives by hand immediately after use; dry thoroughly. Sharpen them regularly (preferably with a steel). Store knives in a knife block (or on a magnetic knife rack), away from other tools/utensils.

Chopping boards
These vary from hard wood chopping boards to toughened plastic (polypropylene) ones (colour-coded) and are readily available in a variety of sizes. They are ideal for safely slicing and chopping foods. Choose thick, sturdy boards to prevent warping.

Spoons and spatulas
Wooden spoons are useful for mixing and stirring food as it cooks, so it's good to have a few in varying sizes. Alternatively, use durable, heat-resistant nylon, silicone or melamine spoons. Flexible rubber, silicone or plastic spatulas are perfect for mixing, stirring and scraping.

Essential cookware
An extensive range of saucepans is readily available and the quality varies enormously. Buy the best quality, durable cookware you can afford; you will be rewarded with a set of pans that should see you through years of daily cooking.

Pans are made of many different materials and come in a range of sizes. Think about what you need; choose pans to suit your requirements.

Make sure they suit the type of heat source/hob you have. Check they are comfortable to hold and are not too heavy when empty (though ideally they should be fairly weighty with a heavy base).

Choose pans with lids and looks that you like. Decide on the type of material and whether you want non-stick ones or not.

Roasting tins
Good-quality metal roasting tins (standard and non-stick) are invaluable for roasts, racks and vegetables, plus other tempting mains like lasagnes and bakes. Heavy-duty, durable ones can be placed over direct heat for making gravy; they also won't warp in the oven.

Meat thermometer/probe
Sharp, pointed thin metal thermometer/probes are used for inserting into the deepest part or centre of a joint of meat, to give accurate internal temperature readings on a dial or digital display.

Specialist equipment

Blender/liquidiser
A large, heat resistant lidded goblet or cylindrical container with a powerful motor (with varying speeds). Whizzes up soups, sauces, batters and purées in next to no time. Hand-held stick blenders are useful for blending smaller portions of food.

Food processor
Available in a range of sizes, colours and capacities, a food processor is a valuable time-saving piece of kit with a variety of attachments – usually a revolving S-shaped blade and various cutting discs. It will essentially save you time and effort with basic tasks such as mixing, chopping, slicing, shredding, puréeing, liquidising, etc.

Wok

Perfect for cooking food such as stir-fries over a high heat. Available in various diameters, woks are usually made from stainless steel or cast iron. Non-stick ones are also obtainable. The unique shape of a wok (rounded bottom with curved sides) allows you to continuously toss or stir-fry food with ease.

Casserole

Cast-iron, enamelled cast-iron or stainless steel covered casseroles can typically be used on the hob or in the oven. Ideal for creating magnificent dinners like stews, casseroles, braises, one-pots and pot roasts. Usually round or oval and available in varying sizes and colours, a casserole is worthy for dinners that require long, slow cooking.

Electric deep-fat fryer

Typically, a long-handled wire mesh basket fits within an insulated metal unit/pan housing a heating element that is thermostatically controlled. Ideal for deep-frying foods safely and effectively.

Ridged griddle pan

Ridged, heavy, cast-iron pan ideal for char-grilling or griddling meat, poultry, fish and vegetables on the hob. Most recipes call for the griddle to be preheated before food is added to the searing hot pan. The food is sealed quickly over a high heat, then cooked over a reduced heat level.

Storecupboard Staples

Keep a range of the following storecupboard staples, as these are useful to have on hand in the kitchen. When they are on offer, stock up on essentials that keep well (canned products, dried pasta, oils, etc.)

Cans, condiments, bottles and jars

Canned tomatoes, sweetcorn, canned beans/pulses (red kidney beans, chickpeas, lentils).
Canned fish (tuna, salmon).
Soy sauce, chilli sauce, tomato purée, passata, pesto, tomato ketchup, mayonnaise, English mustard powder, Dijon or wholegrain mustard, curry paste, Worcestershire sauce.

Rice, grains, beans/pulses and dried pasta

Long-grain brown and white rice, risotto rice, basmati rice, quick-cook polenta, couscous, bulgar wheat, dried lentils, dried beans/pulses, white or wholewheat spaghetti, pasta shapes (such as fusilli and penne).

Stocks

Good quality bouillon powder or stock cubes/granules. Or, try making your own stock – it's easy and costs next to nothing to make. Home-made stock also freezes well.

Oils and vinegars

Olive oil, rapeseed or sunflower oil, sesame oil.
White (and red) wine vinegar, cider vinegar.
Dried herbs and spices and other flavourings
Keep a variety of dried herbs and spices to suit your individual taste, plus other flavourings such as garlic and fresh root ginger (keep these in a cool place or the refrigerator). Sea salt and black peppercorns are invaluable too.

Twice the price but twice as nice!

It's well worth splashing out on a few more expensive ingredients that will enrich your dishes and make a real difference to your cooking.

These include: extra virgin olive oil, good quality balsamic vinegar, Kalamata olives, Puy lentils, sea salt flakes, walnut or hazelnut oil for dressings, fresh pasta, fresh Parmesan cheese, and so on.

Food hygiene, safety & storage

Kitchen and personal hygiene

- Keep the kitchen clean and tidy.
- Keep work surfaces, sinks, walls, floors and kitchen equipment clean; disinfect them regularly or use an antibacterial spray.
- Clean up as you go; wipe up spillages as they occur.
- Keep pets away from food preparation areas.
- Change and wash tea towels, hand towels and cloths regularly.
- Before handling food, remove jewellery; wash your hands in hot, soapy water. Wash your hands again after handling raw food and in between tasks.
- Wear a protective apron, roll up your sleeves, tie long hair back.
- If you are ill, avoid handling food altogether.

Food safety and hygiene

- Wash work surfaces before and after preparing food; clear up as you go along. Wash knives and other utensils between each task.
- Avoid cross-contamination – keep raw and cooked foods separate. Never use the same utensil (such as a knife) for preparing raw and cooked food unless you have washed it thoroughly in between.
- Use different chopping boards for meat, fish, vegetables, etc. Keep separate ones for raw and cooked foods – colour coded chopping boards make this easy. Scrub chopping boards thoroughly after use; dry them before storing.
- Wash fresh/raw produce before preparation. Scrub all fruits and vegetables with plain water to remove any pesticides, dirt or bacterial contamination.
- Use a spoon to taste food while cooking; wash it between tastings.

Cooking food safely

- Follow the cooking time given in the recipe. Preheat the oven before you put the food in and start timing.
- Cook food thoroughly; the centre of the cooked food should be piping hot. The internal temperature of meat joints/poultry can be checked using a meat thermometer/probe.
- With poultry dishes, always make sure the poultry is thoroughly cooked and tender before serving. Ensure the juices run clear and are piping hot and that there are no signs of pinkness when a skewer or tip of a sharp knife is inserted into the thickest part of the meat. If the juices are pink or there are traces of blood, continue cooking until the juices run clear.
- With cooked burgers, sausages and pork, cut into the middle to check that the meat is no longer pink; any juices that run out should be clear and piping hot with visible steam rising. Pork joints and rolled joints should not be eaten pink or rare.

Serving and cooling food safely

- Once food has been cooked, serve and eat it as soon as possible. If it is not for immediate consumption, cool it as quickly as possible, then cover and store in the refrigerator.
- Do not cover hot food with a lid – uncovered food cools more quickly.
- Keep leftovers wrapped or in a covered airtight container in the refrigerator and use within use within 2 days.

Food storage solutions

- Keep dry foods (pasta, rice, etc) in airtight containers or sealed polythene food bags in cool, dry, well-ventilated kitchen cupboards. Don't store food on the floor.
- Store fruit and vegetables either in a cool, dark, dry place or in the refrigerator, depending on type.
- Chilling food helps to keep harmful bacteria at bay. Storage times for chilled foods vary.
- Your refrigerator should be set to a constant temperature of between 0–5°C (32–41°F). Check it regularly with a refrigerator thermometer.
- The coldest part of the refrigerator is towards the bottom above the salad drawer.
- Store raw and cooked foods separately in the refrigerator – store cooked food on a higher shelf and raw food towards the bottom (the coldest part).

- Place raw food (such as meat) on a plate to catch any drips.
- Don't overload your refrigerator – cold air needs to circulate freely for the refrigerator to work efficiently.

Thawing frozen food

- Ideally, thaw frozen food as slowly as possible, for several hours or overnight in the refrigerator (on a low shelf).
- Place frozen food on a plate to catch any juices; keep it covered.
- A microwave oven can be used to thaw some frozen foods; check the manufacturer's guidelines.
- Use or cook thawed food as soon as it is thawed and within a day of removing it from the freezer.

Reheating food

- Always reheat previously cooked food until it is piping hot throughout.
- If you are reheating food in a microwave oven, follow the manufacturer's guidelines.
- Never reheat any type of food more than once. If you have leftovers after reheating, throw them away.

Freezing – secrets for success

Freezing allows food to be kept for longer periods while retaining much of its quality, taste, texture and goodness. A great way to store home-made batch-cooked dinners.

- Your freezer should be set to a constant temperature of –18°C (–0.4°F) or below. Check it regularly with a freezer thermometer.
- Many foods are suitable for freezing, but not all (like bananas, lettuce, etc); check before you freeze. Storage times for frozen foods vary.
- Freeze fresh foods that are in prime condition.
- Wrap and pack food carefully; seal it tightly. Freeze food in suitable wrappings or containers, such as polythene freezer bags, foil containers, freezer wrap, rigid airtight plastic containers, etc.
- Label and date frozen food clearly – strips of masking tape and a permanent marker are ideal.
- Keep your freezer as full as possible – it will work most efficiently if full.
- Don't re-freeze food once it has thawed unless the food has been cooked in the interim, i.e. frozen raw meat which has been thawed then cooked in a casserole, can be cooled and frozen.

Poultry dishes

Serves 4

Cream of chicken soup

Ingredients

3 tbsp butter

4 shallots, chopped

1 leek, sliced

450 g/1 lb skinless chicken breasts, chopped

600 ml/1 pint chicken stock

1 tbsp chopped fresh parsley

1 tbsp chopped fresh thyme, plus extra sprigs to garnish

175 ml/6 fl oz double cream

salt and pepper

1. Melt the butter in a large saucepan over a medium heat. Add the shallots and cook, stirring, for 3 minutes, until soft. Add the leek and cook for a further 5 minutes, stirring occasionally.

2. Add the chicken, stock and herbs, and season to taste with salt and pepper. Bring to the boil, then reduce the heat and simmer for 25 minutes, until the chicken is tender and cooked through. Remove from the heat and leave to cool for 10 minutes. Transfer to a food processor or blender, in batches if necessary, and process until smooth. Return the soup to the rinsed-out pan and heat over a low heat for 5 minutes.

3. Stir in the cream and cook for a further 2 minutes, then remove from the heat and ladle into warmed bowls. Garnish with thyme sprigs and serve immediately.

2

Serves 4

Chicken, rice & vegetable soup

Ingredients

1.5 litres/2¾ pints chicken stock

2 small carrots, very thinly sliced

1 celery stick, finely diced

1 baby leek, halved lengthways and thinly sliced

115 g/4 oz petit pois, thawed if frozen

175 g/6 oz cooked rice

150 g/5½ oz cooked chicken, sliced

2 tsp chopped fresh tarragon

1 tbsp chopped fresh flat-leaf parsley, plus extra sprigs to garnish

1. Put the stock in a large saucepan and add the carrots, celery and leek. Bring to the boil, reduce the heat to low and gently simmer, partially covered, for 10 minutes.

2. Stir in the petit pois, rice and chicken and continue cooking for a further 10–15 minutes, or until the vegetables are tender.

3. Add the chopped tarragon and parsley. Ladle the soup into warmed bowls, garnish with parsley and serve immediately.

#3

Lemon turkey soup with mushrooms

Ingredients

350 g/12 oz skinless, boneless turkey

1 litre/1¾ pints chicken stock

1 onion, quartered

2 carrots, thinly sliced

2 garlic cloves, halved

1 strip pared lemon rind

1 bay leaf

1 tbsp butter

350 g/12 oz small button mushrooms, quartered

4 tbsp cornflour

125 ml/4 fl oz double cream

freshly grated nutmeg

lemon juice

1–2 tbsp chopped fresh flat-leaf parsley

salt and pepper

1. Cut the turkey into 1-cm/½-inch pieces and put into a large saucepan. Add the stock. Bring just to the boil, skimming off any foam that rises to the surface. Add the onion, carrots, garlic, lemon rind and bay leaf. Season to taste with salt and pepper. Reduce the heat and simmer, partially covered, for about 45 minutes, stirring occasionally, until the turkey is cooked. Remove the turkey and carrots with a slotted spoon and reserve, covered. Strain the stock into a clean saucepan. Remove and discard the onion and garlic, lemon rind and bay leaf.

2. Melt the butter in a frying pan over a medium–high heat. Add the mushrooms, season to taste with salt and pepper and gently fry until light golden. Set aside with the turkey and carrots.

3. Mix the cornflour and cream together. Bring the cooking liquid just to the boil and whisk in the cream mixture. Boil very gently for 2–3 minutes until it thickens, whisking almost constantly. Add the reserved meat and vegetables and heat over a low heat for 5 minutes. Add the nutmeg and some lemon juice. Stir in the parsley. Ladle into warmed bowls and serve immediately.

#4

Chicken & lentil soup

Ingredients

3 tbsp olive oil

1 large onion, chopped

2 leeks, chopped

2 carrots, chopped

2 celery sticks, chopped

175 g/6 oz button mushrooms, chopped

4 tbsp dry white wine

1.2 litres/2 pints vegetable stock

1 bay leaf

2 tsp dried mixed herbs

175 g/6 oz Puy lentils

350 g/12 oz boneless cooked chicken, diced

salt and pepper

1. Heat the oil in a large saucepan. Add the onion, leeks, carrots, celery and mushrooms and cook over a low heat, stirring occasionally, for 5–7 minutes, until soft but not coloured.

2. Increase the heat to medium, pour in the wine and cook for 2–3 minutes, until the alcohol has evaporated, then pour in the stock.

3. Bring to the boil, add the bay leaf and herbs, reduce the heat, cover and simmer for 30 minutes. Add the lentils, re-cover the pan and simmer, stirring occasionally, for a further 40 minutes, until they are tender.

4. Stir in the chicken, season to taste with salt and pepper and simmer for a further 5–10 minutes, until heated through. Ladle into warmed bowls and serve immediately.

Serves
2

Spicy chicken noodle soup

Ingredients

300 ml/10 fl oz chicken stock

1 x 18 g/¾ oz sachet miso paste

2-cm/¾-inch piece fresh ginger, peeled and finely grated

1 red chilli, deseeded and thinly sliced

1 carrot, cut into thin strips

200 g/7 oz pak choi, roughly chopped

150 g/5½ oz dried egg thread noodles, cooked

1 cooked chicken breast, shredded

dark soy sauce, to taste

4 spring onions, trimmed and finely chopped

1. Put the stock in a saucepan with 250 ml/9 fl oz boiling water and bring to the boil over a medium-high heat. Add the miso paste and simmer for 1–2 minutes.

2. Add the ginger, chilli, carrot, pak choi, cooked noodles and chicken. Simmer for a further 4–5 minutes. Season to taste with soy sauce.

3. Scatter the spring onions in the base of two warmed bowls, pour the soup over and serve immediately.

6

Serves
6

Turkey, sage & mushroom soup

Ingredients

3 tbsp butter

1 onion, finely chopped

1 stick celery, finely chopped

25 large fresh sage leaves, finely chopped

4 tbsp plain flour

1.2 litres/2 pints chicken stock

100 g/3½ oz brown rice

250 g/9 oz mushrooms, sliced

200 g/7 oz cooked turkey, diced

200 ml/7 fl oz double cream

salt and pepper

fresh sage sprigs, to garnish

freshly grated Parmesan cheese, to serve

1. Melt half the butter in a large saucepan over a medium-low heat. Add the onion, celery and sage and cook for 3–4 minutes, until the onion is soft, stirring frequently. Stir in the flour and cook for a further 2 minutes.

2. Slowly add about one quarter of the stock and stir well, scraping the base of the pan to mix in the flour. Pour in the remaining stock, stirring to combine, and bring just to the boil. Stir in the rice and season to taste with salt and pepper. Reduce the heat and simmer gently, partially covered, for about 30 minutes until the rice is just tender, stirring occasionally.

3. Meanwhile, melt the remaining butter in a large frying pan over a medium heat. Add the mushrooms and season to taste with salt and pepper. Cook for about 8 minutes, until golden brown, stirring occasionally at first, then more often after they start to colour.

4. Add the mushrooms and turkey to the soup and stir in the cream. Simmer for about 10 minutes, until heated through. Taste and adjust the seasoning, if necessary. Ladle into warmed bowls, garnish with sage and serve with Parmesan cheese.

Serves 4

Chicken caesar salad

Ingredients

3 tbsp sunflower oil

2 thick slices of white bread, cubed

3 skinless, boneless chicken breasts, about 140 g/5 oz each

1 garlic clove, crushed

2 canned anchovy fillets, drained and finely chopped

5 tbsp light olive oil

2 tbsp white wine vinegar

2 tbsp mayonnaise

2 tbsp freshly grated Parmesan cheese

2 small heads of cos lettuce, roughly chopped

2 tbsp Parmesan cheese shavings

salt and pepper

1. Preheat the oven to 200°C/400°F/Gas Mark 6. Place 2 tablespoons of the sunflower oil in a bowl, add the bread and toss to coat. Spread out on a baking sheet, season with salt and pepper and bake in the preheated oven for 10 minutes, until crisp and golden brown.

2. Meanwhile, preheat a cast-iron frying pan and brush the chicken with the remaining sunflower oil and season to taste with salt and pepper. Cook on the preheated pan for 8–10 minutes on each side, until the chicken is tender and the juices run clear when a skewer is inserted into the thickest part of the meat.

3. Place the garlic, anchovies, olive oil, vinegar, mayonnaise, grated cheese, and salt and pepper to taste in a small bowl and mix thoroughly until smooth and creamy.

4. Slice the hot chicken and lightly toss with the lettuce and croûtons. Divide the salad between four bowls and drizzle over the dressing. Scatter over the cheese shavings and serve.

8

Serves 4

High-fibre chicken salad

Ingredients

250 g/9 oz easy-cook brown rice

2 tsp harissa

4 tbsp olive oil

juice of 1 lemon

2 tsp tomato purée

500 g/1 lb 2 oz skinless chicken breast fillets

85 g/3 oz ready-to-eat dried apricots, diced

55 g/2 oz raisins

55 g/2 oz preserved lemons, drained and finely chopped

1 small red onion, finely chopped

85 g/3 oz kale, shredded

3 tbsp pine nuts, toasted

salt and pepper

1. Put the rice in a saucepan of boiling water. Bring back to the boil, then simmer for 25—30 minutes, or until tender. Drain, then transfer to a salad bowl.

2. Meanwhile, put the harissa, oil and lemon juice in a jar, season to taste with salt and pepper, screw on the lid and shake well. Spoon 2 tablespoons into a bowl and mix in the tomato purée. Preheat the grill to high and line the grill pan with foil. Put the chicken on the foil in a single layer. Brush some of the tomato dressing over the chicken, then grill for 15—18 minutes, or until golden and cooked through, turning the meat and brushing it with the remaining tomato dressing half-way through cooking. Cover and leave to cool.

3. Drizzle the remaining dressing over the rice in the salad bowl. Add the apricots, raisins, preserved lemons and onion, then gently toss together and leave to cool. Add the kale and pine nuts to the salad and stir well. Thinly slice the chicken, arrange it over the salad and serve.

Grilled chicken & pesto salad

Ingredients

4 large chicken thighs

sunflower oil or olive oil, for brushing

200 g/7 oz dried trifoli or fusilli pasta

200 g/7 oz fine French beans, chopped

300 g/10½ oz ready-made pesto,
plus extra if needed

2 large tomatoes, sliced

salt and pepper

fresh basil leaves, to garnish

1. Preheat the grill to medium–high and position the grill rack about 7.5 cm/3 inches below the heat. Brush the chicken thighs with oil and season to taste. Brush the rack with a little oil, add the chicken, skin-side up, and cook for 20–25 minutes, or until cooked through and the juices run clear when a skewer is inserted into the thickest part of the meat. Remove from the heat and set aside.

2. Meanwhile, bring a large saucepan of lightly salted water to the boil. Add the pasta, return to the boil and cook for 8–10 minutes, or until tender but still firm to the bite. Add the beans 5 minutes before the end of the cooking time. Drain the pasta and beans, shaking off the excess water, and immediately tip into a large bowl. Add the pesto and stir until the pasta and beans are well coated. Set aside to cool.

3. When the chicken is cool enough to handle, remove the skin and bones and cut the flesh into bite-sized pieces. Stir into the pasta mixture and season to taste with salt and pepper. Set aside to cool completely, then cover and chill until required. Remove from the refrigerator 10 minutes before serving. Arrange the tomato slices on a serving platter. Stir the salad and add extra pesto, if needed. Mound the salad on top of the tomatoes, garnish with basil leaves and serve immediately.

Serves
4

Turkey & cranberry salad

Ingredients

150 g/5½ oz brown basmati rice

40 g/1½ oz wild rice

250 g/9 oz raw turkey breast slices

40 g/1½ oz dried cranberries

1½ tbsp cranberry sauce

1½ tbsp sherry vinegar

grated rind and juice of 1 lemon

1 level tsp Dijon mustard

3 spring onions, finely chopped

200 g/7 oz tomatoes, diced

1 small red pepper, halved, deseeded and cut into chunks

55 g/2 oz rocket

40 g/1½ oz sliced ham, cut into strips

salt and pepper

1. Put cold water in the base of a steamer, bring to the boil, then add the brown rice and wild rice and bring back to the boil. Put the turkey in the top of the steamer in a single layer, season with salt and pepper, then put it on the steamer base, cover and steam for 15 minutes, or until the turkey is cooked; cut into the middle of a slice to check that the meat is no longer pink and that the juices are clear and piping hot. Remove the steamer top and cook the rice for 5—10 minutes more, or until tender.

2. Dice the turkey and put it in a bowl. Add the cranberries. Drain and rinse the rice, then add to the bowl.

3. Put the cranberry sauce in a small saucepan and heat over a low heat until just melted. Remove from the heat, then add the vinegar, lemon rind and juice, mustard and a little salt and pepper. Whisk together until smooth, then drizzle over the salad and leave to cool. Add the spring onions, tomatoes and red pepper to the salad. Toss gently together, then divide between four plates. Top with the rocket and ham and serve.

Serves
4

Honey & mustard chicken pasta salad

Ingredients

5 tbsp olive oil

4 tsp clear honey

1 tbsp sherry vinegar

1 tbsp fresh thyme leaves, plus extra to garnish

250 g/9 oz dried fusilli pasta

1 onion, thinly sliced

1 garlic clove, crushed

4 skinless, boneless chicken breasts, about 115 g/4 oz each, thinly sliced

2 tbsp wholegrain mustard

175 g/6 oz cherry tomatoes, halved

handful of mizuna or rocket leaves

salt and pepper

1. Put 3 tablespoons of the oil, 2 tablespoons of the honey, the vinegar and thyme in a small bowl with a little salt and pepper and whisk together until well blended.

2. Bring a large saucepan of lightly salted water to the boil. Add the pasta, bring back to the boil and cook for 8-10 minutes, or until just tender but still firm to the bite.

3. Meanwhile, heat the remaining oil in a large frying pan. Add the onion and garlic and fry for 5 minutes. Add the chicken and cook, stirring frequently, for 3-4 minutes. Stir the mustard and remaining honey into the pan and cook for a further 2-3 minutes until the chicken and onion are golden brown and sticky. Check the chicken is tender and cooked through.

4. Drain the pasta and transfer to a large bowl. Pour over the dressing and toss. Stir in the chicken and onion and leave to cool. Stir in the tomatoes and mizuna. Garnish with thyme and serve.

Serves
6

Barbecue-glazed drumsticks

Ingredients

12 chicken drumsticks, about
1.6 kg/3 lb 8 oz

225 ml/8 fl oz barbecue sauce

1 tbsp soft light brown sugar

1 tbsp cider vinegar

1 tsp salt

½ tsp pepper

½ tsp hot pepper sauce

vegetable oil, for brushing

salad, to serve

1. Using a sharp knife, make two slashes, about 2.5 cm/1 inch apart, into the thickest part of the drumsticks, cutting to the bone. Put the drumsticks into a large, polythene freezer bag. Mix 4 tablespoons of the barbecue sauce, the sugar, vinegar, salt, pepper and hot pepper sauce together in a small bowl. Pour into the bag, press out most of the air and seal tightly. Gently shake the bag to distribute the sauce evenly and leave to marinate in the refrigerator for at least 4 hours.

2. Preheat the oven to 200°C/400°F/Gas Mark 6. Line a baking sheet with foil and lightly brush with oil. Transfer the drumsticks to the prepared sheet. Brush both sides of the drumsticks with some of the remaining barbecue sauce.

3. Bake for 15 minutes, then remove from the oven and brush with more barbecue sauce. Return to the oven and repeat three more times for a total cooking time of 1 hour. Serve with salad.

13

Serves
4

Turkey pasta pesto

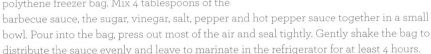

Ingredients

150 g/5½ oz dried trofie pasta or thin penne pasta

100 g/3½ oz new potatoes, scrubbed and thinly sliced

100 g/3½ oz fine French beans, topped and tailed and cut about the same length as the pasta

2 tbsp olive oil

450 g/1 lb fresh turkey mince

2 large garlic cloves, crushed

150 g/5½ oz pesto sauce

salt and pepper

freshly grated Parmesan cheese or pecorino cheese, to serve

1. Bring a large saucepan of lightly salted water to the boil. Add the pasta, bring back to the boil and cook for 12 minutes, or according to the packet instructions. Add the potatoes 7 minutes before the end of the cooking time, then add the beans 2 minutes later.

2. Meanwhile, heat the oil in a large frying pan over a medium–high heat. Add the turkey and fry, stirring with a wooden spoon to break it up into large clumps, for about 5 minutes until just starting to brown. Add the garlic and fry for a further minute, or until the turkey is cooked through. Remove from the pan and keep hot.

3. When the pasta and vegetables are tender, drain, reserving a few tablespoons of the cooking water. Return the pasta and vegetables to the pan, add the turkey and pesto and toss together. Add a little of the reserved cooking water, if necessary. Season to taste with salt and pepper.

4. Divide the mixture between warmed bowls and serve immediately, with plenty of cheese for sprinkling over.

Chicken & lime tacos

Ingredients

4 boneless, skinless chicken thighs

2 tbsp freshly squeezed lime juice

1 tbsp sunflower oil, plus extra for oiling

1 tsp ancho chilli powder or paprika

1 tsp ground cumin

1 tsp ground coriander

175 g/6 oz easy-cook long-grain rice

finely grated rind of 1 lime

2 tbsp finely chopped coriander

salt and pepper

12 crisp corn taco shells, warmed

shredded lettuce, guacamole and tomato salsa, to serve

1. Put the chicken thighs into a non-metallic dish and rub all over with the lime juice. Mix together the oil, chilli powder, cumin and ground coriander and season to taste with salt and pepper. Rub all over the chicken thighs, then set aside to marinate for 2 hours.

2. Meanwhile, cook the rice according to the packet instructions. Drain well and transfer to a bowl. Stir in the lime rind, cover and keep warm while you cook the chicken.

3. Heat a ridged griddle pan over a very high heat. Brush the ridges with oil and reduce the heat to medium. Add the chicken and fry for 4 minutes, brushing once with any leftover marinade. Turn and fry for a further 4 minutes, or until the chicken is cooked through and the juices run clear when a skewer is inserted into the thickest part of the meat. Slice into strips.

4. Stir the coriander into the rice and adjust the seasoning, if necessary. Divide the rice between the taco shells, then add the chicken. Top with lettuce, then add some guacamole and tomato salsa. Serve immediately.

Sticky turkey kebabs

Ingredients

280 g/10 oz turkey breast meat, cubed

3 tbsp soft brown sugar

¼ tsp paprika

¼ tsp ground cumin

¼ tsp salt

¼ tsp black pepper

1 tbsp vegetable oil

1 onion, finely chopped

2 garlic cloves, finely chopped

2.5-cm/1-inch piece of ginger, grated

3 tbsp tomato ketchup

3 tbsp white wine or chider vinegar

3 tbsp soy sauce

200ml/7 fl oz water

watercress and cooked long-grain rice, to serve

1. Put the turkey in a bowl and add 1 tablespoon of the sugar, the paprika, cumin, salt and pepper, mixing well to coat. Chill for at least 1 hour.

2. Meanwhile, heat the oil in a saucepan over a medium heat, add the onion, garlic and ginger and cook for 5 minutes. Add the ketchup, wine, soy sauce, the remaining sugar and the water and bring to the boil. Reduce the heat and simmer for 1 hour, stirring regularly until the mixture is thick and sticky.

3. Preheat the barbecue or grill to hot. Thread the turkey pieces onto two metal skewers and lay them on a sheet of foil. Brush with some of the sauce. Cook on the preheated barbecue for 10–15 minutes, turning and brushing with more of the sticky sauce until cooked. Serve with watercress and cooked rice and any remaining sauce.

Serves
4

Paprika turkey strips

Ingredients

500 g/1 lb 2 oz turkey breast steaks

1 tbsp paprika

1 tsp crushed coriander seeds

½ tsp garlic salt

¼ tsp pepper

2 tbsp olive oil

1 red onion, sliced

3 tbsp chopped fresh coriander

cooked rice, to serve

1. Cut the turkey into long, 1-cm/½-inch thick strips.

2. Put the paprika, coriander seeds, garlic salt and pepper into a large bowl and mix together. Stir in 1 tablespoon of the oil. Add the turkey strips and turn to coat evenly in the mixture.

3. Heat the remaining oil in a large frying pan or wok, add the onion and stir-fry for 1 minute. Add the turkey strips and stir-fry over a fairly high heat for 6–8 minutes until cooked through.

4. Sprinkle over the chopped coriander and serve with rice.

17

Serves
4

Chicken fajitas

Ingredients

3 tbsp olive oil, plus extra for drizzling

3 tbsp maple syrup or honey

1 tbsp red wine vinegar

2 garlic cloves, crushed

2 tsp dried oregano

1–2 tsp dried red pepper flakes

4 skinless, boneless chicken breasts

2 red peppers, deseeded and cut into 2.5-cm/1-inch strips

8 tortillas, warmed

salt and pepper

1. Place the oil, maple syrup, vinegar, garlic, oregano, pepper flakes, and salt and pepper to taste in a large, shallow dish and mix together.

2. Slice the chicken across the grain into 2.5-cm/1-inch thick slices. Toss in the marinade until well coated. Cover and chill in the refrigerator for 2–3 hours, turning occasionally.

3. Heat a griddle pan until hot. Lift the chicken slices from the marinade with a slotted spoon, lay on the pan and cook over a medium–high heat for 3–4 minutes on each side, or until cooked through. Transfer to a warmed serving plate and keep warm. Add the red peppers, skin-side down, to the pan and cook for 2 minutes on each side. Transfer to the serving plate. Serve with the warmed tortillas to be used as wraps.

#18 Jamaican Jerk Turkey Wraps

Serves 4

Ingredients

4 large flour tortillas

1 lime

450 g/1 lb turkey breast meat

2 tbsp soy sauce

3 tbsp vegetable oil

2 tbsp jerk seasoning

1 tbsp soft light brown sugar

½ tsp salt

1 jalapeño chilli

¼ small red onion

125 ml/4 fl oz mayonnaise

8 large cos lettuce leaves

1 mango

1 small red pepper

4 slices havarti cheese

1. Preheat the oven to 200°C/400°F/Gas Mark 6. Wrap the tortillas in foil and place in the oven to heat. Zest the lime into a small bowl. Cut the turkey into 1 x 7.5-cm/ ½ x 3-inch strips. Squeeze the lime into a large bowl, add the soy sauce, 1 tablespoon of the oil, the jerk seasoning, sugar and salt. Add the meat and toss to coat.

2. Deseed and finely chop the chilli and finely chop the onion. Add to the lime zest with the mayonnaise and stir to combine. Shred the lettuce. Peel the mango and slice into strips. Deseed the red pepper and slice into thin strips. Heat the remaining oil in a large frying pan over a medium–high heat. Add the turkey and cook, stirring occasionally, for 5–7 minutes until the meat is cooked through.

3. Remove the tortillas from the oven. Spread the mayonnaise mixture on one side of each tortilla. Top each with a cheese slice. Divide the turkey between the tortillas, making a strip of meat down the centre. Divide the lettuce, mango and red pepper equally between the wraps. Roll up and serve immediately.

#19 Sticky chicken wings

Serves 4

Ingredients

12 chicken wings

2 garlic cloves, crushed

2.5-cm/1-inch piece fresh ginger, chopped

2 tbsp dark soy sauce

2 tbsp lime juice

1 tbsp clear honey

1 tsp chilli sauce

2 tsp sesame oil

lime wedges, to serve

1. Tuck the pointed tip of each of the chicken wings under the thicker end to make a neat triangle.

2. Mix the garlic, ginger, soy sauce, lime juice, honey, chilli sauce and oil together.

3. Spoon the mixture over the chicken and turn to coat evenly. Cover and marinate for several hours or overnight.

4. Preheat the grill to hot. Line the grill pan with foil. Lay the chicken in the pan and cook under the preheated grill for 12–15 minutes, or until the chicken is tender and the juices run clear when a skewer is inserted into the thickest part of the meat.

5. Transfer to a serving dish and serve hot with some lime wedges.

#20

Serves 4

Chicken breasts with creamy peppercorn sauce

Ingredients

1 tbsp olive oil

4 boneless, skinless chicken breasts, about 175 g/6 oz each

25 g/1 oz butter

1 small onion, finely chopped

200 ml/7 fl oz dry white wine

1 bay leaf

200 g/7 oz crème fraîche

2 tbsp green peppercorns, drained and rinsed

500 g/1 lb 2 oz young spinach leaves

rind of 1 lemon, removed with a zester

salt and pepper

1. Heat the oil in a heavy frying pan over a medium-high heat, add the chicken breasts and fry for 4–5 minutes on each side, until golden brown and the juices run clear when a skewer is inserted into the thickest part of the meat. Remove from the pan, set aside and keep warm.

2. Add 15 g/½ oz of the butter to the pan and heat until melted. Add the onion and gently fry, stirring, for about 5 minutes, until soft and pale golden brown.

3. Add the wine and bay leaf to the pan and simmer, stirring occasionally, until the wine has reduced by about half. Stir in the crème fraîche and peppercorns and bring to the boil.

4. Return the chicken breasts to the pan and spoon the sauce over. Gently simmer for about 1 minute to heat through. Remove the bay leaf, then season to taste with salt and pepper. Set aside and keep warm.

5. Place the spinach in a wok or large frying pan and cook over a high heat, stirring, for about 2 minutes, until wilted. Press out any excess liquid and stir in the remaining butter and the lemon rind. Season to taste with salt and pepper.

6. Cut the chicken breasts in half diagonally and serve on the spinach, with the sauce spooned over.

24

Devilled turkey legs

Ingredients

2 turkey legs, skinned

½ tsp cayenne pepper

2 tbsp Dijon mustard or hot mustard

40 g/1½ oz unsalted butter, softened

salt and pepper

salad leaves, to garnish

1. Make deep criss-cross slashes in the turkey legs. Season with salt and pepper and sprinkle with a little cayenne pepper. Spread the mustard all over the legs, pressing it well into the slashes. Place the legs in a large, deep dish, cover with clingfilm and transfer to the refrigerator to marinate for 6–8 hours.

2. Meanwhile, cream the butter in a bowl, then beat in the remaining cayenne pepper to taste. Cover the bowl with clingfilm and set aside until you are ready to serve.

3. Preheat the grill. Place the turkey legs on a grill rack and cook under the grill, turning frequently, for 15–20 minutes, or until golden brown and cooked through and the juices run clear when the thickest part of the meat is pierced with a knife. Transfer to a carving board and carve into slices. Arrange on a serving plate with the cayenne butter and garnished with salad leaves. Serve immediately.

22

Serves 4

Chicken satay skewers

Ingredients

4 skinless, boneless chicken breasts, cut into 2-cm/¾-inch cubes

4 tbsp soy sauce

1 tbsp cornflour

2 garlic cloves, finely chopped

2.5-cm/1-inch piece fresh ginger, peeled and finely chopped

1 cucumber, diced, to serve

Sauce

2 tbsp groundnut oil or vegetable oil

½ onion, finely chopped

1 garlic clove, finely chopped

4 tbsp crunchy peanut butter

4–5 tbsp water

½ tsp chilli powder

1. Put the chicken cubes in a shallow dish. Mix the soy sauce, cornflour, garlic and ginger together in a small bowl and pour over the chicken. Cover and leave to marinate in the refrigerator for at least 2 hours.

2. Meanwhile, soak 12 wooden skewers in cold water for at least 30 minutes. Preheat the grill and thread the chicken pieces onto the wooden skewers. Transfer the skewers to a grill pan and cook under the preheated grill for 3–4 minutes. Turn and cook for a further 3–4 minutes or until cooked through. To test whether the chicken is cooked through, cut into the middle of the cubes to check that there are no remaining traces of pink or red.

3. Meanwhile, to make the sauce, heat the oil in a saucepan, add the onion and garlic and cook over a medium heat, stirring frequently, for 3–4 minutes until soft. Add the peanut butter, water and chilli powder and simmer for 2–3 minutes until soft and thinned. Serve the skewers immediately with the warm sauce and cucumber.

#23 Chicken burrito bowls

Serves 4

Ingredients

6 skinless chicken thighs on the bone
1 litre/1¾ pints water
400 g/14 oz canned chopped tomatoes
2 bay leaves
2 pickled jalapeño chillies, chopped
2 limes, sliced
1 onion, halved
1 tbsp Mexican oregano
2 tsp ancho chilli powder
2 tsp ground coriander
2 tsp ground cumin
300 g/10½ oz easy-cook long-grain rice
salt and pepper
chopped fresh coriander, to garnish
diced avocado, grated cheese and olives, to serve

1. Put the chicken and water into a saucepan and slowly bring to the boil, skimming the surface as necessary. When the foam stops rising, stir in the tomatoes, bay leaves, chillies, lime slices, onion, oregano, chilli powder, ground coriander and cumin and season to taste with salt and pepper. Adjust the heat so the liquid just bubbles, then leave to bubble for about 60 minutes until the liquid evaporates and the meat is very tender. The juices should run clear when a skewer is inserted into the thickest part of the meat.

2. Meanwhile, cook the rice according to the packet instructions, then drain and keep hot.

3. Use a slotted spoon to transfer the chicken to a bowl. Remove the bones and use 2 forks to shred the meat. Adjust the seasoning, if necessary.

4. Divide the rice between four warmed bowls, top with the chicken, sprinkle with chopped coriander and serve with the accompaniments in small bowls for adding at the table.

#24 Duck & pea stir-fry

Serves 2-4

Ingredients

1 tbsp soft light brown sugar
3 tbsp lukewarm water
1–2 red chillies, deseeded and chopped
1 tbsp soy sauce
1 tsp Thai fish sauce
3 tbsp lime juice
450 g/1 lb skinless, duck breasts
6 large spring onions
3 tbsp groundnut oil
1 tsp finely chopped fresh ginger
300 g/10½ oz mangetout, halved
140 g/5 oz shelled peas
3 tbsp whole almonds, halved
55 g/2 oz fresh beansprouts
freshly cooked noodles, to serve

1. Combine the sugar, water, chillies, soy sauce, Thai fish sauce and lime juice in a bowl, stirring to dissolve the sugar. Slice the duck into large pieces and add to the marinade. Leave to stand at room temperature for 30 minutes, or overnight in the refrigerator.

2. Separate the white and green parts of the spring onions and slice into 2-cm/¾-inch pieces. Heat a wok over a high heat, then add the oil. Add the white spring onion and the ginger and stir-fry for a few seconds. Add the duck and the marinade, and stir-fry for about 5 minutes. When the liquid has reduced slightly, add the mangetout and peas and stir-fry for a further 2–3 minutes.

3. Add the almonds, beansprouts and green spring onion, and stir-fry for a few seconds to heat through. Serve immediately with noodles.

#25 Pesto chicken pizza

Serves 6

Ingredients

2 x 26-cm/10½-inch ready-made pizza bases

8 tbsp ready-made pesto

175 g/6 oz cooked chicken, torn into strips

100 g/3½ oz canned sweetcorn, drained

6 cherry tomatoes, thinly sliced

250 g/9 oz mozzarella cheese, drained and roughly torn

salt and pepper

1. Preheat the oven to 220°C/425°F/Gas Mark 7. Place the pizza bases on two baking trays.

2. Divide the pesto between the pizza bases, spreading almost to the edges. Scatter over the chicken, sweetcorn and tomatoes. Top with the cheese and season to taste with salt and pepper.

3. Bake in the preheated oven for 10-12 minutes, or until the cheese is melting and turning golden and the bases are crisp underneath. Serve immediately.

#26 Mexican turkey steak

Serves 4–6

Ingredients

4 turkey steaks, 500 g/1 lb 2 oz in total

olive oil, for brushing and oiling

avocado salsa and warmed tortillas, to serve

Marinade

juice of 1 orange

juice of 2 limes

2 garlic cloves, crushed

1 tsp paprika

½ tsp salt

½ tsp chilli powder

½ tsp cumin seeds, crushed

¼ tsp pepper

4 tbsp olive oil

1. Cut the turkey steaks in half horizontally to make 8 thinner pieces. Place between two sheets of clingfilm and pound with a meat mallet until flattened to a thickness of 1 cm/½ inch. Slice into 4-cm/1½-inch wide strips. Place in a shallow dish in a single layer.

2. Whisk together the marinade ingredients and pour over the turkey. Cover with clingfilm and leave in the refrigerator to marinate for at least 4 hours or overnight. Allow to come to room temperature before cooking. When ready to cook, preheat the barbecue.

3. Drain the turkey. Lightly brush with oil and thread concertina-style onto presoaked wooden skewers or metal skewers. Oil the barbecue rack. Cook for 2–2½ minutes on each side over hot coals until no longer pink in the middle when cut into with a small vegetable knife. Remove from the skewers and serve with avocado salsa and tortillas.

Parmesan chicken tenders

Ingredients

4 boneless, skinless chicken breasts, each about 175 g/6 oz, cut across the grain into 1-cm/½-inch wide strips

55 g/2 oz panko breadcrumbs

55 g/2 oz freshly grated Parmesan cheese

3 tbsp self-raising flour

¼ tsp paprika, or to taste

olive oil or vegetable oil spray

cooked green vegetables, to serve

Marinade

150 ml/5 fl oz buttermilk

1 egg, lightly beaten

salt and pepper

1. To make the marinade, combine the buttermilk and egg in a large bowl and season to taste with salt and pepper. Stir in the chicken strips, then cover the bowl and marinate in the refrigerator for 2–4 hours.

2. When ready to cook, preheat the oven to 190°C/375°F/Gas Mark 5 and line two baking sheets with baking paper. Toss the breadcrumbs, cheese, flour and paprika together in a wide bowl.

3. Remove a piece of chicken from the marinade, allowing the excess to drip back into the bowl. Place in the breadcrumb mixture and toss to coat, then transfer to the prepared baking sheet. Continue until all the chicken pieces are coated. Lightly spray each piece with oil.

4. Bake in the preheated oven for 20–25 minutes until golden brown. Cut into the middle of the chicken to check there are no remaining traces of pink or red. Serve with vegetables.

Grilled turkey breast with lemon

Ingredients

1 lemon

2 tbsp olive oil

1 garlic clove, crushed

4 turkey breast steaks

salt and pepper

salad, to serve

1. Finely grate the rind from the lemon and squeeze the juice. Mix together the lemon rind, lemon juice, oil and garlic in a wide, non-metallic dish.

2. Place the turkey steaks in the lemon marinade, turning to coat evenly. Cover with clingfilm and chill in the refrigerator for 30 minutes. Drain the turkey, discarding the marinade.

3. Preheat a ridged griddle pan to hot. Season the turkey steaks with salt and pepper to taste, place in the pan and cook for about 4 minutes, until golden. Using tongs, turn the turkey steaks over and cook the other side for 3–4 minutes, until the turkey is tender and the juices run clear when a skewer is inserted into the thickest part of the meat.

4. Transfer the turkey to a warmed plate, cover with foil and leave to stand for 3–4 minutes before serving. Serve with salad.

Fried chicken with tomato & bacon sauce

Ingredients

25 g/1 oz butter

2 tbsp olive oil

4 skinless, boneless chicken breasts or 8 skinless, boneless chicken thighs

Sauce

25 g/1 oz butter

2 tbsp olive oil

1 large onion, finely chopped

2 garlic cloves, finely chopped

1 celery stick, finely chopped

4 bacon rashers, diced

400 g/14 oz canned chopped tomatoes

2 tbsp tomato purée

soft light brown sugar, to taste

100 ml/3½ fl oz water

1 tbsp chopped fresh basil

1 tbsp chopped fresh flat-leaf parsley, plus extra to garnish

salt and pepper

1. To make the sauce, melt the butter with the oil in a large saucepan. Add the onion, garlic, celery and bacon and cook over a low heat, stirring occasionally, for 5 minutes, until soft. Stir in the tomatoes, tomato purée, sugar to taste and water and season to taste with salt and pepper. Increase the heat to medium and bring to the boil, then reduce the heat and simmer, stirring occasionally, for 15–20 minutes, until thickened.

2. Meanwhile, melt the butter with the oil in a large frying pan. Add the chicken and cook over a medium–high heat for 4-5 minutes on each side, until evenly browned.

3. Stir the basil and parsley into the sauce. Add the chicken and spoon the sauce over. Cover and simmer for 10–15 minutes. Check the chicken is tender and the juices run clear when a skewer is inserted into the thickest part of the meat. Garnish with parsley and serve immediately.

Chicken Kiev

Ingredients

115 g/4 oz butter, softened

3–4 garlic cloves, very finely chopped

1 tbsp chopped fresh parsley

1 tbsp snipped fresh chives

juice and finely grated rind of ½ lemon

8 skinless, boneless chicken breasts

55 g/2 oz plain flour

2 eggs, lightly beaten

175 g/6 oz dry breadcrumbs

groundnut oil or sunflower oil, for deep-frying

salt and pepper

cooked green vegetables, to serve

1. Beat the butter in a bowl with the garlic, herbs, and lemon juice and rind. Season to taste with salt and pepper. Divide into 8 pieces, then shape into cylinders. Wrap in foil and chill in the refrigerator until firm.

2. Place each chicken breast between two sheets of clingfilm. Gently pound with a meat mallet or rolling pin to flatten to an even thickness. Place a butter cylinder on each chicken piece and roll up. Secure with wooden cocktail sticks.

3. Place the flour, eggs and breadcrumbs in separate shallow dishes. Dip the rolls into the flour, then the egg and, finally, the breadcrumbs. Chill in the refrigerator for 1 hour.

4. Heat enough oil for deep-frying in a saucepan or deep-fat fryer to 180–190°C/ 350–375°F, or until a cube of bread browns in 30 seconds. Remove the cocktail sticks and deep-fry the chicken. Drain on kitchen paper. Serve immediately with green vegetables.

Stir-fried turkey with cranberry glaze

Ingredients

450 g/1 lb skinless, boneless turkey breast

2 tbsp sunflower oil

15 g/½ oz stem ginger, in syrup

50 g/1¾ oz fresh or frozen cranberries

100 g/3½ oz canned chestnuts

4 tbsp cranberry sauce

3 tbsp light soy sauce

salt and pepper

1. Using a sharp knife, thinly slice the turkey breast.

2. Heat the oil in a large preheated wok or frying pan. Add the turkey and stir-fry for 5 minutes, or until cooked through. Drain the syrup from the stem ginger. Using a sharp knife, finely chop the ginger.

3. Add the ginger and the cranberries to the wok and stir-fry for 2–3 minutes, or until the cranberries are soft. Add the chestnuts, cranberry sauce and soy sauce, season to taste with salt and pepper and leave to bubble for 2–3 minutes.

4. Transfer to warmed serving dishes and serve immediately.

Creamed chicken with Jerusalem artichokes

Ingredients

25 g/1 oz butter

1 onion, finely chopped

200 g/7 oz Jerusalem artichokes, sliced

200 ml/7 fl oz water

100 ml/3½ fl oz white wine

2 fresh tarragon sprigs

2 skinless, boneless chicken breasts, about 115 g/4 oz each

1 tsp Dijon mustard

3 tbsp crème fraîche

salt and pepper

chopped fresh tarragon, to garnish

cooked rice, to serve

1. Melt the butter in a large frying pan over a medium heat, add the onion and cook for 4–5 minutes, or until soft. Add the artichokes, water, wine and tarragon. Bring to the boil, then reduce the heat and simmer, covered, for 5 minutes, or until the artichokes are just tender.

2. Cut each chicken breast into 4 pieces and add to the pan. Season with salt and pepper and continue to cook, stirring, for 10 minutes, or until the chicken is cooked through and shows no traces of pink.

3. Remove the tarragon sprigs and stir in the mustard and crème fraîche. Increase the heat and leave the sauce to bubble and thicken. Divide between two warmed plates and garnish with chopped tarragon. Serve immediately with cooked rice.

Turkey stroganoff

Ingredients

3 tbsp sunflower oil

450 g/1 lb fresh turkey mince

30 g/1 oz butter

1 onion, very finely chopped

2 large garlic cloves, very finely chopped

250 g/9 oz chestnut mushrooms, trimmed and thinly chopped

4 tsp Dijon mustard

freshly grated nutmeg, to taste

450 ml/16 fl oz soured cream

freshly squeezed lemon juice, to taste

salt and pepper

finely chopped fresh flat-leaf parsley, to garnish

cooked tagliatelle, to serve

1. Heat the oil in a large frying pan over a medium–high heat. Add the turkey and fry, stirring with a wooden spoon to break up the meat into large clumps, for 4–6 minutes until cooked through. Remove from the pan with a slotted spoon and set aside.

2. Pour off all but 1 tablespoon of the fat remaining in the pan. Add the butter and heat until melted. Add the onion and fry, stirring, for 3–5 minutes until soft. Stir in the garlic and mushrooms and season to taste with salt and pepper. Fry, stirring, for about 5 minutes until the mushrooms re-absorb the liquid they give off.

3. Stir in the mustard and nutmeg, then return the turkey to the pan. Stir in the soured cream and bring to the boil, stirring. Reduce the heat and simmer for a few minutes until slightly reduced. Add lemon juice to taste and adjust the seasoning, if necessary.

4. Divide the pasta between four plates and pour over the sauce. Sprinkle with parsley and serve immediately.

#34 Chicken & mushroom lasagne

Serves 4

Ingredients

600 ml/ 1 pint milk

55 g/2 oz butter

55 g/2 oz plain flour

1 bay leaf

2 tbsp olive oil

1 large onion, finely chopped

500 g/ 1 lb 2 oz fresh chicken mince

100 g/3½ oz pancetta, chopped

350 g/12 oz chestnut mushrooms

150 ml/5 fl oz dry white wine

400 g/14 oz canned chopped tomatoes

3 tbsp chopped fresh basil

9 sheets pre-cooked lasagne

3 tbsp freshly grated Parmesan cheese

salt and pepper

1. Preheat the oven to 190°C/375°F/Gas Mark 5. For the white sauce, heat the milk, butter, flour and bay leaf in a saucepan over a low heat, whisking constantly, until smooth and thick. Season to taste with salt and pepper, cover and leave to stand.

2. Heat the oil in a large saucepan over a medium heat, add the onion and fry, stirring, for 3–4 minutes. Add the chicken and pancetta and cook for 6–8 minutes. Chop and stir in the mushrooms and cook for a further 2–3 minutes. Add the wine and bring to the boil. Pour in the tomatoes, cover and simmer for 20 minutes. Stir in the basil.

3. Spoon a third of the meat sauce into a large baking dish. Remove and discard the bay leaf from the white sauce. Spoon a quarter of the white sauce over the meat sauce. Arrange 3 lasagne sheets over the white sauce. Repeat the layers twice more, finishing with white sauce. Sprinkle with cheese and bake in the preheated oven for 35–40 minutes, until golden brown and bubbling. Serve immediately.

#35 Turkey schnitzel

Serves 4

Ingredients

4 potatoes, unpeeled

2 tbsp olive oil, plus extra for frying

1 tbsp dried sage

55 g/2 oz fresh white breadcrumbs

40 g/1½ oz finely grated Parmesan cheese

4 turkey escalopes, thinly sliced

1 egg, beaten

salt and pepper

lemon wedges, to serve

1. Preheat the oven to 220°C/425°F/Gas Mark 7. Cut each potato into 8 wedges. Place the wedges in a bowl and add the oil, 1 teaspoon of the sage, and salt and pepper to taste. Toss well to coat evenly.

2. Arrange the potatoes in a single layer on a baking sheet. Bake in the preheated oven for about 25 minutes, until golden brown and tender.

3. Meanwhile, mix together the breadcrumbs, cheese, remaining sage, and salt and pepper to taste. Dip the turkey in the beaten egg and then in the crumb mixture, pressing to coat on both sides.

4. Heat a shallow depth of oil in a frying pan over a fairly high heat, add the turkey and fry for 4–5 minutes, turning once, until golden brown and the turkey is cooked through. Serve the turkey hot with the potato and lemon wedges.

Serves
2

Creamy chicken penne

Ingredients

200 g/7 oz dried penne

1 tbsp olive oil

2 skinless, boneless chicken breasts

4 tbsp dry white wine

115 g/4 oz frozen peas

5 tbsp double cream

salt

4–5 tbsp chopped fresh flat-leaf parsley, to garnish

1. Bring a large saucepan of lightly salted water to the boil. Add the pasta, bring back to the boil and cook for about 8–10 minutes, until tender but still firm to the bite.

2. Meanwhile, heat the oil in a frying pan. Add the chicken and cook over a medium heat for about 4 minutes on each side.

3. Pour in the wine and cook over a high heat until it has almost evaporated.

4. Drain the pasta. Add the peas, cream and pasta to the frying pan and stir well. Cover and simmer for 2 minutes.

5. Garnish the chicken and pasta mixture with parsley and serve immediately.

Serves
4

Steamed chicken with chilli & coriander butter

Ingredients

55 g/2 oz butter, softened

1 fresh bird's eye chilli, deseeded and chopped

3 tbsp chopped fresh coriander

4 skinless, boneless chicken breasts

400 ml/14 fl oz coconut milk

350 ml/12 fl oz chicken stock

200 g/7 oz basmati rice

salt and pepper

Pickled vegetables

1 carrot

½ cucumber

3 spring onions

2 tbsp rice vinegar

1. Mix the butter with the chilli and coriander. Cut a deep slash into the side of each chicken breast to form a pocket. Spoon a quarter of the butter into each pocket and place on a 30-cm/12-inch square of baking paper. Season to taste with salt and pepper, then bring two opposite sides of the paper together on top, folding over to seal firmly. Twist the ends to seal.

2. Pour the coconut milk and stock into a large saucepan with a steamer top. Bring to the boil. Stir in the rice with a pinch of salt. Place the chicken parcels in the steamer top, cover and simmer for 15–18 minutes, stirring the rice once, until the rice is tender and the chicken is cooked through.

3. Meanwhile, to make the pickled vegetables, trim the carrot, cucumber and spring onions and cut into fine matchsticks. Sprinkle with the rice vinegar.

4. Unwrap the chicken, reserving the juices, and cut in half diagonally. Serve the chicken over the rice, with the juices spooned over and pickled vegetables on the side.

Garlic chicken with leek

Serves 4

Ingredients

450 g/1 lb chicken breasts, skinned and cut into strips

1 tbsp groundnut oil

6 garlic cloves, thinly sliced

2.5-cm/1-inch piece fresh ginger, finely grated

200 g/7 oz leek, thinly sliced

4 spring onions, chopped

1 tbsp clear honey

Marinade

2 tbsp rice wine

2 tbsp dark soy sauce

1 tsp sesame oil

1. To make the marinade, mix the rice wine, soy sauce and sesame oil in a bowl. Add the chicken strips and stir to coat and leave to marinate for 1 hour.

2. Drain the chicken, reserving the marinade. Heat the oil in a preheated wok or large frying pan over a high heat until smoking. Add the drained chicken and stir-fry for 3 minutes to seal.

3. Add the garlic, ginger, leek and spring onions to the wok and fry for a further 3 minutes to soften. Add the reserved marinade and honey and stir-fry for a further minute to heat through. Serve immediately.

Turkey cutlets with Parma ham

Serves 2

Ingredients

2 skinless, boneless turkey cutlets

2 slices Parma ham, halved

4 fresh sage leaves

2 tbsp plain flour

2 tbsp olive oil

1 tbsp butter

salt and pepper

lemon wedges, to serve

1. Slice each turkey cutlet in half horizontally into 2 thinner escalopes. Place each escalope between two sheets of clingfilm and lightly pound with a rolling pin. Season each escalope with salt and pepper to taste.

2. Lay half a slice of ham on each escalope, put a sage leaf on top and secure with a cocktail stick.

3. Mix the flour with salt and pepper to taste on a large plate. Dust both sides of each escalope with the seasoned flour.

4. Heat the oil in a large frying pan, add the butter and cook until foaming. Add the escalopes and fry over a medium heat for 1½ minutes, sage-side down. Turn the escalopes over and fry for a further 30 seconds, or until golden brown and cooked through. Serve immediately with lemon wedges for squeezing over.

#40

Serves 4

Turkey meatballs with honey-chipotle glaze

Ingredients

2 tbsp olive oil, plus extra for greasing

675 g/1 lb 8 oz fresh turkey mince

½ yellow onion, finely diced

25 g/1 oz fresh breadcrumbs

3 garlic cloves, finely chopped

2 tsp dried oregano

¾ tsp salt

¼ tsp pepper

roasted vegetables and freshly cooked rice, to serve

Glaze

4 tbsp clear honey

2 tbsp tomato ketchup

1 tbsp cider vinegar

¼–½ tsp ground chipotle chilli

1. Preheat the oven to 190°C/375°F/Gas Mark 5 and brush a large baking dish with oil.

2. In a large bowl, combine the mince, onion, breadcrumbs, garlic, oregano, salt and pepper and mix well to combine. Form the mixture into 4-cm/1½-inch balls and place them in the prepared dish. Brush the tops and sides of the meatballs with the remaining oil. Bake in the preheated oven for about 15 minutes.

3. Meanwhile, prepare the glaze. Put the honey, ketchup, vinegar and chilli into a bowl and stir to combine.

4. Remove the meatballs from the oven and increase the oven temperature to 230°C/450°F/Gas Mark 8.

5. Pour off as much liquid as you can from the baking dish. Spoon the glaze over the meatballs, making sure they all get some sauce. Return to the oven and bake for a further 5 minutes, or until the glaze is reduced.

6. Serve immediately with roasted vegetables and freshly cooked rice.

#41 Turkey club burgers

Makes 4

Ingredients

450 g/1 lb fresh turkey mince

1 garlic clove, finely chopped

1½ tsp finely chopped fresh rosemary

1 tsp salt

½ tsp pepper

6 bacon rashers

8 slices white farmhouse bread, toasted

2–3 tbsp ready-made ranch-style dressing

lettuce leaves

tomato slices

1. Preheat a barbecue or grill to medium-high. Combine the turkey mince with the garlic, rosemary, salt and pepper in a bowl. Divide the mixture into 4 equal-sized portions and shape each portion into a thick patty.

2. Cook the bacon in a frying pan over a medium heat for about 8 minutes, or until crisp. Drain on kitchen paper and break the pieces in half. Spread each slice of bread with about ½ teaspoon of the ranch-style dressing.

3. Put the burgers on the rack and cook over a medium heat, covered, for 4–5 minutes on each side, or until cooked through. Place each burger on a slice of the toasted bread, add the bacon, lettuce leaves and tomato slices, drizzle with a little more dressing and top with the remaining toasted bread. Serve immediately.

#42 Cajun chicken

Serves 4

Ingredients

4 chicken drumsticks

4 chicken thighs

2 fresh corn cobs

85 g/3 oz butter, melted

oil, for frying

Spice mix

2 tsp onion powder

2 tsp paprika

1½ tsp salt

1 tsp garlic powder

1 tsp dried thyme

1 tsp cayenne pepper

1 tsp ground black pepper

½ tsp ground white pepper

¼ tsp ground cumin

1. Using a sharp knife, make two or three diagonal slashes in the chicken drumsticks and thighs, then place them in a large dish. Remove the husks and silks from the corn cobs and add the cobs to the dish. Mix all the ingredients for the spice mix together in a small bowl.

2. Brush the chicken and corn with the melted butter and sprinkle with the spice mix. Toss to coat well.

3. Heat the oil in a large griddle pan over a medium–high heat, add the chicken and cook, turning occasionally, for 15 minutes, then add the corn cobs and cook, turning occasionally, for a further 10–15 minutes, or until beginning to blacken slightly at the edges. Check that the chicken is tender and the juices run clear when a skewer is inserted into the thickest part of the meat. Transfer to a serving plate and serve.

#43 Chicken meatball pasta

Serves 4

Ingredients

3 tbsp olive oil

1 red onion, chopped

400 g/14 oz skinless, boneless chicken breasts, chopped

55 g/2 oz fresh white breadcrumbs

2 tsp dried oregano

1 garlic clove, crushed

400 g/14 oz canned chopped tomatoes

1 tbsp sun-dried tomato purée

300 ml/10 fl oz water

225 g/8 oz dried spaghetti or linguine

salt and pepper

Parmesan cheese shavings, to serve

1. Heat 1 tablespoon of the oil in a large frying pan and fry half the chopped onion for 5 minutes, until just soft. Leave to cool.

2. Place the chicken, breadcrumbs, oregano and the fried onion in a food processor or blender. Season to taste well with salt and pepper, and process for 2–3 minutes, until thoroughly combined. Shape into 24 meatballs.

3. Heat the remaining oil in the pan, add the meatballs and fry over a medium–high heat for 3–4 minutes, until golden brown. Remove and set aside. Add the remaining onion and the garlic to the pan and fry for 5 minutes. Stir in the tomatoes, tomato purée and water, and bring to the boil. Add the meatballs and simmer for 20 minutes. Season with salt and pepper.

4. Meanwhile, bring a large saucepan of lightly salted water to the boil. Add the pasta, bring back to the boil and cook for 8–10 minutes, until tender but still firm to the bite. Drain and toss with the meatballs and sauce. Serve immediately with Parmesan cheese shavings.

#44 Crisp-fried spicy turkey

Serves 4

Ingredients

450 g/1 lb turkey steaks

2 tbsp Thai fish sauce

2 tbsp light soy sauce

groundnut oil, for frying

40 g/1½ oz peanuts, roughly chopped

4 tbsp chopped Thai basil and lime wedges, to garnish

Spice paste

2 tsp coriander seeds

1 tsp cumin seeds

2 tsp white peppercorns

seeds from 3 green cardamom pods

1 tsp sugar

2 fresh red chillies, finely chopped

2 garlic cloves, finely chopped

1. To make the spice paste, dry-fry the coriander seeds over a medium–high heat, shaking the pan frequently, for 2 minutes until starting to pop. Dry-fry the cumin seeds for 30 seconds until fragrant, taking care not to let them burn. Grind the seeds to a paste with the remaining ingredients, using a mortar and pestle.

2. Pound the turkey steaks with a mallet until they are 5 mm/¼ inch thick. Slice across the grain into thin strips and put in a shallow bowl. Rub the spice paste into the meat. Add the fish sauce and soy sauce, tossing to coat. Leave to marinate at room temperature for 20 minutes.

3. Heat a large wok over a high heat and add oil to a depth of 2.5 cm/1 inch. Add the turkey and any spice paste from the bowl. Fry for 4 minutes, turning, until beginning to colour. Add the peanuts and fry for a further minute, or until the turkey is cooked through. Remove with a slotted spoon and drain on kitchen paper. Tip into a warmed serving dish and sprinkle with the basil. Garnish with lime wedges and serve.

Italian turkey cutlets

Ingredients

1 tbsp olive oil

4 turkey escalopes or steaks

2 red peppers, deseeded and sliced

1 red onion, sliced

2 garlic cloves, finely chopped

300 ml/10 fl oz passata

150 ml/5 fl oz medium white wine

1 tbsp chopped fresh marjoram

400 g/14 oz canned cannellini beans, drained and rinsed

3 tbsp fresh white breadcrumbs

salt and pepper

fresh basil sprigs, to garnish

1. Preheat the grill to medium. Heat the oil in a large, heavy-based frying pan. Add the turkey and cook over a medium heat for 5–10 minutes, turning occasionally, until golden. Transfer to a plate. Add the red pepper and onion to the pan and cook over a low heat, stirring occasionally, for 5 minutes, or until soft. Add the garlic and cook for a further 2 minutes.

2. Return the turkey to the pan and add the passata, wine and marjoram. Season to taste with salt and pepper. Bring to the boil, then reduce the heat, cover and simmer, stirring occasionally, for 25–30 minutes, or until the turkey is cooked through and tender.

3. Stir in the beans and simmer for a further 5 minutes. Sprinkle the breadcrumbs over the top and place under the preheated grill for 2–3 minutes, or until golden. Serve, garnished with fresh basil sprigs.

Jerk chicken burgers

Ingredients

1 tsp soft light brown sugar

1 tsp ground ginger

½ tsp ground allspice

½ tsp dried thyme

½–1 tsp cayenne pepper

1 tbsp lime juice

2 garlic cloves, finely chopped

450 g/1 lb fresh chicken mince

1 tbsp vegetable oil

1 red pepper, deseeded and cut into large flat pieces

1 tsp olive oil

1 tsp red wine vinegar

4 onion rolls, split

lettuce leaves

salt and pepper

1. Place the sugar, ginger, allspice, thyme, cayenne pepper, lime juice, garlic, ½ teaspoon of salt and ½ teaspoon of pepper into a bowl and mix together. Add the chicken and gently mix to combine. Divide the mixture into 4 equal-sized portions and shape each portion into a patty.

2. Place a griddle pan over a medium–high heat and add the vegetable oil. Add the red pepper and cook for about 5 minutes, turning frequently, until blackened. Transfer to a bowl, cover with clingfilm and leave to steam for 5 minutes. Remove the skin and cut the flesh into strips. Toss with the olive oil, vinegar, and salt and pepper to taste.

3. Put the patties in the pan and cook, covered, for about 5 minutes on each side until brown and cooked through. Place the burgers in the rolls and top with the lettuce and peppers. Serve immediately.

Serves
4

Venetian duck with spaghetti

Ingredients

4 duck legs
1 tbsp duck fat
1 tbsp butter
3 garlic cloves, peeled
450 g/1 lb dried spaghetti
juice and grated rind of ½ lemon
salt and pepper

1. Preheat the oven to 150°C/300°F/Gas Mark 2. Prick the skin on the duck legs all over and season well with salt. Put in a small roasting tin, fitting them snugly in a single layer. Roast in the preheated oven for 1½ hours, then increase the oven temperature to 200°C/400°F/Gas Mark 6 and roast for a further 15 minutes until the skin is golden and crisp. Remove from the oven and leave to cool. Remove the skin from the duck legs and roughly chop, then remove all the meat and roughly chop. Heat a heavy-based saucepan over a medium heat, add the duck skin and meat with the duck fat and butter and cook over a medium–low heat for 10–12 minutes.

2. Add the garlic to the pan with the duck and cook, stirring occasionally, for a few minutes, until the garlic starts to colour, then remove the pan from the heat. Remove and discard the garlic.

3. Meanwhile, bring a large saucepan of lightly salted water to the boil. Add the pasta, bring back to the boil and cook for 8–10 minutes, until tender but still firm to the bite. Drain the pasta, add to the pan and return to a medium heat. Toss together, then add the lemon juice, season with pepper and toss again. Transfer to a warmed serving dish, sprinkle with lemon rind and serve.

48

Serves
2

Yaki soba

Ingredients

400 g/14 oz ramen noodles
1 onion, finely sliced
200 g/7 oz beansprouts
1 red pepper, deseeded and sliced
150 g/5½ oz cooked chicken, sliced
12 cooked peeled prawns
1 tbsp sunflower oil, for stir-frying
2 tbsp shoyu
½ tbsp mirin
1 tsp sesame oil
1 tsp sesame seeds
2 spring onions, finely sliced

1. Cook the noodles according to the packet instructions, drain well and tip into a bowl.

2. Mix together the onion, beansprouts, red pepper, chicken and prawns in a bowl. Stir through the noodles. Meanwhile, preheat a wok over a high heat, add the oil and heat until very hot.

3. Add the noodle mixture and stir-fry for 4 minutes, or until golden, then add the shoyu, mirin and sesame oil and toss together.

4. Divide the noodles between two bowls.

5. Sprinkle with sesame seeds and spring onions and serve.

Chicken Parmesan

Ingredients

100 g/3½ oz plain flour

2 eggs

200 g/7 oz dry breadcrumbs

4 skinless, boneless chicken breasts,
250 g/9 oz each

2 tbsp olive oil, plus extra if needed

250 g/9 oz mozzarella cheese, sliced

125 g/4½ oz Parmesan cheese, grated

salt and pepper

chopped fresh flat-leaf parsley,
to garnish

Simple marinara sauce

2 tbsp olive oil

1 large onion, chopped

2 large garlic cloves, chopped

1 tbsp dried mixed herbs

800 g/1 lb 12 oz canned chopped
tomatoes

250 ml/9 fl oz passata

2 tsp dried oregano

pinch of sugar

salt and pepper

1. To make the sauce, heat the oil in a large saucepan. Add the onion and fry, stirring, for 2 minutes. Add the garlic and cook, stirring, until the onion is soft. Stir in the mixed herbs, tomatoes, passata, oregano and sugar and season to taste. Bring to the boil, then cover and simmer for 15 minutes. Transfer to a blender or food processor and purée.

2. Meanwhile, preheat the oven to 200°C/400°F/Gas Mark 6. Spread the flour on a plate. Beat the eggs in a wide bowl, and put the breadcrumbs on a separate plate. Halve the chicken breasts horizontally, place between sheets of clingfilm and pound with a meat mallet to a thickness of 5 mm/¼ inch. Season all over with salt and pepper. Dust each chicken breast with flour, shaking off the excess, then dip in the egg to coat. Dip in the breadcrumbs to coat both sides.

3. Heat the oil in a frying pan over a medium–high heat. Add as many chicken pieces as will fit in a single layer and fry on each side for 2 minutes, or until golden and cooked through. Fry the remaining pieces. Pour half of the sauce into a baking dish that will hold the chicken in a single layer. Arrange the chicken on top, then pour over the remaining sauce. Arrange the mozzarella cheese on top and sprinkle over the Parmesan cheese. Bake in the preheated oven for 20–25 minutes, or until the cheese is melted, golden and bubbling. Leave to stand for 5 minutes, then garnish with parsley and serve immediately.

Chicken piccata

Serves
4

Ingredients

4 boneless, skinless chicken breasts, flattened to a 5-mm/¼-inch thickness

plain flour, for dusting

4 tbsp olive oil

2 tbsp capers, drained

150 ml/5 fl oz white wine

90 ml/3 fl oz lemon juice

90 ml/3 fl oz chicken stock or water

6 tbsp cold unsalted butter, cut into 5-mm/¼-inch slices

15 g/½ oz fresh flat-leaf parsley, chopped

salt and pepper

lemon slices, to garnish

1. Season the chicken breasts with salt and pepper and dust with the flour until completely covered, shaking off excess. Set aside.

2. Put the oil in a large frying pan and heat over a medium–high heat until hot. Add the chicken and cook for 4 minutes on each side, or until brown and just cooked through. Transfer to a plate, loosely cover with foil and set aside.

3. Finely chop half the capers and add to the pan with the wine. Increase the heat to high, bring to the boil and boil until the wine has reduced by half. Use a spatula to scrape the caramelized bits from the base of the pan. Add the lemon juice and stock, and bring to the boil. Cook for a further 2 minutes, reduce the heat to low, then return the chicken to the pan to heat through.

4. Transfer the chicken to a serving platter. Add the butter and parsley to the pan and whisk until the butter emulsifies into the sauce. Spoon the sauce over the chicken and serve immediately, garnished with lemon slices.

Mexican turkey

Serves
4

Ingredients

55 g/2 oz plain flour

4 turkey breast fillets

3 tbsp corn oil

1 onion, thinly sliced

1 red pepper, deseeded and sliced

300 ml/10 fl oz chicken stock

25 g/1 oz raisins

4 tomatoes, peeled, deseeded and chopped

1 tsp chilli powder

½ tsp ground cinnamon

pinch of ground cumin

25 g/1 oz plain chocolate, grated

salt and pepper

fresh coriander sprigs, to garnish

1. Preheat the oven to 160°C/325°F/Gas Mark 3. Spread the flour on a plate and season with salt and pepper. Coat the turkey in the seasoned flour, shaking off any excess. Set aside any remaining seasoned flour.

2. Heat the oil in a flameproof casserole. Add the turkey and cook over a medium heat, turning occasionally, for 5–10 minutes, or until golden. Transfer to a plate. Add the onion and red pepper to the casserole. Cook over a low heat, stirring occasionally, for 5 minutes, or until soft. Sprinkle in the reserved seasoned flour and cook, stirring constantly, for 1 minute. Gradually stir in the stock, then add the raisins, tomatoes, chilli powder, cinnamon, cumin and chocolate. Season to taste with salt and pepper. Bring to the boil, stirring constantly.

3. Return the turkey to the casserole, cover and cook in the preheated oven for 50 minutes. Serve immediately, garnished with sprigs of coriander.

Baked tapenade chicken

Serves 4

Ingredients

4 skinless, boneless chicken breasts

4 tbsp green olive tapenade

8 thin slices smoked pancetta

2 garlic cloves, chopped

250 g/9 oz cherry tomatoes, halved

100 ml/3½ fl oz dry white wine

2 tbsp olive oil

8 slices ciabatta

salt and pepper

1. Preheat the oven to 220°C/425°F/Gas Mark 7. Place the chicken breasts on a board and cut three deep slashes into each. Spread a tablespoon of the tapenade over each chicken breast, pushing it into the slashes with a palette knife. Wrap each chicken breast in two slices of pancetta. Place the chicken breasts in a shallow ovenproof dish and arrange the garlic and tomatoes around them. Season to taste with salt and pepper, then pour over the wine and 1 tablespoon of the oil. Bake in the preheated oven for about 20 minutes, until the juices run clear when the chicken is pierced with a skewer. Loosely cover with foil and leave to stand for 5 minutes.

2. Meanwhile, preheat the grill to high. Brush the ciabatta with the remaining oil and cook under the preheated grill for 2–3 minutes, turning once, until golden. Transfer the chicken and tomatoes to serving plates and spoon over the juices. Serve with the ciabatta.

Turkey & mushroom cannelloni

Serves 4

Ingredients

2 tbsp olive oil, plus extra for greasing

2 garlic cloves, crushed

1 large onion, finely chopped

225 g/8 oz wild mushrooms, sliced

350 g/12 oz fresh turkey mince

115 g/4 oz prosciutto, diced

150 ml/5 fl oz Marsala

200 g/7 oz canned chopped tomatoes

1 tbsp shredded fresh basil leaves

2 tbsp tomato purée

10–12 dried cannelloni tubes

600 ml/1 pint béchamel sauce

85 g/3 oz freshly grated Parmesan cheese

salt and pepper

1. Preheat the oven to 190°C/375°F/Gas Mark 5. Lightly grease a large ovenproof dish. Heat the oil in a heavy-based frying pan. Add the garlic, onion and mushrooms and cook over a low heat, stirring frequently, for 8–10 minutes. Add the turkey mince and prosciutto and cook, stirring frequently, for 12 minutes, or until browned all over. Stir in the Marsala, tomatoes, basil and tomato purée and cook for 4 minutes. Season to taste with salt and pepper, then cover and simmer for 30 minutes. Uncover, stir and simmer for 15 minutes.

2. Meanwhile, bring a large saucepan of lightly salted water to the boil. Add the cannelloni tubes, bring back to the boil and cook for 8–10 minutes, until tender but still firm to the bite. Using a slotted spoon, transfer the cannelloni tubes to a plate and pat dry with kitchen paper.

3. Using a teaspoon, fill the cannelloni tubes with the turkey and mushroom mixture. Transfer them to the dish. Pour the bechamel sauce over them to cover completely and sprinkle with the grated Parmesan cheese. Bake in the preheated oven for 30 minutes, or until golden and bubbling. Serve immediately.

Serves 4

Turkey steaks with chilli maple glaze

Ingredients

4 turkey breast steaks, about 125 g/4½ oz each

2 tbsp olive oil

1 garlic clove, crushed

4 tbsp maple syrup

2 tbsp tomato purée

2 tbsp Worcestershire sauce

3 tbsp lime juice

1½ tsp hot chilli sauce

salt and pepper

chopped fresh flat-leaf parsley, to garnish

1. Place the turkey breasts between two pieces of clingfilm and beat with a rolling pin until very thin. Season to taste with salt and pepper.

2. Heat the oil in a large frying pan, add the turkey and fry over a fairly high heat, turning once, for 3–4 minutes until golden brown.

3. Mix together the garlic, maple syrup, tomato purée, Worcestershire sauce, lime juice and chilli sauce, then spoon over the turkey.

4. Turn the turkey in the glaze to coat, then reduce the heat to low, cover the pan and cook very gently for 8–10 minutes until the turkey is tender and thoroughly cooked.

5. Adjust the seasoning to taste, sprinkle with parsley and serve.

55

Serves 4

Coq au vin

Ingredients

55 g/2 oz butter

2 tbsp olive oil

1.8 kg/4 lb chicken pieces

115 g/4 oz rindless smoked bacon, cut into strips

115 g/4 oz baby onions

115 g/4 oz chestnut mushrooms, halved

2 garlic cloves, finely chopped

2 tbsp brandy

225 ml/8 fl oz red wine

300 ml/10 fl oz chicken stock

1 bouquet garni

2 tbsp plain flour

salt and pepper

bay leaves, to garnish

1. Melt half the butter with the oil in a large flameproof casserole. Add the chicken and cook over a medium heat, stirring, for 8–10 minutes, or until brown all over. Add the bacon, onions, mushrooms and garlic.

2. Pour in the brandy and set it alight with a match or taper. When the flames have died down, add the wine, stock and bouquet garni and season to taste with salt and pepper. Bring to the boil, reduce the heat and simmer gently for 1 hour, or until the chicken is tender and the juices run clear when a skewer is inserted into the thickest part of the meat.

3. Remove and discard the bouquet garni. Transfer the chicken to a large plate and keep warm. Mix the flour with the remaining butter and whisk into the casserole, a little at a time. Bring to the boil, return the chicken to the casserole and heat through. Garnish with bay leaves and serve immediately (do not eat the bay leaves).

Lemon & tarragon chicken breasts

Ingredients

225 ml/8 fl oz white wine

475 ml/16 fl oz chicken stock

1 tbsp fresh tarragon leaves

½ onion, sliced

½ tsp salt

pinch of black pepper

pinch of cayenne pepper

juice of 1 lemon

4 boneless, skinless chicken breasts

1 tbsp cold unsalted butter

lemon wedges, to garnish

mashed potato, to serve

1. Put the wine, stock, tarragon, onion, salt, black pepper, cayenne paper, and lemon juice into a 25-cm/10-inch frying pan. Bring to a simmer over a high heat, then add the chicken breasts. Reduce the heat to very low and simmer gently for 12 minutes, or until the chicken is cooked through.

2. Transfer the chicken to a plate, and cover with foil. Increase the heat to high and boil the liquid for 5 minutes until reduced slightly. Remove from the heat, add the butter and whisk until it is dissolved.

3. Place a scoop of mashed potato in four warmed bowls. Slice the chicken and arrange on top of the potatoes. Spoon over the hot sauce. Serve immediately with lemon wedges.

Baked chicken & chorizo paella

Ingredients

2 tbsp olive oil

100 g/3½ oz chorizo sausages, sliced

1 onion, finely chopped

1 red pepper, roughly chopped

400 g/14 oz boneless, skinless chicken thighs, cut into bite-sized pieces

4 large garlic cloves, finely chopped

350 g/12 oz paella rice

150 g/5½ oz frozen peas

1 tsp Spanish sweet paprika

large pinch of saffron threads

125 ml/4 fl oz dry white wine

700 ml/1¼ pints chicken stock

200 g/7 oz large raw prawns, peeled

salt and pepper

chopped fresh parsley, to garnish

lemon wedges, to serve

1. Preheat the oven to 220°C/425°F/Gas Mark 7. Heat the oil in a flameproof casserole over a high heat. Reduce the heat to low–medium, add the chorizo and fry, stirring, for 3–4 minutes until it starts to brown and gives off its oil. Remove from the pan and pour off all but 2 tablespoons of the oil. Add the onion and red pepper and fry, stirring, for 3–5 minutes until soft. Add the chicken and garlic and stir until the chicken is coloured all over.

2. Add the rice and peas, gently stirring until the rice is coated in oil. Stir in the paprika and saffron threads, then add the wine and stock and season with salt and pepper. Bring to the boil, stirring occasionally. Transfer to the preheated oven and bake, uncovered, for 15 minutes.

3. Remove from the oven and add the prawns and chorizo, pushing them down into the rice. Return to the oven and bake for a further 10 minutes, or until the rice is tender, the prawns are pink and cooked through and the chicken is cooked through. Cut into the middle of the chicken to check there are no remaining traces of pink. Garnish with parsley and serve with lemon wedges.

#58 Chicken jalfrezi

Serves
4–6

Ingredients

55 g/2 oz ghee or 4 tbsp vegetable oil

8 skinless chicken pieces, sliced

1 large onion, chopped

2 tbsp garlic paste

2 tbsp ginger paste

2 green peppers, chopped

1 large fresh green chilli, finely chopped

1 tsp ground cumin

1 tsp ground coriander

¼–½ tsp chilli powder

½ tsp ground turmeric

¼ tsp salt

400 g/14 oz canned chopped tomatoes

125 ml/4 fl oz water

chopped fresh coriander, to garnish

1. Melt half the ghee in a large frying pan over a medium-high heat. Add the chicken pieces and stir for 5 minutes until brown, then remove from the pan with a slotted spoon and set aside.

2. Melt the remaining ghee in the pan. Add the onion and fry, stirring frequently, for 5–8 minutes until golden brown. Stir in the garlic and ginger paste and fry for a further 2 minutes, stirring frequently.

3. Add the peppers and stir for 2 minutes. Stir in the chilli, cumin, coriander, chilli powder, turmeric and salt. Add the tomatoes with their can juices and the water and bring to the boil.

4. Reduce the heat to low, add the chicken and leave it to simmer, uncovered, for 10 minutes, stirring frequently, until the peppers are tender and the chicken is cooked through. Garnish with the coriander and serve immediately.

#59 Peking duck

Serves
6–10

Ingredients

1 duck, weighing 2 kg/4 lb 8 oz

1.5 litres/2¾ pints boiling water

1 tbsp honey

1 tbsp Shaoxing rice wine

1 tsp white rice vinegar

1 cucumber, peeled, deseeded and julienned

10 spring onions, white parts only, shredded

30 pancakes

plum or hoisin sauce, to serve

1. To prepare the duck, massage the skin to separate it from the meat. Pour the boiling water into a large saucepan, add the honey, rice wine and vinegar and lower in the duck. Baste in the mixture for about 1 minute. Remove the duck and hang it to dry for 2 hours, or overnight.

2. Preheat the oven to 200°C/400°F/Gas Mark 6. Place the duck on a rack above a roasting tin and roast in the preheated oven for at least 1 hour until the skin is very crispy and the duck is cooked through.

3. Place the duck on a chopping board, together with the cucumber, spring onions and pancakes, and carve off the duck skin. Arrange a little duck skin on a pancake with some cucumber and spring onion. Top with a little plum sauce. Roll up and eat. Repeat the process with the lean meat.

Serves
4

Mustard-crusted turkey breast

Ingredients

1 x 650 g/1 lb 7 oz turkey breast joint, skin removed

25 g/1 oz fresh white breadcrumbs (preferably ciabatta)

40 g/1½ oz butter, softened

2 tbsp wholegrain mustard

1 tbsp finely chopped fresh rosemary

1 garlic clove, crushed

1 tbsp fresh lemon juice

salt and pepper

fresh rosemary sprigs, to garnish

1. Preheat the oven to 190°C/375°F/Gas Mark 5. Place the turkey in a small roasting tin and season with salt and pepper.

2. Mix the breadcrumbs, butter, mustard, rosemary, garlic and lemon juice together to make a thick paste. Season with salt and pepper.

3. Spread the mustard mixture over the surface of the turkey, pressing out with your fingers to make an even crust.

4. Cook the turkey in the preheated oven for about 40 minutes, until golden brown and thoroughly cooked – the juices should run clear when the thickest part of the meat is pierced with a sharp knife.

5. Remove from the oven, loosely cover with foil and leave to stand for about 10 minutes. Serve sliced, with the pan juices spooned over. Garnish with fresh rosemary sprigs.

Serves
4

Chicken with goat's cheese & mushroom sauce

Ingredients

4 boneless, skinless chicken breasts, halved horizontally

2 tbsp olive oil

115 g/4 oz button mushrooms, sliced

1 tbsp unsalted butter

50 ml/2 fl oz chicken stock

125 ml/4 fl oz double cream

85 g/3 oz goat's cheese

15 g/½ oz fresh flat-leaf parsley, chopped

salt and pepper

1. Place the chicken between two pieces of clingfilm and pound with a meat mallet to a thickness of 5 mm/ ¼ inch. Season to taste with salt and pepper.

2. Heat the oil in a large frying pan over a medium–high heat. Add the chicken and cook for about 3 minutes on each side, or until brown and cooked through. Transfer to a plate.

3. Add the mushrooms and butter to the pan and cook, stirring occasionally, until the liquid has evaporated, and the mushrooms are brown. Stir in the stock, cream, cheese and parsley. Bring to a simmer, add the chicken and cook until heated through. Season to taste with salt and pepper and serve immediately.

62

Serves
4

Chicken with mustard cream sauce

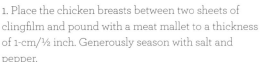

Ingredients

4 boneless, skinless chicken breasts

1 tbsp unsalted butter

1 tbsp olive oil

125 ml/4 fl oz chicken stock

75 ml/2½ fl oz double cream

2 tbsp whole-grain mustard

2 tbsp chopped fresh flat-leaf parsley

salt and pepper

1. Place the chicken breasts between two sheets of clingfilm and pound with a meat mallet to a thickness of 1-cm/½ inch. Generously season with salt and pepper.

2. Add the butter and oil to a large frying pan over a medium–high heat. Add the chicken and sauté for about 5 minutes on each side until cooked through. Cut into the middle of the chicken to check there are no remaining traces of pink or red. Remove to a plate, and cover with foil.

3. Add the stock to the pan. Whisk in the cream, mustard and parsley and cook for 3 minutes, or until thickened. Pour the sauce over the chicken and serve immediately.

#63 Turkey breast with bacon, leeks & prunes

Serves 6–8

Ingredients

115 g/4 oz bacon rashers

2 leeks, trimmed, white and light green parts, thinly sliced

1 skinless, bone-in turkey breast, about 1.8 kg/4 lb

30 g/1 oz plain flour

1 tbsp olive oil, if needed

12 stoned prunes, halved

1 tsp crumbled dried thyme or 1 tbsp finely chopped fresh thyme

225 ml/8 fl oz chicken stock

salt and pepper

1. Heat a frying pan over a medium–high heat, then add the bacon and cook until just crisp. Remove from the pan, drain on kitchen paper, then chop or crumble into small pieces.

2. Add the leeks to the pan and cook, stirring frequently, for about 5 minutes, or until soft.

3. Season the turkey with salt and pepper and dredge with the flour. If needed, add the oil to the pan, then add the turkey and cook on one side for 4–5 minutes, until brown. Turn and cook on the other side for a further 4–5 minutes, until brown.

4. Place the turkey in a slow cooker with the leeks, bacon, prunes and thyme. Add the stock, cover and cook on high for about 5 hours or on low for about 9 hours.

5. Remove the turkey from the slow cooker and leave to rest for 5 minutes. Slice and serve with some of the sauce, including the prunes and bits of bacon, spooned over the top.

#64 Chicken mole poblano

Serves 4

Ingredients

3 tbsp olive oil

4 x 175 g/6 oz chicken pieces, halved

1 onion, chopped

2 garlic cloves, finely chopped

1 dried red chilli, finely chopped

1 tbsp sesame seeds, toasted, plus extra to garnish

1 tbsp chopped almonds

½ tsp each ground cinnamon, cumin and cloves

3 tomatoes, peeled and chopped

2 tbsp raisins

350 ml/12 fl oz chicken stock

1 tbsp peanut butter

25 g/1 oz plain chocolate

salt and pepper

1. Heat the oil in a large frying pan. Add the chicken and cook until browned on all sides. Remove the chicken pieces with a slotted spoon and set aside.

2. Add the onion, garlic and chilli and cook for 5 minutes, or until soft. Add the sesame seeds, almonds and spices and cook, stirring, for 2 minutes. Add the tomatoes, raisins, stock and peanut butter. Grate in the chocolate and stir well.

3. Season to taste with salt and pepper and simmer for 5 minutes. Transfer the mixture to a food processor and process until smooth Return to the pan, add the chicken and bring to the boil. Reduce the heat, cover and simmer for 1 hour, or until the chicken is very tender, adding more liquid if necessary. Check the juices run clear when a skewer is inserted into the thickest part of the meat. Garnish with sesame seeds and serve.

51

#65 Turkey & barley stew

Serves 4

Ingredients

15 g/½ oz dried ceps

2 tbsp olive oil

1 onion, diced

450 g/1 lb button mushrooms, sliced

4 carrots, sliced

1 tsp salt

½ tsp pepper

200 g/7 oz barley

600 ml/1 pint vegetable stock

1 tbsp fresh thyme leaves

450 g/1 lb turkey breast meat

grated Parmesan cheese and chopped fresh parsley, to garnish

1. Place the ceps in a small bowl and cover with hot water. Heat the oil in a large saucepan over a medium-high heat. Add the onion and cook, stirring frequently, for about 4 minutes until soft. Add the mushrooms and carrots to the pan with the salt and pepper. Cook, stirring occasionally, for 4 minutes until the vegetables are tender. Add the barley and stir to mix well. Add the stock.

2. Remove the ceps from the soaking water, reserving the soaking liquid, and chop. Add to the pan with the soaking liquid and bring to the boil. Meanwhile, finely chop the thyme and add to the pan. Reduce the heat to low and simmer, uncovered, for about 5 minutes.

3. Cut the turkey into 1-cm/½-inch cubes and add to the stew, stir to mix, then cover and simmer for 15 minutes, until the turkey is cooked through, the barley is tender, and most of the liquid has evaporated. Serve in bowls, garnished with the cheese and parsley.

#66 Chicken pot pies

Serves 6

Ingredients

1 tbsp olive oil

225 g/8 oz button mushrooms, sliced

1 onion, finely chopped

350 g/12 oz carrots, sliced

115 g/4 oz celery, sliced

1 litre/1¾ pints chicken stock

85 g/3 oz butter

55 g/2 oz plain flour, plus extra for dusting

900 g/2 lb skinless, boneless chicken breasts, cut into 2.5-cm/1-inch cubes

115 g/4 oz frozen peas

1 tsp chopped fresh thyme

675 g/1 lb 8 oz shortcrust pastry

1 egg, lightly beaten

salt and pepper

1. Heat the oil in a large saucepan over a medium heat. Add the mushrooms and onion and cook for about 8 minutes, until golden. Add the carrots, celery and half the stock and bring to the boil. Reduce the heat and simmer for 12–15 minutes.

2. Melt the butter in a separate large saucepan over a medium heat. Whisk in the flour and cook, stirring constantly, for 4 minutes. Gradually whisk in the remaining stock. Reduce the heat to medium–low and simmer, stirring, until thickened. Stir in the vegetable mixture, add the chicken, peas and thyme and season with salt and pepper. Bring back to a simmer and cook, stirring constantly, for 5 minutes. Remove from the heat.

3. Preheat the oven to 200°C/400°F/Gas Mark 6. Divide the filling between six large ramekins. Roll out the pastry on a lightly floured work surface and cut out 6 rounds 2.5 cm/1 inch larger than the diameter of the ramekins. Place on top of the filling, then fold over 1 cm/½ inch all the way around. Cut a small cross in the centre of each crust. Put the ramekins on a baking sheet and brush with the beaten egg. Bake in the preheated oven for 35–40 minutes, until golden brown and bubbling. Leave to cool for 15 minutes before serving.

#67 Thai green chicken curry

Serves 4

Ingredients

2 tbsp groundnut oil

4 spring onions, roughly chopped

2 tbsp green curry paste

700 ml/1¼ pints canned coconut milk

1 chicken stock cube

6 skinless chicken breasts, cut into 2.5-cm/1-inch cubes

large handful of fresh coriander, chopped

½ tsp salt

cooked rice, to serve

1. Heat a wok over a medium–high heat, then add the oil. Add the spring onions and stir-fry for 30 seconds, or until starting to soften.

2. Add the curry paste, coconut milk and stock cube and bring gently to the boil, stirring occasionally.

3. Add the chicken, half the coriander and the salt and stir well. Reduce the heat and simmer gently for 8–10 minutes, or until the chicken is cooked through. Cut into the middle of the chicken to check that there are no traces of pink or red. Stir in the remaining coriander. Serve immediately with rice.

#68 Duck stew with pancetta & olives

Serves 4

Ingredients

2 tbsp olive oil

1.8 kg/4 lb oven-ready duck, cut into 8 pieces

150 g/5½ oz pancetta, diced

1 large onion, diced

1 celery stick, diced

1 carrot, diced

1 garlic clove, crushed

175 ml/6 fl oz red wine

400 ml/14 fl oz passata

1 fresh red chilli, finely chopped

3 fresh rosemary sprigs

12 black olives

salt and pepper

chopped fresh flat-leaf parsley, to garnish

1. Heat the oil in a large saucepan and fry the duck pieces, in batches, until golden brown. Remove and set aside. Tip out all but 1 tablespoon of the oil and fry the pancetta, stirring, until golden. Add the onion, celery, carrot and garlic and fry gently, stirring, for 3–4 minutes.

2. Stir in the wine and boil for 1 minute, then add the passata, chilli, rosemary and olives with salt and pepper to taste.

3. Return the duck pieces to the pan, spooning over the sauce to cover. Cover and simmer gently for about 1 hour, or until the duck is tender.

4. Sprinkle with parsley and serve.

#69 Chicken gumbo

Serves 4–6

Ingredients

1 chicken, weighing 1.5 kg/3 lb 5 oz, cut into 6 pieces

2 celery sticks, 1 broken in half and 1 finely chopped

1 carrot, chopped

2 onions, 1 sliced and 1 chopped

2 bay leaves

¼ tsp salt

4 tbsp corn oil or groundnut oil

50 g/1¾ oz plain flour

2 large garlic cloves, crushed

1 green pepper, cored, deseeded and diced

450 g/1 lb fresh okra, trimmed, then cut crossways into 1-cm/½-inch slices

225 g/8 oz andouille sausage or Polish kielbasa, sliced

2 tbsp tomato purée

1 tsp dried thyme

½ tsp salt

½ tsp cayenne pepper

¼ tsp pepper

400 g/14 oz canned plum tomatoes

cooked long-grain rice and hot pepper sauce, to serve

1. Put the chicken into a large saucepan with water to cover over a medium–high heat and bring to the boil, skimming the surface to remove the foam. When the foam stops rising, reduce the heat to medium, add the celery stick halves, carrot, sliced onion, 1 bay leaf and salt and simmer for 20 minutes, or until the chicken is tender and the juices run clear when a skewer is inserted into the thickest part of the meat. Strain the chicken, reserving 1 litre/1¾ pints of the liquid. When the chicken is cool enough to handle, remove and discard the skin, bones and flavourings. Cut the flesh into bite-sized pieces and reserve.

2. Heat the oil in a large saucepan over a medium–high heat for 2 minutes. Reduce the heat to low, sprinkle in the flour and stir. Stir constantly for 20 minutes, or until hazelnut-brown. Add the chopped celery, chopped onion, garlic, green pepper and okra. Increase the heat to medium–high and cook, stirring frequently, for 5 minutes. Add the sausage and cook, stirring frequently, for 2 minutes. Stir in the remaining ingredients and the reserved cooking liquid. Bring to the boil, crushing the tomatoes with a wooden spoon. Reduce the heat to low–medium and simmer, uncovered, for 30 minutes, stirring occasionally.

3. Add the chicken and simmer for 30 minutes. Remove and discard the bay leaves and spoon the gumbo over the rice. Serve with a bottle of hot pepper sauce on the side.

Serves
4

Parma ham-wrapped chicken with pesto

Ingredients

4 skinless chicken breast fillets

4 tsp green pesto

125 g/4½ oz mozzarella cheese

4 thin slices Parma ham

250 g/9 oz cherry plum tomatoes, halved

75 ml/2½ fl oz dry white wine or chicken stock

1 tbsp olive oil

salt and pepper

fresh ciabatta, to serve

1. Preheat the oven to 220°C/425°F/Gas Mark 7. Place the chicken breasts on a board and cut a deep pocket into each with a sharp knife. Place a teaspoonful of pesto in each pocket.

2. Cut the cheese into 4 equal pieces and divide between the chicken breasts, tucking into the pockets. Wrap a slice of ham around each chicken breast to enclose the filling, with the join underneath. Place the chicken in a shallow ovenproof dish and arrange the tomatoes around it. Season to taste with salt and pepper, pour over the wine and drizzle with the oil.

3. Bake in the preheated oven for 15–20 minutes, until the chicken is tender and the juices run clear when a skewer is inserted into the thickest part of the meat.

4. Cut the chicken breasts in half diagonally, place on serving plates with the tomatoes and spoon over the juices. Serve with chunks of ciabatta on the side.

71

Serves
4

Chicken with creamed shallots

Ingredients

1 whole chicken, cut into quarters

1 tbsp unsalted butter

1 tbsp olive oil

225 g/8 oz shallots, peeled and cut in thick 1-cm/½-inch-wide slices

2 tbsp plain flour

50 ml/2 fl oz white wine

225 ml/8 fl oz chicken stock

50 ml/2 fl oz double cream

1 tbsp snipped fresh chives

salt and pepper

1. Generously season the chicken with salt and pepper on both sides. Heat the butter and oil in a casserole over a medium–high heat. Add the chicken and sear for about 4 minutes on each side. Transfer to a plate and add the shallots to the casserole. Reduce the heat and cook for 5 minutes, or until golden. Add the flour and stir in. Cook for 2 minutes.

2. Add the wine and stock and bring to the boil, scraping any sediment from the base of the casserole. Return the chicken to the casserole. Cover tightly, and simmer over a low heat for about 40 minutes, until the chicken is cooked through.

3. Transfer the chicken to a serving platter and loosely cover with foil. Increase the heat to high, add the cream, bring to the boil and cook for 5 minutes, or until reduced and slightly thickened. Add the chives, and salt and pepper to taste. Pour the sauce over the chicken, and serve immediately.

Creamy turkey & broccoli gnocchi

Ingredients

1 tbsp sunflower oil

500 g/1 lb 2 oz turkey stir-fry strips

2 small leeks, sliced diagonally

500 g/1 lb 2 oz ready-made fresh gnocchi

200 g/7 oz broccoli, cut into bite-sized pieces

85 g/3 oz crème fraîche

1 tbsp wholegrain mustard

3 tbsp orange juice

salt and pepper

3 tbsp toasted pine nuts, to serve

1. Heat the oil in a wok or large frying pan, then add the turkey and leeks and stir-fry over a high heat for 5–6 minutes.

2. Meanwhile, bring a saucepan of lightly salted water to the boil. Add the gnocchi and broccoli, bring back to the boil and cook for 3–4 minutes.

3. Drain the gnocchi and broccoli and stir into the turkey mixture.

4. Mix together the crème fraîche, mustard and orange juice in a small bowl. Season to taste with salt and pepper, then stir into the wok.

5. Sprinkle with pine nuts and serve immediately.

Chicken, mushroom & tarragon pie

Ingredients

1 chicken, about 1.5 kg/3 lb 5 oz

2 fresh tarragon sprigs

1 Spanish onion, cut into wedges

300 ml/10 fl oz water

25 g/1 oz butter

175 g/6 oz chestnut mushrooms, sliced

2 tbsp plain flour

55 g/2 oz frozen or shelled fresh peas

1 tbsp chopped fresh tarragon

400 g/14 oz ready-made puff pastry, chilled

1 egg, lightly beaten

salt and pepper

1. Preheat the oven to 200°C/400°F/Gas Mark 6. Put the chicken, tarragon sprigs and onion into a casserole, add the water and season. Cover and bake in the preheated oven for 1½ hours. Remove the chicken. Strain the juices into a jug and chill. Discard the chicken skin, cut off the meat and dice. Skim the fat from the juices and make up to 300 ml/10 fl oz with water.

2. Melt the butter in a saucepan. Add the mushrooms and cook over a medium heat for 3 minutes. Stir in the flour for 1 minute, then gradually stir in the cooking juices. Bring to the boil, add the chicken, peas and chopped tarragon and season to taste. Transfer to a large pie dish and leave to cool.

3. Preheat the oven to 200°C/400°F/Gas Mark 6. Roll out the pastry to 2.5 cm/1 inch larger than the top of the dish. Cut out a 15-mm/⅝-inch strip all the way around. Brush the rim of the dish with water and press the strip onto it. Brush with water and lift the remaining dough on top. Trim the excess, crimping the edges to seal. Make a slit in the centre and brush with beaten egg. Roll out the trimmings and use to decorate the pie, then brush with beaten egg. Bake in the preheated oven for 40 minutes, until golden. Serve immediately.

#74 Duck legs with olives

Serves 4

Ingredients

4 duck legs, all visible fat trimmed off

800 g/1 lb 12 oz canned tomatoes, chopped

8 garlic cloves, peeled but left whole

1 large onion, chopped

1 carrot, finely chopped

1 celery stick, finely chopped

3 sprigs fresh thyme

100 g/3½ oz Spanish green olives in brine, stuffed with pimientos, garlic or almonds, drained and rinsed

1 tsp finely grated orange rind

salt and pepper

1. Put the duck legs in the base of a large, heavy-based frying pan with a tight-fitting lid. Add the tomatoes, garlic, onion, carrot, celery, thyme and olives and stir together. Season with salt and pepper.

2. Increase the heat to high and cook, uncovered, until the ingredients begin to bubble. Reduce the heat to low, cover tightly and simmer for 1¼–1½ hours until the duck is very tender. Check occasionally and add a little water if the mixture appears to be drying out.

3. When the duck is tender, transfer it to a serving platter, cover and keep warm. Increase the heat to medium and cook the liquid, stirring, for about 10 minutes until it forms a sauce. Stir in the orange rind, then taste and adjust the seasoning if necessary.

4. Mash the tender garlic cloves with a fork and spread over the duck legs. Spoon the sauce over the top. Serve immediately.

#75 Turkey tagliatelle with lemon pepper cream sauce

Serves 4

Ingredients

450 g/1 lb turkey steaks

grated zest of 1 lemon

2 tsp cracked black peppercorns

1 tbsp olive oil

55 g/2 oz butter

juice of ½ lemon

250 ml/9 fl oz double cream

350 g/12 oz egg tagliatelle

4 tbsp chopped fresh flat-leaf parsley

salt

1. Place the turkey between two sheets of clingfilm and flatten with a meat mallet. Slice across the grain into 1 x 9-cm/½ x 3½-inch thin strips. Transfer to a shallow dish and toss with the lemon zest and pepper.

2. Heat the oil and half the butter in a saucepan, add the turkey strips and fry for 5 minutes until no longer pink. Season to taste with salt, then transfer to a plate and keep warm. Add the remaining butter to the pan. Stir in the lemon juice and simmer for a few seconds. Pour in the cream, bring to the boil, then reduce the heat and simmer for 5 minutes, stirring often. Return the turkey to the pan, stirring until well coated with the cream.

3. Meanwhile, bring a large saucepan of lightly salted water to the boil. Add the pasta, bring back to the boil and cook for 8–10 minutes, or until tender but still firm to the bite. Drain the pasta, reserving 4 tablespoons of the cooking water. Tip the pasta into a warmed serving dish. Stir the cooking water into the turkey mixture, then add the parsley. Pour the sauce over the pasta, and toss to mix. Serve immediately.

#76 Rolled Stuffed turkey breast

Serves 4–6

Ingredients

1.6 kg/3 lb 8 oz boneless turkey breast, butterflied

4–6 slices Parma ham

1 tbsp olive oil, plus extra if needed

200 g/7 oz spicy Italian sausage meat, crumbled

1 shallot, finely chopped

2 garlic cloves, chopped

100 g/3½ oz fine breadcrumbs

2 tbsp chopped fresh flat-leaf parsley

2 chargrilled red peppers in olive oil, drained and sliced

salt and pepper

1. Preheat the oven to 190°C/375°F/Gas Mark 5. Open out the turkey, cover with clingfilm and pound with a meat mallet to a 1-cm/½-inch thick rectangle. Season, cover with the ham, then set aside. Heat half the oil in a frying pan. Add the sausage meat and fry, stirring, for 3–5 minutes. Use a slotted spoon to remove the meat, leaving 1 tablespoon of oil in the pan. Add the shallot and fry, stirring, for 1–2 minutes. Add the garlic and stir for 1 minute. Add the breadcrumbs and season with salt and pepper. Stir in the parsley.

2. Place the turkey ham-side down on a board. Cut along the length of the breast without cutting all the way through. Mound the stuffing into the centre, then spread over the top of the breast leaving a 1-cm/½-inch border. Arrange the red pepper slices on top. Roll up Swiss-roll fashion and tie it in three or four places with string. Add the remaining oil to the pan and heat over a high heat. Add the turkey and fry for 3–5 minutes. Transfer to a roasting tin and roast in the preheated oven for 35–40 minutes, or until the juices run clear. Cover and leave to rest for 8–10 minutes before slicing and serving.

#77 Chicken in Riesling

Serves 4–6

Ingredients

1 chicken, about 1.6 kg/3 lb 8 oz, cut into 8 pieces

2 tbsp plain flour, seasoned with salt and pepper

55 g/2 oz butter, plus extra for the pasta

1 tbsp sunflower oil, plus extra if needed

4 shallots, finely chopped

400 g/14 oz chestnut mushrooms, sliced

2 tbsp brandy

300 ml/10 fl oz Riesling wine

2 carrots, thinly sliced

200 g/7 oz dried ribbon pasta

100 ml/3½ fl oz crème fraîche

salt and pepper

1. Coat the chicken pieces with the seasoned flour. Melt 30 g/1 oz of the butter with the oil in a casserole over a medium heat. Add the chicken and fry for 3–5 minutes until golden brown. Remove the chicken and set aside, then wipe out the casserole. Melt the remaining butter in the casserole. Add the shallots and fry, stirring, for 2–3 minutes, or until soft. Add the mushrooms and a pinch of salt and fry until they absorb their liquid. Return the chicken to the casserole.

2. Light the brandy in a ladle and pour over the chicken. When the flames have died down, add the wine, carrots and enough water to cover. Bring to the boil, reduce the heat and simmer for 20–25 minutes. Preheat the oven to 110°C/225°F/Gas Mark ¼.

3. Bring a large saucepan of lightly salted water to the boil. Add the pasta, bring back to the boil and cook for 8–10 minutes, or until just tender but still firm to the bite. Drain, toss with butter and keep warm in the preheated oven. Transfer the chicken and the vegetables to a platter and keep warm in the oven. Skim any fat off the cooking juices, stir in the crème fraîche and bring to the boil, stirring, for 2–3 minutes to reduce. Taste and adjust the seasoning, if necessary, then pour the sauce over the chicken. Serve with the pasta.

#78 Chicken, pumpkin & chorizo casserole

Serves 4

Ingredients

1 small pumpkin

200 g/7 oz fresh chorizo sausage

3 tbsp olive oil

2.25 kg/5 lb chicken, cut into 8 pieces and dusted in flour

small bunch of fresh sage leaves

1 onion, chopped

6 garlic cloves sliced

2 celery sticks, sliced

200 ml/7 fl oz dry sherry

600 ml/1 pint chicken stock

400 g/14 oz chopped tomatoes

2 bay leaves

salt and pepper

1 tbsp chopped fresh parsley, to garnish

1. Preheat the oven to 180°C/350°F/Gas Mark 4.

2. Peel and roughly chop the pumpkin and chop the chorizo. Heat the oil in a casserole, add the chicken, chorizo and sage leaves and fry until golden brown. Remove with a slotted spoon and reserve. You may need to do this in two batches.

3. Add the onion, garlic, celery and pumpkin to the casserole and cook for 20 minutes or until the mixture is golden brown.

4. Add the sherry, chicken stock, tomatoes and bay leaves and season with salt and pepper.

5. Put the reserved chicken, chorizo and sage into the casserole dish. Cover with a lid and cook in the oven for 1 hour.

6. Remove from the oven and remove and discard the bay leaf. Stir in the chopped parsley and serve immediately.

#79 Moroccan-style turkey

Serves 4

Ingredients

400 g/14 oz skinless, boneless turkey breasts, diced

1 onion, sliced

1 tsp ground cumin

½ tsp ground cinnamon

1 tsp hot chilli sauce

240 g/8½ oz canned chickpeas, drained and rinsed

600 ml/1 pint chicken stock

12 dried apricots

40 g/1½ oz cornflour

75 ml/2½ fl oz cold water

2 tbsp chopped fresh coriander

cooked couscous, rice or jacket sweet potatoes, to serve

1. Put the turkey, onion, cumin, cinnamon, chilli sauce, chickpeas and stock into a large saucepan. Bring to the boil, reduce the heat, cover and simmer for 15 minutes.

2. Stir in the apricots and return to the boil. Reduce the heat, cover and simmer for a further 15 minutes, or until the turkey is cooked through.

3. Blend the cornflour with the water in a small bowl and stir into the casserole. Return to the boil, stirring constantly, and cook until the casserole thickens. Reduce the heat, cover and simmer for a further 5 minutes.

4. Stir half of the coriander into the casserole. Transfer to a warmed serving dish and sprinkle over the remaining coriander. Serve immediately with cooked couscous.

Duck breasts with pomegranate & walnut sauce

Ingredients

4 duck breasts, about 175 g/6 oz each

juice of 1 lime

1 tbsp olive oil

4 shallots, finely chopped

1½ tsp ground allspice

3 tbsp pomegranate molasses

140 g/5 oz walnut pieces, chopped

300 ml/10 fl oz chicken stock

2 tbsp chopped fresh mint

salt and pepper

seeds from 1 pomegranate, to garnish

green salad, to serve

1. Use a sharp knife to score the skin of the duck breasts in a diamond pattern. Sprinkle with the lime juice and leave to stand for about 15 minutes.

2. Heat the oil in a large saucepan over a medium heat, add the shallots and fry for 3–4 minutes, stirring, until soft and golden brown. Stir in the allspice, molasses and walnuts and stir-fry for 30 seconds.

3. Add the stock to the pan, bring to the boil and gently simmer, uncovered, for 4–5 minutes until reduced by about half. Remove from the heat, set aside and keep warm.

4. Heat a large, heavy frying pan over a high heat. Season the duck breasts with salt and pepper and place in the pan, skin side down. Cook over a medium-high heat for about 10 minutes, until most of the fat is released and the skin is brown. Drain off the excess fat, then turn over the duck breasts and cook for a further 4–5 minutes, until they are lightly browned and the juices are still pink, or until cooked to your liking.

5. Remove the pan from the heat, loosely cover the duck breasts with foil and leave to rest for about 10 minutes.

6. Meanwhile, add the mint to the sauce and gently heat, stirring, until boiling. Season to taste with salt and pepper.

7. Slice the duck breasts and arrange on warmed plates, then spoon the sauce over and sprinkle with pomegranate seeds. Serve with a fresh green salad.

#81 Chicken with forty cloves of garlic

Serves 6

Ingredients

1 whole chicken,
about 1.6 kg/3 lb 8 oz

3 large garlic bulbs, separated into
cloves but unpeeled

6 fresh thyme sprigs

2 fresh tarragon sprigs

2 bay leaves

300 ml/10 fl oz dry white wine

salt and pepper

1. Preheat the oven to 180°C/350°F/Gas Mark 4. Season the chicken inside and out with salt and pepper, then truss with kitchen string. Place on a rack in a casserole and arrange the garlic and herbs around it.

2. Pour the wine over the chicken and cover with a tight-fitting lid. Cook in the preheated oven for 1½–1¾ hours, or until the chicken is tender and the juices run clear when a skewer is inserted into the thickest part of the meat. Remove and discard the bay leaves. Transfer the chicken and garlic to a dish and keep warm. Strain the cooking juices into a jug. Skim off any fat on the surface of the cooking juices.

3. Carve the chicken and transfer to serving plates with the garlic. Spoon over a little of the cooking juices and serve immediately.

#82 Roast turkey with cider sauce

Serves 8

Ingredients

25 g/1 oz butter

3 shallots, finely chopped

1 celery stick, finely chopped

1 apple, peeled, cored and diced

115 g/4 oz stoned prunes, chopped

55 g/2 oz raisins

175 ml/6 fl oz chicken stock

350 ml/12 fl oz dry cider

1 tbsp chopped fresh parsley

1 boneless turkey breast roast, about
1 kg/2 lb 4 oz

1 tbsp sunflower oil or corn oil

salt and pepper

1 tsp cider vinegar

1. Melt the butter in a pan. Add 2 of the shallots and cook, for 5 minutes. Add the celery and apple and cook for 5 minutes. Add the prunes, raisins, 3 tablespoons of the stock, 4 tablespoons of the cider and the parsley, cover, and simmer for 5 minutes, or until the liquid has been absorbed. Transfer to a bowl and leave to cool.

2. Preheat the oven to 190°C/375°F/Gas Mark 5. Place the turkey on a board and slice almost completely through, from the thin side towards the thicker side. Open out, place between two sheets of clingfilm, and flatten with a meat mallet to an even thickness. Season to taste with salt. Spoon on the cooled stuffing, roll the roast around it, and tie with kitchen string. Heat the oil in a roasting tin, add the turkey and brown all over. Transfer to the preheated oven and roast for 1 hour 10 minutes, or until cooked through. Remove from the tin and cover with foil.

3. Pour off any fat from the tin and place over a medium heat. Add the remaining shallot and half the remaining cider and cook for 1–2 minutes. Add the remaining cider, remaining stock and vinegar and cook for 10 minutes, or until reduced and thickened. Remove and discard the string from the turkey and cut into slices. Serve with the cider sauce.

Serves
6–8

Boned & stuffed roast duck

Ingredients

1.8 kg/4 lb duck (dressed weight), ask your butcher to bone the duck and cut off the wings at the first joint

450 g/1 lb flavoured sausage meat, such as pork and apricot

1 small onion, finely chopped

1 Cox's apple, cored and finely chopped

85 g/3 oz ready-to-eat dried apricots, finely chopped

85 g/3 oz chopped walnuts

2 tbsp chopped fresh parsley

1 large or 2 smaller duck breasts, skin removed

salt and pepper

ready-made apricot sauce, to serve

1. Wipe the duck inside and out with kitchen paper. Lay it on a board, skin-side down, and season well with salt and pepper.

2. Mix the sausage meat, onion, apple, apricots, walnuts and parsley together and season well with salt and pepper. Form into a large sausage shape. Lay the duck breast on the whole duck and cover with the stuffing. Wrap the whole duck around the filling and tuck in any leg and neck flaps.

3. Preheat the oven to 190°C/375°F/Gas Mark 5. Sew the duck up the back and across both ends with fine string. Mould the duck into a good shape and place, sewn-side down, on a wire rack over a roasting tin. Roast in the preheated oven for 1½–2 hours, basting occasionally, until golden brown and crispy.

4. Carve the duck into thick slices at the table and serve with apricot sauce.

84

Serves
4

Turkey & peppercorn sauce

Ingredients

1 tbsp vegetable oil

25 g/1 oz butter

2 shallots, chopped

700 g/1 lb 9 oz lb turkey escalopes, cut into thin strips

225 g/8 oz button mushrooms, sliced

300 ml/10 fl oz soured cream

1 tbsp green peppercorns in brine, drained

finely grated rind of ½ lemon

salt and pepper

snipped fresh chives, to garnish

1. Heat the oil and butter in a large heavy-based frying pan, add the shallots and cook until soft. Add the turkey and cook over a medium–high heat until golden. Remove the turkey from the pan with a slotted spoon and keep warm.

2. Add the mushrooms to the pan and cook for 5 minutes, stirring, until soft. Return the turkey to the pan and season to taste with salt and pepper. Stir in the soured cream, peppercorns and lemon rind, and warm through gently.

3. Transfer to a warmed serving dish, garnish with chives and serve.

Moroccan chicken stew

Ingredients

1 whole chicken, cut into quarters

2 tbsp olive oil

1 large onion, sliced

4 garlic cloves, sliced

1 tsp ground cumin

1 tsp dried coriander

½ tsp cinnamon

½ tsp dried red chilli flakes

175 g/6 oz tomatoes, diced

125 ml/4 fl oz chicken stock

1 green pepper, sliced

2 tbsp currants

2 tbsp flaked almonds

salt and pepper

1. Preheat oven to 180°C/350°F/Gas Mark 4.

2. Generously season the chicken with salt and pepper.
Heat the oil in a casserole over a medium-high heat,
add the chicken and brown well all over. Remove the chicken, and add onions and garlic.
Reduce the heat to medium, and sauté for about 5 minutes, until the onions are translucent.

3. Stir in the remaining ingredients. Place the chicken and any juices over the mixture. Cover
and bake in the preheated oven for 1 hour 15 minutes. Leave to rest for 15 minutes.
Season to taste with salt and pepper and serve.

Chicken risotto with saffron

Ingredients

125 g/4½ oz butter

900 g/2 lb skinless, boneless chicken breasts, thinly sliced

1 large onion, chopped

500 g/1 lb 2 oz risotto rice

150 ml/5 fl oz white wine

1 tsp crumbled saffron threads

1.3 litres/2¼ pints hot chicken stock

55 g/2 oz freshly grated Parmesan cheese

salt and pepper

1. Heat 55 g/2 oz of the butter in a deep saucepan. Add
the chicken and onion and cook, stirring frequently, for
8 minutes, or until golden brown and cooked through.
Add the rice and mix to coat in the butter. Cook,
stirring constantly, for 2–3 minutes, or until the grains are
translucent. Add the wine and cook, stirring constantly, for 1 minute, until reduced.

2. Mix the saffron with 4 tablespoons of the hot stock. Add the liquid to the rice and cook,
stirring constantly, until it is absorbed. Gradually add the remaining hot stock, a ladleful at
a time. Add more liquid as the rice absorbs each addition. Cook, stirring, for 20 minutes, or
until all the liquid is absorbed and the rice is creamy.

3. Remove from the heat and add the remaining butter. Mix well, then stir in the Parmesan
cheese until it melts. Season to taste with salt and pepper. Spoon the risotto into warmed
serving dishes and serve immediately.

Garlic & rosemary roast chicken with gravy

Ingredients

6 garlic cloves, very finely chopped

4 tbsp olive oil

2 tbsp finely chopped fresh rosemary leaves

1 tsp dried mixed herbs

1 whole chicken, about 2.25 kg/5 lb

350 ml/12 fl oz chicken stock

1 tbsp unsalted butter

salt and pepper

1. Add a pinch of salt to the garlic and use the flat of a knife blade to scrape and press the garlic against a board to make a smooth paste. Mix the oil, garlic, rosemary and mixed herbs together in a large bowl. Add the chicken and rub all over, inside and out, with the oil.

2. Preheat the oven to 200°C/400°F/Gas Mark 6. Place the chicken in a large, ovenproof frying pan. Generously season the cavity with salt and pepper. Tie the legs together with kitchen string. Generously season the outside with salt and pepper. Roast in the centre of the preheated oven for 1 hour, or until cooked through. Carefully transfer the chicken to a serving platter, and loosely cover with foil. Leave to rest for 10 minutes before serving.

3. Meanwhile, pour off the excess fat from the pan and add the chicken stock to the pan. Place over high heat and bring to a boil, scraping up the sediment from the base of the pan with a whisk. Boil for 2 minutes, remove from the heat and whisk in the butter. Season with salt and pepper. Serve alongside the chicken.

Chicken in a salt crust

Ingredients

bunch of fresh flat-leaf parsley

1 chicken, about 1.5 kg/3 lb 5 oz

1.5 kg/3 lb 5 oz sea salt

1 egg white

fresh thyme sprigs, to garnish

1. Preheat the oven to 180°C/350°F/Gas Mark 4. Line a large roasting tin with a double thickness of foil, letting it overhang the sides. Put the parsley in the cavity of the chicken and tie the legs with kitchen string.

2. Mix the salt and egg white together in a bowl until thoroughly combined and the salt is moist. Spoon a layer of the salt mixture into the prepared tin, spreading it out evenly. Place the chicken on top and cover with the remaining salt mixture to cover it completely. Fold the overhanging sides of foil over the chicken to enclose it completely and bake for 1½ hours.

3. Remove the chicken, still wrapped in foil, from the roasting tin. Open the foil and break the salt crust with the back of a large knife. Brush away all traces of salt and transfer the chicken to a carving board. Serve immediately, garnished with thyme.

#89

Serves
6

Chicken in a pot

Ingredients

1.5 litres/2¾ pints chicken stock

1.5 litres/2¾ pints water

bouquet garni of 4 parsley sprigs, 4 thyme sprigs and 4 bay leaves tied with string

1 tsp black peppercorns

150 g/5½ oz smoked streaky bacon, chopped into chunks

1 whole garlic bulb, halved

3 small leeks, cut into large chunks

3 carrots, cut into large chunks

3 celery sticks, cut into large chunks

3 turnips, cut into large chunks

6 baby onions

1 chicken, 2–2.5 kg/4 lb 8 oz–5 lb 8 oz

1 small head of cabbage, cut into 6 pieces

12 small new potatoes, scrubbed

salt and pepper

Stuffing

125 g/4½ oz stale bread or breadcrumbs

125 g/4½ oz chicken livers, finely chopped

1 shallot, finely chopped

1 egg

handful of fresh flat-leaf parsley, chopped

125 g/4½ oz sausage meat

3 garlic cloves, crushed

Sauce

125 g/4½ oz gherkins, finely chopped

4 tbsp extra virgin olive oil

1 tbsp Dijon mustard

1. Put the stock, water, bouquet garni, peppercorns, bacon, garlic and all the vegetables, except the potatoes and cabbage, into a very large saucepan and season to taste with salt and pepper. Place over a low heat and bring to a very gentle simmer.

2. Meanwhile, put all the stuffing ingredients in a bowl and mix thoroughly. Season the chicken cavity with salt and pepper. Spoon in the stuffing and truss the chicken closed with string. Place the chicken in the pan, cover and simmer very gently for 1½ hours. Add the cabbage and potatoes, bring to the boil and simmer for a further 20 minutes.

3. Combine all the sauce ingredients in a bowl and mix well. Check that the chicken is cooked through and the juices run clear when a skewer is inserted into the thickest part of the meat. Remove the chicken from the pan, wrap in foil and leave to rest. Carve the chicken and serve with the vegetables, broth (removing the bouquet garni) and sauce.

66

Spatchcocked chicken with lemon & honey

Ingredients

2 tbsp clear honey

1 tbsp freshly squeezed lemon juice

¼ tsp hot or sweet paprika, to taste

1 chicken, about 1.5 k g/3 lb 5 oz, spatchcocked

sunflower oil, for greasing

salt and pepper

finely chopped fresh flat-leaf parsley and finely grated lemon rind, to garnish

1. Mix together the honey, lemon juice, paprika, and salt and pepper to taste in a wide, non-metallic bowl, large enough to hold the chicken flat. Add the chicken and rub in the mixture all over, then leave to stand for 30 minutes at room temperature.

2. Meanwhile, preheat the oven to 190°C/375°F/Gas Mark 5. Put a greased rack into a large roasting tin. When ready to cook, grease two long metal skewers. Place the chicken on a chopping board and run the skewers through the body in an X shape.

3. Place the chicken on the prepared rack, skin side up, and brush with the marinade. Roast in the preheated oven for 45–55 minutes, basting twice during cooking, until golden brown and the juices run clear when the thickest part of the meat is pierced with a skewer.

4. Remove from the oven, cover with foil and leave to rest for 5 minutes. Skim the fat off the pan juices. Carve the chicken, spoon over the juices and garnish with parsley and lemon rind.

Chipotle chicken stew

Ingredients

200 g/7 oz dried haricot beans, soaked overnight

1 large onion, sliced

1 dried chipotle pepper, soaked for 20 minutes, then drained and finely chopped

1 whole chicken, about 1.5 kg/3 lb 5 oz

200 ml/7 fl oz hot chicken stock

400 g/14 oz canned chopped tomatoes

1 tsp ground cumin

salt and pepper

1. Drain and rinse the beans, place in a saucepan, cover with cold water and bring to the boil. Boil rapidly for 10 minutes, then remove from the heat and drain and rinse again.

2. Transfer the beans to a slow cooker and add the onion and chipotle pepper. Place the chicken on top, pour over the stock and the tomatoes with their can juices, sprinkle with cumin and season to taste with salt and pepper.

3. Cover and cook for 4 hours on high. Carefully remove the chicken and cut into 8 pieces. Skim the excess fat from the juices and adjust the seasoning.

4. Spoon the beans into a warmed serving dish, top with the chicken and spoon the juices over. Serve immediately.

#92

Serves 4

Duck breasts with citrus glaze

Ingredients

55 g/2 oz light brown sugar, plus extra if needed

finely grated rind and juice of 1 large lemon

finely grated rind and juice of 1 orange

finely grated rind and juice of 1 lime

4 duck breasts, skin on

2 tbsp olive oil

salt and pepper

freshly cooked sugar snap peas and orange wedges, to serve

1. Put the sugar in a small saucepan, add just enough water to cover and heat gently until dissolved. Add the citrus rinds and juices and bring to the boil. Reduce the heat and simmer for about 10 minutes, until syrupy. Remove from the heat. Taste and add extra sugar if needed. Keep warm.

2. Meanwhile, score the skin of the duck breasts with a sharp knife in a diamond pattern and rub with salt and pepper. Heat the oil in a frying pan. Place the duck breasts in the pan, skin-side down, and cook for 5 minutes on each side, until the flesh is just pink.

3. Slice the duck breasts diagonally into 5–6 slices, then transfer to warmed plates. Arrange some sugar snap peas and orange wedges on each plate, then spoon over the glaze and serve immediately.

#93

Serves 4

Chicken & apple pot

Ingredients

1 tbsp olive oil

4 x 175-g/6-oz chicken portions,

1 onion, chopped

2 celery sticks, roughly chopped

1½ tbsp plain flour

300 ml/10 fl oz clear apple juice

150 ml/5 fl oz chicken stock

1 cooking apple, cored and quartered

2 bay leaves

1–2 tsp clear honey

1 yellow pepper, deseeded and cut into chunks

1 large eating apple, cored and sliced

1 tbsp melted butter

2 tbsp demerara sugar

salt and pepper

1 tbsp chopped fresh mint, to garnish

1. Heat the oil in a heavy-based frying pan. Add the chicken and cook over a medium–high heat, turning frequently, for 10 minutes, until golden brown. Transfer to a slow cooker. Add the onion and celery to the pan and cook over a low heat for 5 minutes, until soft. Sprinkle in the flour and cook for 2 minutes, then remove the pan from the heat.

2. Gradually stir in the apple juice and stock, then return the pan to the heat and bring to the boil. Stir in the cooking apple, bay leaves and honey and season to taste. Pour the mixture over the chicken in the slow cooker, cover and cook on low for 6½ hours, until the chicken is tender and cooked through. Stir in the pepper, re-cover and cook on high for 45 minutes.

3. Shortly before serving, preheat the grill. Brush one side of the eating apple slices with half the melted butter and sprinkle with half the sugar. Cook under the preheated grill for 2–3 minutes, until the sugar has caramelized. Turn the slices over with tongs, brush with the remaining butter and sprinkle with the remaining sugar. Grill for a further 2 minutes. Transfer the stew to warmed plates and garnish with the caramelized apple slices and the mint. Serve immediately.

#94 Chicken with sweet & sour apricot sauce

Serves 8

Ingredients

325 g/11½ oz apricot jam

2 tbsp rice wine vinegar

1 tbsp water

1 tsp fresh thyme leaves

8 chicken legs, skin on, bone in

1 tbsp olive oil

1 yellow onion, sliced

1 carrot, sliced

1 celery stick, sliced

6 whole garlic cloves, peeled and bruised

6 fresh thyme sprigs

225 ml/8 fl oz chicken stock

salt and pepper

1. Put the jam, vinegar, and water into a small saucepan over a medium heat and bring to a simmer, stirring. Remove from heat and stir in the thyme, and salt and pepper to taste. Set aside and keep warm until ready to serve.

2. Preheat oven to 160°C/325°F/Gas Mark 3. Generously season the chicken legs on both sides with salt and pepper. Heat the oil in a large ovenproof frying pan over a medium heat and place chicken in it, skin-side down. Cook for 5 minutes, or until the skin is well browned. Turn and brown the other side for 3 minutes.

3. Transfer to a plate, pour off the excess fat and add the vegetables, garlic, and thyme to the pan. Arrange the chicken on the vegetables, skin-side up. Pour in the stock, cover with foil and place in the preheated oven. Roast for 1 hour, then uncover and increase the oven temperature to 220°C/425°F/Gas Mark 7. Roast for a further 10 minutes. Remove from oven and let rest for 10 minutes before serving, topped with the apricot sauce.

#95 Cheddar & apple-stuffed chicken breasts

Serves 4

Ingredients

4 thick boneless, skinless chicken breasts, about 200 g/7 oz each

1 tbsp sunflower oil, plus extra for oiling

1 small onion, finely chopped

1 celery stick, finely chopped

¼ tsp dried sage

1 eating apple, cored and diced

85 g/3 oz mature Cheddar cheese, coarsely grated

2 tbsp finely chopped parsley, plus extra to garnish

6 slices Parma ham

salt and pepper

cooked green vegetables, to serve

1. Preheat the oven to 190°C/375°F/Gas mark 5 and lightly oil a small roasting tin. Put a chicken breast on a chopping board, rounded side up. use a small, sharp knife to cut a pocket along the length of the breast, cutting as deep as you can without cutting through to the other side or the ends. Repeat with the remaining chicken breasts, then set aside.

2. Heat the oil in a frying pan, add the onion, celery and sage and fry, stirring, for 3–5 minutes until soft. Stir in the apple and fry for a further 2 minutes until it is soft but not falling apart. stir in the cheese and parsley and season with salt and pepper. Divide the stuffing between the breast pockets. wrap 1½ slices of ham around each breast, then rub the tops with a little oil.

3. Transfer to the prepared tin and roast in the preheated oven for 20–25 minutes, or until the chicken is cooked through and the juices run clear when a skewer is inserted into the thickest part of the meat. Remove from the oven, cover with foil and leave to stand for 3–5 minutes before serving with green vegetables.

Turkey meatloaf

Ingredients

oil, for greasing

600 g/1 lb 5 oz fresh turkey mince

1 onion, finely chopped

55 g/2 oz porridge oats

2 tbsp chopped fresh sage

2 tbsp Worcestershire sauce

1 egg, beaten

salt and pepper

1. Grease and line a 900-g/2-lb loaf tin, or a tin that fits into your slow cooker.

2. Mix together the turkey mince, onion, oats, sage, Worcestershire sauce and egg, and season well with salt and pepper.

3. Spoon the mixture into the tin and smooth the top level with a palette knife.

4. Place the loaf in the slow cooker and place a piece of baking paper on top. Cover and cook on low for 4 hours, until firm and the juices are clear, not pink.

5. Turn out the loaf and serve sliced.

Classic roast chicken

Ingredients

1 whole free-range chicken, about 2.25 kg/5 lb

55 g/2 oz butter

2 tbsp chopped fresh lemon thyme

1 lemon, quartered

125 ml/4 fl oz white wine

roasted vegetables, to serve

salt and pepper

1. Preheat the oven to 220°C/425°F/Gas Mark 7. Place the chicken in a roasting tin.

2. Soften the butter with a fork, mix in the thyme and season well with salt and pepper. Butter the chicken all over with the herb butter, inside and out, and place the lemon pieces inside the body cavity. Pour the wine over the chicken and roast in the centre of the preheated oven for 20 minutes. Reduce the oven temperature to 190°C/375°F/Gas Mark 5 and roast for a further 1¼ hours, basting frequently. Cover with foil if the skin begins to brown too much. If the liquid in the tin dries out, add a little more wine or water.

3. Test that the chicken is cooked by piercing the thickest part of the leg with a sharp knife or skewer and making sure the juices run clear. Remove from the oven. Place the chicken on a warmed serving plate, cover with foil and leave to rest for 10 minutes before carving.

4. Place the tin on the hob and gently bubble the pan juices over a low heat until reduced, thick and glossy. Season to taste with salt and pepper. Serve the chicken with the pan juices and roasted vegetables.

Serves
4

Roast duck with onion marmalade

Ingredients

4 duck breasts, skin on, about 185 g/6½ oz each

2 tbsp clear honey

salt and pepper

freshly cooked vegetables, to serve

Onion marmalade

50 g/1¾ oz butter

2 firm ripe pears, peeled, cored and sliced

6 onions, sliced

2 tbsp dark chestnut honey

2 pieces stem ginger

2 tbsp stem ginger syrup

1. To make the marmalade, melt the butter in a saucepan over a medium-high heat, add the pears and onions and cook, stirring occasionally, for 10 minutes, or until soft and golden. Add the honey, stem ginger and ginger syrup and bubble gently for 15–20 minutes until the mixture is sticky and caramelized. Season to taste with salt and pepper. Keep warm until ready to serve.

2. Meanwhile, preheat the oven to 200°C/400°F/Gas Mark 6. Heat a frying pan over a medium-high heat until hot. Add the duck breasts, skin-side down, to the dry pan. Cook for 2–3 minutes until golden brown. Turn and cook for a further 2–3 minutes. Transfer the breasts to a roasting dish, brush with the honey and season to taste with salt and pepper. Roast in the preheated oven for 12 minutes. Remove from the oven and leave to rest in a warm place for 5 minutes.

3. To serve, cut each duck breast into slices and fan out on each of four warmed dinner plates. Serve immediately with the onion marmalade and freshly cooked vegetables.

99

Serves
4–6

Traditional roast turkey

Ingredients

1 oven-ready turkey, about 5 kg/11 lb

1 garlic clove, finely chopped

100 ml/3½ fl oz red wine

75 g/2¾ oz butter

seasonal vegetables and cranberry sauce, to serve

Stuffing

100 g/3½ oz button mushrooms

1 onion, chopped

1 garlic clove, chopped

85 g/3 oz butter

100 g/3½ oz fresh breadcrumbs

2 tbsp finely chopped fresh sage

1 tbsp lemon juice

salt and pepper

1. Preheat the oven to 200°C/400°F/Gas Mark 6.

2. To make the stuffing, clean and chop the mushrooms, put them in a saucepan with the onion, garlic and butter and salt and pepper to taste and cook for 3 minutes. Remove from the heat and stir in the remaining stuffing ingredients. Rinse the turkey and pat dry with kitchen paper. Fill the neck end with stuffing and truss with string.

3. Put the turkey in a roasting tin. Rub the garlic over the bird and pour the wine over. Add the butter and roast in the preheated oven for 30 minutes. Baste, then reduce the temperature to 180°C/350°F/Gas Mark 4 and roast for a further 40 minutes. Baste again and cover with foil. Roast for a further 2 hours, basting regularly. Check that the bird is cooked by inserting a knife between the legs and body. If the juices run clear, it is cooked. Remove from the oven, cover with foil and leave to stand for 25 minutes.

4. Serve the turkey with seasonal vegetables and cranberry sauce.

Meat meals

#100 Ham & lentil soup

Ingredients

200 g/7 oz cooked ham

1 tbsp vegetable oil

1 onion, finely chopped

1 garlic clove, finely chopped

1 carrot, finely diced

1 celery stick, thinly sliced

400 g/14 oz canned cooked green lentils, drained

1 tsp finely chopped fresh rosemary leaves

600 ml/1 pint vegetable stock or ham stock

pepper

1. Using two forks, finely shred the ham and set aside.

2. Heat the oil in a saucepan over a medium–high heat. Add the onion, garlic, carrot and celery and sauté for 4–5 minutes, or until starting to soften.

3. Add the lentils, rosemary, shredded ham and stock and season to taste with pepper. Cover and simmer for 20 minutes, or until the vegetables are just tender. Ladle into warmed bowls and serve immediately.

#101 Sausage & red cabbage soup

Ingredients

2 tbsp olive oil

1 garlic clove, chopped

1 large onion, chopped

1 large leek, sliced

2 tbsp cornflour

1 litre/1¾ pints vegetable stock

450 g/1 lb potatoes, sliced

200 g/7 oz skinless sausages, sliced

150 g/5½ oz red cabbage, chopped

200 g/7 oz canned black-eye beans, drained

125 ml/4 fl oz double cream

salt and pepper

ground paprika, to garnish

1. Heat the oil in a large saucepan. Add the garlic and onion and cook over a medium heat, stirring, for 3 minutes, until slightly softened. Add the leek and cook for a further 3 minutes, stirring.

2. Mix the cornflour with enough stock to make a smooth paste, then stir into the pan. Cook, stirring, for 2 minutes. Stir in the remaining stock, then add the potatoes and sausages. Season to taste with salt and pepper. Bring to the boil, then reduce the heat and simmer for 25 minutes.

3. Add the cabbage and beans and cook for 10 minutes, then stir in the cream and cook for a further 5 minutes.

4. Ladle into warmed bowls. Garnish with ground paprika and serve immediately.

#102 Scotch broth

Serves 8

Ingredients

700 g/1 lb 9 oz neck of lamb

1.7 litres/3 pints water

55 g/2 oz pearl barley

2 onions, chopped

1 garlic clove, finely chopped

3 small turnips, diced

3 carrots, finely sliced

2 celery sticks, sliced

2 leeks, sliced

salt and pepper

2 tbsp chopped fresh parsley, to garnish

1. Cut the meat into small pieces, removing as much fat as possible. Put into a large saucepan and cover with the water. Bring to the boil over a medium heat and skim off any foam that appears.

2. Add the barley, reduce the heat and cook gently, covered, for 1 hour. Add the onion, garlic and vegetables and season to taste with salt and pepper. Continue to cook for a further hour.

3. Remove the meat from the pan using a slotted spoon and strip the meat from the bones. Discard the bones and any fat or gristle. Return the meat to the pan and leave to cool completely, then chill in the refrigerator overnight.

4. Scrape the fat off the surface of the soup. Reheat, season with salt and pepper to taste and ladle into warmed bowls. Serve immediately, garnished with the parsley.

#103 Chunky potato & beef soup

Serves 4

Ingredients

2 tbsp vegetable oil

225 g/8 oz lean braising steak, cut into strips

225 g/8 oz new potatoes, halved

1 carrot, diced

2 celery sticks, sliced

2 leeks, sliced

850 ml/1½ pints beef stock

8 baby sweetcorn cobs, sliced

1 bouquet garni

2 tbsp dry sherry

salt and pepper

chopped fresh flat-leaf parsley, to garnish

1. Heat the oil in a large saucepan. Add the strips of meat to the pan and cook for 3 minutes, turning constantly. Add the potatoes, carrot, celery and leeks and cook for a further 5 minutes, stirring.

2. Pour the stock into the pan and bring to the boil. Reduce the heat until the liquid is simmering, then add the sweetcorn and the bouquet garni. Cook for a further 20 minutes, or until cooked through.

3. Remove and discard the bouquet garni. Stir the sherry into the soup and season to taste with salt and pepper.

4. Ladle the soup into warmed bowls, garnish with chopped parsley and serve immediately.

#104 Beef & bean soup

Serves 6

Ingredients

2 tbsp vegetable oil

1 large onion, finely chopped

2 garlic cloves, finely chopped

1 green pepper, deseeded and sliced

2 carrots, sliced

400 g/14 oz canned black-eye beans

225 g/8 oz fresh beef mince

1 tsp each ground cumin, chilli powder and paprika

¼ head of cabbage, sliced

225 g/8 oz tomatoes, peeled and chopped

600 ml/1 pint beef stock

salt and pepper

1. Heat the oil in a large saucepan over a medium heat. Add the onion and garlic and cook, stirring frequently, for 5 minutes, or until soft. Add the green pepper and carrots and cook for a further 5 minutes.

2. Meanwhile, drain the beans, reserving the can liquid. Place two thirds of the beans in a food processor or blender with the can liquid and process until smooth.

3. Add the beef to the pan and cook, stirring constantly, to break up any lumps, until well browned. Add the spices and cook, stirring, for 2 minutes. Add the cabbage, tomatoes, stock and puréed beans and season to taste with salt and pepper. Bring to the boil, then reduce the heat, cover and simmer for 15 minutes, or until the vegetables are tender. Stir in the remaining beans, cover and simmer for a further 5 minutes. Ladle the soup into warmed bowls and serve immediately.

#105 Chestnut & pancetta soup

Serves 6

Ingredients

3 tbsp olive oil

175 g/6 oz pancetta, cut into strips

2 onions, finely chopped

2 carrots, finely chopped

2 celery sticks, finely chopped

350 g/12 oz dried chestnuts, soaked overnight

2 garlic cloves, finely chopped

1 tbsp finely chopped fresh rosemary

1 litre/1¾ pints chicken stock

salt and pepper

extra virgin olive oil, for drizzling

1. Heat the olive oil in a large saucepan, add the pancetta and cook over a medium heat, stirring frequently, for 2–3 minutes, until starting to brown.

2. Add the onions, carrots and celery and cook, stirring frequently, for 10 minutes, or until soft and slightly golden.

3. Drain the chestnuts, add to the pan with the garlic and rosemary, and stir well. Pour in the stock, bring to a simmer and cook, uncovered, for 30–35 minutes, until the chestnuts are beginning to soften and break down.

4. Season to taste with salt and pepper. Ladle the soup into warmed bowls, drizzle with extra virgin olive oil and serve immediately.

#106 Parma ham, melon & pecorino salad

Serves 4

Ingredients

400 g/14 oz watermelon flesh, thinly sliced

400 g/14 oz honeydew melon flesh, thinly sliced

400 g/14 oz canteloupe melon flesh, thinly sliced

140 g/5 oz sliced Parma ham

25 g/1 oz pecorino cheese shavings

25 g/1 oz fresh basil

Dressing

4 tbsp light olive oil

4 tbsp aged sherry vinegar

salt and pepper

1. Arrange the watermelon, honeydew melon and canteloupe melon slices on a large serving platter. Tear any large ham slices in half, then fold them all over and around the melon.

2. To make the dressing, put the oil and vinegar in a jar, season well with salt and pepper, screw on the lid and shake well. Drizzle over the melon and ham.

3. Sprinkle with the cheese shavings and basil. Serve immediately.

#107 Warm shredded beef tabbouleh salad

Serves 4

Ingredients

100 g/3½ oz bulgar wheat

400 g/14 oz lean beef fillet

200 g/7 oz fresh flat-leaf parsley, finely chopped

140 g/5 oz fresh mint, finely chopped

1 red onion, thinly sliced

2 tomatoes, diced

1 tbsp extra virgin olive oil, plus extra for brushing

juice of 2 lemons

salt and pepper

1. Place the bulgar wheat in a bowl and pour over boiling water to cover. Leave to soak for 10 minutes. Drain thoroughly, pressing out any excess moisture.

2. Meanwhile, place a griddle pan over a high heat. Season the beef with salt and pepper, lightly brush with oil and cook for 2–3 minutes on each side, turning once. Remove from the heat, cover with foil and set aside for 5 minutes.

3. Mix together the parsley, mint, onion, tomatoes and bulgar wheat in a bowl. Stir in the oil and lemon juice and season to taste with salt and pepper.

4. Slice the beef into 2.5-cm/1-inch strips. Place the bulgar wheat salad on warmed plates and arrange the beef slices on top. Pour over the meat juices and serve immediately.

Sweet & sour crispy pork noodle salad

Ingredients

600 g/1 lb 5 oz lean pork leg escalopes

200 g/7 oz dried wholewheat Chinese noodles

200 g/7 oz Chinese leaves, shredded

115 g/4 oz carrots, cut into thin matchsticks

115 g/4 oz mangetout, thinly sliced

2 spring onions, finely chopped

2-cm/¾-inch piece fresh ginger, peeled and finely grated

Dressing

finely grated rind and juice of ½ orange

2 tbsp sunflower oil

2 tbsp soy sauce

1 tbsp clear honey

1 tbsp rice vinegar

1 tsp star anise pieces, ground

2 garlic cloves, finely chopped

1. Preheat the grill to high and line the grill pan with foil. To make the dressing, put all the ingredients into a jar, screw on the lid and shake well.

2. Arrange the pork on the grill pan in a single layer and spoon over 3 tablespoons of the dressing. Place under the grill and cook for 12—15 minutes, turning the pork and spooning over the juices once or twice, until brown and cooked through.

3. Meanwhile, cook the noodles according to the packet instructions. Drain into a sieve, rinse with cold water, then drain again. Put them in a salad bowl, pour over the remaining dressing and leave to cool.

4. Add the Chinese leaves, carrots, mangetout, spring onions and ginger to the salad bowl and toss gently together. Thinly slice the pork and arrange it over the salad, then serve.

#109 Seared beef salad with horseradish ricotta dressing

Ingredients

500 g/1 lb 2 oz baby new potatoes, thickly sliced

225 g/8 oz cherry tomatoes, halved

115 g/4 oz baby spinach

1 red onion, finely chopped

225 g/8 oz cooked beetroot, drained and diced

2 tbsp balsamic vinegar

2 x 250 g/9 oz sirloin steaks

2 tsp olive oil

1 tsp mixed peppercorns, crushed

115 g/4 oz ricotta cheese

4 tbsp low-fat natural yogurt

1—2 tsp horseradish sauce

salt and pepper

1. Put the potatoes in the top of a steamer, cover and set over a saucepan of simmering water. Steam for 6—8 minutes, or until tender. Leave to cool.

2. Put the tomatoes, spinach, onion and beetroot in a salad bowl. Drizzle over the vinegar and gently toss together.

3. Preheat a ridged griddle pan over a high heat. Brush the steaks with the oil, then sprinkle with the peppercorns. Cook for 2 minutes on each side for medium rare, 3 minutes for medium and 4 minutes for well done. Transfer to a plate and leave to rest for a few minutes.

4. Put the ricotta cheese and yogurt in a salad bowl, stir in the horseradish, then season to taste with salt and pepper. Add the potatoes and gently toss together. Divide the spinach salad between four plates, then spoon the potato salad in the centre. Thinly slice the steak and arrange it over the top, then serve.

#110 Grilled lamb salad

Ingredients

2 tbsp sunflower oil, plus extra for brushing

1 tbsp tomato purée

½ tbsp ground cumin

2½ tbsp lemon juice

1 garlic clove, crushed

pinch of cayenne pepper

500 g/1 lb 2 oz lamb neck fillets

1 tsp clear honey

85 g/3 oz Greek yogurt

2 tbsp finely shredded fresh mint

2 tbsp chopped fresh flat-leaf parsley, plus extra sprigs to garnish

salt and pepper

toasted sesame seeds, to garnish

1. Mix together the oil, tomato purée, cumin, 1 teaspoon of the lemon juice, the garlic, cayenne pepper, and salt and pepper to taste in a non-metallic bowl. Add the lamb fillets and rub all over with the marinade. Cover and marinate in the refrigerator for at least 2 hours, but ideally overnight.

2. Whisk the remaining lemon juice and honey together until the honey dissolves. Whisk in the yogurt until well blended. Stir in the mint and parsley and add salt and pepper to taste. Cover and chill until required. Preheat the grill to high.

3. Remove the lamb from the refrigerator 15 minutes before you are ready to cook. Brush the grill rack with oil. Grill the lamb, turning once, for 10 minutes for medium and 12 minutes for well done. Leave to cool completely, then cover and chill until required. Thinly slice the lamb then divide between four plates. Pour over the dressing, sprinkle with toasted sesame seeds and parsley and serve.

#111 Beef wraps with lime & honey

Serves 4

Ingredients

finely grated rind and juice of 1 lime

1 tbsp clear honey

1 garlic clove, crushed

450 g/1 lb sirloin steak

oil, for brushing

4 tbsp mayonnaise

4 large wheat tortillas

1 red onion, thinly sliced

7.5-cm/3-inch piece cucumber, sliced into ribbons

salt and pepper

1. Mix together the lime juice, honey and garlic in a bowl and add the steak. Cover and leave to marinate in the refrigerator for 20 minutes.

2. Remove the steak from the marinade and season to taste with salt and pepper. Heat a griddle pan and brush with oil. Add the steak to the pan and cook, turning once, for 5–6 minutes until golden brown. Remove from the heat, leave to stand for 2 minutes, then cut into thin strips.

3. Mix together the mayonnaise and grated lime rind and spread over the tortillas. Scatter the onion over and add the steak strips and cucumber. Wrap the sides over, turn over one end and serve immediately.

#112 Monster hot dogs

Serves 4

Ingredients

2 tbsp vegetable oil

2 large onions, sliced

4 large frankfurters

To serve

4 hot dog rolls

sliced gherkins

American mustard

sweet pickle relish

grated Cheddar cheese

1. Heat the oil in a medium-sized saucepan over a medium heat, add the onions and gently fry for 20 minutes, or until soft and caramelized. Remove from the heat, set aside and keep warm.

2. Meanwhile, cook the frankfurters according to the packet instructions.

3. To serve, split the hot dog rolls and divide the frankfurters between them. Top with the onions, gherkins, mustard, relish and grated cheese and serve immediately.

80

#113 Meatball subs

Ingredients

450 g/1 lb lean beef mince

1 small onion, grated

2 garlic cloves, crushed

25 g/1 oz fine white breadcrumbs

1 tsp hot chilli sauce

salt and pepper

wholemeal flour, for dusting

groundnut oil, for frying

1 tbsp olive oil

1 small onion, sliced

To serve

4 sub rolls or small baguettes

4 tbsp mayonnaise

55 g/2 oz sliced jalapeño chillies

2 tbsp American mustard

1. Place the beef, onion, garlic, breadcrumbs and chilli sauce in a bowl. Season to taste with salt and pepper and mix thoroughly. Shape the mixture into 20 small equal-sized balls using floured hands. Cover and chill in the refrigerator for 10 minutes or until required.

2. Heat a shallow depth of groundnut oil in heavy-based frying pan until very hot, then add the meatballs in batches and fry for 6–8 minutes, turning frequently, until golden brown and firm. Remove with a slotted spoon, drain on kitchen paper and keep hot.

3. To make the sandwich, heat the olive oil in a clean frying pan over a medium heat, add the onions and fry, stirring occasionally, until soft and golden brown.

4. Split the rolls lengthways and spread with mayonnaise. Arrange the onions, meatballs and chillies over the bottom half, squeeze the mustard over, and serve immediately.

#114 Fiery beef tacos

Serves
4

Ingredients

2 tbsp corn oil

1 small onion, finely chopped

2 garlic cloves, finely chopped

280 g/10 oz fresh beef mince

1½ tsp hot chilli powder

1 tsp ground cumin

8 taco shells

1 avocado

2 tbsp lemon juice

¼ head of lettuce, shredded

4 spring onions, thinly sliced

2 tomatoes, peeled and diced

125 ml/4 fl oz soured cream

115 g/4 oz Cheddar cheese, grated

salt and pepper

1. Heat the oil in a frying pan. Add the onion and garlic and cook over a low heat, stirring occasionally, for 5 minutes until soft. Add the mince, increase the heat to medium and cook, stirring frequently and breaking up the meat with a wooden spoon, for 8–10 minutes, until brown all over. Drain off as much fat as possible.

2. Stir in the chilli powder and cumin, season to taste with salt and pepper and cook over a low heat, stirring frequently, for a further 8 minutes, then remove from the heat.

3. Heat the taco shells according to the packet instructions. Meanwhile, peel, stone and slice the avocado and gently toss with the lemon juice in a bowl.

4. Divide the lettuce, spring onions, tomatoes and avocado slices between the taco shells. Add a tablespoon of soured cream to each, then divide the beef mixture among them. Sprinkle with the cheese and serve immediately.

81

Serves
4

Lamb with Roquefort cheese & walnut butter

Ingredients

55 g/2 oz unsalted butter

140 g/5 oz Roquefort cheese, crumbled

2 tbsp finely chopped walnuts

8 lamb noisettes

salt and pepper

snipped fresh chives, to garnish (optional)

1. Cream half the butter in a bowl with a wooden spoon. Beat in the cheese and walnuts until thoroughly combined and season to taste with salt and pepper. Turn out onto a sheet of greaseproof paper and shape into a cylinder. Wrap in foil and chill in the refrigerator until firm.

2. Heat a ridged griddle pan, add the remaining butter and, as soon as it has melted, add the lamb and cook for 4–5 minutes on each side.

3. Transfer the lamb to warmed serving plates and top each noisette with a slice of the cheese and walnut butter. Serve immediately, garnished with snipped chives, if using.

116

Serves
4

Hot sesame beef

Ingredients

500 g/1 lb 2 oz fillet steak

1½ tbsp sesame seeds

125 ml/4 fl oz beef stock

2 tbsp soy sauce

2 tbsp grated fresh ginger

2 garlic cloves, finely chopped

1 tsp cornflour

½ tsp chilli flakes

3 tbsp sesame oil

1 large head of broccoli, cut into florets

1 yellow pepper, deseeded and sliced

1 fresh red chilli, finely sliced

1 tbsp chilli oil, or to taste

salt and pepper

cooked wild rice, to serve

chopped fresh coriander, to garnish

1. Cut the steak into thin strips and mix with 1 tablespoon of the sesame seeds in a small bowl.

2. In a separate bowl, stir together the stock, soy sauce, ginger, garlic, cornflour and chilli flakes. Heat 1 tablespoon of the sesame oil in a large wok. Add the beef strips and stir-fry for 2–3 minutes. Remove and set aside, then wipe out the wok with kitchen paper.

3. Heat the remaining sesame oil in the wok, add the broccoli, yellow pepper, chilli and chilli oil and stir-fry for 2–3 minutes. Stir in the stock mixture, cover and simmer for 2 minutes.

4. Return the beef to the wok and simmer until the juices thicken, stirring occasionally. Cook for a further 1–2 minutes. Sprinkle with the remaining sesame seeds and season to taste with salt and pepper. Serve with wild rice and garnish with coriander.

#117 Thin ribs

Ingredients

1 onion, finely chopped
2 garlic cloves, crushed
2 tbsp English mustard
1 tbsp smoked paprika
1 tbsp dried oregano
1 tbsp smoked chipotle sauce
1 tsp fennel seeds
100 ml/3½ fl oz light soy sauce
100 g/3½ oz dark muscovado sugar
100 ml/3½ fl oz tomato ketchup
100 ml/3½ fl oz cider vinegar
200 ml/7 fl oz water
1 tsp celery salt
1 tsp pepper
2 kg/4 lb 8 oz beef short ribs

1. Place all of the ingredients, except the beef ribs, into a large non-metallic bowl and mix together.

2. Add the ribs to the marinade, cover and chill in the refrigerator for at least 4 hours, or for up to 12 hours. Turn every couple of hours to coat.

3. Preheat the oven to 180°C/350°F/Gas Mark 4. Place all of the ribs, with the marinade, in a large flameproof casserole with a tight-fitting lid. Cover and cook in the preheated oven for 3 hours.

4. Remove from the oven and leave to cool slightly, then remove the ribs from the sauce and set aside to keep warm. Skim off any excess fat from the surface of the remaining marinade, then place the casserole dish over a medium heat until the marinade is reduced to a sticky consistency. Serve with the reduced marinade drizzled over the ribs.

#118 Cheese & bacon burgers

Ingredients

6 bacon rashers
450 g/1 lb fresh beef mince
Cheddar cheese slices
4 burger buns, split
2 tbsp mayonnaise
lettuce leaves
tomato slices
salt and pepper

1. Preheat the barbecue to medium–high. Put the bacon in a frying pan over a medium heat and cook for about 8 minutes, or until crisp. Drain on kitchen paper and break the rashers in half.

2. Place the beef in a bowl and season to taste with salt and pepper. Divide into 4 equal-sized portions and shape each portion into a patty.

3. Place the patties on the preheated rack and cook, covered, for 4 minutes. Turn, top each burger with a slice of cheese, re-cover and cook for a further 4 minutes, or until the burgers are cooked to your liking and the cheese is melted.

4. Spread both halves of the buns with mayonnaise, then place each burger on a bun base. Top with the bacon pieces, lettuce and tomato slices and finish with the top halves of the buns. Serve immediately.

119

Serves 4

Charcoal-cooked Argentine steaks with chimichurri sauce

Ingredients

6 garlic cloves

1 shallot

40 g/1½ oz fresh flat-leaf parsley, chopped

40 g/1½ oz fresh coriander, chopped

2 tbsp chopped fresh oregano

225 ml/8 fl oz olive oil

125 ml/4 fl oz red wine vinegar, white wine vinegar or sherry vinegar

4 tbsp lemon juice

¾ tsp pepper

2½ tsp salt

¼ tsp chilli flakes

1 sirloin steak, about 750–900 g/ 1 lb 10 oz–2 lb

1. Put the garlic, shallot, parsley, coriander and oregano into a food processor and pulse until roughly chopped. Add the oil, vinegar and lemon juice and pulse until the herbs, garlic and shallot are finely chopped and the mixture is well blended, but not puréed. Add ¼ teaspoon of the pepper, ½ teaspoon of the salt and the chilli flakes.

2. Transfer 225 ml/8 fl oz of the sauce to a non-metallic bowl, cover and set aside. Sprinkle the remaining salt and pepper over the steak, seasoning both sides. Put the steak into a large, re-sealable polythene bag with the remaining sauce and turn it a few times to make sure the meat is well coated. Refrigerate for at least 2 hours. Remove from the refrigerator and leave to stand at room temperature for 30 minutes before cooking.

3. To cook the steak, prepare a very hot bed of charcoal in a barbecue. Remove the steak from the marinade, brushing off any herbs, and place on the rack. Cook for 6 minutes, then turn the steak 45 degrees to create hatch marks and continue to cook on the first side for a further 6 minutes. Turn over and cook for a further 8 minutes for medium-rare.

4. Transfer the steak to a board and leave to rest for 5–10 minutes before slicing. Slice against the grain into 5-mm/¼-inch thick slices. Serve topped with the reserved sauce.

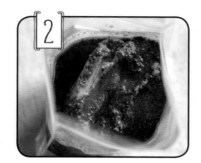

#120 Pork with mixed green beans

Serves 4

Ingredients

2 tbsp vegetable or groundnut oil

2 shallots, chopped

225 g/8 oz pork fillet, thinly sliced

2.5-cm/1-inch piece fresh galangal or ginger, thinly sliced

2 garlic cloves, chopped

300 ml/10 fl oz chicken stock

4 tbsp chilli sauce

4 tbsp crunchy peanut butter

115 g/4 oz fine French beans

115 g/4 oz frozen broad beans

115 g/4 oz runner beans, sliced

crispy noodles, to serve

1. Heat the oil in a preheated wok or large frying pan over a high heat.

2. Add the shallots, pork, galangal and garlic and stir-fry for 3–4 minutes until the pork is lightly browned all over.

3. Add the stock, chilli sauce and peanut butter and cook, stirring, until the peanut butter has melted. Add all the beans, stir well and simmer for 3–4 minutes, or until the beans are tender and the pork is cooked through. Serve immediately with crispy noodles.

#121 Beef enchiladas

Serves 6

Ingredients

1 tbsp corn oil, plus extra for brushing

2 onions, finely chopped

3 fresh green chillies, chopped

280 g/10 oz fresh beef mince

115 g/4 oz Cheddar cheese, grated

25 g/1 oz butter

2 tbsp olive oil

2 garlic cloves, finely chopped

400 g/14 oz canned chopped tomatoes

2 tbsp tomato purée

1 tsp dried oregano

½ tsp cayenne pepper

125 ml/4 fl oz double cream

18 tortillas

salt and pepper

chopped fresh coriander, to garnish

1. Heat the corn oil in a frying pan. Add half the onion and two thirds of the chillies and cook over a low heat, stirring occasionally, for 5 minutes. Add the beef, increase the heat to medium and cook, stirring frequently and breaking it up with the spoon, for 8–10 minutes. Remove the pan from the heat and stir in half the cheese. Melt the butter with the olive oil in a saucepan. Add the remaining onion, chillies and the garlic and cook over a medium heat, stirring occasionally, for 5–8 minutes, until the onion is golden brown. Stir in the tomatoes, tomato purée, oregano and cayenne pepper and season to taste with salt and pepper. Increase the heat to medium and bring to the boil. Reduce the heat, stir in the cream and simmer for 15–20 minutes, until thickened. Remove from the heat and leave to cool slightly.

2. Meanwhile, preheat the oven to 180°C/350°F/Gas Mark 4. Heat a frying pan and brush with corn oil. Dip the tortillas in the sauce, shake off any excess and cook in the pan for 30 seconds on each side. Transfer to a large plate, put a tablespoon of the meat mixture in the centre and roll up. Place the filled tortillas, seam-side down, in an ovenproof dish and pour over the remaining sauce. Sprinkle with the remaining cheese and bake in the preheated oven for 15–20 minutes. Garnish with coriander and serve.

#122 Bacon-wrapped pork fillet with lentils

Serves 2

Ingredients

1 pork fillet, about 280 g/10 oz

4 rindless streaky bacon rashers

4 small sage leaves

1 apple, cored and sliced

2 small onions, 1 sliced, 1 finely chopped

2 tbsp olive oil

2 garlic cloves, finely chopped

115 g/4 oz Puy lentils

200 ml/7 fl oz red wine, plus extra if needed

400 g/14 oz canned chopped tomatoes

25 g/1 oz butter

salt and pepper

1. Preheat the oven to 190°C/375°F/Gas Mark 5. Wrap the pork with bacon, slotting the sage leaves evenly along the meat. Arrange the apple and onion slices in a small roasting tin and lay the pork on top. Season to taste with salt and pepper and roast in the preheated oven for 40 minutes.

2. Meanwhile, heat the oil in a small saucepan, add the chopped onion and cook gently for 5 minutes. Add the garlic and cook for 3–4 minutes, or until golden. Add the lentils and stir to coat with the oil, then add the wine and tomatoes. Stir well and leave to simmer for 40–45 minutes, or until the lentils are tender. Add a little water or wine if the liquid evaporates before the lentils are cooked.

3. Remove the meat from the oven and transfer to a board. Loosely cover with foil. Add a little water to the tin and stir well to loosen the apple and onion. Stir in the butter and keep warm.

4. Spoon some of the lentil mixture into the centre of each plate and top with the pork, cut diagonally into slices, with the apple and onion on the side. Drizzle with the pan juices.

#123 Pork chops with apple sauce

Serves 4

Ingredients

4 thick pork rib chops on the bone

1½ tbsp sunflower oil or rapeseed oil

salt and pepper

Sauce

450 g/1 lb cooking apples, such as Bramley, peeled, cored and diced

4 tbsp caster sugar, plus extra if needed

finely grated zest of ½ lemon

½ tbsp lemon juice, plus extra if needed

4 tbsp water

¼ tsp ground cinnamon

knob of butter

1. Preheat the oven to 200°C/400°F/Gas Mark 6. To make the sauce, put the apples, sugar, lemon zest, lemon juice and water into a heavy-based saucepan over a high heat and bring to the boil, stirring to dissolve the sugar. Reduce the heat to low, cover and simmer for 15–20 minutes, until the apples are tender and fall apart when mashed against the side of the pan. Stir in the cinnamon and butter and beat until as smooth or chunky as you like. Add sugar or lemon juice to taste. Remove from the heat, cover and keep warm.

2. Meanwhile, season the chops with salt and pepper to taste. Heat the oil in a large ovenproof frying pan over a medium-high heat. Add the chops and fry for 3 minutes on each side to brown. Transfer the pan to the preheated oven and cook for 7–9 minutes until the juices run clear when you cut the chops. Remove from the oven, cover with foil and leave to stand for 3 minutes. Transfer the chops to warmed plates and spoon over the pan juices. Serve immediately with the apple sauce.

Beef chop suey

Ingredients

1 tbsp Chinese rice wine

1 tbsp light soy sauce

½ tsp sesame oil

450 g/1 lb rib-eye steak, sliced

1 head broccoli, cut into florets

225 g/8 oz mangetout

55 g/2 oz canned bamboo shoots

2 tbsp vegetable oil

1 onion, sliced

2 sticks celery, sliced

8 water chestnuts, sliced

225 g/8 oz mushrooms, sliced

1 tbsp oyster sauce

salt and white pepper

1. Mix the rice wine, ½ teaspoon white pepper, ½ teaspoon of salt, the soy sauce and sesame oil together in a bowl, add the beef and marinate for at least 20 minutes.

2. Bring a large saucepan of water to the boil, add the broccoli and blanch for 30 seconds. Drain and set aside. Slice the mangetout lengthways and shred the bamboo shoots.

3. Preheat a wok over a high heat, add 1 tablespoon of the vegetable oil, then add the beef and stir-fry until the colour has changed. Remove and set aside. Clean out the wok, heat the remaining oil and stir-fry the onion for 1 minute. Add the celery and broccoli and cook for 2 minutes. Add the mangetout, bamboo shoots, water chestnuts and mushrooms and cook for 1 minute. Add the beef and season to taste with the oyster sauce and salt. Transfer to bowls and serve immediately.

Spaghetti Bolognese

Ingredients

1 tbsp olive oil

1 onion, finely chopped

2 garlic cloves, chopped

1 carrot, chopped

1 celery stick, chopped

50 g/1¾ oz pancetta, diced

350 g/12 oz fresh beef mince

400 g/14 oz canned chopped tomatoes

2 tsp dried oregano

125 ml/4 fl oz red wine

2 tbsp tomato purée

350 g/12 oz dried spaghetti

salt and pepper

chopped fresh flat-leaf parsley, to garnish

1. Heat the oil in a large frying pan. Add the onion and cook for 3 minutes. Add the garlic, carrot, celery and pancetta and sauté for 3–4 minutes, or until just beginning to brown.

2. Add the beef and cook over a high heat for a further 3 minutes, or until all of the meat is brown. Stir in the tomatoes, oregano and red wine and bring to the boil. Reduce the heat and leave to simmer for about 45 minutes. Stir in the tomato purée and season to taste with salt and pepper.

3. Bring a large, heavy-based saucepan of lightly salted water to the boil. Add the spaghetti, bring back to the boil and cook for 8–10 minutes, or until just tender but still firm to the bite. Drain well.

4. Transfer the spaghetti to serving plates and pour over the meat sauce. Toss to mix well, garnish with parsley and serve hot.

#126 Marinated lamb brochettes

Makes 4

Ingredients

700 g/1 lb 9 oz boned leg of lamb, cut into 2.5-cm/1-inch cubes

2 tbsp light malt vinegar

½ tsp salt, or to taste

1 tbsp garlic paste

1 tbsp ginger paste

115 g/4 oz Greek-style yogurt

1 tbsp gram flour

1 tsp ground cumin

1 tsp garam masala

½–1 tsp chilli powder

½ tsp ground turmeric

3 tbsp vegetable oil, plus extra for brushing

½ red pepper, deseeded and sliced

½ green pepper, deseeded and sliced

8 shallots, halved

1. Put the lamb in a large, non-metallic bowl. Add the vinegar, salt, garlic paste and ginger paste. Mix well, cover and marinate in the refrigerator for 30 minutes.

2. Put the yogurt and gram flour in a separate bowl and beat with a fork until smooth. Add the cumin, garam masala, chilli powder, turmeric and oil and mix well. Add to the lamb, then add the red and green peppers and shallots and stir until well blended. Cover and leave to marinate in the refrigerator for at least 2–3 hours. Return to room temperature before cooking.

3. Preheat the grill to high. Brush the grill rack and four metal skewers with oil. Thread the lamb, red and green peppers and shallots alternately onto the prepared skewers. Place on the prepared rack and cook under the preheated grill for 4 minutes. Generously brush with oil and cook for a further 2 minutes. Turn and cook for 3–4 minutes. Brush with oil and cook for a further 2 minutes.

4. Balance the brochettes over a large saucepan and leave to stand for 5–6 minutes before sliding off the skewers with a knife. Serve immediately.

#127 Grilled Italian sausages with double chilli salsa

Serves 4

Ingredients

8 Italian-style sausages

oil, for brushing

crusty bread rolls, to serve

Salsa

1 red pepper, deseeded and finely diced

2 tomatoes, finely diced

1 red finger chilli, finely chopped

2 jalapeño chillies, finely chopped

2 tbsp extra virgin olive oil

1 tbsp balsamic vinegar

salt and pepper

1. To make the salsa, put the red pepper, tomatoes and chillies into a bowl and mix together. Stir in the oil and vinegar, then season to taste with salt and pepper. Cover and chill in the refrigerator for at least 1 hour, or until required.

2. Preheat the grill to medium. Arrange the sausages on the grill rack and brush lightly with oil. Cook under the preheated grill, turning occasionally, for 12–15 minutes until golden and thoroughly cooked.

3. Halve the bread rolls and place 2 sausages on each roll bottom. Spoon a little of the salsa over and replace the roll lid. Serve immediately.

Caramelized swede, onion & ham pie

Ingredients

600 g/1 lb 5 oz cooked
ham, cubed

85 g/3 oz butter

2 onions, chopped

450 g/1 lb swede, cubed

1 tsp chopped fresh sage

25 g/1 oz plain flour,
plus extra for dusting

600 ml/1 pint milk

325 g/11½ oz ready-made puff pastry,
thawed if frozen

beaten egg, to glaze

salt and pepper

1. Put the ham into a large bowl and set aside. Melt 55 g/2 oz of the butter in a large frying pan over a medium heat. Add the onions, swede and sage and season to taste with salt and pepper. Stir well and cook over a medium–high heat for 35–40 minutes, occasionally turning over the pieces using a wide spatula, until golden brown.

2. Meanwhile, melt the remaining butter in a small saucepan over a medium heat. Add the flour and cook, stirring, for 1–2 minutes. Gradually add the milk, stirring to make a smooth sauce. Remove from the heat and season to taste with salt and pepper.

3. Preheat the oven to 220°C/425°F/Gas Mark 7. Roll out the pastry on a lightly floured surface to a rectangle slightly larger than the top of a 26 x 18-cm/10½ x 7-inch pie dish.

4. When the vegetables are caramelized, add to the bowl with the ham, then add the white sauce, stirring gently to combine. Transfer the mixture to a pie dish, brush the rim with the beaten egg and then lay the pastry over the filling. Press the pastry to the rim, then trim off the excess and cut out shapes to decorate the top, if liked. Brush the pastry with the beaten egg and cook in the oven for 15–20 minutes, or until the pastry is puffed and golden. Serve immediately.

#129 Pork chops with tomato & mushroom sauce

Serves 4

Ingredients

4 boneless pork chops
2 tbsp sunflower oil
1 tsp dried sage
25 g/1 oz butter
2 tbsp olive oil
2 shallots, finely chopped
2 garlic cloves, finely chopped
1 celery stick, finely chopped
115 g/4 oz mushrooms, sliced
400 g/14 oz canned chopped tomatoes
2 tbsp tomato purée
brown sugar, to taste
2 tbsp chopped fresh flat-leaf parsley
100 ml/3½ fl oz water
salt and pepper

1. Preheat the grill to high. Brush the chops with sunflower oil, sprinkle with sage and season well with salt and pepper. Cook under the preheated grill for 5 minutes on each side, then reduce the heat and grill for a further 10–15 minutes on each side, until cooked through and tender.

2. Melt the butter with the olive oil in a saucepan. Add the shallots, garlic and celery and cook over a low heat, stirring occasionally, for 5 minutes, until soft. Add the mushrooms and cook, stirring occasionally, for a further 3 minutes. Stir in the tomatoes, tomato purée, sugar to taste, parsley and water and season to taste with salt and pepper. Increase the heat to medium and bring to the boil, then reduce the heat and simmer, stirring occasionally, for 15–20 minutes, until thickened.

3. Transfer the chops to warmed serving plates. Pour the sauce over them and serve immediately.

#130 Indonesian beef with red pepper & chilli sauce

Serves 4

Ingredients

70 g/2½ oz tamarind pulp
3 garlic cloves, crushed
1 tsp turmeric
¼ tsp chilli powder
4½ tbsp groundnut oil
4 small sirloin steaks, trimmed
4 shallots, finely chopped
2 thin-skinned red peppers, chopped
1–2 fresh red chillies, chopped
2.5-cm/1-inch piece fresh ginger, finely chopped
3 lemon grass stalks, thinly sliced
150 ml/5 fl oz beef stock
25 g/1 oz creamed coconut, crumbled
juice of 1½ limes
salt

1. Mix the tamarind pulp with hot water to cover and soak for 15 minutes, breaking it up as it softens. Push through a sieve and mix with the garlic, turmeric, chilli powder and 1 teaspoon of the oil. Trim any excess fat from the steak and slice the meat crossways into 3 pieces. Put into a shallow dish and pour over the marinade. Marinate for at least 4 hours or up to 24 hours. Preheat a wok over a medium–low heat. Add 1 tablespoon of the oil, the shallots, red peppers, chillies, ginger and lemon grass and fry for 10 minutes, stirring occasionally, until soft but not brown. Pour in the stock. Bring to the boil, then reduce the heat and simmer for 15–20 minutes, until very soft. Transfer to a food processor and process to a smooth purée.

2. Preheat a large wok over a high heat. Add the remaining oil and heat until very hot. Add the beef, in batches and fry for 4 minutes on each side. Remove with a slotted spoon and set aside. Pour the sauce into the wok and mix with the cooking juices. Add the coconut and stir until melted. Add the lime juice and check the seasoning. Return the beef to the wok. Stir for 1 minute, then tip into a warmed serving dish and serve immediately.

#131 Pork meatballs with tomato sauce

Ingredients

400 g/14 oz lean pork fillet

4 pork sausages, skinned and roughly chopped

3-4 tsp sunflower oil

1 onion, finely chopped

800 g/1 lb 12 oz canned chopped tomatoes

150 ml/5 fl oz chicken stock

1 carrot, finely chopped

1 celery stick, finely chopped

1 tsp dried oregano

250 g/9 oz dried spaghetti

salt and pepper

1. Place the pork in a food processor and process until finely chopped. Transfer to a bowl. Add the sausage meat and mix well, then roll into 20 walnut-sized balls.

2. Heat 2 teaspoons of the oil in a large saucepan. Add the onion, cover and cook over a low heat for 2–3 minutes, or until soft. Stir in the tomatoes, stock, carrot, celery and oregano. Simmer uncovered for 15–20 minutes, or until the sauce has reduced and thickened slightly.

3. Meanwhile, heat 1 teaspoon of oil in a large frying pan. Add the meatballs in batches and fry for 2–3 minutes, turning several times, until brown all over. Transfer to a plate.

4. Season the sauce to taste with salt and pepper. Add the meatballs, then cover the pan and simmer for 8–10 minutes, or until cooked through. Cook the spaghetti according to the packet instructions. Drain and return to the pan. Add the meatballs and sauce and toss well to mix. Serve immediately.

#132 Lasagne

Ingredients

2 tbsp olive oil

55 g/2 oz pancetta, chopped

1 onion, chopped

1 garlic clove, finely chopped

225 g/8 oz fresh beef mince

2 celery sticks, chopped

2 carrots, chopped

pinch of sugar

½ tsp dried oregano

400 g/14 oz canned chopped tomatoes

2 tsp Dijon mustard

450 ml/16 fl oz ready-made cheese sauce

225 g/8 oz no pre-cook lasagne sheets

115 g/4 oz freshly grated Parmesan cheese, plus extra for sprinkling

salt and pepper

1. Preheat the oven to 190°C/375°F/Gas Mark 5. Heat the oil in a large, heavy-based saucepan. Add the pancetta and cook over a medium heat, stirring occasionally, for 3 minutes.

2. Add the onion and garlic and cook, stirring occasionally, for 5 minutes, or until soft. Add the mince and cook, breaking it up with a wooden spoon, until brown all over. Stir in the celery and carrots and cook for 5 minutes. Season to taste with salt and pepper. Add the sugar, oregano and tomatoes and their can juices. Bring to the boil, reduce the heat and simmer for 30 minutes. Meanwhile, stir the mustard into the cheese sauce.

3. In a large, rectangular ovenproof dish, make alternate layers of meat sauce, lasagne sheets and cheese. Pour the cheese sauce over the layers, covering them completely, and sprinkle with cheese.

4. Bake in the preheated oven for 30 minutes, or until golden brown and bubbling. Serve immediately.

#133 Pork & sausage bake

Serves 4

Ingredients

2 tbsp sunflower oil

25 g/1 oz butter

450 g/1 lb pork fillet, cut into thin strips

1 large onion, chopped

1 red pepper, deseeded and sliced

1 orange pepper, deseeded and sliced

115 g/4 oz mushrooms, sliced

140 g/5 oz long-grain rice

425 ml/15 fl oz beef stock

225 g/8 oz smoked sausage, sliced

¼ tsp mixed spice

salt and pepper

2 tbsp chopped fresh parsley, to garnish

1. Preheat the oven to 180°C/350°F/Gas Mark 4. Heat the oil and butter in a large, flameproof casserole. Add the pork and cook over a medium heat, stirring, for 5 minutes, until brown. Transfer to a plate.

2. Add the onion and cook over a low heat, stirring occasionally, for 5 minutes, or until soft. Add the peppers and cook, stirring frequently, for a further 4–5 minutes. Add the mushrooms and cook for 1 minute, then stir in the rice. Cook for 1 minute, or until the grains are well coated, then add the stock and bring to the boil.

3. Return the pork to the casserole, add the sausage and mixed spice and season to taste with salt and pepper. Mix thoroughly, cover and cook in the preheated oven for 1 hour, or until all the liquid has been absorbed and the meat is tender. Serve immediately, garnished with chopped parsley.

#134 Beef in black bean sauce

Serves 4

Ingredients

3 tbsp groundnut oil

450 g/1 lb beef sirloin, thinly sliced

1 red pepper, deseeded and thinly sliced

1 green pepper, deseeded and thinly sliced

6 spring onions, sliced

2 garlic cloves, crushed

1 tbsp grated fresh ginger

2 tbsp black bean sauce

1 tbsp sherry

1 tbsp soy sauce

1. Heat 2 tablespoons of the oil in a wok and add the beef. Stir-fry over a high heat for 1–2 minutes. Remove from the wok and set aside.

2. Add the remaining oil, then add the red and green peppers and stir-fry for 2 minutes. Add the spring onions, garlic and ginger and stir-fry for 30 seconds.

3. Add the black bean sauce, sherry and soy sauce, then stir in the beef and heat until bubbling.

4. Transfer to warmed bowls and serve immediately.

#135 Chorizo, chilli & chickpea casserole

Serves 4

Ingredients

2 tbsp olive oil

1 onion, sliced

1 large yellow pepper, deseeded and sliced

1 garlic clove, crushed

1 tsp chilli flakes

225 g/8 oz chorizo sausage

400 g/14 oz canned chopped tomatoes

400 g/14 oz canned chickpeas, drained and rinsed

200 g/7 oz basmati rice

handful of rocket leaves

salt and pepper

chopped fresh basil, to garnish

1. Heat the oil in a flameproof casserole and fry the onion over a medium heat, stirring occasionally, for 5 minutes.

2. Add the yellow pepper, garlic and chilli flakes and cook for 2 minutes, stirring. Chop the chorizo into bite-sized chunks and stir into the casserole. Add the tomatoes and chickpeas and season to taste with salt and pepper. Bring to the boil, cover and simmer for 10 minutes.

3. Meanwhile, bring a saucepan of lightly salted water to the boil, add the rice, bring back to the boil and cook for 10–12 minutes until tender. Drain.

4. Stir the rocket into the casserole. Serve spooned over the rice, garnished with fresh basil.

#136 Pad noodles with pork strips & prawns

Serves 4

Ingredients

250 g/9 oz flat rice noodles

200 g/7 oz pork fillet

3 tbsp groundnut oil

2 shallots, finely chopped

2 garlic cloves, finely chopped

175 g/6 oz raw prawns, peeled and deveined

2 eggs, beaten

2 tbsp Thai fish sauce

juice of 1 lime

1 tbsp tomato ketchup

2 tsp light muscovado sugar

½ tsp dried chilli flakes

100 g/3½ oz beansprouts

4 tbsp roasted peanuts, chopped

6 spring onions, diagonally sliced

1. Soak the noodles in hot water for 10 minutes, or according to the packet instructions. Drain well.

2. Slice the pork into 5-mm/¼-inch thick strips. Heat the oil in a wok, add the shallots and stir-fry for 1–2 minutes until soft. Add the pork strips and stir-fry for 2–3 minutes.

3. Add the garlic and prawns and stir-fry for 1–2 minutes. Pour in the beaten egg and stir for a few seconds until lightly set.

4. Reduce the heat and add the noodles, fish sauce, lime juice, ketchup and sugar. Toss together and heat through.

5. Sprinkle with the chilli flakes, beansprouts, peanuts and spring onions. Transfer to bowls and serve.

94

Ginger pork with shiitake mushrooms

Ingredients

2 tbsp vegetable oil

3 shallots, finely chopped

2 garlic cloves, crushed

5-cm/2-inch piece fresh ginger, thinly sliced

500 g/1 lb 2 oz pork stir-fry strips

250 g/9 oz shiitake mushrooms, sliced

4 tbsp soy sauce

4 tbsp rice wine

1 tsp light muscovado sugar

1 tsp cornflour

2 tbsp cold water

3 tbsp chopped fresh coriander, to garnish

1. Heat a wok over a high heat, then add the oil. Add the shallots and stir-fry for 2–3 minutes, then add the garlic and ginger and stir-fry for 1 minute.

2. Add the pork strips and stir-fry for a further minute, then add the mushrooms and stir-fry for 2–3 minutes until the pork is cooked through.

3. Stir in the soy sauce, rice wine and sugar. Blend the cornflour and water until smooth, add to the pan, stirring, and cook until the juices are thickened and clear. Transfer to warmed serving dishes, garnish with coriander and serve immediately.

Bangers & mash

Ingredients

1 tbsp olive oil

8 good-quality sausages

3 onions, halved and thinly sliced

70 g/2½ oz butter

125 ml/4 fl oz Marsala or port

125 ml/4 fl oz vegetable stock

salt and pepper

Mash

900 g/2 lb floury potatoes, peeled and cut into chunks

55 g/2 oz butter

3 tbsp hot milk

2 tbsp chopped fresh parsley

salt and pepper

1. Place a frying pan over a low heat with the oil and add the sausages. Cover the pan and cook for 25–30 minutes, turning the sausages from time to time, until brown all over.

2. Put the onions in a frying pan with the butter and fry over a low heat until soft, stirring constantly. Continue to cook for around 30 minutes, or until the onions are brown and have started to caramelize. Pour in the Marsala and stock and bubble until the really thick. Season to taste with salt and pepper.

3. To make the mash, bring a large saucepan of lightly salted water to the boil. Add the potatoes, bring back to the boil and cook for 15–20 minutes. Drain well and mash until smooth. Season to taste with salt and pepper. Add the butter, milk and parsley and stir well.

4. Serve the sausages with the mash, and the onion gravy spooned over the top.

Yam & beef stew with couscous

Ingredients

800 g/1 lb 12 oz stewing beef

2 onions, chopped

200 g/7 oz yams, cubed

200 g/7 oz new potatoes, halved

400 g/14 oz canned chickpeas, drained and rinsed

400 g/14 oz canned chopped tomatoes

200 ml/7 fl oz red wine or water

200 g/7 oz couscous

250 ml/9 fl oz boiling water

1 tbsp roughly chopped fresh flat-leaf parsley

1 small bunch spring onions, trimmed and chopped

juice of 1 lemon

2 tbsp olive oil

salt and pepper

Marinade

2 tbsp vegetable oil

2 tbsp chopped fresh coriander

2 cinnamon sticks

1 tbsp clear honey

1 tsp ground paprika

1 tsp ground cumin

1 tsp harissa paste

1 tsp salt

1. Trim the beef, cut into 2.5-cm/1-inch pieces and put into a large bowl. Add the marinade ingredients and stir well to combine. Cover and chill in the refrigerator for 6 hours or overnight.

2. Preheat the oven to 190°C/375°F/Gas Mark 5. Transfer the meat and the marinade to a casserole dish and add the onions, yams, new potatoes and chickpeas. Pour over the tomatoes and wine and stir well. Cook in the preheated oven for 1 hour.

3. Remove from the oven, stir well and check the seasoning. If all the liquid has been absorbed, add enough water to create a generous sauce. Return the casserole to the oven and cook for a further 30 minutes, or until the meat is tender.

4. Meanwhile, put the couscous into a bowl and pour over the boiling water. Season to taste with salt and leave to stand for 5 minutes. Stir in the parsley and spring onions and drizzle over the lemon juice and oil. Remove the cinnamon sticks from the stew and serve immediately with the couscous.

#140 Braised lamb with garlic & orange

Serves 4–6

Ingredients

1 boned, rolled shoulder of lamb, weighing 1.5–2 kg/3 lb 5 oz–4 lb 8 oz

12–18 garlic cloves, unpeeled

finely grated rind and juice of 2 bitter oranges

½ tsp allspice berries, crushed

1 cinnamon stick, roughly crushed

150 ml/5 fl oz dry white wine

large handful fresh coriander leaves

2 green chillies, deseeded and roughly chopped

salt and pepper

cooked corn cobs and butternut squash, to serve

1. Season the lamb with salt and pepper and put into a flameproof casserole. Pack the garlic cloves around the side. Scatter over the orange rind, allspice and cinnamon and drizzle with the orange juice. Add the wine and enough water to come half-way up the meat. Bring to the boil, then reduce the heat, cover tightly with foil and the lid, and simmer very gently for 1½–2 hours, or until the meat is perfectly tender. Check every now and again, adding a little boiling water if the juices are drying out.

2. Transfer the meat to a warmed serving dish. Squeeze the garlic flesh from the skins into a food processor, add the coriander, chillies and cooking juices and purée. Return to the casserole and reheat gently, diluting with boiling water if necessary.

3. Carve the lamb into thick slices and serve with corn, butternut squash and the sauce.

#141 Pasta & pork in a red wine sauce

Serves 4

Ingredients

450 g/1 lb pork fillet, thinly sliced

4 tbsp olive oil

225 g/8 oz button mushrooms, sliced

1 tbsp lemon juice

pinch of saffron threads

350 g/12 oz dried orecchiette

4 tbsp double cream

12 quail eggs

salt

Sauce

1 tbsp olive oil

1 onion, chopped

1 tbsp tomato purée

200 ml/7 fl oz red wine

1 tsp finely chopped fresh oregano

1. To make the sauce, heat the oil in a small heavy-based saucepan, add the onion and cook until translucent. Stir in the tomato purée, red wine and oregano. Heat gently to reduce and set aside.

2. Put the slices of pork between two sheets of clingfilm and pound with a meat mallet until wafer thin, then cut into strips. Heat the oil in a frying pan, add the pork and cook for 5 minutes. Add the mushrooms and cook for a further 2 minutes. Strain and pour over the red wine sauce. Reduce the heat and simmer for 20 minutes.

3. Meanwhile, bring a large heavy-based saucepan of lightly salted water to the boil. Add the lemon juice, saffron and pasta, return to the boil and cook for 8–10 minutes, or until tender but still firm to the bite. Drain thoroughly, return to the pan and keep warm.

4. Stir the cream into the pan with the pork and heat for a few minutes. Boil the quail eggs for 3 minutes, cool them in cold water and remove the shells. Transfer the pasta to a large warmed plate, top with the pork and the sauce and garnish with the eggs. Serve immediately.

#142 Pork chops with puy lentils

Ingredients

1 tbsp olive oil, plus extra
for brushing

85 g/3 oz lardons

1 onion, chopped

2 large garlic cloves, crushed

2 large carrots, peeled and diced

250 g/9 oz Puy lentils,
picked over and rinsed

bouquet garni, made with a bay leaf,
parsley sprigs and thyme sprigs

4 loin pork chops,
about 150 g/5½ oz each

2 chargrilled red peppers in olive oil,
drained and sliced

2 tbsp chopped fresh parsley

salt and pepper

1. Heat the oil in a large saucepan over a medium-high heat. Add the lardons and cook, stirring, for 5 minutes, or until brown and giving off their fat. Add the onion and cook, stirring, for 3 minutes, then add the garlic and continue to cook, stirring, for about 2 minutes, or until the onion is soft, but not brown. Add the carrot and stir, then add the lentils and enough water to cover by 4 cm/1½ inches. Add the bouquet garni and bring to the boil. Cover, reduce the heat to low and leave to simmer for 20–30 minutes until the liquid has been absorbed and the lentils are tender.

2. Meanwhile, preheat the grill to high. Brush the grill rack with oil. Brush the pork chops with a little oil and season with salt and pepper. Place the chops under the grill and cook for 4 minutes. Turn and cook for a further 4 minutes, or until cooked to your liking.

3. The lentils should have absorbed all the water by the time they are tender, but if any liquid remains on the surface drain them. Return to the pan, stir in the red peppers, season to taste with salt and pepper and stir through the parsley. Serve the lentils immediately with the pork chops.

#143 Orange & lemon crispy lamb cutlets

Ingredients

1 garlic clove, crushed

1 tbsp olive oil

2 tbsp finely grated orange rind

2 tbsp finely grated lemon rind

6 lamb cutlets

salt and pepper

orange wedges, to garnish

1. Preheat a ridged griddle pan over a medium-high heat.

2. Mix together the garlic, olive oil, orange rind and lemon rind in a bowl and season to taste with salt and pepper.

3. Brush the mixture over the lamb cutlets and turn to coat evenly.

4. Cook the lamb cutlets in the preheated pan for 4–5 minutes on each side, or until cooked to your liking.

5. Transfer the cutlets to warmed serving plates. Garnish with orange wedges and serve immediately.

#144 Tartiflette

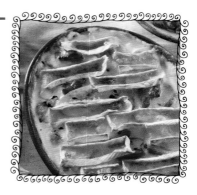

Ingredients

1 kg/2 lb 4 oz small waxy potatoes, sliced

2 tbsp olive oil

3 garlic cloves, peeled but kept whole

150 g/5½ oz bacon lardons

600 ml/1 pint double cream

2 tbsp fresh thyme leaves

200 g/7 oz Reblochon cheese or any other good melting cheese, sliced

salt

1. Preheat the oven to 180°C/350°F/Gas Mark 4.

2. Bring a large saucepan of lightly salted water to the boil, add the potato slices, bring back to the boil and cook for 10–15 minutes until just tender. Drain.

3. Heat the oil in a large frying pan over a medium heat. Hit the garlic cloves with the back of a sturdy knife to split them and add to the pan. Add the bacon lardons and cook for 3–4 minutes until just cooked. Add the potato slices and cook for 3–4 minutes. Pour in the cream, add the thyme leaves and stir well. Transfer the mixture to a gratin dish and top with the cheese slices. Bake in the preheated oven for 20 minutes, or until golden and bubbling.

#145 New York strip steak with tarragon mushrooms

Serves
4

Ingredients

4 tbsp olive oil

3 tbsp butter

900 g/2 lb large button mushrooms, thickly sliced

2 garlic cloves, finely chopped

3 tbsp sherry vinegar

1 tbsp chopped fresh tarragon

4 x 280-g/10-oz sirloin steaks, 280 g/10 oz each

1 tbsp vegetable oil

4 tbsp chicken stock

1 tbsp butter, chilled

salt and pepper

1. Put the olive oil and 2 tablespoons of the butter into a large frying pan over a medium-high heat. Add the mushrooms and cook, stirring, for 10–15 minutes, or until brown. Stir in the garlic and cook for 2 minutes.

2. Pour in the vinegar and as soon as it starts to boil remove the pan from the heat. Transfer the mushrooms to a bowl, add the tarragon and season to taste with salt and pepper. Leave to cool, then cover with clingfilm and set aside.

3. Season the steaks on both sides with the salt and pepper. Heat the vegetable oil in a large frying pan over a high heat. Add the steaks and cook for 5–6 minutes on each side for medium-rare, or until cooked to your liking. Set aside to rest for 5 minutes before serving.

4. Add the stock to the hot pan and use a wooden spoon to scrape the sediment from the base. When the stock has deglazed the pan, add the remaining butter and stir until melted. Add the mushrooms and stir until heated through. Taste and adjust the seasoning if necessary. Serve the steaks with the butter and mushrooms.

#146 Spaghetti & meatballs

Serves 4

Ingredients

2 tbsp olive oil, plus extra for brushing

1 onion, finely diced

4 garlic cloves, finely chopped

½ tsp dried mixed herbs

140 g/5 oz fine breadcrumbs

4 tbsp milk

900 g/2 lb beef mince, well chilled

2 large eggs, lightly beaten

5 tbsp chopped fresh flat-leaf parsley

55 g/2 oz freshly grated Parmesan cheese, plus extra to serve

1.5 litres/2¾ pints ready-made tomato pasta sauce

225 ml/8 fl oz water

450 g/1 lb thick dried spaghetti

salt and pepper

1. Heat the oil in a saucepan. Add the onion, garlic and a pinch of salt, cover and cook over a medium–low heat for 6–7 minutes, until soft. Remove from the heat, stir in the herbs and leave to cool. Put the breadcrumbs into a bowl, toss with the milk and leave to soak for 10 minutes. Preheat the oven to 220°C/425°F/Gas Mark 7. Brush a baking sheet with oil.

2. Put the beef, eggs, parsley, cheese, breadcrumbs, cooled onion mixture, 2 teaspoons of salt and 1 teaspoon of pepper into a bowl. Mix well with your hands until thoroughly combined. Dampen your hands and roll pieces of the mixture into golf-ball sized balls. Put them on the prepared tray and bake in the preheated oven for 20 minutes. Meanwhile, pour the pasta sauce into a saucepan, stir in the water and bring to a simmer. Transfer the cooked meatballs into the hot sauce, reduce the heat to very low, cover and simmer gently for 45 minutes.

3. Bring a large saucepan of lightly salted water to the boil, add the spaghetti, bring back to the boil and cook for 10–12 minutes, until tender but still firm to the bite. Drain the spaghetti and tip into a large serving dish. Ladle over some of the sauce from the meatballs and toss to coat. Top with the meatballs and the remaining sauce, sprinkle with cheese and serve.

#147 Shepherd's pie

Serves 6

Ingredients

1 tbsp olive oil

2 onions, finely chopped

2 garlic cloves, finely chopped

675 g/1 lb 8 oz minced lamb

2 carrots, finely chopped

1 tbsp plain flour

225 ml/8 fl oz beef stock, plus extra if needed

125 ml/4 fl oz red wine

675 g/1 lb 8 oz floury potatoes, peeled and cut into chunks

55 g/2 oz butter

2 tbsp single cream or milk

salt and pepper

1. Preheat the oven to 180°C/350°F/Gas Mark 4. Heat the oil in a casserole dish, add the onions and fry until soft, then add the garlic and stir well. Increase the heat and add the meat. Cook quickly to brown the meat all over, stirring constantly. Add the carrots and season well with salt and pepper. Stir in the flour and add the stock and wine. Stir well and heat until simmering and thickened. Cover the casserole dish and cook in the oven for about 1 hour. Check the consistency from time to time and add a little more stock if needed. The mixture should be quite thick but not dry.

2. Meanwhile, bring a large saucepan of lightly salted water to the boil, add the potatoes and cook for 15–20 minutes. Drain well and mash with a potato masher until smooth. Add the butter and cream and season to taste with salt and pepper. Spoon the lamb mixture into an ovenproof serving dish and spread or pipe the potato on top. Increase the oven temperature to 200°C/400°F/Gas Mark 6 and cook the pie for 15–20 minutes at the top of the oven until golden brown. Serve immediately.

#148 Meatloaf

Ingredients

25 g/1 oz butter

1 tbsp olive oil, plus extra for brushing

3 garlic cloves, chopped

100 g/3½ oz carrots, very finely diced

55 g/2 oz celery, very finely diced

1 onion, very finely diced

1 red pepper, deseeded and diced

4 large white mushrooms, diced

1 tsp dried thyme

2 tsp finely chopped rosemary

1 tsp Worcestershire sauce

6 tbsp tomato ketchup

½ tsp cayenne pepper

1.1 kg/2 lb 8 oz beef mince, chilled

2 eggs, beaten

55 g/2 oz fresh breadcrumbs

2 tbsp brown sugar

1 tbsp Dijon mustard

salt and pepper

1. Melt the butter with the oil and garlic in a large frying pan. Add the vegetables and cook over a medium heat, stirring frequently, for 10 minutes until most of the moisture has evaporated. Remove from the heat and stir in the herbs, Worcestershire sauce, 4 tablespoons of tomato ketchup and the cayenne pepper. Leave to cool.

2. Preheat the oven to 160°C/325°F/Gas Mark 3. Brush a loaf tin with oil. Put the beef into a large bowl and gently break it up with your fingertips. Add the vegetable mixture, eggs, and salt and pepper to taste and mix with your fingers. Add the breadcrumbs and mix.

3. Transfer the meatloaf mixture to the loaf tin. Smooth the surface and bake in the preheated oven for 30 minutes. Meanwhile, make a glaze by whisking together the sugar, the remaining tomato ketchup, the mustard and a pinch of salt.

4. Remove the meatloaf from the oven and spread the glaze evenly over the top. Return to the oven and bake for a further 35-45 minutes. Cut into the middle to check that the meat is no longer pink. Any juices that run out should be clear and piping hot with steam rising.

5. Remove from the oven and leave to rest for at least 15 minutes. Slice thickly to serve.

#149 Gammon steaks with fried egg & chips

Serves 4

Ingredients

vegetable oil, for frying and brushing

6 large floury potatoes, peeled and cut into even-sized chips

4 x 175 g/6 oz gammon steaks

4 eggs

1. Heat the oil in a deep-fat fryer or a large saucepan to 120°C/250°F. Add the chips and fry for 8–10 minutes until soft but not coloured. Remove from the oil and increase the temperature to 180–190°C/350–375°F.

2. Meanwhile, preheat the grill, place the steaks on a grill pan and brush with a little oil. Grill for 3–4 minutes on each side, turning occasionally, until the fat is crisp. Set aside and keep warm.

3. Return the chips to the fryer and cook for a further 2–3 minutes until golden brown and crisp. Drain, season well and keep warm.

4. Put 2 tablespoons of oil into a frying pan and heat over a medium heat. Break two eggs into the pan and cook for a few seconds until the white is setting. Tip the pan and spoon the hot oil over the egg yolks until firm but still soft. Remove from the pan and drain on kitchen paper. Keep warm and repeat with the other eggs. Arrange the steaks, egg and chips on warmed plates and serve immediately.

#150 Pork hot pot

Serves 6

Ingredients

85 g/3 oz plain flour

1.3 kg/3 lb pork fillet, cut into 5-mm/¼-inch slices

4 tbsp sunflower oil

2 onions, thinly sliced

2 garlic cloves, finely chopped

400 g/14 oz canned chopped tomatoes

350 ml/12 fl oz dry white wine

1 tbsp torn fresh basil leaves

2 tbsp chopped fresh parsley

salt and pepper

fresh oregano, to garnish

fresh crusty bread, to serve

1. Spread the flour on a plate and season with salt and pepper. Coat the pork slices in the flour, shaking off any excess. Heat the oil in a casserole. Add the pork slices and cook over a medium heat, turning occasionally, for 4–5 minutes, or until brown. Transfer to a plate with a slotted spoon.

2. Add the onion slices to the casserole and cook over a low heat, stirring occasionally, for 10 minutes, or until golden brown. Add the garlic and cook for a further 2 minutes, then add the tomatoes, wine and basil and season to taste with salt and pepper. Cook, stirring frequently, for 3 minutes.

3. Return the pork to the casserole, cover and simmer gently for 1 hour, or until the meat is tender. Stir in the parsley, garnish with oregano and serve with fresh crusty bread.

#151 Honeyed apricot lamb with lemon couscous

Ingredients

4 lamb leg steaks

4 tsp ground coriander

1 tbsp ground cumin

1 small butternut squash

1 tbsp olive oil

1 onion, chopped

600 ml/1 pint chicken stock

2 tbsp chopped fresh ginger

100 g/3½ oz dried apricots

2 tbsp clear honey

finely grated rind and juice of 1 lemon

200 g/7 oz couscous

salt and pepper

3 tbsp chopped fresh mint, to garnish

1. Sprinkle the lamb steaks with the coriander and cumin.

2. Peel and deseed the squash and cut into bite-sized chunks. Heat the oil in a flameproof casserole. Add the lamb and cook over a high heat for 2–3 minutes, turning once.

3. Stir in the squash, onion and half the stock, then bring to the boil. Add the ginger, apricots, honey and lemon juice and season to taste with salt and pepper. Cover and cook over a medium heat for about 20 minutes, stirring occasionally.

4. Meanwhile, bring the remaining stock to the boil in a small saucepan, then stir in the couscous and lemon rind with salt and pepper to taste. Remove from the heat, cover and leave to stand for 5 minutes. Serve the lamb with the couscous, sprinkled with fresh mint.

#152 Kashmiri lamb & fennel stew

Ingredients

4 tbsp vegetable or groundnut oil

2 onions, halved and thinly sliced

600 g/1 lb 5 oz lamb shoulder, trimmed and cut into bite-sized pieces

4 garlic cloves, crushed

2 tsp finely grated fresh ginger

1 tbsp ground coriander

1 tsp Kashmiri chilli powder

1 tsp salt

300 g/10½ oz potatoes, halved

500 ml/18 fl oz lamb or chicken stock

200 ml/7 fl oz single cream

4 tbsp ground almonds

2 tbsp crushed fennel seeds

6 tbsp finely chopped fresh coriander

2 tbsp finely chopped fresh mint

1. Heat the oil in a non-stick saucepan, add the onions and cook over a low heat, stirring frequently, for about 15–20 minutes, until lightly browned.

2. Increase the heat to high, add the lamb and stir-fry for 4–5 minutes, until sealed. Reduce the heat to medium and add the garlic, ginger, ground coriander, chilli powder and salt. Stir and cook for 1–2 minutes. Add the potatoes and stock, then cover and simmer over a low heat for about 1½ hours, or until the lamb is tender.

3. Uncover the pan, increase the heat slightly and stir in the cream and ground almonds. Cook for a further 8–10 minutes, until thickened and reduced. Take care not to boil or the cream will curdle.

4. Add the crushed fennel seeds to the pan and cook for a further 3–4 minutes. Remove from the heat and stir in the chopped coriander and mint. Serve immediately.

Pork with borlotti beans

Ingredients

250 g/9 oz dried borlotti beans, soaked overnight

800 g/1 lb 12 oz pork shoulder

1 large onion, chopped

2 celery sticks, chopped

1 large carrot, chopped

1 fresh red chilli, finely chopped

2 garlic cloves, finely chopped

large sprig of each fresh rosemary, thyme and bay leaves

about 600 ml/1 pint chicken stock

salt and pepper

crusty bread, to serve

1. Preheat the oven to 160°C/325°F/Gas Mark 3. Drain the beans and cook in a saucepan of boiling water for 10 minutes. Drain and tip into a wide ovenproof casserole.

2. Cut the pork into bite-sized chunks, leaving on any skin.

3. Layer the pork and vegetables over the beans, sprinkling the layers with the chilli, garlic, and salt and pepper to taste. Tuck in the herb sprigs.

4. Pour over just enough stock to cover, then cover and bake in the preheated oven, without stirring, for 3 hours until tender.

5. Serve the pork and beans with chunks of bread to soak up the juices.

Beef Stroganoff

Ingredients

15 g/½ oz dried ceps

350 g/12 oz beef fillet

2 tbsp olive oil

115 g/4 oz shallots, sliced

175 g/6 oz chestnut mushrooms

½ tsp Dijon mustard

5 tbsp double cream

salt and pepper

freshly cooked pasta, to serve

fresh chives, to garnish

1. Place the ceps in a bowl, cover with hot water and leave to soak for 20 minutes. Meanwhile, cut the beef against the grain into 5-mm/¼-inch-thick slices, then into 1-cm/½-inch-long strips, and reserve. Drain the ceps, reserving the soaking liquid, and chop. Strain the soaking liquid through a fine-mesh sieve or coffee filter and reserve.

2. Heat half the oil in a large frying pan. Add the shallots and cook over a low heat, stirring occasionally, for 5 minutes, or until soft. Add the soaked ceps, reserved soaking water and chestnut mushrooms and cook, stirring frequently, for 10 minutes, or until almost all of the liquid has evaporated, then transfer the mixture to a plate.

3. Heat the remaining oil in the pan, add the beef and cook, stirring frequently, for 4 minutes, or until brown all over. You may need to do this in batches. Return the mushroom mixture to the pan and season to taste with salt and pepper. Place the mustard and cream in a small bowl and stir to mix, then fold into the meat and mushroom mixture. Heat through gently, then serve with freshly cooked pasta, garnished with chives.

#155 Chilli con carne

Serves
4–6

Ingredients

2 tbsp corn oil

2 onions, thinly sliced

2 garlic cloves, finely chopped

650 g/1 lb 7 oz fresh beef mince

200 g/7 oz canned chopped tomatoes

1 tsp ground cumin

1 tsp cayenne pepper

1 tbsp chilli powder

1 tsp dried oregano

1 bay leaf

350 ml/12 fl oz beef stock

400 g/14 oz canned red kidney beans

salt

cooked rice, to serve

1. Heat the oil in a large saucepan. Add the onions and garlic and cook over a low heat, stirring occasionally, for 5 minutes, until soft. Add the beef, increase the heat to medium and cook, stirring frequently and breaking it up with a wooden spoon, for 8–10 minutes, until evenly browned.

2. Stir in the tomatoes, cumin, cayenne pepper, chilli powder, oregano, bay leaf and stock, then season to taste with salt and bring to the boil. Reduce the heat, cover and simmer, stirring occasionally, for 1 hour.

3. Drain and rinse the beans and add them to the pan, re-cover and simmer, stirring occasionally, for a further 30 minutes. Remove and discard the bay leaf and serve immediately with rice..

#156 Pork goulash with paprika

Serves
6

Ingredients

1 x 1-kg/2 lb 4-oz pork shoulder

2 tbsp sweet paprika

1 tsp dried marjoram

1 tbsp plain flour, for dusting

300 g/10½ oz onions

3 garlic cloves

20 g/¾ oz fresh parsley sprigs

40 g/1½ oz pork lard

1 strip lemon zest

½ tsp caraway seeds

4 tsp butter, softened, plus extra to serve

1 tbsp tomato purée

500 ml/18 fl oz chicken stock

salt and pepper

snipped fresh chives, to garnish

500 g/1 lb 2 oz cooked pasta, to serve

1. Cut the pork shoulder into 4-cm/1½-inch cubes. Put the meat into a bowl, season with salt, pepper, paprika and marjoram and dust with the flour. Mix together well using your hands. Cut the onions into strips. Peel and finely dice 2 garlic cloves. Tie the parsley sprigs together with string.

2. Heat the lard in a large saucepan, then add the diced garlic, followed by the onions. Gently sauté until the onions are translucent. Finely chop the remaining garlic clove, the lemon zest and the caraway seeds, then combine them with the butter. Chill in the refrigerator.

3. Add the meat to the pan and gently sauté for 10 minutes, being careful not to brown it. Push the meat to the side, add the tomato purée to the centre of the pan and lightly cook. Mix it with the meat, cover the pan and cook for a further 10 minutes. Pour in the stock, re-cover the pan and cook over a low heat for 1 hour. Stir occasionally, adding water, if necessary. After 45 minutes' cooking, add the parsley and cook for a further 15 minutes. Remove the parsley, add the chilled herb butter and mix well. Serve immediately with pasta and chives to garnish.

#157 Beef with cracked black pepper & chillies

Serves 2

Ingredients

400 g/14 oz beef fillet

2 tbsp cornflour

groundnut oil, for deep-frying

4 small shallots, halved and thinly sliced

1–3 fresh red chillies, deseeded and very thinly sliced crossways

3 tbsp beef stock

3 garlic cloves, very finely chopped

2.5-cm/1-inch piece fresh ginger, very finely chopped

1½ tbsp ketjap manis soy sauce

½ tbsp sugar

1–2 tbsp black peppercorns, cracked

3 tbsp mint leaves

3 tbsp chopped coriander leaves

salt

1. Slice the meat into 2.5-cm/1-inch cubes and put in a shallow dish. Toss with cornflour and season to taste with salt. Heat enough oil for deep-frying in a large wok to 180–190°C/350–375°F, or until a cube of bread browns in 30 seconds. Add the beef and fry for 2½–3 minutes, turning with tongs, until brown and starting to crisp at the edges. Remove with a slotted spoon and drain briefly on kitchen paper. Tip onto a warmed plate.

2. Pour all but 1 tablespoon of the oil from the wok. Place the wok over a medium–low heat, add the shallots and chillies and fry for 5–7 minutes, until soft but not coloured. Stir in the stock, then add the garlic and ginger. Gently fry for a further 3–4 minutes, stirring occasionally, until the mixture is very soft. Add the soy sauce, sugar and cracked pepper and stir for a few seconds.

3. Return the beef and any juices to the wok. Increase the heat to medium and stir for 1–2 minutes, until heated through. Check the seasoning and stir in the mint and chopped coriander.

4. Transfer to a warmed serving dish and serve immediately.

#158 Spanish rice with pork

Serves 1

Ingredients

½ tsp olive oil

75 g/2¾ oz lean pork fillet, cut into small cubes

1 small onion, or 2 shallots, finely chopped

1 garlic clove, chopped

1 red pepper, deseeded and chopped into 1-cm/½-inch cubes

200 g/7 oz canned chopped tomatoes

1 tbsp chopped fresh parsley

pinch of saffron threads

60 g/2¼ oz brown basmati rice

225 ml/8 fl oz chicken stock

pepper

1. Heat the oil in a large, heavy-based saucepan with a lid over a high heat, add the pork and brown all over. Remove with a slotted spoon and keep warm.

2. Reduce the heat to medium–high and add the onion, garlic and pepper, and stir-fry for a few minutes until everything is soft and turning golden.

3. Return the meat to the pan and add the tomatoes, parsley, saffron, rice and stock, and season to taste with pepper. Stir well to combine and to break up the tomatoes a little, and bring to a simmer. Reduce the heat to low and cover.

4. Simmer for 30–40 minutes, or until the rice is tender and all the stock is absorbed. (If the rice is not cooked but the dish looks dry, add a little more hot water.) Remove from the heat and serve.

#159 Beer-braised beef short ribs

Serves 4

Ingredients

6 fresh thyme sprigs

6 fresh oregano sprigs

3 fresh rosemary sprigs

3 tbsp olive oil

900 g/2 lb thin ribs of beef (bone in), cut into 8 pieces

2 carrots, peeled and roughly chopped

1 onion, roughly chopped

2 celery sticks, roughly chopped

2 garlic cloves, crushed

350 ml/12 fl oz beer, at room temperature

425 g/15 oz canned tomato purée

225 ml/8 fl oz beef stock

rock salt

pepper

15 g/½ oz fresh flat-leaf parsley, finely chopped, to garnish

1. Preheat the oven to 140°/275°F/Gas Mark 1 and make a bouquet garni by tying the thyme, oregano and rosemary together with string.

2. Heat 2 tablespoons of the oil in a casserole over a medium-high heat. Generously season the meat all over with salt and pepper. When the oil is very hot, add the ribs to the casserole, in batches to avoid overcrowding. Cook, turning occasionally, for about 8 minutes, until brown all over. Remove the ribs and pour the fat out of the casserole.

3. Add the remaining oil to the casserole and heat over a medium-high heat. Add the carrots, onion and celery and cook for about 3 minutes, until they are beginning to brown. Stir in the garlic and cook for a further minute.

4. Add the beer and bring to the boil, stirring and scraping up the sediment from the base of the casserole. Boil for 3–5 minutes, until the beer is reduced by half. Stir in the tomato purée and stock. Return the ribs to the casserole and add the bouquet garni.

5. Bring to the boil, cover and transfer to the preheated oven. Cook for 2–2½ hours until the meat is very tender.

6. Just before serving, remove and discard the bouquet garni. Serve immediately garnished with chopped parsley.

#160 Rump steak in a lemon & thyme marinade

Ingredients

2 rump steaks, 280 g/10 oz each

2 tbsp extra virgin olive oil

juice and zest of 1 lemon

1 small bunch thyme, leaves picked

Marinade

4 tbsp olive oil

1 small bunch thyme, leaves picked

2 garlic cloves, crushed

juice and zest of 1 lemon

1 tsp salt

1 tsp pepper

1. Place all of the marinade ingredients into a shallow non-metallic dish, large enough to hold both steaks in a single layer. Mix the ingredients together.

2. Add the steaks to the marinade, turning a few times to coat. Cover and chill in the refrigerator for at least 4 hours, turning once. Remove from the refrigerator 1 hour before cooking, to allow the meat to return to room temperature.

3. Preheat a griddle pan over a high heat, add the steaks and cook for 5 minutes on each side for medium rare, or until cooked to your liking. Leave to rest for 5 minutes.

4. Slice the steaks and serve drizzled with the extra virgin olive oil and lemon juice, and sprinkled with the lemon zest and thyme leaves.

#161 Steak & chips

Ingredients

85 g/3 oz unsalted butter, softened

4 tbsp finely chopped watercress

4 x 225 g/8 oz sirloin steaks

4 tsp Tabasco sauce

salt and pepper

Chips

450 g/1 lb potatoes, peeled

2 tbsp sunflower oil

1. To make the chips, preheat the oven to 200°C/400°F/Gas Mark 6. Cut the potatoes into thick, even-sized chips. Rinse them under cold running water and then dry well on a clean tea towel. Place in a bowl, add the oil and toss together until coated. Spread the chips on a baking sheet and cook in the preheated oven for 40–45 minutes, turning once, until golden.

2. Place the butter in a small bowl and beat in the chopped watercress with a fork until fully incorporated. Cover with clingfilm and chill in the refrigerator until required.

3. Preheat a griddle pan to high. Sprinkle each steak with 1 teaspoon of the Tabasco sauce, rubbing it in well. Season to taste with salt and pepper.

4. Add the steaks to the preheated pan and cook for 2½ minutes each side for rare, or until cooked to your liking. Transfer to warmed serving plates and serve immediately, topped with the watercress butter and accompanied by the chips.

162 Saltimbocca

Ingredients

4 pork chops, bones and fat removed

4 large, thin slices Parma ham or San Daniele prosciutto

4 large sage leaves

100 g/3½ oz unsalted butter

200 ml/7 fl oz Marsala, Madeira or dry white wine

salt and pepper

sautéed potatoes and a green salad, to serve

1. Lay the pork chops on a board and flatten them with a meat mallet or rolling pin until they are the same size as the ham slices. Lay down a piece of ham, put a piece of pork on top and place a sage leaf at the edge nearest to you. Season with salt and pepper then roll the meat around the sage leaf and secure it with a cocktail stick. The ham should be on the outside. Repeat with all four chops.

2. Place a wide, heavy-based saucepan over a high heat. Add the butter and then the meat rolls and brown them quickly all over. Add the Marsala and reduce the heat to a simmer.

3. Cover and cook for about 10–15 minutes, until the meat is cooked through. The pork should not show any pink traces and the juices should run clear when pierced with a sharp knife.

4. Remove the rolls with a slotted spoon and keep them warm. Increase the heat and reduce the liquid for 2 minutes to thicken. Serve the rolls immediately with sautéed potatoes and a green salad and pour over a little of the sauce.

163 Beef medallions with orange, lime & honey

Ingredients

4 fillet steaks

2 oranges

juice of 1 lime

1 tbsp olive oil

15 g/½ oz butter

1 fresh thyme sprig

2 tbsp clear honey

salt and pepper

1. Place the steaks in a wide, non-metallic dish. Squeeze the juice from 1 orange and pour over the steak with the lime juice. Cover and leave to stand in a cool place for 20 minutes. Drain, reserving the juices. Cut all the peel and white pith from the remaining orange and remove the segments, catching any juice in a bowl.

2. Heat a heavy-based frying pan over a medium–high heat. Brush the steaks with oil and season to taste with salt and pepper. Place in the pan and cook for 2–2½ minutes on each side for medium-rare, or until cooked to your liking. Remove, cover and keep warm.

3. Melt the butter in the pan, then stir in the marinade and reserved citrus juice, thyme and honey. Bring to the boil and stir for 1 minute. Season to taste with salt and pepper and add the orange segments. Arrange the steaks on serving plates, spoon over the juices and the orange segments and serve.

#164 Lamb shanks with roasted onions

Serves 4

Ingredients

4 x 350 g/12 oz lamb shanks, trimmed of any excess fat

6 garlic cloves, quartered lengthways

2 tbsp extra virgin olive oil

1 tbsp fresh rosemary, very finely chopped

4 red onions

350 g/12 oz carrots, cut into thin batons

4 tbsp water

salt and pepper

1. Preheat the oven to 180°C/350°F/Gas Mark 4. Make 6 incisions in each lamb shank and insert 1 garlic slice in each incision. Place the lamb in a single layer in a roasting tin, drizzle with the oil, sprinkle with the rosemary and season with pepper. Roast in the preheated oven for 45 minutes. Wrap each onion in foil. Remove the lamb from the oven and season with salt. Return to the oven and place the onions on the shelf next to it. Roast for a further 1–1¼ hours until the lamb is very tender. Meanwhile, bring a large saucepan of water to the boil. Add the carrot batons and blanch for 1 minute. Drain and refresh in cold water.

2. Remove the lamb from the oven and transfer to a warmed serving dish. Skim off the fat and place the tin over a medium heat. Add the carrots and cook for 2 minutes. Add the water, bring to the boil and simmer, stirring constantly and scraping up the glazed bits from the base of the roasting tin. Transfer the carrots and sauce to the serving dish. Remove the onions from the oven and unwrap. Cut off and discard about 1 cm/½ inch off the tops and add the onions to the dish. Serve immediately.

#165 Winter beef stew with herb dumplings

Serves 4

Ingredients

3 tbsp plain flour

800 g/1 lb 12 oz braising steak, cubed

3 tbsp olive oil

12 shallots, peeled and halved

2 carrots, cut into batons

1 parsnip, sliced

2 bay leaves

1 tbsp chopped fresh rosemary

450 ml/16 fl oz cider

450 ml/16 fl oz beef stock

1 tbsp soy sauce

200 g/7 oz canned chestnuts, drained

115 g/4 oz self-raising flour,

50 g/1¾ oz vegetable suet

2 tbsp chopped fresh thyme

salt and pepper

1. Preheat the oven to 160°C/325°F/Gas Mark 3. Put the plain flour on a plate and season generously with salt and pepper. Toss the beef in the flour until coated.

2. Heat 1 tablespoon of the oil in a large, flameproof casserole over a medium–high heat. Add one third of the beef and cook for 5–6 minutes, turning occasionally, until brown all over. Remove the beef with a slotted spoon. Cook the remaining two batches, adding another tablespoon of oil, if needed. Set aside. Add the remaining oil to the casserole with the shallots, carrots, parsnip and herbs and cook for 3 minutes, stirring occasionally. Pour in the cider and beef stock and bring to the boil. Cook over a high heat until the alcohol has evaporated and the liquid reduced. Add the soy sauce, then cook for a further 3 minutes. Stir in the chestnuts and beef, cover and cook in the preheated oven for 1 hour 35 minutes.

3. Meanwhile, combine the self-raising flour, suet and thyme in a bowl and season to taste with salt and pepper. Mix in enough water to make a soft dough. Divide into walnut-sized pieces and roll each piece into a ball. Add to the casserole, cover and cook for a further 25 minutes, or until the dumplings are cooked, the stock has formed a thick, rich gravy and the meat is tender. Remove the bay leaves, season to taste with salt and pepper and serve.

Serves
4

Pork, tarragon & mushroom pies

Ingredients

2 tbsp sunflower oil

6 shallots, cut into wedges

600 g/1 lb 5 oz diced lean pork

250 g/9 oz chestnut mushrooms, quartered

150 ml/5 fl oz apple juice

2 tbsp chopped tarragon

400 g/14 oz potatoes, cut into even chunks

85 g/3 oz olive spread

125 g/4½ oz rice flour

1 tsp baking powder

beaten egg, to glaze

salt and pepper

1. Preheat the oven to 200°C/400°F/Gas Mark 6. Heat the oil in a large pan and fry the shallots for 2–3 minutes, stirring occasionally.

2. Add the pork and fry for 6–8 minutes, stirring, until brown. Add the mushrooms and cook for 2 minutes to soften. Stir in the apple juice, half the tarragon and season with salt and pepper. Divide the mixture between four 300-ml/10-fl oz ovenproof dishes.

3. Bring a large saucepan of lightly salted water to the boil. Add the potatoes, bring back to the boil and cook for 10 minutes until tender. Drain and leave to cool, uncovered. Mash the potatoes, then stir in the olive spread, the remaining tarragon and salt and pepper to taste. Sift in the flour and baking powder and stir in lightly and evenly to make a soft dough, pressing together with your hands.

4. Divide the dough into four pieces and roll out each piece to cover the pie dishes, pinching the edges to seal. Place the pies on a baking sheet, brush the tops with beaten egg and bake for 35–40 minutes, until golden. Serve hot.

Serves
1

Large Mixed Grill

Ingredients

1 x 225 g/8 oz fillet steak

2 small lamb chops

2 large field mushrooms

1 large beef tomato, cut in half

6 tbsp vegetable oil

2 pork sausages

1 x 225 g/8 oz gammon steak

55 g/2 oz chorizo, sliced

2 eggs

salt and pepper

chips, to serve

1. Season the fillet steak, lamb chops, mushrooms and tomato with salt and pepper to taste. Heat 4 tablespoons of the oil in a large frying pan over a high heat. When the oil starts to smoke, add the lamb chops and sausages to the pan and cook the chops for 2 minutes on each side until seared and brown. Reduce the heat and continue to cook the chops until done to your liking. Remove the chops and keep warm on a large plate.

2. Increase the heat to high and add the gammon steak and fillet steak. Cook the gammon for 3–4 minutes on each side and the fillet steak for 2 minutes on each side, or until cooked to your liking. Turn the sausages every now and then to ensure even cooking. Remove all of the meat from the pan, apart from the sausages, and add to the warmed plate. Add the chorizo, mushrooms and tomato to the pan and cook for 4 minutes on each side, then add to the plate.

3. Heat the remaining oil in a non-stick frying pan over a medium heat and fry the eggs for 2–3 minutes. Add to the plate. Remove the sausages from the pan, slicing one open to ensure that no traces of pink remain. Add to the plate and serve the mixed grill with chips.

#168 Pork medallions in a creamy mustard sauce

Serves 4

Ingredients

500 g/1 lb 2 oz pork fillet
1 tbsp olive oil
15 g/½ oz butter
1 onion, finely chopped
200 ml/7 fl oz dry cider
1 tbsp Dijon mustard
150 ml/5 fl oz crème fraîche
salt and pepper
chopped fresh flat-leaf parsley,
to garnish

1. Trim the pork fillet of any fat, then cut into 2.5-cm/1-inch thick slices. Place between two sheets of clingfilm and beat with a meat mallet until the meat is about half its original thickness. Lightly season on both sides with salt and pepper.

2. Heat the oil and butter in a wide frying pan, add the pork slices and fry over a medium–high heat for 3–4 minutes, turning once, until golden brown. Remove from the pan, set aside and keep warm.

3. Add the onion to the pan and fry gently, stirring, for 3–4 minutes, until soft. Add the cider, stirring with a wooden spoon to scrape up any sediment from the base of the pan, then boil rapidly for about 1 minute until slightly reduced. Stir in the mustard and crème fraîche, and gently simmer, stirring, until the sauce is smooth and slightly thickened.

4. Return the pork medallions to the pan and bring the sauce back to the boil. Season to taste with salt and pepper, sprinkle with chopped parsley and serve immediately.

#169 Herbed leg of lamb with vegetables

Ingredients

1 tbsp sunflower oil

1 onion, thinly sliced

2 leeks, thinly sliced

2 carrots, thinly sliced

2 celery sticks, thinly sliced

1.5-kg/3 lb 5-oz leg of lamb, boned

4 garlic cloves, thinly sliced

2 fresh rosemary sprigs,
plus extra to garnish

150 ml/5 fl oz beef stock

50 ml/2 fl oz rosé wine

2 tbsp mint or redcurrant jelly

salt and pepper

1. Heat the oil in a frying pan. Add the onion, leeks, carrots and celery and cook over a low heat, stirring occasionally, for 5 minutes. Using a slotted spoon, transfer the vegetables to a large sheet of foil. Meanwhile, make small slits all over the lamb with a small sharp knife. Push a slice of garlic and a few rosemary leaves into each slit. Add to the pan, increase the heat to medium and cook, turning occasionally, for about 8 minutes. Put the lamb on top of the vegetables. Fold up the sides of the foil but do not seal the parcel.

2. Pour the stock into the pan and bring to the boil. Add the wine and mint jelly and season with salt and pepper. Spoon over the lamb and seal the edges of the foil. Place in a steamer, cover and steam for 1½ hours. Remove the parcel from the steamer and unwrap. Put the lamb on a plate and leave to rest for 10–15 minutes. Meanwhile, tip the stock and vegetables into a saucepan and bring to the boil, then boil until reduced and thickened. Remove from the heat. Carve the lamb into medium-thick slices and place on a warmed serving dish. Spoon over the vegetables and sauce, garnish with rosemary and serve immediately.

#170 Beef & ale pie

Ingredients

900 g/2 lb stewing steak, trimmed and cut into 2.5-cm/1-inch cubes

4 tbsp plain flour, plus extra for dusting

1 tsp dried thyme

115 g/4 oz butter

2 onions, thinly sliced

2 carrots, thinly sliced

140 g/5 oz mushrooms, thinly sliced

500 ml/18 fl oz beef stock

400 ml/14 fl oz brown ale or stout

400 g/14 oz ready-made puff pastry

beaten egg, for brushing and glazing

salt and pepper

1. Mix the steak, flour, thyme and salt and pepper to taste together. Melt the butter in a large pan, add the meat and cook over a medium heat, stirring frequently, for 10 minutes, until brown. Add the onions, carrots and mushrooms, pour in the stock and ale and bring to the boil. Reduce the heat, cover and simmer, stirring occasionally, for 1½–2 hours, until the meat is tender. Season and transfer the mixture to a large pie dish. Leave to cool.

2. Preheat the oven to 200°C/400°F/Gas Mark 6. Roll out the pastry on a floured surface to 2.5 cm/1 inch larger than the top of the dish. Cut out a 15-mm/⅝-inch strip all the way around. Brush the rim of the dish with water and press the strip onto it. Brush with water and lift the remaining dough o n top. Trim off the excess and crimp the edges to seal. Make a small slit in the centre and brush with beaten egg. Roll out the trimmings and use to decorate the pie, then brush with beaten egg. Bake in the preheated oven for 35–40 minutes, until golden brown. Serve immediately.

171 Drunk chuck steak in a red wine marinade

Serves 4

Ingredients

4 chuck steaks, 350 g/12 oz each

Marinade

4 tbsp olive oil

100 ml/3½ fl oz red wine

1 small bunch thyme, leaves picked

1 small bunch rosemary, leaves picked

2 garlic cloves, crushed

1 tbsp Dijon mustard

1 tsp salt

1 tsp pepper

1. Place all of the marinade ingredients in a shallow non-metallic dish, large enough to hold all of the steaks in a single layer. Mix well to combine.

2. Add the steaks to the marinade, turning a few times to coat. Cover and chill in the refrigerator for at least 4 hours. Turn once, half-way through marinating.

3. Remove from the refrigerator 1 hour before cooking, to allow the meat to return to room temperature. Discard the marinade.

4. Preheat a griddle pan over a high heat, add the steaks and cook for 5 minutes on each side for medium rare, or until cooked to your liking. Cook the steaks in batches if necessary. Set aside to rest for 5 minutes before serving.

172 Pork hocks with sauerkraut

Serves 6

Ingredients

6 pork hocks, cleaned, split and rinsed under cold running water

1 onion, peeled and left whole

2 bay leaves

1 tbsp pickling spice

8 black peppercorns, lightly crushed

salt

sauerkraut, to serve

fresh parsley, finely chopped, to garnish

1. Place the pork hocks in a large, heavy-based saucepan and pour over water to cover.

2. Add the onion, bay leaves, pickling spice and peppercorns and season to taste with salt. Cover the pan, bring to the boil, reduce the heat and simmer over a medium–low heat for about 3 hours, or until the meat is tender but still clinging to the bone. Remove the hocks from the pan and drain well.

3. Divide the pork hocks between individual plates and serve with sauerkraut, garnished with fresh parsley.

#173 Lamb Stew

Ingredients

1 tbsp sunflower oil
4 lamb chump chops
1 garlic clove, crushed
2 small onions, quartered
300 g/10½ oz small whole carrots
2 small turnips, quartered
1 tbsp plain flour
300 ml/10 fl oz lamb stock
1 tbsp wholegrain mustard
salt and pepper
chopped fresh flat-leaf parsley,
to garnish

1. Heat the oil in a flameproof casserole, add the lamb chops and fry until golden brown, turning once. Remove from the pan and keep warm.

2. Add the garlic and onions to the pan and fry, stirring, for 2–3 minutes. Stir in the carrots and turnips.

3. Stir the flour into the vegetables and add the stock. Cook, stirring, until boiling, then add the chops. Season to taste with salt and pepper, then cover and simmer gently for 35 minutes, stirring occasionally.

4. Stir in the mustard and adjust the seasoning to taste. Sprinkle with the parsley and serve.

#174 Beef Bourguignon

Serves 2–4

Ingredients

1.3 kg/3 lb stewing beef
2 tbsp olive oil
175 g/6 oz bacon, sliced into thin strips
2 carrots, sliced
2 onions, chopped
2 garlic cloves, very finely chopped
3 tbsp plain flour
700 ml/1¼ pints red wine
350–450 ml/12–16 fl oz beef stock
bouquet garni sachet
3 tbsp butter
350 g/12 oz pickling onions
350 g/12 oz button mushrooms
chopped fresh parsley, to garnish
mashed potatoes, to serve
salt and pepper

1. Cut the beef into 5-cm/2-inch pieces. Heat the oil in a large casserole over a medium heat. Add the bacon and brown for 2–3 minutes. Remove with a slotted spoon. Add the beef in batches and cook until brown. Drain and set aside with the bacon. Add the carrots and onions to the casserole and cook for 5 minutes. Add the garlic and fry until just coloured. Return the beef and bacon to the casserole. Sprinkle in the flour and cook for 1 minute, stirring. Add the wine, enough stock to cover, the bouquet garni, and salt and pepper to taste. Bring to the boil, cover and simmer gently for 3 hours.

2. Heat half the butter in a frying pan. Add the pickling onions, cover and cook until soft. Remove with a slotted spoon and keep warm. Heat the remaining butter in the pan. Add the mushrooms and fry briefly. Set aside and keep warm. Remove the casserole from the heat and strain the liquid into a clean saucepan. Wipe out the casserole and tip in the meat mixture, mushrooms and onions. Discard the bouquet garni. Remove the surface fat from the casserole liquid, simmer for 1–2 minutes to reduce, then pour over the meat and vegetables. Serve immediately, garnished with parsley and with mashed potatoes on the side.

#175 Pork with mango, basil & green peppercorns

Serves 6

Ingredients

60 g/2¼ oz butter

1 white onion, finely chopped

1 ripe mango, peeled and chopped into 5-mm/¼-inch cubes

zest of 1 orange

1 tbsp honey

6 green peppercorn clusters

juice of 2 oranges

600 g/1 lb 5 oz pork fillet

2 tbsp vegetable oil

salt and pepper

fresh Thai basil leaves, to garnish

1. Melt 40 g/1½ oz of the butter in a saucepan. Add the onion and gently sauté until translucent, then add the mango. Add the orange zest and honey and gently sauté for a further 5 minutes.

2. Strip the green peppercorns from 2 of the clusters, reserving the remaining clusters to garnish. Add the peppercorns and the orange juice to the sauce, season with salt and simmer for about 10 minutes. Meanwhile, cut the pork fillet into 8 medallions.

3. Add the oil and the remaining butter to a non-stick frying pan and heat until foaming. Season the pork medallions on both sides with salt and pepper and add them to the pan. Fry on each side for about 5 minutes, basting with the pan juices from time to time.

4. Put portions of mango sauce on four serving plates and lay 2 medallions on top of each portion. Garnish each serving with a green pepper cluster and some Thai basil leaves.

#176 Pork braised with celeriac & orange

Serves 4

Ingredients

500 g/1 lb 2 oz celeriac

2 small leeks

3 carrots

900 g/2 lb pork shoulder, cubed

3 tbsp olive oil

200 ml/7 fl oz chicken stock

cooked rice, to serve

Marinade

pared rind and juice of 1 orange

1–2 whole star anise

2 tbsp dark soy sauce

1 tbsp honey

2.5 cm/1-inch piece fresh ginger, grated

3 garlic cloves, finely chopped

2 tsp Chinese chilli bean sauce

1. Cut the celeriac, leeks and carrots into 5-cm/2-inch strips. Place the pork in a large bowl. Add all the marinade ingredients, stir well, cover and chill in the refrigerator for 3 hours or overnight.

2. Preheat the oven to 120°C/250°F/Gas Mark ½. Transfer the pork to a plate using a slotted spoon, discarding the orange peel and star anise. Reserve the marinade.

3. Heat 1 tablespoon of the oil in a large frying pan and add half the pork pieces. Cook for 2 minutes, then turn the pieces over and cook for a further 2 minutes. Transfer the pork and the cooking juices to a casserole dish. Repeat with 1 tablespoon of the oil and the remaining pork and transfer to the casserole dish. Add the remaining oil to the pan, then add the celeriac, leeks and carrots and cook, stirring occasionally, until the leeks are soft.

4. Transfer the vegetables to the casserole dish, strain the marinade over the vegetables and add the stock. Cover and cook in the preheated oven for 1 hour. Stir, cover and return to the oven for a further 1 hour. Serve immediately with cooked rice.

Daube of beef

Serves
6

Ingredients

750 g/1 lb 10 oz beef topside

350 ml/12 fl oz dry white wine

2 tbsp brandy

1 tbsp white wine vinegar

4 shallots, sliced

4 carrots, sliced

1 garlic clove, finely chopped

6 black peppercorns

1 bouquet garni

2 tbsp olive oil

800 g/1 lb 12 oz canned chopped tomatoes

225 g/8 oz mushrooms, sliced

strip of finely pared orange rind

55 g/2 oz Bayonne ham, cut into strips

12 black olives

salt

1. Cut the beef into 2.5-cm/1-inch cubes. Combine the wine, brandy, vinegar, shallots, carrots, garlic, peppercorns and bouquet garni and season to taste with salt. Add the beef, stirring to coat, then cover with clingfilm and chill in the refrigerator for 8 hours, or overnight.

2. Preheat the oven to 150°C/300°F/Gas Mark 2. Drain the beef, reserving the marinade, and pat dry on kitchen paper. Heat half the oil in a large, flameproof casserole. Add the beef in batches and cook over a medium heat, stirring, for 3–4 minutes, or until browned. Transfer the beef to a plate with a slotted spoon. Brown the remaining beef, adding more oil, if necessary. Return all of the beef to the casserole and add the tomatoes and their juices, mushrooms and orange rind. Strain the reserved marinade into the casserole. Bring to the boil, cover and cook in the oven for 2½ hours.

3. Remove the casserole from the oven, add the ham and olives and return it to the oven to cook for a further 30 minutes, or until the beef is very tender. Discard the orange rind and serve straight from the casserole, garnished with parsley.

178 Caribbean beef stew

Serves
6

Ingredients

450 g/1 lb braising steak

450 g/1 lb diced pumpkin

1 onion, chopped

1 red pepper, deseeded and chopped

2 garlic cloves, finely chopped

2.5-cm/1-inch piece fresh ginger, finely chopped

1 tbsp sweet or hot paprika

225 ml/8 fl oz beef stock

400 g/14 oz canned chopped tomatoes

400 g/14 oz canned pigeon peas or chickpeas, drained and rinsed

400 g/14 oz canned black-eyed beans, drained and rinsed

salt and pepper

1. Trim off any visible fat from the steak, then dice the meat. Heat a large heavy-based saucepan without adding any extra fat. Add the meat and cook, stirring constantly, for a few minutes, until evenly browned.

2. Stir in the pumpkin, onion and red pepper and cook for 1 minute, then add the garlic, ginger and paprika. Pour in the stock and tomatoes and bring to the boil.

3. Transfer the mixture to a slow cooker, cover and cook on low for 7 hours. Add the pigeon peas and black-eyed beans to the stew and season to taste with salt and pepper. Re-cover and cook on high for 30 minutes. Serve immediately.

Serves
4

Roasted rack of lamb with whisky sauce

Ingredients

2 x 6-8-rib racks of lamb, trimmed
2 tbsp vegetable oil
salt and pepper

Sauce

1 shallot, finely diced
1 tsp finely chopped garlic
1 fresh rosemary sprig
1 tsp plain flour
4 tbsp whisky
225 ml/8 fl oz chicken stock
¼ tsp salt
¼ tsp pepper
1 tbsp unsalted butter
1 tbsp chopped fresh parsley
juice of ½ lemon

1. Preheat the oven to 220°C/425°F/Gas Mark 7.

2. Pat the lamb dry with kitchen paper and generously season all over with salt and pepper.

3. Heat the oil in a large frying pan over a medium–high heat. When the oil is very hot, add the lamb, meat side down, and cook for about 5 minutes until well browned. Stand the racks in the pan and cook for a further 2–3 minutes. Transfer to a large roasting tin and roast in the preheated oven for about 15 minutes, until a meat thermometer reads 51°C/125°F for medium-rare. Remove from the oven, tent with foil and leave to rest for at least 10 minutes.

4. While the meat is resting, make the sauce. Pour all but about 1 tablespoon of the fat from the pan and heat over a medium–high heat. Add the shallot and cook, stirring frequently, for about 5 minutes, until soft. Stir in the garlic and rosemary and cook for a further minute. Stir in the flour, add the whisky and reduce the heat to low. Cook, stirring, for about 3 minutes, until most of the liquid has evaporated, then add the stock, salt and pepper. Increase the heat to medium–high and bring to the boil. Cook for about 5 minutes, until the sauce has thickened. Remove from the heat and immediately stir in the butter, parsley, and lemon juice.

5. Cut the rack into individual chops and serve immediately, topped with the whisky sauce. Hand any extra sauce at the table, if desired.

#180 Steak medallions with beef & beer sauce

Serves 4–6

Ingredients

4 tbsp olive oil

2 tbsp butter

2 shallots, finely chopped

2 garlic cloves, crushed

2 tbsp flour

300 ml/10 fl oz beer

300 ml/10 fl oz hot beef stock

2 tbsp Worcestershire sauce

1 tbsp chopped thyme

1 tbsp chopped parsley

1.5 kg/3 lb 5 oz beef fillet

salt and pepper

1. Place a saucepan over a medium heat, add half the oil and the butter and cook the shallots and garlic for 5–10 minutes, or until translucent. Add the flour and cook for a few minutes, until the flour is beginning to brown. Gradually whisk in the beer, then add the stock and Worcestershire sauce. Reduce the sauce until it is the consistency of double cream, then add the thyme, parsley, and salt and pepper to taste. Set aside and keep warm.

2. Brush the meat with the remaining olive oil and season with salt and pepper.

3. Preheat a griddle pan over a medium-high heat, add the beef and cook for 15–20 minutes, ensuring that it is sealed all over. Set aside to rest for 10 minutes before serving, then slice and serve with the beer sauce.

#181 Peppered lamb fillet

Serves 4

Ingredients

900 g/2 lb lamb fillet

3 tbsp olive oil

2–3 tbsp black peppercorns, coarsely ground

salt and pepper

cooked broccoli, to serve

Onion gratin

butter, for greasing

6 onions, sliced

3–4 tbsp dry sherry or white wine

1 tbsp fresh thyme leaves

3–4 tbsp mascarpone cheese

150 g/5½ oz Gorgonzola cheese, crumbled

salt and pepper

1. To make the onion gratin, preheat the oven to 180°C/350°F/Gas Mark 4. Lightly grease a gratin dish.

2. Lay the onions in an even layer in the prepared dish. Pour over the sherry, scatter with thyme leaves and season to taste with salt and pepper. Dot the mascarpone cheese evenly over the onions, then scatter over the Gorgonzola cheese. Bake in the preheated oven for 30–40 minutes until the onions are soft and the gratin is golden and bubbling.

3. Meanwhile, brush the lamb with 1 tablespoon of the oil and season to taste with a little salt. Roll in the ground peppercorns. Heat the remaining oil in a frying pan over a high heat, add the lamb fillet and cook for 3–4 minutes on each side. Leave to rest for 5 minutes, then slice and serve immediately with the onion gratin and broccoli.

#182 Cassoulet of pork & lamb

Serves
6

Ingredients

500 g/1 lb 2 oz dried haricot beans, soaked overnight, drained and rinsed

1 bouquet garni

1 celery stick, roughly chopped

3 onions, 1 quartered, 2 thinly sliced

4 garlic cloves, 2 whole, 2 chopped

2 litres/3½ pints water

500 g/1 lb 2 oz pork belly, skin removed

400 g/14 oz lamb shoulder, boned

200 g/7 oz thick-cut bacon

2 tbsp duck fat or vegetable oil

400 g/14 oz Toulouse sausage, sliced

2 tbsp tomato purée

150 g/5½ oz fresh breadcrumbs

salt and pepper

1. Put the beans into a large saucepan with the bouquet garni, celery, onion quarters and whole garlic and season to taste with salt and pepper. Add the water and bring to the boil. Skim off any foam, then reduce the heat to low. Gently simmer for 1 hour, uncovered.

2. Meanwhile, cut the pork and lamb into pieces 4 cm/1½ inches square and cut the bacon into chunks, then add the duck fat to a large heavy-based saucepan over a high heat. Add the pork belly and bacon and brown all over. Remove and set aside, then repeat with the sausage, then the lamb and set aside. Add the sliced onions, chopped garlic and tomato purée and cook in the remaining fat for 2 minutes. Remove from the heat and leave to cool.

3. Preheat the oven to 180°C/350°F/Gas Mark 4. Drain the beans, reserving the liquid but discarding the vegetables. Layer the beans and meat alternately in a large casserole,. Add the fried garlic, onion and tomato purée mixture and enough of the bean liquid to almost cover the beans. Sprinkle over the breadcrumbs, cover and cook in the preheated oven, for 1 hour. Reduce the oven temperature to 140°C/275°F/Gas Mark 1, uncover and cook for a further hour. Serve immediately.

#183 Pork & potatoes in red wine

Serves
4

Ingredients

4 pork chops

700 g/1 lb 9 oz waxy potatoes, cut into large pieces

1 tsp coriander seeds, crushed

400 ml/14 fl oz red wine

salt and pepper

1. Trim the fat from the chops and melt it in a non-stick frying pan. Add the potatoes and cook over a medium–low heat, stirring and turning occasionally, for 20 minutes until golden brown. Remove from the pan with a slotted spoon and place in a flameproof casserole.

2. Add the chops to the pan and cook over a medium heat, turning occasionally, for 8–10 minutes until brown all over. Transfer to the casserole.

3. Gently stir the coriander seeds into the casserole, season to taste with salt and pepper and pour in the red wine. Bring to the boil, then reduce the heat, cover and simmer for 40 minutes, or until the meat is tender. Serve immediately,

184 Roast gammon

Serves 6

Ingredients

1.3 kg/3 lb boneless gammon, pre-soaked if necessary

2 tbsp Dijon mustard

85 g/3 oz demerara sugar

½ tsp ground cinnamon

½ tsp ground ginger

18 whole cloves

ready-made Cumberland sauce, to serve

1. Place the gammon in a large saucepan, cover with cold water and slowly bring to the boil over a gentle heat. Cover the pan and simmer very gently for 1 hour. Preheat the oven to 200°C/400°F/Gas Mark 6.

2. Remove the gammon from the pan and drain. Remove the rind from the gammon and discard. Score the fat into a diamond-shaped pattern with a sharp knife. Spread the mustard over the fat. Mix the sugar and the ground spices together on a plate and roll the gammon in the mixture, pressing down well to coat evenly. Stud the diamond shapes with cloves and place the joint in a roasting tin. Roast in the preheated oven for 20 minutes, until the glaze is a rich golden colour.

3. To serve hot, leave to stand for 20 minutes before carving. If the gammon is to be served cold, it can be cooked a day ahead. Serve with Cumberland sauce.

185 Lamb & turnip stew

Serves 4–6

Ingredients

40 g/1½ oz butter

2 tbsp sunflower oil

900 g/2 lb boned shoulder of lamb, trimmed and cut into large chunks, any bones reserved

2 shallots, finely chopped

1 tbsp sugar

1 litre/1¾ pints lamb stock

2 tbsp tomato purée

1 bouquet garni

8 new potatoes, halved, if large

4 young turnips, quartered

12 baby carrots, scrubbed

140 g/5 oz frozen peas

salt and pepper

chopped fresh parsley, to garnish

1. Melt 30 g/1 oz of the butter with the oil in a large frying pan over a medium heat. Add the lamb, in batches, and fry, stirring, until coloured on all sides, adding extra oil, if necessary. Transfer the meat to a large casserole.

2. Melt the remaining butter with the fat left in the pan. Add the shallots and stir for 3 minutes, or until beginning to soften. Sprinkle with the sugar, increase the heat and continue stirring until the shallots caramelize, taking care that they do not burn. Transfer to the casserole and remove any charred bits from the base of the pan. Add half the stock to the pan and bring to the boil, then tip this mixture into the casserole. Add the remaining stock, tomato purée, bouquet garni and bones, if any, to the casserole. Season to taste with salt and pepper. Cover and bring to the boil. Reduce the heat and simmer for 45 minutes.

3. Add the potatoes, turnips and carrots and continue simmering for 15 minutes. Add the peas, then uncover and simmer for a further 5–10 minutes, or until the meat and all the vegetables are tender. Remove and discard the bones, if used, and the bouquet garni. Taste and adjust the seasoning, if necessary. Garnish with parsley and serve immediately.

#186 Pork steaks baked with pears & Gorgonzola

Serves 4

Ingredients

2 ripe pears

1 tbsp butter

1 tbsp sugar

2 fresh thyme sprigs, plus extra to garnish

4 pork neck steaks, about 125 g/4½ oz each

1 tbsp vegetable oil

125 g/4½ oz Gorgonzola cheese

salt and pepper

1. Peel, halve and core the pears. Cut lengthways into segments. Melt the butter with the sugar in a frying pan. Add the pear segments, season to taste with pepper and add the thyme, then toss until the mixture is slightly caramelized.

2. Season the pork with salt and pepper. Heat the oil in a non-stick frying pan, then add the steaks and sear on both sides. Transfer them to a baking dish.

3. Preheat the grill to high. Lay the pear segments on top of the steaks. Put the cheese on top of the pear segments, place under the preheated grill and cook for 2–3 minutes.

4. Arrange the steaks on plates and pour over the pan scrapings. Garnish with thyme sprigs and serve immediately.

#187 Braised beef with red wine & cranberries

Serves 4

Ingredients

2 tbsp olive oil

6 shallots, quartered

600 g/1 lb 5 oz braising beef, cubed

1 tbsp plain flour

300 ml/10 fl oz red wine

2 tbsp tomato purée

1 tbsp Worcestershire sauce

2 bay leaves

100 g/3½ oz fresh or frozen cranberries

salt and pepper

mashed potatoes and seasonal vegetables, to serve

1. Heat the oil in a large casserole, add the shallots and fry, stirring, for 2–3 minutes until beginning to brown. Remove from the pan and keep warm.

2. Add the beef and cook, stirring, for 3–4 minutes, or until evenly coloured. Stir in the flour and cook for 1 minute.

3. Add the wine and bring to the boil, then boil for 1 minute. Return the shallots to the pan with the tomato purée, Worcestershire sauce, bay leaves, and salt and pepper to taste. Stir in the cranberries.

4. Reduce the heat to low, cover tightly and leave to simmer very gently for 1–1½ hours until the beef is tender. Remove the bay leaves, adjust the seasoning to taste and serve with mashed potatoes and vegetables.

Serves
6

Roast pork loin with salted fennel crackling

Ingredients

1 x 7-rib loin of pork

2 tbsp fennel seeds

2 tbsp coriander seeds

2 small dried chillies, crushed

3 star anise pods

1 tsp ground cinnamon

2 tsp coarse sea salt

2 tbsp olive oil

100 ml/3½ fl oz water

pepper

Crisp cabbage salad

1 hard white cabbage, tough outer leaves removed, quartered

2 green chillies, deseeded and finely chopped

juice and zest of 1 lemon

3 tbsp olive oil

1 tbsp sesame oil

1 tbsp light soy sauce

4 spring onions, finely sliced

bunch of fresh coriander, chopped

1. Preheat the oven to 220°C/425°F/Gas Mark 7. Using a very sharp knife, make a gap between the meat and the ribs. Score the skin of the pork through the fat and almost to the meat, at intervals of 1 cm/½ inch. Grind the fennel seeds, coriander seeds, dried chillies and star anise pods until medium fine. Mix with the cinnamon, salt and pepper to taste, then rub into the scores in the skin and the gaps between the meat and the bone. Rub in a little oil. Use string to fasten the meat to the bone in three or four places. Place on a rack in a roasting tin and cook in the preheated oven for 50–60 minutes, basting regularly with the pan juices. Remove from the oven and leave to rest on the rack.

2. To make the cabbage salad, finely shred the cabbage and place in a bowl. Mix the chillies with the lemon juice and zest, olive oil, sesame oil and soy sauce.

3. When ready to serve, remove the pork from the rack. Pour off any liquid fat. Add the water to the tin and place over a medium heat. Stir to make gravy, scraping up the sediment from the base of the tin. Carve the meat into thick slices along the scores. Add the gravy to the chilli dressing. Taste and adjust the seasoning – it will be sweet, salty, hot and sour. Mix the shredded cabbage with the spring onions and the coriander, and dress the salad with the warm dressing and gravy mixture. Serve with the pork.

Chilli Lamb Cutlets

Ingredients

60 g/2¼ oz fresh parsley leaves

2 garlic cloves

juice of 1 lemon

1–2 red chillies or green chillies

1 tbsp sweet paprika

4 tbsp olive oil

4 x 5-cm/2-inch thick
lamb cutlets

salt and pepper

pittas, to serve

Salad

1 cucumber

1 tbsp fresh parsley leaves

225 g/8 oz cherry tomatoes

juice of 1 lemon

1. Put the parsley, garlic, lemon juice, chillies, paprika and 1 teaspoon of salt into a food processor and process until smooth. Add the oil and process to combine. Season the lamb with salt and pepper, then coat them on both sides with some of the sauce. Reserve the remaining sauce.

2. To make the salad, dice the cucumber, finely chop the parsley and halve the tomatoes, then put them all into a medium-sized bowl. Toss with the lemon juice and set aside until ready to serve.

3. Heat a ridged griddle pan over a medium–high heat. Add the chops and cook for about 6 minutes on each side for medium-rare, or a bit longer for medium. Remove from the heat and leave to rest for a few minutes before serving. Meanwhile, warm the bread under the grill. Serve the chops with the bread, salad and reserved sauce.

Lamb roasted with lemon & thyme

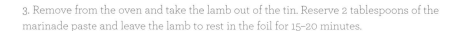

Ingredients

1 leg of lamb, 2.5–3 kg/
5 lb 8 oz -6 lb 8 oz

250 ml/9 fl oz chicken stock

250 ml/9 fl oz red wine

1 tbsp redcurrant jelly

seasonal vegetables and mint sauce,
to serve

Marinade

1 garlic bulb, cloves separated
but unpeeled

5 lemons or blood oranges

1 tbsp fresh rosemary leaves, chopped

1 tbsp fresh thyme leaves

2 tbsp salt

1. Pat the lamb dry with kitchen paper. Put the marinade ingredients in a food processor and blend to a paste.

2. Place the lamb in a roasting tin and cover with the paste so that it is completely encased. Loosely cover with foil and set aside in a cool place for 1 hour or in the refrigerator overnight. Remove from the refrigerator 30 minutes before cooking. Preheat the oven to 200°C/400°F/ Gas Mark 6. Cook the foil-covered lamb in the preheated oven for 1¾ hours.

3. Remove from the oven and take the lamb out of the tin. Reserve 2 tablespoons of the marinade paste and leave the lamb to rest in the foil for 15–20 minutes.

4. Meanwhile, place the roasting tin over a medium–high heat, add the marinade paste, stock, wine and jelly and simmer until reduced by about half. Carve the lamb, discarding most of the paste, and serve with the gravy, vegetables and mint sauce.

#191 Stuffed beef fillet

Serves 4

Ingredients

1 beef fillet, about 600 g/1 lb 5 oz

5 tbsp finely chopped sun-dried tomatoes in oil

bunch of fresh mixed herbs, finely chopped

1 tbsp sunflower oil

1. Preheat the oven to 160°C/325°F/Gas Mark 3. Using a knife with a strong, thin blade, pierce the centre of the beef from one side. Twist the knife in circles until you have drilled a tunnel about 1 cm/½ inch wide all the way through.

2. Mix the sun-dried tomatoes and herbs together in a bowl. Spoon the mixture into the tunnel, pushing it in with your fingers or the handle of a wooden spoon.

3. Heat the oil in a flameproof casserole, add the beef and cook over a high heat, turning frequently, for 5–8 minutes, or until brown all over. Transfer the casserole to the oven and roast, basting occasionally, for 20–25 minutes for rare beef, 30–35 minutes for medium rare and 45–55 minutes for well done.

4. Remove the beef from the oven, leave to cool completely, then slice and serve.

#192 Soy & ginger pork fillets

Serves 4

Ingredients

2 tsp sunflower oil

500 g/1 lb 2 oz lean pork fillet

4 shallots, thinly sliced

2 tsp soy sauce

1 garlic clove, crushed

1 tbsp honey

2.5-cm/1-inch piece fresh ginger, grated

150 ml/5 fl oz chicken stock

250 g/9 oz closed-cup mushrooms, sliced

250 g/9 oz pak choi, quartered

salt and pepper

1. Place a wide, heavy-based frying pan over a high heat. Brush the oil over the surface of the pork. Place the pork in the hot pan and fry, turning occasionally, for about 10 minutes, or until golden brown all over. Add the shallots to the pan and fry for 1 minute, stirring constantly.

2. Mix the soy sauce, garlic, honey and ginger together in a small bowl. Spread the soy mixture evenly over the pork in the pan. Pour the stock into the pan and bring to the boil. Reduce the heat to low and simmer gently for about 20 minutes, turning the pork occasionally in the juices. Remove the pork from the pan with a slotted spoon and leave to rest on a warmed dish. Check that the pork is cooked through, with no traces of pink, and that the juices run clear when you cut into the meat.

3. Add the mushrooms and pak choi to the pan, increase the heat and bring to the boil. Reduce the heat and simmer for 4–5 minutes, or until tender. Season to taste with salt and pepper. Slice the pork diagonally, returning the juices to the pan.

4. Serve the sliced pork on top of the vegetables, with the juices spooned over.

#193 Lamb shanks with gremolata

Serves 4

Ingredients

4 lamb shanks, trimmed

2 tbsp olive oil

6 garlic cloves, halved

1 dried chilli, crushed

3 sprigs rosemary

6 ripe plum tomatoes

2 large onions, finely chopped

4 strips orange zest

2 bay leaves

1 tsp brown sugar

100 ml/3½ fl oz red wine

500 ml/18 fl oz water

100 g/3½ oz blanched skinned almonds

zest of 2 lemons

small bunch of flat-leaf parsley

salt and pepper

1. Preheat the oven to 180°C/350°F/Gas Mark 4. Season the lamb with salt and pepper. Heat a little oil in a flameproof casserole. Add the meat and brown all over, then remove from the heat. Chop 4 garlic cloves, the chilli and rosemary. Cut the tomatoes in half and, with the skin side in your hand, grate the flesh on a cheese grater to form a rough tomato pulp.

2. Remove the meat from the casserole and return the casserole to the heat with a little oil. Add the garlic, chilli and rosemary mixture and fry for 2 minutes until fragrant and aromatic. Add the onions and cook for about 5 minutes, until soft. Season to taste with salt and pepper. Return the meat to the casserole with the orange zest, bay leaves, sugar, tomato pulp, wine and water. Cover and bring to a simmer on the hob, then transfer to the preheated oven and cook for a further 2½ hours, basting regularly.

3. Meanwhile, roast the almonds in the oven until golden brown. Finely chop the remaining garlic. Add the almonds and the lemon zest. When ready to serve, chop the parsley, add to the gremolata and scatter the gremolata over the cooked lamb and the rest of the plate.

#194 Pot-roast pork

Serves 4

Ingredients

1 tbsp sunflower oil

55 g/2 oz butter

1 kg/2 lb 4 oz boned and rolled pork loin joint

4 shallots, chopped

6 juniper berries

2 fresh thyme sprigs, plus extra to garnish

150 ml/5 fl oz dry cider

150 ml/5 fl oz chicken stock or water

8 celery sticks, chopped

2 tbsp plain flour

150 ml/5 fl oz double cream

salt and pepper

freshly cooked peas, to serve

1. Heat the oil with half the butter in a heavy-based saucepan or flameproof casserole. Add the pork and cook over a medium heat, turning frequently, for 5–10 minutes, or until brown. Transfer to a plate. Add the shallots to the pan and cook, stirring frequently, for 5 minutes, or until soft. Add the juniper berries and thyme sprigs and return the pork to the pan, with any juices that have collected on the plate. Pour in the cider and stock, season to taste with salt and pepper, then cover and simmer for 30 minutes. Turn the pork over and add the celery. Re-cover the pan and cook for a further 40 minutes.

2. Meanwhile, make a beurre manié by mashing the remaining butter with the flour in a small bowl. Transfer the pork to a platter with a slotted spoon and keep warm. Remove and discard the juniper berries and thyme. Whisk the beurre manié, a little at a time, into the simmering cooking liquid. Cook, stirring constantly, for 2 minutes, then stir in the cream and bring to the boil. Slice the pork and spoon a little of the sauce over it. Garnish with thyme sprigs and serve immediately with freshly cooked peas and the remaining sauce.

#195 Crown of roast lamb

Serves 6

Ingredients

1.6 kg/3 lb 8 oz crown of lamb

2 tbsp olive oil

salt and pepper

100 g/3½ oz long-grain rice

2 tbsp vegetable oil

1 onion, finely chopped

2 celery sticks, finely chopped

2 garlic cloves, crushed

25 g/1 oz shelled pistachios

zest of 1 lemon, juice of ½ lemon

2 tbsp finely chopped mint

2 tbsp finely chopped parsley

100 g/3½ oz raisins

1. Place the lamb in a deep roasting tin, brush the outside with the oil and season with salt and pepper. Preheat the oven to 180°C/350°F/Gas Mark 4.

2. Cook the rice until tender but still firm to the bite. Drain and cool. Heat the oil in a frying pan, add the onion and celery and sauté for 4–5 minutes. Add the garlic and cook for a further 1 minute until soft. Stir into the rice, pistachio nuts, lemon zest and juice, herbs and raisins.

3. Fill the centre of the lamb with the stuffing, cover the ends of the bones with foil, then cover the whole joint with foil. Roast in the preheated oven for 25 minutes per 450 g/1 lb plus 25 minutes for medium, 30 minutes per 450 g/1 lb plus 30 minutes for well done, removing the foil for the last 10–15 minutes. At the end of the cooking time, remove from the oven, lift out of the tin, re-cover completely with foil and leave to rest for 20 minutes. Serve with the stuffing.

#196 Pork with roasted rhubarb

Serves 4

Ingredients

800 g/1 lb 12 oz boned loin of pork

olive oil, for brushing

1 tsp sea salt flakes

½ tsp pepper

10 small rosemary sprigs

125 ml/4 fl oz chicken stock

3½ pink rhubarb stalks, trimmed and diagonally sliced into 4-cm/1½-inch lengths

1 tbsp clear honey

1. Preheat the oven to 190°C/375°F/Gas Mark 5. Use the tip of a sharp knife to score the pork fat at 1-cm/½-inch intervals. Tie into a neat roll with kitchen string.

2. Place the meat in a small roasting tin. Rub with oil, salt and pepper, rubbing in well. Insert the rosemary sprigs into the slits in the fat. Roast in the preheated oven for 40 minutes.

3. Pour in the stock. Arrange the rhubarb around the meat and drizzle with the honey. Roast for a further 10–15 minutes, until the rhubarb is tender and starting to colour at the edges.

4. Transfer the pork and rhubarb to a warmed serving platter, reserving the pan juices. Make a tent over the meat with foil, and leave to rest for 10 minutes in a warm place.

5. Place the roasting tin over a medium–high heat. Bubble rapidly to reduce the pan juices, for 3–4 minutes, until slightly thickened. Season to taste, strain into a sauce boat and serve with the meat.

197 Roast pork with gingered apples

Serves 4

Ingredients

2 garlic cloves, crushed

4 tbsp red wine

3 tbsp soft brown sugar

1 tbsp tamari

1 tsp sesame oil

½ tsp ground cinnamon

¼ tsp ground cloves

1 star anise pod, broken into pieces

½ tsp pepper

350 g/12 oz pork fillet

4 Bramley apples, roughly chopped

1 tbsp rice vinegar

4 tbsp apple juice

1 tbsp fresh ginger, finely chopped

French beans, to serve

1. In a large bowl combine the garlic, wine, 2 tablespoons of the brown sugar, the tamari, oil, cinnamon, cloves, star anise and pepper. Add the pork and toss to coat. Cover and chill in the refrigerator overnight.

2. Preheat the oven to 190°C/375°F/Gas Mark 5. Heat a non-stick frying pan over a high heat. Remove the pork from the marinade and sear in the hot pan. Cook for about 8 minutes or until brown all over. Transfer to an ovenproof dish and drizzle with half the marinade. Roast in the preheated oven for 15 minutes. Turn the meat, drizzle the remaining marinade and roast for 30 minutes, or until cooked through.

3. Put the apples, vinegar, apple juice, ginger and the remaining sugar into a saucepan and cook over a medium-high heat until the liquid begins to boil. Reduce the heat to medium-low and simmer, stirring occasionally, for about 20 minutes or until the apples are soft.

4. Remove the pork from the oven and leave to rest for 5 minutes. Slice the meat and serve with the apples and French beans.

198 Roast venison with brandy sauce

Serves 4

Ingredients

6 tbsp vegetable oil

1.7 kg/3 lb 12 oz saddle of fresh venison, trimmed

salt and pepper

fresh thyme sprigs, to garnish

roast potatoes, to serve

Sauce

1 tbsp plain flour

4 tbsp vegetable stock

175 ml/6 fl oz brandy

100 ml/3½ fl oz double cream

1. Preheat the oven to 180°C/350°F/Gas Mark 4.

2. Heat half the oil in a frying pan over a high heat. Season the venison with salt and pepper, add to the pan and cook until lightly browned all over. Pour the remaining oil into a roasting tin. Add the venison, cover with foil and roast in the preheated oven, basting occasionally, for 1½ hours, or until cooked through. Remove from the oven and transfer to a warmed serving platter. Cover with foil and set aside.

3. To make the sauce, stir the flour into the roasting tin and cook over a medium heat for 1 minute. Pour in the stock and heat, scraping the sediment from the base of the tin Gradually stir in the brandy and bring to the boil, then reduce the heat and simmer, stirring, for 10–15 minutes until the sauce has thickened. Remove from the heat and stir in the cream.

4. Garnish the venison with thyme and serve with the brandy sauce and roast potatoes.

#199 Beef Wellington

Serves 4–6

Ingredients

2 tbsp olive oil

1.5 kg/3 lb 5 oz beef fillet, trimmed

55 g/2 oz butter

150 g/5½ oz mushrooms, chopped

2 garlic cloves, crushed

150 g/5½ oz smooth liver pâté

1 tbsp finely chopped fresh parsley

2 tsp English mustard

500 g/1 lb 2 oz ready-made puff pastry

1 egg, lightly beaten

salt and pepper

1. Place a large frying pan over a high heat and add the oil. Rub salt and pepper into the beef, add to the pan and seal. Set aside to cool. Heat the butter in a separate frying pan over a medium heat, add the mushrooms and fry for 5 minutes. Reduce the heat, add the garlic and fry for a further 5 minutes. Transfer the mushrooms and garlic to a bowl, add the pâté and parsley, mix with a fork and leave to cool.

2. Rub the mustard into the beef. Roll out the pastry into a rectangle large enough to wrap the whole fillet with some to spare. Spread the mushroom paste in the middle, leaving a 5-cm/ 2-inch border, and lay the beef on top. Brush the edges of the pastry with beaten egg and fold it over, edges overlapping, and across the meat to completely enclose it.

3. Preheat the oven to 220°C/425°F/Gas Mark 7. Place the beef in a roasting tin, join underneath, and brush the surface with beaten egg. Chill in the refrigerator for 15 minutes, then bake in the preheated oven for 50 minutes. Leave to rest for 15 minutes before serving.

#200 Rack of lamb

Serves 2

Ingredients

1 x 500-g/1 lb 2-oz rack of lamb, trimmed

salt and pepper

new potatoes and green vegetables, to serve

Sauce

1 tbsp extra virgin olive oil

1 small onion, finely chopped

1 garlic clove, crushed

1–2 tbsp redcurrant jelly

1 tbsp soy sauce

200 ml/7 fl oz orange juice

150 ml/5 fl oz red wine

1 fresh rosemary sprig

salt and pepper

1. To make the sauce, heat the oil in a small saucepan. Add the onion and garlic and cook for 3 minutes, stirring occasionally. Add the redcurrant jelly, soy sauce, orange juice, wine and rosemary and bring to the boil, stirring until the jelly has dissolved. Reduce the heat and simmer for 20 minutes, or until the sauce has reduced by half and is slightly syrupy. Season to taste with salt and pepper.

2. Preheat the oven to 200°C/400°F/Gas Mark 6. Lightly season the meat with salt and pepper and sear on all sides in a hot frying pan. Transfer the meat to a roasting tin and brush with some of the sauce. Roast in the preheated oven for 8 minutes for medium rare, 15 minutes for medium and 20–25 minutes for well done. Remove from the oven and transfer to a board. Cover loosely with foil and leave to stand for 10 minutes.

3. Meanwhile strain the sauce and reheat. Slice the rack through into individual chops and arrange on serving plates. Drizzle with the sauce and serve with new potatoes and green vegetables.

#201 Pot roast with potatoes & dill

Serves 6

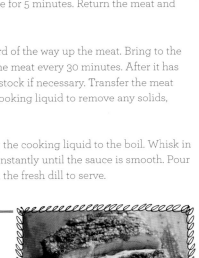

Ingredients

2½ tbsp plain flour

1 tsp salt

¼ tsp pepper

1 x 1- kg/3 lb 8-oz rolled brisket joint

2 tbsp vegetable oil

2 tbsp butter

1 onion, finely chopped

2 celery sticks, diced

2 carrots, peeled and diced

1 tsp dill seed

1 tsp dried thyme or oregano

350 ml/12 fl oz red wine

150–225 ml/5–8 fl oz beef stock

4–5 potatoes, cut into large chunks and boiled until just tender

2 tbsp chopped fresh dill, to serve

1. Preheat the oven to 140°C/275°F/Gas Mark 1. Mix 2 tablespoons of the flour with the salt and pepper in a shallow dish. Dip the meat to coat. Heat the oil in a flameproof casserole and brown the meat all over. Transfer to a plate. Add half the butter to the casserole and cook the onion, celery, carrots, dill seed and thyme for 5 minutes. Return the meat and juices to the casserole.

2. Pour in the wine and enough stock to reach one third of the way up the meat. Bring to the boil, cover and cook in the oven for 3 hours, turning the meat every 30 minutes. After it has been cooking for 2 hours, add the potatoes and more stock if necessary. Transfer the meat and vegetables to a warmed serving dish. Strain the cooking liquid to remove any solids, then return the liquid to the casserole.

3. Mix the remaining butter and flour to a paste. Bring the cooking liquid to the boil. Whisk in small pieces of the flour and butter paste, whisking constantly until the sauce is smooth. Pour the sauce over the meat and vegetables. Sprinkle with the fresh dill to serve.

#202 Roast pork belly

Serves 4

Ingredients

15 dried bay leaves

5 x 2.5-cm/1-inch pieces of fresh ginger, grated

15 garlic cloves, peeled and roughly chopped

100 ml/3½ fl oz olive oil

½ tsp pepper

2 tsp salt

1 tbsp whole star anise (optional)

1 tbsp whole cardamom seeds, cracked (optional)

3 kg/6 lb 8 oz pork belly, complete with skin and bones (make sure there are 8 ribs), skin scored with a knife every 1 cm/½ inch

1. Combine all of the ingredients, except the pork, in a small food processor and process to a thick paste. Put the pork into a roasting tin that will fit in your refrigerator, then rub the paste into it on all sides, making sure you get some into the cuts through the fat. Place in the refrigerator for at least 1 hour and up to 2 days.

2. Preheat the oven to 160°C/325°F/Gas Mark 3. Roast the pork, uncovered, in the preheated oven for 2 hours. Increase the oven temperature to 240°C/475°F/Gas Mark 9. Cook for a further 20–30 minutes to crisp the skin, checking every 10 minutes to make sure the pork doesn't burn.

3. If the pork skin hasn't turned into good crackling, preheat the grill to high and place the pork under the grill, making sure that it doesn't burn. Cut off the crackling in one large piece and set aside, uncovered. Cover the meat with foil and leave to rest for 15 minutes before serving. Carve it at the table, giving each person 2 whole ribs and a chunk of crackling.

Vegetable garden

#203 Tomato soup

Serves 4

Ingredients

2 tbsp olive oil

1 large onion, chopped

400 g/14 oz canned whole plum tomatoes

300 ml/10 fl oz vegetable stock

1 tbsp tomato purée

1 tsp hot pepper sauce

handful of fresh basil leaves

salt and pepper

1. Heat the oil in a large saucepan over a medium heat, then add the onion and fry for 4–5 minutes, stirring, until soft. Add the tomatoes, stock, tomato purée, hot pepper sauce and half the basil leaves.

2. Process using a hand-held blender until smooth. Stir the soup over a medium heat until just boiling, then season to taste with salt and pepper.

3. Serve the soup in warmed serving bowls, garnished with the remaining basil leaves.

#204 Broccoli & Stilton soup

Serves 4

Ingredients

40 g/1½ oz butter

2 onions, chopped

1 large potato, chopped

750 g/1 lb 10 oz broccoli florets

1.5 litres/2¾ pints vegetable stock

150 g/5½ oz Stilton cheese, diced

pinch of ground mace

salt and pepper

croûtons, to garnish

1. Melt the butter in a large saucepan. Add the onions and potato and stir well. Cover and cook over a low heat for 7 minutes. Add the broccoli and stir well, then re-cover the pan and cook for a further 5 minutes.

2. Increase the heat to medium, pour in the stock and bring to the boil. Reduce the heat, season to taste with salt and pepper and re-cover. Simmer for 15–20 minutes until the vegetables are tender.

3. Remove the pan from the heat, strain into a bowl, reserving the vegetables, and leave to cool slightly. Transfer the vegetables to a food processor or blender, add 1 ladleful of the stock and process until smooth. Gradually add the remaining stock.

4. Return the soup to the rinsed-out pan and reheat gently. Remove from the heat and stir in the cheese until melted and thoroughly combined. Stir in the mace and taste and adjust the seasoning, if necessary. Ladle into warmed bowls, sprinkle with the croûtons and serve immediately.

#205 French onion soup

Ingredients

3 tbsp olive oil

675 g/1 lb 8 oz onions, thinly sliced

4 garlic cloves, 3 chopped and
1 halved

1 tsp sugar

2 tsp chopped fresh thyme, plus extra
sprigs to garnish

2 tbsp plain flour

125 ml/4 fl oz dry white wine

2 litres/3½ pints vegetable stock

6 slices French bread

300 g/10½ oz Gruyère cheese, grated

1. Heat the oil in a large, heavy-based saucepan over a medium–low heat, add the onions and cook, stirring occasionally, for 10 minutes, or until they are just beginning to brown. Stir in the chopped garlic, sugar and chopped thyme, then reduce the heat and cook, stirring occasionally, for 30 minutes, or until the onions are golden brown. Sprinkle in the flour and cook, stirring constantly, for 1–2 minutes. Stir in the wine. Gradually stir in the stock and bring to the boil, skimming off any foam that rises to the surface, then reduce the heat and simmer for 45 minutes.

2. Meanwhile, preheat the grill to medium. Toast the bread on both sides under the grill, then rub the toast with the cut edges of the halved garlic clove.

3. Ladle the soup into six flameproof bowls set on a baking tray. Float a piece of toast in each bowl and divide the grated cheese between them. Place under the grill for 2–3 minutes, or until the cheese has just melted. Garnish with thyme sprigs and serve immediately.

#206 Barley, lentil & onion soup

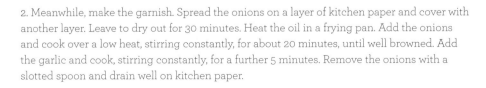

Ingredients

25 g/1 oz pearl barley

150 ml/5 fl oz water

1.7 litres/3 pints vegetable stock

500 g/1 lb 2 oz onions, sliced into rings

140 g/5 oz Puy lentils

½ tsp ground ginger

1 tsp ground cumin

3 tbsp lemon juice

2 tbsp chopped fresh coriander

salt and pepper

Garnish

2 onions, halved and thinly sliced

5 tbsp vegetable oil

2 garlic cloves, finely chopped

1. Put the barley into a large saucepan, pour in the water and bring to the boil. Reduce the heat, cover and simmer gently, stirring frequently, for about 30 minutes, until all the liquid has been absorbed. Add the stock, onions, lentils, ginger and cumin and bring to the boil over a medium heat. Reduce the heat, cover and simmer, stirring occasionally, for 1½ hours, adding a little more stock if necessary.

2. Meanwhile, make the garnish. Spread the onions on a layer of kitchen paper and cover with another layer. Leave to dry out for 30 minutes. Heat the oil in a frying pan. Add the onions and cook over a low heat, stirring constantly, for about 20 minutes, until well browned. Add the garlic and cook, stirring constantly, for a further 5 minutes. Remove the onions with a slotted spoon and drain well on kitchen paper.

3. Season the soup to taste with salt and pepper, stir in the lemon juice and coriander and simmer for a further 5 minutes. Serve immediately, garnished with the browned onions.

#207 Roast pumpkin, garlic & thyme soup

Serves 6

Ingredients

4 tbsp olive oil, plus extra
for drizzling

2 garlic bulbs

900 g/2 lb pumpkin or butternut
squash, peeled, deseeded and cut
into large chunks

2 tbsp fresh thyme leaves,
plus extra sprigs to garnish

25 g/1 oz butter

1 onion, chopped

1 tbsp plain flour

1.2 litres/2 pints chicken stock

100 g/3½ oz crème fraîche

salt and pepper

1. Preheat the oven to 190°C/375°F/Gas Mark 5. Pour ½ tablespoon of the oil over each garlic bulb, sprinkle with salt and pepper, wrap in foil and place in a roasting tin. Toss the pumpkin in the remaining oil and sprinkle with salt and pepper to taste and half the thyme. Place in the tin in a single layer. Cook in the preheated oven for 1 hour. Meanwhile, melt the butter in a large saucepan. Add the onion and cook over a medium heat for 5 minutes, until soft. Stir in the flour and cook for 2 minutes. Gradually add the stock. Add the pumpkin to the pan and simmer for 10 minutes.

2. Open the garlic packages and leave to cool. Break up the bulbs and press down on each clove until the pulp squeezes out. Remove the soup from the heat and leave to cool slightly. Stir in the garlic pulp and the remaining thyme, then transfer to a food processor and process until smooth. Return to the rinsed-out pan and reheat gently. Ladle into warmed bowls and top with crème fraîche. Drizzle over a little oil, garnish with thyme and serve immediately.

#208 Minestrone soup

Serves 4

Ingredients

2 tbsp olive oil

2 garlic cloves, chopped

2 red onions, chopped

75 g/2¾ oz Parma ham, sliced

1 red pepper and 1 orange pepper

400 g/14 oz canned chopped tomatoes

1 litre/1¾ pints vegetable stock

1 celery stick, chopped

400 g/14 oz canned borlotti beans

100 g/3½ oz leafy green cabbage

75 g/2¾ oz frozen peas

1 tbsp chopped fresh parsley

75 g/2¾ oz dried vermicelli pasta

salt and pepper

freshly grated Parmesan cheese,
to serve

1. Heat the oil in a large saucepan. Add the garlic, onions and ham and cook over a medium heat, stirring, for 3 minutes, until slightly softened.

2. Deseed and chop the red pepper and orange pepper, add to the pan with the chopped tomatoes and cook for a further 2 minutes, stirring. Stir in the stock, then add the celery.

3. Drain and rinse the beans and shred the cabbage, then add to the pan with the peas and parsley. Season to taste with salt and pepper. Bring to the boil, then reduce the heat and simmer for 30 minutes.

4. Add the pasta to the pan. Cook for a further 8–10 minutes, then remove from the heat and ladle into bowls. Sprinkle with Parmesan cheese and serve.

#209 Greek feta salad

Ingredients

handful of vine leaves

4 tomatoes, sliced

½ cucumber, peeled and sliced

1 small red onion, thinly sliced

115 g/4 oz feta cheese, drained and cubed

8 black olives

salt and pepper

Dressing

3 tbsp extra virgin olive oil

1 tbsp lemon juice

½ tsp dried oregano

salt and pepper

1. To make the dressing, put the olive oil, lemon juice, dried oregano and salt and pepper to taste in a small screw-top jar. Mix well until blended and set aside.

2. Arrange the vine leaves on a serving dish, then add the tomatoes, cucumber and onion. Scatter the cheese and olives on top. Pour the dressing over the salad, season to taste with salt and pepper and serve immediately.

#210 Waldorf salad

Ingredients

100 g/3½ oz pecan nuts

4 dessert apples, such as Cox or Granny Smith

juice of 1 lemon

4 celery sticks, thinly sliced

75 g/2¾ oz red seedless grapes, halved

250 g/9 oz natural yogurt

70 g/2½ oz rocket

pepper

1. Toast the pecan nuts in a frying pan for a few minutes to bring out their flavour. When they are cool enough to handle, roughly chop them.

2. Peel and chop the apples, then toss them in a bowl with the lemon juice to prevent discoloration.

3. Add the celery, grapes and half the pecan nuts to the apples and mix well. Stir in the yogurt, and pepper to taste and gently toss together.

4. Divide the rocket between four serving plates and spoon over the salad mixture. Sprinkle with the remaining pecan nuts.

Bean salad with feta

Ingredients

350 g/12 oz French beans, topped and tailed

1 red onion, chopped

3–4 tbsp chopped fresh coriander

2 radishes, thinly sliced

75 g/2¾ oz feta cheese, drained and crumbled

1 tsp chopped fresh oregano or ½ tsp dried oregano

2 tbsp red wine vinegar or fruit vinegar

5 tbsp extra virgin olive oil

3 ripe tomatoes, cut into wedges

pepper

1. Place the beans in a saucepan and cover with cold water. Bring to the boil, cover and simmer for 5 minutes, or until tender when pierced with a fork. Drain and halve.

2. Transfer the beans to a bowl and add the onion, coriander, radishes and cheese.

3. Sprinkle the oregano over the salad, then grind pepper over to taste. Whisk together the vinegar and oil and pour over the salad. Gently toss to mix well.

4. Transfer to a serving platter, add the tomato wedges and serve at once or chill until ready to serve.

Serves
4

Avocado, feta & rocket salad

Ingredients

2 ripe avocados

100 g/3½ oz rocket leaves

250 g/9 oz feta cheese, crumbled

Dressing

6 tbsp olive oil

2 tbsp white wine vinegar

1 shallot, finely chopped

2 large ripe tomatoes, deseeded and diced

1 tbsp lemon juice

1 tsp caster sugar

salt and pepper

1. Halve, stone, peel and slice the avocados and arrange on a serving dish together with the rocket leaves. Top with the cheese.

2. To make the dressing, put the oil and vinegar into a saucepan and gently heat, then add the shallot and cook, stirring, for 2–3 minutes until soft. Add the tomatoes, lemon juice and sugar and gently heat, stirring, for 30 seconds.

3. Season the dressing to taste with salt and pepper, then spoon it over the salad and serve.

Serves
4

Green & white asparagus salad with poached eggs

Ingredients

400 g/14 oz white asparagus

400 g/14 oz green asparagus

2 shallots

2 fresh mint sprigs

½ bunch fresh parsley

½ bunch fresh chervil

½ bunch fresh chives

2 tbsp sugar

2 tbsp salt

juice of ½ lemon

150 ml/5 fl oz ready-made vinaigrette

4 eggs

2 tbsp water

2 tbsp cream

1½ tbsp mayonnaise

1. Peel the asparagus. Peel the shallots and finely chop. Cut the mint leaves, parsley and chervil into thin ribbons and finely snip the chives.

2. Put the white asparagus, sugar, half the salt and the lemon juice into a saucepan, cover with water and bring to the boil. Cook for around 8 minutes, or until tender. Put the green asparagus into a separate saucepan with the remaining salt. Cover with water and bring to the boil. Cook for around 5 minutes, or until tender. Refresh the asparagus in cold water and arrange in a dish. Sprinkle with the shallot and herb mixture and drizzle over the vinaigrette. Leave to marinade for 10 minutes. Meanwhile, poach the eggs in an egg poacher, following the manufacturers instructions.

3. Meanwhile, bring a saucepan of water to the boil and stir well. Crack the eggs one at a time and carefully drop them into the water. Cook for 1–2 minutes, or until the white has set. Divide the asparagus between plates and top each with an egg. Mix together the water, cream and mayonnaise and drizzle over. Serve immediately.

#214 Roasted vegetable & feta cheese wraps

Ingredients

1 red onion, cut into eighths

1 red pepper, cored and cut into eighths

1 small aubergine, cut into eighths

1 courgette, cut into eighths

4 tbsp extra virgin olive oil

1 garlic clove, crushed

100 g/3½ oz feta cheese, crumbled

small bunch fresh mint, shredded

4 x 25-cm/10-inch sun-dried tomato wraps

salt and pepper

1. Preheat the oven to 220°C/425°F/Gas Mark 7. Mix all of the vegetables, olive oil, garlic and salt and pepper to taste together and place in a non-stick baking tray. Roast in the preheated oven for 15–20 minutes or until golden and cooked through.

2. Remove from the oven and leave to cool, then mix in the cheese and mint.

3. Preheat a non-stick frying pan until almost smoking, then cook the wraps, one at a time, for 10 seconds on each side.

4. Divide the vegetable and cheese mixture between the wraps, placing it along the middle of each wrap. Roll up the wraps, cut them in half and serve.

#215 Falafel pittas

Ingredients

1 onion, finely chopped

1 garlic clove, chopped

400 g/14 oz canned chickpeas, drained and rinsed

1 tsp ground cumin

1 tsp ground coriander

¼ tsp chilli powder

1 tbsp chopped fresh coriander

1 egg, beaten

2 tbsp vegetable oil, plus extra for frying

2 pitta breads

salt and pepper

coleslaw, to serve

1. To make the falafel, heat some oil in a small frying pan, add the onion and garlic and cook for 3 minutes.

2. Meanwhile put the chickpeas in a bowl and roughly mash with a fork. Add the onion and garlic, cumin, ground coriander, chilli and fresh coriander. Taste the mixture and add seasoning to taste. Stir in the egg and mix well. Divide the mixture into 6 falafel shapes and chill in the refrigerator.

3. Heat the oil in a frying pan and cook the falafel for 2–3 minutes on each side, or until golden. Warm the pitta breads and split them open. Fill each one with coleslaw and falafel and serve immediately.

#216 Egg tortilla with feta & sweetcorn

Ingredients

350 g/12 oz potatoes

2 tbsp olive oil

1 onion, chopped

1 courgette, coarsely grated

200 g/7 oz canned sweetcorn, drained

6 eggs

100 g/3½ oz feta cheese (drained weight), crumbled

salt and pepper

paprika, to garnish

1. Peel or scrub the potatoes and cut into 1-cm/½-inch dice. Bring a saucepan of lightly salted water to the boil, add the potatoes, bring back to the boil and cook for 5 minutes, or until just tender. Drain.

2. Heat the oil in a large ovenproof frying pan over a medium heat, add the onion and fry for about 5 minutes, until soft.

3. Stir in the courgette and potatoes, then cook for 2 minutes. Stir in the sweetcorn. Lightly beat the eggs with salt and pepper to taste. Stir into the pan, then scatter over the feta cheese. Cook for 4–6 minutes, until almost set.

4. Meanwhile, preheat the grill to high. Place the tortilla under the preheated grill for 2–3 minutes until set and golden brown. Sprinkle the tortilla with paprika. Cut into 4–6 wedges and serve hot or cold.

#217 Wholewheat spaghetti with edamame beans

Ingredients

350 g/12 oz wholewheat spaghetti

200 g/7 oz frozen edamame (soya) beans

2 tbsp extra virgin olive oil

2 garlic cloves, thinly sliced

finely grated rind of 1 lemon

salt and pepper

1. Bring a saucepan of lightly salted water to the boil over a high heat. Add the spaghetti, bring back to the boil and cook for 10–12 minutes, or until tender but still firm to the bite. Add the beans to the pan for the final 3 minutes. Drain the spaghetti and beans and keep warm in the pan.

2. Meanwhile, place the oil in a small frying pan over a low heat and stir in the garlic. Reduce the heat to very low and leave to infuse for about 10 minutes, stirring occasionally, without allowing the garlic to sizzle or brown.

3. Add the lemon rind, garlic and oil to the spaghetti and beans and toss to combine evenly. Season to taste with salt and pepper and serve immediately.

Potato kebabs with feta

Serves
4–6

Ingredients

4 large garlic cloves, peeled

1 tsp sea salt flakes

1 tbsp finely chopped fresh rosemary

½ tsp pepper

4 tbsp olive oil, plus extra for greasing

850 g/1 lb 14 oz oval red-skinned salad potatoes, about 5 cm/
2 inches long

40 g/1½ oz crumbled feta cheese

1 tbsp chopped fresh flat-leaf parsley

1. Preheat the barbecue. Crush the garlic cloves with the sea salt until smooth and creamy. Add the rosemary and pepper, and pound to a paste. Whisk in the oil, then pour the mixture into a large bowl and leave to stand.

2. Scrub the potatoes and cut in half crossways. Steam for 7 minutes until just tender. Spread out on a clean tea towel to dry. Add to the garlic mixture in the bowl and toss to coat. Arrange on a board, cut-side down, reserving the remaining garlic mixture in the bowl. Thread onto six presoaked wooden skewers, piercing through the middle so that the cut sides face downwards.

3. Grease the barbecue rack. Cook the kebabs over hot coals, cut-side down, for 3–4 minutes, turning when each side is striped from the grill. Brush the upper surface with the garlic oil as you turn. Move to the cooler zone and cook for a further 5–7 minutes, turning and brushing, until tender. Arrange on a serving platter, sprinkle with the cheese and parsley and serve.

Goat's cheese & red pepper tarts

Makes
2

Ingredients

200 g/7 oz ready-made puff pastry

flour, for dusting

1 egg, beaten

2 red peppers

4 tbsp ready-made pesto

115 g/4 oz goat's cheese, sliced

fresh basil sprigs, to garnish

1. Preheat the oven to 200°C/400°F/Gas Mark 6. Roll out the pastry on a lightly floured surface. Cut the pastry into two equal pieces and transfer to a baking sheet. With the tip of a sharp knife, score a line about 1 cm/½ inch inside the edge all the way round.
Make diagonal scores on the outside rim of the pastry and brush this with beaten egg. Bake in the preheated oven for 10 minutes, or until risen and golden.

2. Meanwhile, char the red peppers under a preheated grill until blackened all over. Put the peppers in a polythene bag or wrap in kitchen paper and leave to cool a little. Scrape off the charred skin, rinse under cold water and remove the stalk and seeds. Thinly slice the red peppers.

3. Cut along the inner line of the pastry cases to loosen the centre part and push down gently. Spread 2 tablespoons of pesto in the centre part of each tart, then arrange the sliced peppers on top. Lay slices of goat's cheese on each one and return to the oven for 5 minutes, or until the goat's cheese has melted. Serve the tarts immediately, garnished with basil sprigs.

#220 Sweet potato hash

Serves 2

Ingredients

500 g/1 lb 2 oz sweet potato, cubed

2 tbsp extra virgin olive oil

1 small red onion, chopped

1 garlic clove, chopped

½ red, ½ green and
½ yellow pepper, diced

1 tbsp chopped pickled jalapeños

2 tbsp chopped fresh coriander

1 tbsp vinegar

2 eggs

salt and pepper

1. Bring a large saucepan of lightly salted water to the boil, add the sweet potato, bring back to the boil and cook for 5 minutes, or until tender. Meanwhile, heat the oil in a large, heavy-based frying pan, add the onion and fry for 4 minutes. Add the garlic and cook for a further minute.

2. Drain the sweet potato and add to the pan with the peppers, jalapeños and 1 tablespoon of the coriander. Cook, stirring occasionally, for 8–10 minutes. Transfer to warmed plates.

3. Meanwhile, bring a saucepan of water to the boil. Add the vinegar and stir well. Crack the eggs one at a time and carefully drop them into the water. Cook for 1–2 minutes, or until the white has set. Top the sweet potato hash with the poached eggs, sprinkle the remaining coriander over the top and season to taste. Serve immediately.

#221 Tacos with chickpea salsa

Serves 4

Ingredients

2 firm, ripe avocados

1 tbsp lime juice

1 tomato, diced

1 tbsp olive oil

1 small onion, sliced

400 g/14 oz canned chickpeas, drained

1 tsp mild chilli powder

8 tacos

8 cos lettuce leaves

2 tbsp chopped fresh coriander, plus extra sprigs to garnish

salt and pepper

150 ml/5 fl oz soured cream, to serve

1. Halve, stone, peel and dice the avocados and toss with the lime juice. Stir in the tomato and season well with salt and pepper.

2. Heat the oil in a saucepan, add the onion and fry for 3–4 minutes, or until golden brown. Mash the chickpeas with a fork and stir into the pan with the chilli powder. Gently heat, stirring, for 2 minutes.

3. Divide the lettuce between the tacos. Stir the chopped coriander into the avocado and tomato mixture, then spoon into the tacos.

4. Add a spoonful of the chickpea mixture to each taco and top with a spoonful of soured cream. Garnish with coriander sprigs and serve immediately.

Serves 4

Penne with halloumi & cherry tomatoes

Ingredients

400 g/14 oz dried penne

2 tbsp olive oil

1 red onion, thinly sliced

1 garlic clove, finely chopped

250 g/9 oz cherry plum tomatoes, halved lengthways

250 g/9 oz halloumi cheese, cut into 1-cm/½-inch cubes

3 tbsp chopped fresh basil

salt and pepper

1. Bring a large saucepan of lightly salted water to the boil. Add the pasta, bring back to the boil and cook for 10 minutes until tender but still firm to the bite.

2. Meanwhile, heat the oil in a large frying pan, add the onion and garlic and gently fry, stirring occasionally, for 5–6 minutes, until soft but not brown. Add the tomatoes and cook over a fairly high heat, shaking the pan occasionally, for 2–3 minutes, or until soft. Remove from the pan, set aside and keep warm.

3. Add the halloumi to the pan and fry over a medium heat, stirring, for 2–3 minutes, or until golden brown. Return the tomato mixture to the pan with the basil and season to taste with salt and pepper.

4. Drain the pasta, then add to the pan and toss with the tomato mixture until evenly combined. Serve immediately.

#223 Pasta all' arrabbiata

Serves 4

Ingredients

5 tbsp extra virgin olive oil

450 g/1 lb plum tomatoes, chopped

150 ml/5 fl oz dry white wine

1 tbsp sun-dried tomato purée

2 fresh red chillies

2 garlic cloves, finely chopped

4 tbsp chopped fresh
flat-leaf parsley

400 g/14 oz dried penne

salt and pepper

fresh pecorino cheese shavings, to
garnish

1. Heat the oil in a frying pan over a high heat until almost smoking. Add the tomatoes and cook, stirring frequently, for 2–3 minutes. Reduce the heat to low and cook for about 20 minutes. Season to taste with salt and pepper. Using a wooden spoon, press through a non-metallic sieve into a saucepan.

2. Add the wine, tomato purée, whole chillies and garlic to the pan and bring to the boil. Reduce the heat and simmer gently, then remove the chillies. Check and adjust the seasoning, then stir in half the parsley.

3. Meanwhile, bring a large saucepan of lightly salted water to the boil. Add the pasta, bring back to the boil and cook for 8–10 minutes, or until tender but still firm to the bite. Add the sauce and toss to coat. Sprinkle with the remaining parsley, garnish with cheese and serve.

#224 Jamaican rice & peas with tofu

Serves 4

Ingredients

250 g/9 oz firm tofu

2 tbsp chopped fresh thyme,
plus extra sprigs to garnish

2 tbsp olive oil

1 onion, sliced

1 garlic clove, crushed

1 small fresh red chilli, chopped

400 ml/14 fl oz vegetable stock

200 g/7 oz basmati rice

4 tbsp coconut cream

400 g/14 oz canned red kidney beans,
drained

salt and pepper

1. Cut the tofu into bite-sized cubes. Toss with half the chopped thyme and sprinkle with salt and pepper to taste. Heat 1 tablespoon of the oil in a frying pan, add the tofu and fry, stirring occasionally, for 2 minutes. Remove and keep warm.

2. Add the onion to the remaining oil and fry, stirring, for 3–4 minutes. Stir in the garlic, chilli and the remaining chopped thyme, then add the stock and bring to the boil.

3. Stir in the rice, then reduce the heat, cover and simmer for 12–15 minutes, until the rice is tender. Stir in the coconut cream and beans, season to taste with salt and pepper and cook gently for 2–3 minutes.

4. Spoon the tofu over the rice and serve hot, garnished with thyme sprigs.

#225 Tofu stir-fry

Serves 4

Ingredients

2 tbsp sunflower oil
350 g/12 oz firm tofu, cubed
225 g/8 oz pak choi, roughly chopped
1 garlic clove, chopped
4 tbsp sweet chilli sauce
2 tbsp light soy sauce

1. Heat 1 tablespoon of the oil in a wok. Add the tofu to the wok in batches and stir-fry for 2–3 minutes, until golden. Remove and set aside.

2. Add the pak choi to the wok and stir-fry for a few seconds, until tender and wilted. Remove and set aside.

3. Heat the remaining oil in the wok, then add the garlic and stir-fry for 30 seconds. Stir in the chilli sauce and soy sauce and bring to the boil.

4. Return the tofu and pak choi to the wok and toss gently until coated in the sauce. Transfer to individual dishes and serve immediately.

#226 Pasta pesto

Serves 4

Ingredients

2 garlic cloves
25 g/1 oz pine nuts
115 g/4 oz fresh basil leaves, plus extra to garnish
125 ml/4 fl oz olive oil
55 g/2 oz freshly grated Parmesan cheese
450 g/1 lb dried tagliatelle
salt

1. Put the garlic, pine nuts and a pinch of salt into a food processor and briefly process. Add the basil and process to a paste.

2. With the motor still running, gradually add the oil. Scrape into a bowl and beat in the cheese. Season to taste with salt.

3. Bring a large saucepan of lightly salted water to the boil. Add the pasta, bring back to the boil and cook for 8–10 minutes, until tender but still firm to the bite.

4. Drain well, return to the saucepan and toss with half the pesto.

5. Divide between warmed serving dishes and top with the remaining pesto. Garnish with basil and serve immediately.

149

#227 New potato, feta & herb frittata

Serves 4

Ingredients

250 g/9 oz new potatoes, scrubbed

85 g/3 oz baby spinach leaves

5 eggs

1 tbsp chopped fresh dill, plus extra to garnish

1 tbsp snipped fresh chives, plus extra to garnish

115 g/4 oz feta cheese, crumbled

10 g/¼ oz butter

1 tbsp olive oil

salt and pepper

1. Bring a saucepan of lightly salted water to the boil, add the potatoes, bring back to the boil and cook for 25 minutes until tender. Place the spinach in a colander and drain the potatoes over the top to wilt the spinach. Set aside until cool enough to handle. Cut the potatoes lengthways into 5-mm/¼-in thick slices. Squeeze the excess water from the spinach leaves. Preheat the grill to high.

2. Lightly beat the eggs, dill and chives together. Season with pepper and add 85 g/3 oz of the cheese. Heat the butter and oil in a 20-cm/8-inch frying pan until foaming. Add the potato slices and spinach and cook, stirring, for 1 minute. Pour the egg and cheese mixture over the top. Cook, stirring, over a medium heat for 1 minute until half set, then continue to cook for a further 2–3 minutes, without stirring, until set and golden brown underneath. Sprinkle the remaining cheese over the top, place under the preheated grill and cook for 2 minutes until golden brown on top. Serve hot or cold, sprinkled with chives and dill.

#228 Tomato tart

Serves 4

Ingredients

Pastry

250 g/9 oz plain flour

pinch of salt

140 g/5 oz butter

1 tbsp chopped oregano, plus extra to garnish

5–6 tbsp cold water

Filling

25 g/1 oz butter

1 tbsp caster sugar

500 g/1 lb 2 oz tomatoes, halved

1 garlic clove, crushed

2 tsp white wine vinegar

salt and pepper

1. Preheat the oven to 200°C/400°F/Gas Mark 6. To make the filling, melt the butter in a heavy-based saucepan. Add the sugar and stir over a fairly high heat until just turning golden brown. Remove from the heat and quickly add the tomatoes, garlic and vinegar, stirring to coat evenly. Season with salt and pepper. Tip into a 23-cm/9-inch cake tin, spreading evenly.

2. To make the pastry, place the flour, salt, butter and oregano in a food processor and process until the mixture resembles fine breadcrumbs. Add just enough water to bind to a soft, but not sticky, dough. Roll out the pastry to a 25-cm/10-inch round and place over the tomatoes, tucking in the edges. Pierce with a fork to let out steam. Bake in the preheated oven for 25–30 minutes, or until firm and golden. Leave to rest for 2–3 minutes, then run a knife around the edge and turn out onto a warmed serving plate.

3. Sprinkle the tart with chopped oregano, and serve immediately.

Caponata

Ingredients

4 tbsp olive oil

2 celery sticks, sliced

2 red onions, sliced

450 g/1 lb aubergines, diced

1 garlic clove, finely chopped

5 plum tomatoes, chopped

3 tbsp red wine vinegar

1 tbsp sugar

3 tbsp stoned green olives

2 tbsp capers

4 tbsp chopped fresh flat-leaf parsley

salt and pepper

ciabatta bread, to serve

1. Heat half the oil in a large, heavy-based saucepan. Add the celery and onions and cook over a low heat, stirring occasionally, for 5 minutes, until soft but not coloured. Add the remaining oil and the aubergines. Cook, stirring frequently, for about 5 minutes, until the aubergine starts to colour.

2. Add the garlic, tomatoes, vinegar and sugar and mix well. Cover the mixture with a round of greaseproof paper and gently simmer for about 10 minutes.

3. Remove the greaseproof paper, stir in the olives and capers and season to taste with salt and pepper. Pour into a serving dish and set aside to cool to room temperature. When cool, sprinkle over the parsley and serve immediately with ciabatta bread.

Thai tofu cakes with chilli dip

Ingredients

3 tbsp white distilled vinegar

2 spring onions, finely sliced

1 tbsp caster sugar

4 fresh red chillies, deseeded and finely chopped

6 tbsp chopped fresh coriander

300 g/10½ oz drained firm tofu

1 lemon grass stalk, finely chopped

2 garlic cloves, chopped

2.5-cm/1-inch piece fresh ginger, grated

2 kaffir lime leaves, finely chopped

2 shallots, finely chopped

90 g/3¼ oz plain flour

corn oil, for cooking

salt

1. Mix the vinegar, spring onions, sugar, half the chopped chillies, 2 tablespoons of the chopped coriander and a pinch of salt together in a small bowl and set aside until ready to serve.

2. Coarsely grate the tofu and mix with the lemon grass, garlic, ginger, lime leaves, shallots and the remaining chillies and coriander in a mixing bowl. Stir in the flour and ½ teaspoon of salt to make a coarse, sticky paste. Cover and chill in the refrigerator for 1 hour to allow the mixture to firm up slightly.

3. Form the mixture into 8 large walnut-sized balls and flatten into rounds. Heat enough oil to cover the base of a large, heavy-based frying pan and set over a medium heat. Cook the cakes in two batches, turning halfway through, for 4–6 minutes, or until golden brown. Drain on kitchen paper and serve warm with the chilli dip.

#231 French onion tart

Serves
4

Ingredients

Pastry

200 g/7 oz plain flour, plus extra
for dusting

pinch of salt

100 g/3½ oz butter, diced, plus extra
for greasing

1 egg yolk

Filling

75 g/2¾ oz butter

4 onions, thinly sliced

2 tsp thyme leaves

2 eggs

225 ml/8 fl oz double cream

50 g/1¾ oz Gruyère cheese, grated

½ tsp fresh grated nutmeg

salt and pepper

1. To make the pastry, sift the flour and salt into a large bowl, add the butter, then rub with your fingertips until the mixture resembles fine breadcrumbs. Add the egg yolk and just enough water to bind to a soft, but not sticky, dough. Roll into a ball, wrap in clingfilm and chill in the refrigerator for 15 minutes before using.

2. Preheat the oven to 180°C/350°F/Gas Mark 4. Grease a 20-cm/8-inch loose-based tart tin. Roll out the pastry on a lightly floured surface. Press the pastry into the prepared tin, line with baking paper, fill with baking beans and bake in the preheated oven for 15 minutes. Remove from the oven. Increase the oven temperature to 200°C/400°F/Gas Mark 6. Remove the beans and paper and bake the pastry case for a further 5 minutes. Do not switch off the oven.

3. To make the filling, melt the butter in a large, heavy-based frying pan over a low–medium heat, then add the onions and thyme and fry gently, stirring frequently until lightly browned. Season with salt and pepper, remove from the heat and leave to cool for 10 minutes.

4. Reduce the oven temperature to 190°C/375°F/Gas Mark 5. In a large bowl, beat the eggs and cream together. Add the cheese, nutmeg and onion mixture and stir. Pour the mixture into the pastry case and bake for 30–40 minutes, or until golden brown. Serve immediately.

152

#232 Cheese & tomato pizza

Serves 4

Ingredients

225 g/8 oz plain flour,
plus extra for dusting

1 tsp salt

1 tsp easy-blend dried yeast

3 tbsp olive oil, plus extra for oiling

6 tbsp lukewarm water

6 tomatoes, thinly sliced

175 g/6 oz mozzarella cheese, drained
and thinly sliced

2 tbsp shredded fresh basil

salt and pepper

1. Sift the flour and salt into a bowl and stir in the yeast. Make a well in the centre and pour in 1 tablespoon of the oil and the water. Gradually incorporate the dry ingredients into the liquid, using floured hands. Turn out the dough onto a lightly floured surface and knead for 5 minutes, until smooth and elastic. Return the dough to a clean bowl, cover with lightly oiled clingfilm and leave to rise in a warm place for about 1 hour, or until doubled in size.

2. Preheat the oven to 230°C/450°F/Gas Mark 8. Lightly oil a baking sheet. Turn out the dough onto a lightly floured surface and knock back. Knead briefly, then roll out into a round about 5 mm/¼ inch thick. Transfer the pizza base to the prepared baking sheet and push up the edges with your fingers to form a small rim.

3. Scatter the tomatoes and cheese over the pizza base, Season to taste with salt and pepper, sprinkle with the basil and drizzle with the remaining oil. Bake in the preheated oven for 20–25 minutes, until golden brown. Cut into slices and serve immediately.

#233 Fusilli with courgettes & lemon

Serves 4

Ingredients

6 tbsp olive oil

1 small onion, very thinly sliced

2 garlic cloves, very finely chopped

2 tbsp chopped fresh rosemary

1 tbsp chopped fresh flat-leaf parsley

450 g/1 lb small courgettes,
cut into 4-cm/1½-inch strips

finely grated rind of 1 lemon

450 g/1 lb dried fusilli

salt and pepper

freshly grated Parmesan cheese,
to serve

1. Heat the oil in a large frying pan over a medium–low heat. Add the onion and cook gently, stirring occasionally, for about 10 minutes, until golden.

2. Increase the heat to medium–high. Add the garlic, rosemary and parsley. Cook for a few seconds, stirring.

3. Add the courgettes and lemon rind. Cook for 5–7 minutes, stirring occasionally, until just tender. Season to taste with salt and pepper. Remove from the heat.

4. Bring a large saucepan of lightly salted water to the boil. Add the fusilli, bring back to the boil and cook for 8–10 minutes, or until just tender but still firm to the bite.

5. Drain the pasta and transfer to a serving dish. Briefly reheat the courgette sauce. Pour over the pasta and toss well to mix. Sprinkle with the Parmesan cheese and serve.

#234 Asparagus & tomato tart

Serves 4

Ingredients

butter, for greasing

375 g/13 oz ready-made shortcrust pastry, thawed, if frozen

1 bunch thin asparagus spears

250 g/9 oz spinach leaves

3 large eggs, beaten

150 ml/5 fl oz double cream

1 garlic clove, crushed

10 small cherry tomatoes, halved

handful fresh basil, chopped

25 g/1 oz freshly grated Parmesan cheese

salt and pepper

1. Preheat the oven to 190°C/375°F/Gas Mark 5. Grease a 25–30-cm/10–12-inch tart tin, then roll out the pastry and use to line the tin. Cut off any excess pastry and prick the base with a fork. Line with baking paper, fill with baking beans and bake in the preheated oven for 20–30 minutes until lightly browned. Remove from the oven and take out the paper and beans. Reduce the oven temperature to 180°C/350°F/Gas Mark 4.

2. Meanwhile, bend the asparagus spears until they snap. Discard the woody bases. Bring a saucepan of lightly salted water to the boil, add the asparagus, blanch for 1 minute, then remove and drain. Add the spinach to the boiling water, remove immediately and drain very well. Mix together the eggs, cream and garlic and season to taste with salt and pepper. Lay the spinach in the pastry case. Add the asparagus and tomatoes, cut side up. Scatter over the basil, then pour the egg mixture on top. Transfer to the oven and bake for about 35 minutes, or until the filling has set. Sprinkle the cheese on top, leave to cool to room temperature and serve.

#235 Brown rice lunchbowl

Serves 4

Ingredients

300 g/10½ oz brown basmati rice

1 bay leaf

600 ml/1 pint vegetable stock or water

250 g/9 oz asparagus, cut into 3-cm/1¼-inch chunks

juice of 1 lime

2 tbsp extra virgin olive oil

70 g/2½ oz Brazil nuts, roughly chopped

salt and pepper

1. Place the rice, bay leaf and stock in a large saucepan and bring to the boil over a high heat. Lightly stir, then reduce the heat. Cover and simmer for about 35 minutes, stirring occasionally to prevent sticking, until all the liquid is absorbed and the rice is just tender. Remove and discard the bay leaf.

2. Meanwhile, bring a saucepan of water to the boil over a high heat. Add the asparagus and boil for 3–5 minutes, or until just tender. Alternatively, steam the asparagus for 5–6 minutes over the boiling water to preserve more nutrients. Drain well.

3. Combine the rice and asparagus in a large bowl and pour over the lime juice and oil. Mix well to combine

4. Stir in the nuts and season to taste with salt and pepper. Serve warm or cold.

#236 Bean burgers

Serves
4

Ingredients

1 tbsp sunflower oil,
plus extra for brushing

1 onion, finely chopped

1 garlic clove, finely chopped

1 tsp ground coriander

1 tsp ground cumin

115 g/4 oz button mushrooms,
finely chopped

425 g/15 oz canned red kidney beans,
drained and rinsed

2 tbsp chopped fresh
flat-leaf parsley

plain flour, for dusting

salt and pepper

burger buns and salad leaves,
to serve

1. Heat the oil in a heavy-based frying pan over a medium heat. Add the onion and cook, stirring frequently, for 5 minutes, or until soft. Add the garlic, coriander and cumin and cook, stirring, for a further minute. Add the mushrooms and cook, stirring frequently, for 4–5 minutes, until all the liquid has evaporated. Transfer to a bowl.

2. Put the beans into a bowl and mash with a potato masher. Stir into the mushroom mixture with the parsley and season to taste with salt and pepper.

3. Preheat the grill to medium–high. Divide the mixture into 4 equal portions. Lightly dust with flour and shape into flat patties. Brush with oil and cook under the grill for 4–5 minutes on each side. Serve in the burger buns with the salad leaves.

#237 Lattice flan

Serves
8

Ingredients

450 g/1 lb frozen spinach, thawed

2 tbsp olive oil

1 large onion, chopped

2 garlic cloves, finely chopped

2 eggs, lightly beaten

225 g/8 oz ricotta cheese

55 g/2 oz freshly grated
Parmesan cheese

400 g/14 oz ready-made rich
shortcrust pastry

plain flour, for dusting

pinch of freshly grated nutmeg

salt and pepper

1. Wash the spinach and drain very well. Heat the oil in a large frying pan over a medium heat. Add the onion and cook, stirring frequently, for 5 minutes, or until soft. Add the garlic and spinach and cook, stirring occasionally, for 10 minutes. Remove from the heat and leave to cool slightly, then beat in the eggs (reserving a little for glazing), the ricotta cheese and the Parmesan cheese. Season to taste with salt and pepper and nutmeg.

2. Preheat the oven to 200°C/400°F/Gas Mark 6. Lightly grease a 23-cm/9-inch loose-based flan tin. Roll out two thirds of the dough on a lightly floured work surface and use to line the tin. Spoon in the spinach mixture, spreading it evenly over the base.

3. Roll out the remaining dough and cut into 5-mm/¼-inch strips. Arrange the strips in a lattice pattern on top of the flan, pressing the ends securely to seal. Trim any excess pastry. Brush with the egg to glaze and bake in the preheated oven for 45 minutes, or until golden brown. Transfer to a wire rack to cool slightly before removing from the tin.

#238 Lentils with cumin & shallots

Serves 4

Ingredients

200 g/7 oz split red lentils

850 ml/1½ pints cold water

1 tsp salt, or to taste

2 tsp vegetable or groundnut oil

½ tsp black or brown mustard seeds

½ tsp cumin seeds

4 shallots, finely chopped

2 fresh green chillies, chopped

1 tsp ground turmeric

1 tsp ground cumin

1 fresh tomato, chopped

2 tbsp chopped fresh coriander

1. Rinse the lentils under cold running water. Drain and put into a saucepan. Add the water and bring to the boil. Reduce the heat to medium and skim the surface to remove the foam. Cook, uncovered, for 10 minutes. Reduce the heat to low, cover and cook, stirring occasionally to ensure that the lentils do not stick to the base of the pan as they thicken, for 45 minutes. Stir in the salt.

2. Meanwhile, heat the oil in a small saucepan over a medium heat. When hot, but not smoking, add the mustard seeds, followed by the cumin seeds. Add the shallots and chillies and cook, stirring, for 2–3 minutes, then add the turmeric and ground cumin. Add the tomato and cook, stirring, for 30 seconds.

3. Fold the shallot mixture into the cooked lentils. Stir in the chopped coriander, remove from the heat and serve immediately.

#239 Sichuan mixed vegetables

Serves 4

Ingredients

2 tbsp chilli oil

4 garlic cloves, crushed

5-cm/2-inch piece fresh ginger, grated

250 g/9 oz carrots, cut into thin strips

1 red pepper, cut into thin strips

150 g/5½ oz shiitake mushrooms, sliced

150 g/5½ oz mangetout, halved diagonally

3 tbsp soy sauce

3 tbsp peanut butter

350 g/12 oz beansprouts

cooked rice, to serve

1. Heat the chilli oil in a preheated wok and fry the garlic, ginger and carrots for 3 minutes. Add the red pepper and stir-fry for a further 2 minutes. Add the mushrooms and mangetout and stir-fry for 1 minute.

2. Mix the soy sauce and peanut butter together in a small bowl until combined. Using a wooden spoon, make a space in the centre of the stir-fried vegetables so that the base of the wok is visible. Pour in the peanut butter mixture and bring to the boil, stirring constantly, until it starts to thicken. Add the beansprouts and toss the vegetables to coat thoroughly with the sauce.

3. Transfer to a warmed serving dish and serve immediately with freshly cooked rice.

156

#240 Polenta tart with a herb crust

Serves 4

Ingredients

olive oil, for greasing and brushing

850 ml/1½ pints boiling water

250 g/9 oz quick-cook polenta

1 tbsp chopped fresh oregano, plus extra to garnish

1 small yellow pepper, deseeded and thinly sliced

1 small red onion, thinly sliced

1 small courgette, thinly sliced

2 tomatoes, sliced

100 g/3½ oz half-fat mozzarella cheese, diced

8 black olives, stoned and halved

salt and pepper

1. Preheat the oven to 200°C/400°F/Gas Mark 6. Grease a large baking sheet. Pour the water into a large pan, add a pinch of salt, and bring to the boil over a high heat. Add the polenta in a steady stream, stirring constantly until smooth.

2. Reduce the heat and stir constantly for 4–5 minutes, or until thick and smooth. Remove from the heat and stir in the oregano. Season to taste with pepper. Spoon the polenta onto the prepared baking sheet and spread out in a 30-cm/12-inch round, raising the edges slightly.

3. Arrange the yellow pepper, onion, courgette and tomatoes over the polenta and add the mozzarella cheese. Top the tart with the olives and lightly brush with oil.

4. Bake in the preheated oven for 15–20 minutes, or until bubbling and golden brown. Garnish with oregano and serve immediately.

#241 Baked pasta with mushrooms

Serves 4

Ingredients

140 g/5 oz fontina cheese, thinly sliced

300 ml/10 fl oz béchamel sauce

6 tbsp butter, plus extra for greasing

350 g/12 oz mixed wild mushrooms, sliced

350 g/12 oz dried tagliatelle

2 egg yolks

4 tbsp freshly grated Romano cheese

salt and pepper

1. Preheat the oven to 200°C/400°F/Gas Mark 6 Stir the fontina cheese into the béchamel sauce and set aside.

2. Melt 2 tablespoons of the butter in a large saucepan. Add the mushrooms and cook over low heat, stirring occasionally, for 10 minutes.

3. Meanwhile, bring a large saucepan of lightly salted water to the boil over a medium heat. Add the pasta, bring back to the boil and cook for 8–10 minutes, or until tender but still firm to the bite. Drain, return to the pan and add the remaining butter, the egg yolks and about one third of the sauce, then season with salt and pepper. Toss well to mix, then gently stir in the mushrooms.

4. Lightly grease a large, ovenproof dish and spoon in the pasta mixture. Pour over the remaining sauce and sprinkle with the Romano cheese. Bake in the preheated oven for 15–20 minutes, or until golden brown. Spoon out into serving bowls and serve immediately.

Lemon, chilli & thyme marinated tofu with wild rice

Ingredients

400 g/14 oz firm tofu, drained
1 tbsp chopped fresh thyme
finely grated rind of 1 lemon
1 tsp crushed dried chillies
3 tbsp extra virgin olive oil
300 g/10½ oz wild rice
6 spring onions, sliced diagonally
salt and pepper

1. Place the tofu on a clean tea towel and lightly press to remove as much excess moisture as possible. Cut the tofu into 2-cm/¾-inch thick strips and place in a non-metallic dish.

2. Mix the thyme, lemon rind and chillies with about half the oil and spread over the tofu, gently turning to coat evenly. Cover with clingfilm and leave to marinate in the refrigerator for about 1 hour, or overnight.

3. Cook the rice according to the packet instructions. Drain well.

4. Meanwhile, heat the remaining oil in a wok or large frying pan, add the spring onions and stir-fry for 30 seconds. Remove and reserve the spring onions, add the tofu to the pan and cook for a further 4–5 minutes, turning occasionally, until golden brown.

5. Season to taste with salt and pepper and serve the tofu and reserved spring onions on top of the rice.

#243 Rigatoni with roasted courgettes

Serves 4

Ingredients

4 courgettes, roughly chopped

2½ tbsp olive oil

1 onion, finely chopped

1 garlic clove, crushed

800 g/1 lb 12 oz canned chopped tomatoes

6 sun-dried tomatoes, chopped

225 ml/8 fl oz vegetable stock

½ tsp dried oregano

280 g/10 oz dried rigatoni pasta

125 g/4½ oz mascarpone cheese

salt and pepper

large handful of fresh basil leaves, torn into pieces

1. Preheat the oven to 200°C/400°F/Gas Mark 6. Place the courgettes and 1½ tablespoons of the oil in a large ovenproof dish. Toss together and spread out in a single layer. Roast in the preheated oven for 15–20 minutes until tender and lightly browned.

2. Meanwhile, heat the remaining oil in a saucepan. Add the onion and garlic and cook very gently for 5 minutes until soft. Add the canned tomatoes, sun-dried tomatoes, stock and oregano. Simmer for 10 minutes until the liquid has reduced slightly.

3. Bring a large saucepan of lightly salted water to the boil. Add the rigatoni, bring back to the boil and cook for 11–13 minutes, or until tender but still firm to the bite. Drain, then return to the pan.

4. Add the mascarpone cheese to the hot sauce and stir until melted and smooth. Season well with salt and pepper. Add to the pasta with the courgettes and the basil leaves. Toss together until the pasta is well coated in sauce. Serve immediately.

#244 Bean casserole with potatoes, corn & pumpkin

Serves 4–6

Ingredients

250 g/9 oz dried butter beans

500 g/1 lb 2 oz yellow-fleshed potatoes, peeled and cubed

500 g/1 lb 2 oz pumpkin or butternut squash, deseeded and cubed

500 ml/18 fl oz fresh or frozen sweetcorn kernels

salt and pepper

chopped fresh basil leaves and crumbled feta cheese, to serve

Flavouring salsa

2–3 yellow or red chillies, deseeded and chopped

1 small onion, finely chopped

6 spring onions, finely chopped

2–3 garlic cloves, finely chopped

2 tbsp olive oil

1. Soak the beans in cold water overnight. Drain, rinse and transfer to a large saucepan with enough water to cover by two fingers' width. Do not add salt. Bring to the boil, then reduce the heat and simmer very gently for 1½–2 hours, or until the beans are tender.

2. Meanwhile, put all the flavouring salsa ingredients in a small saucepan and cook over a medium heat, stirring frequently, for 5 minutes. Set aside.

3. When the beans are tender, add the potatoes and pumpkin and top up with enough boiling water to submerge all the ingredients. Return to the boil, then reduce the heat, cover and cook gently for 20–30 minutes, or until the vegetables are tender. Season to taste with salt and pepper.

4. Stir in the sweetcorn kernels and reheat until bubbling. Stir in the flavouring salsa and cook for a further 10 minutes to marry the flavours and reduce the cooking juices. The dish should be juicy but not soupy. Sprinkle with the chopped basil and crumbled cheese and serve.

#245 Courgette, cherry tomato & Brie pasta bake

Serves 4–6

Ingredients

1 small red onion, chopped

3 small courgettes, sliced

2 tbsp olive oil, plus extra for greasing

450 g/1 lb cherry tomatoes, halved

500 g/1 lb 2 oz fresh pasta shapes such as fusilli or riccioli

250 g/9 oz mascarpone

3 tbsp snipped fresh chives, plus extra to garnish

225 g/8 oz mild Brie (weight without rind), rind removed and cheese diced

55 g/2 oz Cheddar cheese, finely grated

salt and pepper

1. Preheat the oven to 190°C/375°F/Gas Mark 5. Grease an ovenproof dish. Put the onion and courgettes in a large roasting tin, drizzle over 1 tablespoon of the oil and toss to coat. Roast in the oven for 15 minutes, stirring once or twice. Reduce the oven temperature to 180°C/350°F/Gas Mark 4. Add the cherry tomatoes to the tin, placing them in a single layer, cut-side up, on top of the vegetables, then drizzle with the remaining oil. Roast for a further 10 minutes, then remove from the oven and set aside.

2. Meanwhile, bring a large saucepan of lightly salted water to the boil, add the pasta and cook for 3–5 minutes or until tender but still firm to the bite. Drain and return to the rinsed pan. Add the mascarpone cheese, chives, and salt and pepper to taste and toss to mix well. Add the roasted vegetables and their juices and gently stir to mix, then gently fold in the Brie.

3. Transfer to the prepared dish. Sprinkle the Cheddar cheese over the top. Bake in the oven for 15–20 minutes or until hot and bubbling. Garnish with chives and serve.

#246 Warm vegetable medley

Serves 4

Ingredients

4 tbsp olive oil

2 celery sticks, sliced

2 red onions, sliced

450 g/1 lb aubergines, diced

1 garlic clove, finely chopped

5 plum tomatoes, chopped

3 tbsp red wine vinegar

1 tbsp sugar

3 tbsp stoned green olives

2 tbsp drained capers

salt and pepper

4 tbsp chopped fresh flat-leaf parsley, to garnish

ciabatta bread, to serve

1. Heat half the oil in a large, heavy-based saucepan. Add the celery and onions and cook over a low heat, stirring occasionally, for 5 minutes, until soft but not coloured. Add the remaining oil and the aubergines. Cook, stirring frequently, for about 5 minutes, until the aubergines begin to colour.

2. Add the garlic, tomatoes, vinegar and sugar and mix well. Cover the mixture with a round of greaseproof paper and simmer gently for about 10 minutes.

3. Remove and discard the greaseproof paper, then stir in the olives and capers. Season to taste with salt and pepper.

4. Tip the mixture into a serving dish and leave to cool slightly. Garnish with the parsley and serve with ciabatta.

#247 Macaroni with chickpeas, herbs & garlic

Serves 4

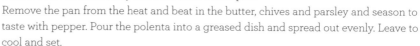

Ingredients

350 g/12 oz dried macaroni

3 tbsp olive oil

1 onion, finely chopped

1 garlic clove, crushed

400 g/14 oz canned chickpeas, drained

4 tbsp passata

2 tbsp chopped fresh oregano

small handful of basil leaves, shredded, plus extra sprigs to garnish

salt and pepper

1. Bring a large saucepan of lightly salted water to the boil. Add the pasta, bring back to the boil and cook for 8–10 minutes, until tender but still firm to the bite. Drain.

2. Meanwhile, heat the oil in a saucepan, add the onion and garlic and fry, stirring occasionally, for 4–5 minutes, until golden.

3. Add the chickpeas and passata to the pan and stir until heated through.

4. Stir the pasta into the pan with the oregano and shredded basil. Season to taste with salt and pepper and serve immediately, garnished with a sprig of basil.

#248 Polenta with tomatoes & garlic sauce

Serves 4

Ingredients

700 ml/1¼ pints vegetable stock

175 g/6 oz quick-cook polenta

25 g/1 oz butter

3 tbsp snipped fresh chives

2 tbsp chopped fresh flat-leaf parsley

2 thick slices of French bread, crusts removed

3 garlic cloves, chopped

115 g/4 oz walnut pieces

3 tbsp lemon juice

7 tbsp olive oil, plus extra for brushing

4 plum tomatoes, sliced

salt and pepper

1. Pour the stock into a large saucepan, bring to the boil and add 1 teaspoon of salt. Add the polenta and cook over a medium heat, stirring constantly, for 5 minutes, until it starts to come away from the sides of the pan. Remove the pan from the heat and beat in the butter, chives and parsley and season to taste with pepper. Pour the polenta into a greased dish and spread out evenly. Leave to cool and set.

2. Tear the bread into pieces and place in a bowl. Cover with cold water and soak for 10 minutes. Put the garlic cloves into a mortar with ½ teaspoon of salt and pound with a pestle to make a paste. Work in the walnuts. Squeeze out the bread, work it into the paste, then work in the lemon juice. Stir in the oil until the sauce is thick and creamy. Transfer to a bowl, cover with clingfilm and set aside.

3. Brush the grill with oil and preheat. Cut the polenta into wedges or rounds. Season the tomatoes with salt and pepper. Place the polenta and tomatoes under the preheated grill and cook for 4–5 minutes. Divide between warmed plates, spoon over the sauce and serve.

#249 Spicy fried eggs

Ingredients

2 tbsp olive oil

1 large onion, finely chopped

2 green or red peppers, deseeded and roughly chopped

1 garlic clove, finely chopped

½ tsp dried chilli flakes

4 plum tomatoes, peeled and roughly chopped

2 eggs

salt and pepper

1. Heat the oil in a large, non-stick frying pan. Add the onion and cook until golden. Add the green peppers, garlic and chilli flakes and cook until the peppers are soft.

2. Stir in the tomatoes and season to taste with salt and pepper. Simmer over a low heat for 10 minutes.

3. Using the back of a spoon, make two depressions in the mixture in the pan. Break the eggs into the depressions, season to taste, cover and cook for 3–4 minutes until set. Serve.

#250 Tofu parcels

Serves 4

Ingredients

2 tbsp olive oil, plus extra for brushing

1 garlic clove, crushed

250 g/9 oz firm tofu, cut into chunks

250 g/9 oz cherry tomatoes, halved

1 small red onion, thinly sliced

handful of fresh basil leaves

salt and pepper

crusty bread, to serve

1. Preheat the oven to 220°C/425°F/Gas Mark 7. Grease 4 x 30-cm/12-inch squares of double-thickness foil Mix the oil with the garlic.

2. Divide the tofu, tomatoes, onion and basil between the foil squares, sprinkle with salt and pepper to taste and spoon over the garlic-flavoured oil.

3. Fold over the foil to enclose the filling and seal. Place on a baking sheet in the preheated oven and cook for 10–15 minutes until heated through.

4. Carefully open the parcels and serve with crusty bread to mop up the juices.

Sweet potato ravioli

Ingredients

Pasta

400 g/14 oz type 00 pasta flour

4 eggs, beaten

semolina, for dusting

Filling

400 g/14 oz sweet potatoes, peeled and cut into chunks

3 tbsp olive oil

1 large onion, finely chopped

1 garlic clove, crushed

1 tsp fresh thyme leaves, chopped

2 tbsp runny honey

salt and pepper

Sage butter

50 g/1¾ oz butter

1 bunch fresh sage leaves finely chopped, reserving a few leaves to garnish

1. To make the pasta, sift the flour into a bowl or food processor. Add the eggs and combine to make a soft but not sticky dough. Dust a surface with semolina and knead the dough for 4–5 minutes until smooth. Cover with clingfilm and refrigerate for at least 30 minutes.

2. To make the filling, bring a large saucepan of lightly salted water to the boil, add the sweet potatoes, bring back to the boil and cook for 20 minutes, or until tender. Drain and mash. Heat the oil in a frying pan over a medium heat, add the onion and cook for 4–5 minutes until soft but not coloured. Stir into the sweet potatoes and add the garlic and thyme. Drizzle with the honey and season to taste with salt and pepper. Set aside.

3. Using a pasta machine, very thinly roll out the dough, then cut it in half. Place teaspoons of filling at intervals across one piece of the pasta. Brush around the filling with water and cover with the remaining piece of pasta. Lightly press around the filling to seal and cut into squares with a sharp knife. Lay the ravioli on a sheet of paper lightly dusted with semolina. Bring a large saucepan of lightly salted water to the boil, drop in the ravioli and cook for 2–3 minutes until it rises to the surface and is tender but still firm to the bite.

4. Meanwhile, melt the butter with the sage in a small saucepan over a low heat. Drain the ravioli and toss with the sage butter. Serve immediately, garnished with sage leaves.

#252 Broccoli, pancetta & blue cheese galette

Ingredients

1 sheet ready-rolled puff pastry

225 g/8 oz small broccoli florets, halved if necessary

125 g/4½ oz diced pancetta

1 small red onion, sliced

100 g/3½ oz Gorgonzola cheese or Roquefort cheese, chopped

pepper

toasted pine nuts, to garnish

1. Preheat the oven to 200°C/400°C/Gas Mark 6. Place the pastry on a baking sheet and lightly score a line all around, cutting only halfway through, to within 1 cm/½ inch of the edge.

2. Bring a saucepan of lightly salted water to the boil, add the broccoli and cook for 4–5 minutes, or until just tender. Drain.

3. Fry the pancetta with the onion, stirring, until golden. Stir in the broccoli and season with pepper. Spread the filling over the pastry, leaving a border. Scatter the cheese over the top.

4. Bake in the preheated oven for 25–30 minutes, until the pastry is risen and golden. Garnish with toasted pine nuts and serve.

#253 Leafy greens, leek & asparagus stir-fry

Ingredients

500 g/1 lb 2 oz mixed leafy greens

225 g/8 oz asparagus

5 tbsp groundnut oil

3-cm/1¼-inch piece fresh ginger, diced

½–1 fresh green or red chilli, deseeded and diced

3 large garlic cloves, thinly sliced

6 baby leeks, sliced into rounds

3–4 tbsp vegetable stock or water

2 tbsp soy sauce

½ tsp salt

small handful fresh coriander leaves

1 tsp sesame seeds

1 tbsp toasted sesame oil

pepper

boiled rice or noodles, to serve

1. Cut away the stalks and large central ribs from the greens. Slice the stalks into 1-cm/½-inch pieces. Stack the leaves and slice into ribbons.

2. Snap off the woody ends from the asparagus and discard. Chop the stems into 2-cm/¾-inch pieces. Leave the tips whole.

3. Heat a large wok over a high heat and add the groundnut oil. When almost smoking, add the ginger, chilli and garlic. Stir-fry for 30 seconds. Add the leeks, asparagus and the chopped stalks from the greens. Add stock to moisten and stir-fry for a further 2 minutes. Add the sliced leaves, soy sauce, salt and a little pepper and stir-fry for 3 minutes.

4. Stir in the coriander, sesame seeds and sesame oil and stir-fry for 30 seconds. Serve immediately with boiled rice.

#254 Falafel burgers

Ingredients

800 g/1 lb 12 oz canned chickpeas, drained

1 small onion, chopped

grated rind and juice of 1 lime

2 tsp ground coriander

2 tsp ground cumin

6 tbsp plain flour

4 tbsp olive oil

salt and pepper

4 sprigs fresh basil, to garnish

tomato salsa, to serve

1. Put the chickpeas, onion, lime rind and juice and the spices into a food processor and process to a coarse paste. Season to taste with salt and pepper.

2. Tip the mixture out onto a clean work surface and shape into 4 patties.

3. Spread out the flour on a large plate and use to coat the patties.

4. Heat the oil in a large frying pan, add the burgers and cook over a medium heat for 2 minutes on each side, or until crisp.

5. Garnish with basil sprigs and serve with tomato salsa.

#255 Bengali vegetable curry

Serves
4

Ingredients

6 tbsp white poppy seeds

3 tbsp black mustard seeds

2 tsp grated fresh ginger

200 g/7 oz fresh bittergourd

2 potatoes, peeled

1 aubergine

1 courgette

1 carrot

4 tbsp vegetable or groundnut oil

2 fresh green chillies, split lengthways

1 tbsp panch phoran

1 tomato, finely chopped

100 g/3½ oz fresh or frozen peas

¼ tsp ground turmeric

2 tsp salt

1 tsp palm sugar

125 ml/4 fl oz milk

1. Soak the white poppy seeds and 2 tablespoons of the mustard seeds in warm water for 1 hour. Drain and blend with the ginger to make a paste. Cut the bittergourd, potatoes, aubergine, courgette and carrot into 1.5-cm/⅝- inch cubes.

2. Heat the oil in a large frying pan and add the remaining mustard seeds and the chillies. When the mustard seeds start to pop, add the panch phoran and all the vegetables. Add 200 ml/7 fl oz water and stir to mix well, then cover tightly and cook, stirring frequently, over a medium heat for 10–12 minutes.

3. Add half the white poppy seed and mustard seed paste, the turmeric and salt. Add more water and cook, stirring frequently, over a low–medium heat for a further 10–15 minutes.

4. Add the remaining white poppy seed and mustard seed paste, the palm sugar and milk and cook for a further 5 minutes, or until the vegetables are tender. Serve hot.

#256 Lentil Bolognese

Serves 6

Ingredients

175 g/6 oz green lentils
2 tbsp olive oil
1 large onion, chopped
2 garlic cloves, crushed
2 carrots, chopped
2 celery sticks, chopped
800 g/1 lb 12 oz canned chopped tomatoes
150 ml/5 fl oz vegetable stock
1 red pepper, deseeded and chopped
2 tbsp tomato purée
2 tsp chopped fresh rosemary
1 tsp dried oregano
280 g/10 oz dried spaghetti
handful of basil leaves, torn
salt and pepper
freshly grated Parmesan cheese, to serve

1. Put the lentils in a saucepan and cover with cold water. Bring to the boil and simmer for 20–30 minutes until just tender. Drain well.

2. Meanwhile, heat the oil in a large saucepan. Add the onion, garlic, carrots and celery. Cover and cook over a low heat for 5 minutes. Stir in the tomatoes, stock, red pepper, tomato purée, rosemary and oregano. Cover and simmer for 20 minutes until the sauce is thickened and the vegetables are tender. Add the lentils and cook, stirring, for a further 5 minutes. Season with salt and pepper.

3. Meanwhile, bring a large saucepan of lightly salted water to the boil. Add the spaghetti, bring back to the boil and cook for 10 minutes, or until tender but still firm to the bite. Drain well, then divide between four warmed bowls. Spoon the sauce over the top and scatter with the basil leaves. Serve immediately with the grated cheese on the side.

#257 Cabbage & walnut stir-fry

Serves 4

Ingredients

4 tbsp groundnut oil
1 tbsp walnut oil
2 garlic cloves, crushed
350 g/12 oz white cabbage, thinly shredded
350 g/12 oz red cabbage, thinly shredded
8 spring onions, trimmed
225 g/8 oz firm tofu, cubed
2 tbsp lemon juice
100 g/3½ oz walnut halves
2 tsp Dijon mustard
salt and pepper
2 tsp poppy seeds, to garnish

1. Preheat a wok. Add the groundnut oil and walnut oil and heat. Add the garlic, white cabbage, red cabbage, spring onions and tofu and cook for 5 minutes, stirring.

2. Add the lemon juice, walnuts and mustard and stir to combine thoroughly.

3. Season the mixture to taste with salt and pepper and cook for a further 5 minutes, or until the cabbage is tender.

4. Transfer the stir-fry to a warmed serving bowl, garnish with poppy seeds and serve immediately.

#258 Vegetable chilli

Ingredients

1 aubergine, cut into 2.5-cm/1-inch slices

1 tbsp olive oil, plus extra for brushing

1 large red onion, finely chopped

2 red peppers, finely chopped

3–4 garlic cloves, finely chopped

800 g/1 lb 12 oz canned chopped tomatoes

1 tbsp mild chilli powder

½ tsp ground cumin

2 small courgettes, sliced

400 g/14 oz canned kidney beans

1 tbsp tomato purée

6 spring onions, finely chopped

115 g/4 oz Cheddar cheese, grated

salt and pepper

1. Brush the aubergine slices on one side with olive oil. Heat half the oil in a large, heavy-based frying pan over a medium–high heat. Add the aubergine slices, oiled-side up, and cook for 5–6 minutes, or until browned on one side. Turn the slices over, cook on the other side until browned and transfer to a plate. Cut into bite-sized pieces.

2. Heat the remaining oil in a saucepan over a medium heat. Add the onion and red peppers and cook, stirring occasionally, for 3–4 minutes. Add the garlic and cook for a further 2–3 minutes. Add the tomatoes, chilli powder and cumin. Season to taste with salt and pepper. Bring just to the boil, reduce the heat, cover and simmer for 15 minutes.

3. Add the courgettes, aubergine pieces and beans. Stir in 450 ml/16 fl oz water and the tomato purée. Bring back to the boil, cover and simmer for 45 minutes, or until the vegetables are tender. Adjust the seasoning. Ladle into serving bowls, top with spring onions and cheese and serve.

#259 Vegetables à la grecque

Ingredients

25 g/1 oz butter

2 tbsp olive oil

1 onion, finely chopped

2 garlic cloves, finely chopped

1 celery stick, finely chopped

500 g/1 lb 2 oz plum tomatoes, peeled, cored and chopped

2 tbsp tomato purée

brown sugar, to taste

150 ml/5 fl oz dry white wine

1 tbsp lemon juice

1 tbsp chopped fresh parsley

8 shallots, trimmed and peeled

225 g/8 oz cauliflower florets

8 button mushrooms

salt and pepper

1. Melt the butter with the oil in a saucepan. Add the onion, garlic and celery and cook over a low heat, stirring occasionally, for 5 minutes until soft. Stir in the tomatoes, tomato purée, sugar to taste, wine, lemon juice and parsley and season to taste with salt and pepper. Increase the heat to medium and bring to the boil, then reduce the heat and simmer, stirring occasionally, for 15–20 minutes, until thickened.

2. Add the shallots and cauliflower and simmer for 10 minutes, then stir in the mushrooms and simmer for a further 5 minutes.

3. Using a slotted spoon, transfer the shallots, cauliflower and mushrooms to a serving dish. Increase the heat to medium–high and cook the sauce, stirring constantly, until reduced and thickened. Remove from the heat and pour it over the vegetables.

4. Leave to cool, then cover and chill in the refrigerator for at least 2 hours before serving.

#260 Tandoori mushroom curry

Serves 4

Ingredients

2 tbsp vegetable or groundnut oil

1 tsp cumin seeds

1 tsp coriander seeds

1 onion, finely chopped

1 tsp ground cumin

6 black peppercorns

½ tsp ground cardamom seeds

1 tsp ground turmeric

1 tbsp tandoori masala

1 fresh red chilli, finely chopped

2 garlic cloves, crushed

2 tsp grated fresh ginger

600 g/1 lb 5 oz chestnut mushrooms

800 g/1 lb 12 oz canned chopped tomatoes

2 tsp salt

200 g/7 oz fresh or frozen peas

1. Heat the oil in a large saucepan over a medium heat. Add the cumin seeds and coriander seeds and cook for 1 minute, or until sizzling.

2. Add the onion, ground cumin, peppercorns, ground cardamom seeds, turmeric, tandoori masala, chilli, garlic and ginger. Cook, stirring, for 2–3 minutes, or until onion is soft and the mixture is aromatic.

3. Slice the mushrooms and add to the pan with the tomatoes and salt. Stir until well combined. Bring to the boil, then reduce the heat to low and cook, uncovered, for 25 minutes.

4. Add the peas and stir to mix well. Cook for a further 4–5 minutes, or until piping hot.

5. Remove from the heat and serve immediately.

#261 Jerusalem artichokes with tomato sauce

Serves 4

Ingredients

450 g/1 lb Jerusalem artichokes, sliced

juice of ½ lemon

Sauce

2 tbsp olive oil

1 large red onion, finely chopped

2 garlic cloves, finely chopped

500 g/1 lb 2 oz baby plum tomatoes, halved

3 sun-dried tomatoes, chopped, or 1 tbsp sun-dried tomato purée

200 ml/7 fl oz dry white wine

salt and pepper

2 tbsp chopped fresh basil leaves, to garnish

1. Put the artichokes into a bowl with the lemon juice, stir to coat, then set aside until ready to cook.

2. To make the sauce, heat the oil in a frying pan, add the onion and cook over a low heat, stirring occasionally, for 5 minutes. Add the garlic and cook for a further 2 minutes. Add the plum tomatoes, sun-dried tomatoes and wine. Season to taste, bring to the boil then reduce the heat and simmer, shaking the pan occasionally, for 10 minutes.

3. Meanwhile, bring a large saucepan of lightly salted water to the boil, add the artichokes and cook for 5–8 minutes, or until tender. Drain and transfer to a warmed serving dish. Top with the tomato mixture and garnish with basil. Serve immediately.

#262 Stilton & mushroom tart

Serves 4

Ingredients

Pastry

280 g/10 oz plain flour, plus extra for dusting

pinch of salt

1 tbsp fresh chopped thyme, or 1 tsp dried thyme

140 g/5 oz butter

3 tbsp cold water

Filling

2 tbsp olive oil

3 shallots, finely chopped

15 g/½ oz butter

350 g/12 oz closed-cup mushrooms, sliced

140 g/5 oz Stilton cheese, crumbled

2 tbsp snipped fresh chives

2 large eggs

200 ml/7 fl oz milk

½ tsp grated nutmeg

salt and pepper

mixed salad, to serve

1. To make the pastry, sift together the flour and salt into a large bowl, add the thyme and rub in the butter using your fingertips. Stir in just enough water to mix to a firm dough. Wrap in clingfilm and chill in the refrigerator for about 10 minutes.

2. Preheat the oven to 200°C/400°F/Gas Mark 6. Roll out the pastry on a lightly floured surface and use to line a 23-cm/9-inch round, loose-based flan tin. Line with baking paper and fill with baking beans, then place on a baking sheet and bake blind in the preheated oven for about 10 minutes. Remove the paper and beans and bake for a further 5 minutes. Reduce the oven temperature to 180°C/350°F/Gas Mark 4.

3. Meanwhile, to make the filling, heat the oil in a frying pan over a medium heat, add the shallots and gently fry for 3–4 minutes, stirring frequently, until soft not brown. Add the butter, then add the mushrooms and fry, stirring frequently, until soft and any liquid has evaporated. Spoon into the pastry case and top with the cheese and chives.

4. Beat together the eggs, milk, nutmeg, and salt and pepper to taste, then pour the mixture over the filling. Bake the tart for 20–25 minutes, or until golden brown and just set.

5. Remove from the oven and leave to cool slightly in the tin, then remove from the tin and serve warm or cold, with a mixed salad.

#263 Roasted squash with risotto & asparagus

Serves 4

Ingredients

200 g/7 oz acorn squash, peeled, deseeded and cut into 4 wedges

1 tsp vegetable oil

100 g/3½ oz onion, finely chopped

1 tsp crushed garlic

70 g/2½ oz three-grain risotto mix

600 ml/1 pint vegetable stock

235 g/8¼ oz asparagus tips

2 tbsp finely chopped fresh marjoram, plus extra to garnish

3 tbsp low-fat fromage frais

2 tbsp finely chopped parsley

pepper

1. Preheat the oven to 200°C/400°F/Gas Mark 6. Spread out the squash wedges on a non-stick baking tray and roast in the oven for 20 minutes, or until tender. Meanwhile, heat the oil in a medium saucepan over a high heat, add the onion and garlic and cook, stirring, until softened but not coloured. Add the risotto mix and stir in half the stock. Simmer, stirring occasionally, until the stock has reduced in the pan. Pour in the remaining stock and continue to cook, stirring occasionally, until the grains are tender.

2. Cut 175 g/6 oz of the asparagus into 10-cm/4-inch lengths and blanch in a saucepan of boiling water for 2 minutes. Drain and keep warm. Cut the remaining asparagus into 5-mm/¼-inch slices and add to the risotto for the last 3 minutes of the cooking time.

3. Remove the risotto from the heat and stir in the marjoram, fromage frais and parsley. Season with pepper. To serve, lay the squash wedges on warmed serving plates, then spoon over the risotto and top with the asparagus. Garnish with marjoram.

#264 Kale pesto & spaghetti

Serves 4

Ingredients

225 g/8 oz kale

450 g/1 lb dried spaghetti

40 g/1½ oz toasted pine nuts

1 large garlic clove

1 lemon

125 ml/4 fl oz olive oil

30 g/1 oz grated Parmesan cheese, plus extra to garnish

400 g/14 oz canned cannellini beans

2 tbsp chia seeds, to garnish

salt

1. Bring a large saucepan of lightly salted water to the boil and fill a medium-sized bowl with iced water. Trim the stems and centre ribs from the kale and blanch the leaves in the boiling water for 45 seconds. Using a slotted spoon, transfer the kale to the iced water. Bring the salted water back to the boil. Drain the kale, place it in a clean tea towel and squeeze to remove any excess water.

2. Add the pasta to the boiling water and cook for 8–10 minutes, until tender but still firm to the bite. Meanwhile, combine the kale, pine nuts, garlic and ¾ teaspoon of salt in a food processor. Zest the lemon into the bowl of the processor, then halve the lemon and squeeze in the juice of one half. Pulse until smooth. With the motor running, drizzle in the oil until it is fully incorporated. Add the cheese and pulse until incorporated.

3. Drain and rinse the beans, then toss into the pasta. Immediately drain the pasta, reserving some of the cooking water. Toss the pasta and beans with the pesto. Add a little of the reserved cooking water if needed to coat the pasta nicely. Serve immediately with a generous dusting of cheese and a sprinkling of chia seeds.

#265 Couscous with cherry tomatoes & pine nuts

Serves 4

Ingredients

300 g/10½ oz cherry tomatoes

3 tbsp olive oil

125 g/4½ oz couscous

200 ml/7 fl oz boiling water

30 g/1 oz pine nuts, toasted

5 tbsp roughly chopped fresh mint

finely grated rind of 1 lemon

½ tbsp lemon juice

salt and pepper

crisp green salad and feta cheese, to serve

1. Preheat the oven to 220°C/425°F/Gas Mark 7. Place the tomatoes and 1 tablespoon of the oil in an ovenproof dish. Toss together, then roast for 7–8 minutes in the preheated oven until the tomatoes are soft and the skins have burst. Leave to stand for 5 minutes.

2. Put the couscous in a heatproof bowl. Pour over the boiling water, cover and leave to stand for 8–10 minutes, until soft and the liquid has been absorbed. Fluff up the couscous with a fork. Add the tomatoes and their juices, the pine nuts, mint, lemon rind, lemon juice and the remaining oil. Season to taste with salt and pepper, then gently toss together.

3. Serve the couscous warm or cold, with a green salad and some feta cheese.

#266 Asparagus gratin

Serves 4–6

Ingredients

butter, for greasing

1 kg/2 lb 4 oz asparagus spears

pinch of sugar

100 g/3½ oz fontina cheese, sliced

50 g/1¾ oz Parmesan cheese, grated

100 ml/3½ fl oz double cream

salt and pepper

1. Preheat the oven to 240°C/475°F/Gas Mark 9. Grease a large baking dish.

2. Wash the asparagus, then cut off and discard the woody ends. Bring a large saucepan of lightly salted water to the boil. Add the asparagus and sugar, bring back to the boil and simmer for about 15 minutes, until tender but still firm to the bite. Drain.

3. Transfer the asparagus to the prepared baking dish. Place the fontina cheese on top, sprinkle over the Parmesan cheese and pour over the cream. Bake in the preheated oven for 8 minutes, until the topping is golden brown. Sprinkle with pepper and serve immediately.

#267 Macaroni cheese

Ingredients

250 g/9 oz dried macaroni pasta

55 g/2 oz butter, plus extra for cooking the pasta

600 ml/1 pint milk

½ tsp grated nutmeg

55 g/2 oz plain flour

200 g/7 oz mature Cheddar cheese, grated

55 g/2 oz freshly grated Parmesan cheese

200 g/7 oz baby spinach

salt and pepper

1. Cook the macaroni according to the instructions on the packet. Remove from the heat, drain, add a small knob of butter to keep it soft, return to the saucepan and cover to keep warm.

2. Put the milk and nutmeg into a saucepan over a low heat and heat until warm, but do not boil. Put the butter into a heavy-based saucepan over a low heat, melt the butter, add the flour and stir to make a roux. Cook gently for 2 minutes. Add the milk a little at a time, whisking it into the roux, then cook for about 10–15 minutes to make a loose, custard-style sauce. Add three quarters of the Cheddar cheese and Parmesan cheese and stir through until they have melted in, then add the spinach, season with salt and pepper and remove from the heat.

3. Preheat the grill to high. Put the macaroni into a shallow heatproof dish, then pour the sauce over. Scatter the remaining cheese over the top and place under the preheated grill. Grill until the cheese begins to brown, then serve.

#268 Tofu steak with fennel & orange

Ingredients

350 g/12 oz extra firm tofu, drained

1 tbsp harissa paste

2 tsp extra virgin olive oil

1 large orange

1 fennel bulb, very thinly sliced

1 small red onion, thinly sliced

8 stoned black olives, halved

chopped fresh mint, to garnish

1. Preheat the grill to high. Place the tofu on a clean tea towel and press lightly to remove any excess moisture.

2. Cut the tofu into 4 thick triangles. Mix the harissa with the oil. Brush this mixture over the tofu.

3. Lift the tofu steaks onto a baking sheet and cook under the preheated grill for 6–8 minutes, turning once, until golden brown.

4. Meanwhile, use a sharp knife to cut all the rind and white pith from the orange and carefully remove the segments from the membranes, catching the juice in a bowl.

5. Place the orange segments, fennel, onion and olives in bowl. Mix thoroughly to combine and then divide the mixture between four serving plates.

6. Place the tofu steaks on top, drizzle with the reserved orange juice and garnish with chopped fresh mint to serve.

Potato gnocchi with walnut pesto

Serves 4

Ingredients

450 g/1 lb floury potatoes, washed

55 g/2 oz freshly grated Parmesan cheese

1 egg, beaten

200 g/7 oz plain flour, plus extra for dusting

salt and pepper

Pesto

40 g/1½ oz fresh flat-leaf parsley, chopped

2 tbsp capers, rinsed and chopped

2 garlic cloves, chopped

175 ml/6 fl oz extra virgin olive oil

70 g/2½ oz walnut pieces

40 g/1½ oz freshly grated Parmesan cheese

salt and pepper

1. Bring a saucepan of lightly salted water to the boil. Add the potatoes, bring back to the boil and cook for 30–35 minutes, until tender. Drain and leave to cool.

2. Meanwhile, to make the pesto, put the parsley, capers and garlic into a mortar with the oil, walnuts, and salt and pepper to taste. Pound to a coarse paste using a pestle. Add the cheese and stir well.

3. Peel off the potato skins and pass the flesh through a sieve into a large bowl. Season with salt and pepper and add the cheese. Beat in the egg and sift in the flour. Lightly mix together, then turn out onto a lightly floured work surface. Lightly knead until smooth. Using your hands, roll out on a lightly floured surface into a long log. Cut into 2.5-cm/1-inch pieces and gently press with a fork. Transfer to a floured baking sheet and cover with a clean tea towel.

4. Bring a large saucepan of water to the boil, add the gnocchi, in small batches, and cook for 1–2 minutes. Remove with a slotted spoon and transfer to a warmed dish to keep warm while you cook the remaining gnocchi. Serve on warmed plates, topped with the pesto.

Vegetable cannelloni

Serves 4

Ingredients

12 dried cannelloni tubes

olive oil, for brushing and frying

1 aubergine, diced

225 g/8 oz spinach

2 garlic cloves, crushed

1 tsp ground cumin

85 g/3 oz mushrooms, chopped

1 onion, chopped

2 garlic cloves, crushed

800 g/1 lb 12 oz canned chopped tomatoes

1 tsp caster sugar

2 tbsp chopped fresh basil

55 g/2 oz mozzarella cheese, sliced

salt and pepper

lamb's lettuce, to garnish

1. Preheat the oven to 190°C/375°F/Gas Mark 5. Bring a large heavy-based saucepan of lightly salted water to the boil. Add the cannelloni tubes, return to the boil and cook for 8–10 minutes, or until tender but still firm to the bite. Transfer to a plate and pat dry with kitchen paper. Brush a large ovenproof dish with oil.

2. Heat some oil in a frying pan over a medium heat. Add the aubergine and cook, stirring frequently, for about 2–3 minutes, adding more oil if needed. Add the spinach, garlic, cumin and mushrooms and reduce the heat. Season to taste with salt and pepper and cook, stirring, for about 2–3 minutes. Spoon into the cannelloni tubes and put into the dish in a single layer.

3. Heat some oil in a saucepan over a medium heat. Add the onion and garlic and cook for 1 minute. Add the tomatoes, sugar and basil and bring to the boil. Reduce the heat and simmer for about 5 minutes. Spoon over the cannelloni tubes. Arrange the mozzarella cheese on top and bake in the preheated oven for about 30 minutes, or until golden brown and bubbling. Serve garnished with lamb's lettuce.

#271 Courgette, pepper & tomato gratin

Serves
4–6

Ingredients

25 g/1 oz butter

2 tbsp olive oil

1 onion, thinly sliced

2 garlic cloves, finely chopped

1 celery stick, finely chopped

700 g/1 lb 9 oz courgettes, sliced

2 large red peppers, deseeded and sliced

400 g/14 oz canned chopped tomatoes

2 tbsp tomato purée

brown sugar, to taste

1 tbsp chopped fresh basil

1 bay leaf

100 ml/3½ fl oz water

6 canned anchovy fillets, drained and chopped

55 g/2 oz freshly grated Parmesan cheese

salt and pepper

1. Melt the butter with the oil in a large saucepan. Add the onion, garlic, celery, courgettes and red peppers and cook over a low heat, stirring occasionally, for 5 minutes, until soft.

2. Stir in the tomatoes, tomato purée, sugar to taste, basil, bay leaf and water and season to taste with salt and pepper. Increase the heat to medium and bring to the boil, then reduce the heat and simmer, stirring occasionally, for 30 minutes, until thickened and the vegetables are tender.

3. Meanwhile, preheat the grill. Remove and discard the bay leaf and spoon the vegetable mixture into a flameproof dish. Sprinkle with the anchovies and cheese and cook under the preheated grill for 3–5 minutes, until the top is golden brown and bubbling. Serve immediately.

#272 Parsnip & tomato casserole

Serves 4

Ingredients

3 tbsp olive oil

600 g/1 lb 5 oz parsnips, peeled and thinly sliced

1 tsp fresh thyme leaves

1 tsp caster sugar

300 ml/10 fl oz double cream

600 g/1 lb 5 oz tomatoes, thinly sliced

1 tsp dried oregano

150 g/5½ oz Cheddar cheese, grated

salt and pepper

1. Preheat the oven to 180°C/350°F/Gas Mark 4.

2. Heat the oil in a frying pan over a medium heat, add the parsnips, thyme, sugar and salt and pepper to taste and cook, stirring frequently, for 6–8 minutes until golden and soft.

3. Spread half the parsnips over the base of a gratin dish. Pour over half the cream, then arrange half the tomatoes in an even layer across the parsnips. Season to taste with salt and pepper and scatter over half the oregano. Sprinkle over half the cheese. Top with the remaining parsnips and tomatoes. Sprinkle with the remaining oregano, season to taste with salt and pepper and pour over the remaining cream. Scatter over the remaining cheese.

4. Cover with foil and bake in the preheated oven for 40 minutes, or until the parsnips are tender. Remove the foil and return to the oven for a further 5–10 minutes until the top is golden and bubbling. Serve.

#273 Potato & red onion pie

Serves 6

Ingredients

butter, for greasing

750 g/1 lb 10 oz potatoes, peeled and thinly sliced

2 spring onions, finely chopped

1 red onion, finely chopped

150 ml/5 fl oz double cream

500 g/1 lb 2 oz fresh ready-made puff pastry

2 eggs, beaten

salt and pepper

1. Preheat the oven to 200°C/400°F/Gas Mark 6. Lightly grease a baking tray. Bring a saucepan of water to the boil, add the sliced potatoes, bring back to the boil and then simmer for a few minutes. Drain the potato slices and leave to cool. Dry off any excess moisture with kitchen paper. Mix the spring onions, red onion and the cooled potato slices together. Stir in 2 tablespoons of the cream and season well with salt and pepper.

2. Divide the pastry in half and roll out one piece to a 23-cm/9-inch round. Roll the remaining pastry to a 25-cm/10-inch round. Place the smaller round on the baking tray and top with the potato mixture, leaving a 2.5-cm/1-inch border. Brush the border with a little beaten egg. Top with the larger round of pastry, seal well and crimp the edges of the pastry. Cut a steam vent in the middle of the pastry and, using the back of a knife, mark with a pattern. Brush with some of the beaten egg and bake in the preheated oven for 30 minutes. Mix the remaining beaten egg with the remaining cream and pour into the pie through the steam vent. Return to the oven for 15 minutes. Leave to cool for 30 minutes. Serve warm or cold.

177

#274 Mushroom stroganoff

Ingredients

25 g/1 oz butter

1 onion, finely chopped

450 g/1 lb closed-cup mushrooms, quartered

1 tsp tomato purée

1 tsp wholegrain mustard

150 ml/5 fl oz crème fraîche

1 tsp paprika, plus extra to garnish

salt and pepper

fresh flat-leaf parsley sprigs, to garnish

1. Heat the butter in a large, heavy-based frying pan. Add the onion and cook gently for 5–10 minutes until soft.

2. Add the mushrooms to the pan and stir-fry for a few minutes until they begin to soften.

3. Stir in the tomato purée and mustard, then add the crème fraîche. Cook gently, stirring constantly, for 5 minutes.

4. Stir in the paprika and season to taste with salt and pepper.

5. Garnish with paprika and parsley sprigs and serve immediately.

#275 Aubergine tagine with polenta

Ingredients

1 aubergine, diced

3 tbsp olive oil

1 large onion, thinly sliced

1 carrot, diced

2 garlic cloves, chopped

115 g/4 oz mushrooms, sliced

2 tsp ground coriander

2 tsp cumin seeds

1 tsp chilli powder

1 tsp ground turmeric

600 ml/1 pint canned chopped tomatoes

1.5 litres/2¾ pints hot vegetable stock

70 g/2½ oz dried apricots, chopped

400 g/14 oz canned chickpeas,

200 g/7 oz quick-cook polenta

2 tbsp coriander, to garnish

1. Preheat the grill to medium. Toss the aubergine in 1 tablespoon of the oil and arrange in the grill pan. Cook under the preheated grill for 20 minutes, turning occasionally, until soft and beginning to blacken around the edges – brush with more oil if the aubergine becomes too dry.

2. Heat the remaining oil in a heavy-based saucepan over a medium heat. Add the onion and fry, for 8 minutes, or until soft and golden. Add the carrot, garlic and mushrooms and cook for 5 minutes. Add the spices and cook, stirring constantly, for a further minute. Add the tomatoes and 300 ml/10 fl oz of the stock and bring to the boil. Reduce the heat and simmer for 10 minutes, or until the sauce begins to thicken and reduce. Add the aubergine, apricots and chickpeas, partially cover and cook for a further 10 minutes, stirring occasionally.

3. Meanwhile, pour the remaining stock into a large saucepan and bring to the boil. Pour in the polenta in a steady stream, stirring constantly with a wooden spoon. Reduce the heat to low and cook for 1–2 minutes, or until the polenta thickens to a mashed potato-like consistency. Serve the tagine with the polenta, sprinkled with the fresh coriander.

#276 Bean & tomato casserole with Parmesan toasts

Serves 4

Ingredients

4 tbsp extra virgin olive oil, plus extra for drizzling

25 g/1 oz butter

1 large onion, thinly sliced

15–20 fresh sage leaves, sliced

2 large garlic cloves, thinly sliced

1 tbsp tomato purée

800 g/1 lb 12 oz canned chopped tomatoes

350 g/12 oz canned borlotti beans, drained and rinsed

300 ml/10 fl oz vegetable stock

4 tbsp chopped fresh flat-leaf parsley

50 g/1¾ oz grated Parmesan cheese

8 thin slices ciabatta, toasted

sea salt and pepper

small fresh sage sprigs, to garnish

1. Heat the oil and butter in a large saucepan over a medium heat. Add the onion and sage and fry for 5 minutes, until the onion is translucent. Add the garlic and fry for 2 minutes, until just coloured. Add the tomato purée and fry for 1 minute, stirring.

2. Stir in the tomatoes, beans and stock and season with salt and pepper. Bring to the boil, then reduce the heat and simmer, partially covered, for 20 minutes. Add the parsley and half the cheese.

3. Ladle the beans into warmed bowls. Top each plate with 2 slices of toasted ciabatta. Drizzle the bread with oil and sprinkle over the remaining cheese. Garnish with sage sprigs and serve immediately.

#277 Butternut squash & lentil stew

Serves 4

Ingredients

1 tbsp olive oil

1 onion, diced

3 garlic cloves, finely chopped

2 tbsp tomato purée

2 tsp ground cumin

1 tsp ground cinnamon

1 tsp salt

¼ tsp cayenne pepper

450 g/1 lb butternut squash, diced

100 g/3½ oz brown lentils

450 ml/16 fl oz vegetable stock

1 tbsp lemon juice

2 tbsp finely chopped coriander and 2 tbsp flaked almonds, to garnish

4 tbsp natural yogurt, to serve

1. Heat the oil in a large saucepan over a medium–high heat. Add the onion and garlic and cook, stirring occasionally, for about 5 minutes or until soft.

2. Add the tomato purée, cumin, cinnamon, salt and cayenne and give it a quick stir. Add the squash, lentils and stock and bring to the boil. Reduce the heat to low and simmer, uncovered, stirring occasionally, for about 25 minutes until the squash and lentils are tender.

3. Just before serving, stir in the lemon juice. Serve hot with the yogurt and a sprinkling of the coriander and almonds.

#278 Baked root vegetable & rosemary cake

Serves 4

Ingredients

olive oil, for greasing

300 g/10½ oz parsnips, roughly grated

300 g/10½ oz carrots, roughly grated

300 g/10½ oz celeriac, roughly grated

1 onion, roughly grated

2 tbsp chopped fresh rosemary

3 tbsp lemon juice

salt and pepper

rosemary sprigs, to garnish

1. Preheat the oven to 190°C/375°F/Gas Mark 5. Grease a 20-cm/8-inch springform cake tin and line with baking paper. Place the parsnip, carrot and celeriac in separate, small bowls.

2. Mix together the onion, rosemary and lemon juice in a small bowl. Add a third of the onion mixture to each vegetable bowl, season to taste with salt and pepper, and stir to mix evenly. Spoon the parsnips into the prepared tin, spreading evenly and pressing down lightly. Top with the carrots, press lightly, then add the celeriac. Top the cake with a piece of lightly oiled kitchen foil and press down to condense the contents. Tuck the foil over the edges of the tin to seal. Place on a baking sheet and bake in the preheated oven for 1 hour, or until tender.

3. Remove the foil and turn out the cake onto a warmed plate. Leave to cool for 5 minutes and then slice and serve, garnished with rosemary sprigs.

#279 Potato & lemon casserole

Serves 4

Ingredients

100 ml/3½ fl oz olive oil

2 red onions, cut into 8 wedges

3 garlic cloves, crushed

2 tsp ground cumin

2 tsp ground coriander

pinch of cayenne pepper

1 carrot, thickly sliced

2 small turnips, quartered

1 courgette, sliced

500 g/1 lb 2 oz potatoes, thickly sliced

juice and grated rind of 2 large lemons

300 ml/10 fl oz vegetable stock

2 tbsp chopped fresh coriander

salt and pepper

1. Heat the oil in a flameproof casserole. Add the onions and sauté over a medium heat, stirring frequently, for 3 minutes.

2. Add the garlic and cook for 30 seconds. Stir in the ground cumin, ground coriander and cayenne pepper and cook, stirring constantly, for 1 minute.

3. Add the carrot, turnips, courgette and potatoes and stir to coat in the oil.

4. Add the lemon juice and rind and the stock. Season to taste with salt and pepper. Cover and cook over a medium heat, stirring occasionally, for 20–30 minutes until tender.

5. Remove the lid, sprinkle in the chopped fresh coriander and stir well. Serve immediately.

#280 Pasta & broccoli gratin

Serves 4

Ingredients

butter, for greasing

250 g/9 oz dried fusilli pasta

450 g/1 lb purple sprouting broccoli

6 tbsp olive oil, plus extra for drizzling

2 shallots, thinly sliced

1 fresh red chilli, deseeded and finely chopped

2 garlic cloves, finely chopped

70 g/2½ oz coarse fresh breadcrumbs (from a ciabatta loaf)

55 g/2 oz roughly grated Parmesan cheese

salt and pepper

1. Preheat the oven to 200°C/400°F/Gas Mark 6. Butter a high-sided 2.5-litre/4½-pint baking dish. Bring a pan of lightly salted water to the boil over a medium heat. Add the pasta and cook for 8–10 minutes, or until tender but still firm to the bite. Drain thoroughly and tip into the baking dish.

2. Meanwhile, steam the broccoli florets, leaves and stems for 4 minutes until just tender. Remove from the heat and set aside, reserving the water in the pan.

3. Heat a frying pan over medium–low heat. Add the oil and the shallots, chilli and garlic and gently fry for 5 minutes until soft and just starting to colour. Add the broccoli and 150 ml/ 5 fl oz of the broccoli cooking water to the dish. Season to taste with salt and pepper and toss to mix. Add the shallot mixture and the oil from the pan. Toss again to mix.

4. Scatter the breadcrumbs over the top, then sprinkle with the cheese and a little more salt and pepper. Drizzle the crumbs with more oil. Bake in the oven for 15–20 minutes until golden and crisp.

#281 Umbrian-style lentils with artichokes

Serves 4

Ingredients

200 g/7 oz Puy lentils

2 tbsp olive oil

2 celery sticks, chopped

2 leeks, sliced

1 garlic clove, crushed

55 g/2 oz sun-dried tomatoes, chopped

2 tbsp chopped fresh sage

1 tbsp chopped fresh rosemary

500 ml/18 fl oz ham or vegetable stock

280 g/10 oz bottled artichoke hearts, drained

salt and pepper

1. Place the lentils in a pan and cover with boiling water. Bring to the boil and boil for 10 minutes. Drain and set aside.

2. Heat the oil in a large saucepan , add the celery and leeks and fry for 2–3 minutes, until soft but not brown. Stir in the garlic, sun-dried tomatoes, sage and rosemary.

3. Add the cooked lentils, the stock and salt and pepper to taste, then bring the boil. Reduce the heat, cover and simmer gently for 25–30 minutes, or until the lentils are tender.

4. Stir in the artichokes and heat gently for 2–3 minutes. Serve immediately.

#282 Kale, sweet potato & peanut stew

Serves 4

Ingredients

2 tbsp olive oil

1 large onion, sliced

1 garlic clove, crushed

2 tsp ground coriander

1 tsp ground cumin

400 g/14 oz sweet potatoes,
cut into 2-cm/¾-inch chunks

400 g/14 oz canned chopped tomatoes

2 bay leaves

300 ml/10 fl oz vegetable stock

140 g/5 oz crunchy peanut butter

200 g/7 oz curly kale, thickly sliced

salt and pepper

55 g/2 oz salted peanuts, lightly toasted,
to garnish

crusty bread, to serve

1. Heat the oil in a large saucepan over a medium heat, add the onion and fry, stirring occasionally, for about 5 minutes, until soft but not brown. Stir in the garlic, coriander and cumin and gently fry, stirring, for about 30 seconds.

2. Stir in the sweet potatoes, tomatoes, bay leaves and stock and bring to the boil. Reduce the heat to low, cover with a lid and simmer gently for 15–20 minutes, until the potatoes are tender.

3. Stir in the peanut butter and season to taste with salt and pepper. Stir in the kale, cover and simmer for a further 5–6 minutes, stirring occasionally, until just tender.

4. Spoon into a serving dish and scatter with toasted peanuts. Serve hot, with crusty bread.

Courgette & cheese gratin

Ingredients

55 g/2 oz butter, plus extra for greasing

6 courgettes, sliced

2 tbsp chopped fresh tarragon or a mixture of fresh mint, tarragon and flat-leaf parsley

200 g/7 oz Gruyère cheese or Parmesan cheese, grated

125 ml/4 fl oz milk

125 ml/4 fl oz double cream

2 eggs, beaten

freshly grated nutmeg

salt and pepper

1. Preheat the oven to 180°C/350°F/Gas Mark 4. Grease a large baking dish.

2. Melt the butter in a large sauté pan or frying pan over a medium-high heat. Add the courgettes and sauté for 4–6 minutes, turning the slices over occasionally, until coloured on both sides. Remove from the pan and drain on kitchen paper, then season to taste with salt and pepper.

3. Spread half the courgettes over the base of the prepared dish. Sprinkle with half of the herbs and 85 g/3 oz of the cheese. Repeat these layers once more.

4. Mix the milk, cream and eggs together in a jug and add nutmeg and salt and pepper to taste. Pour this liquid over the courgettes, then sprinkle the top with the remaining cheese. Bake in the preheated oven for 35–45 minutes, or until set in the centre and golden brown. Remove from the oven and leave to stand for 5 minutes before serving straight from the dish.

Pumpkin & Gruyère stew

Ingredients

1 large pumpkin

300 ml/10 fl oz double cream

3 garlic cloves, thinly sliced

1 tbsp fresh thyme leaves

125 g/4½ oz Gruyère cheese, grated

salt and pepper

crusty bread, to serve

1. Preheat the oven to 180°C/350°F/Gas Mark 4.

2. Cut horizontally straight through the top quarter of the pumpkin to form a lid. Scoop out the seeds. Put the pumpkin in a large, deep ovenproof dish. Heat the cream and garlic in a saucepan until just below boiling point. Remove from the heat, season to taste with salt and pepper and stir in the thyme. Pour into the pumpkin and pop the lid on top.

3. Bake in the preheated oven for 1 hour, or until the flesh is tender – the exact cooking time will depend on the size of the pumpkin. Take care not to overcook the pumpkin, or it may collapse. Remove from the oven, lift off the lid and scatter over the Gruyère cheese. Return to the oven and bake for a further 10 minutes.

4. Serve the soft pumpkin flesh with a generous portion of the cheesy cream and some crusty bread.

#285 Aubergine gratin

Serves 2

Ingredients

4 tbsp olive oil

2 onions, finely chopped

2 garlic cloves, very finely chopped

2 aubergines, thickly sliced

3 tbsp chopped fresh flat-leaf parsley, plus extra sprigs to garnish

½ tsp dried thyme

400 g/14 oz canned chopped tomatoes

175 g/6 oz mozzarella cheese, coarsely grated

6 tbsp freshly grated Parmesan cheese

salt and pepper

1. Heat the oil in a flameproof casserole over a medium heat. Add the onions and cook for 5 minutes, or until soft.

2. Add the garlic and cook for a few seconds, or until just beginning to colour. Using a slotted spoon, transfer the onion mixture to a plate. Add the aubergine slices to the casserole in batches and cook until lightly browned. Transfer to a separate plate.

3. Preheat the oven to 200°C/400°F/Gas Mark 6. Arrange a layer of aubergine slices in the base of the casserole. Sprinkle with some of the parsley, thyme, and salt and pepper to taste.

4. Add layers of onion, tomatoes and mozzarella cheese, sprinkling parsley, thyme, and salt and pepper to taste over each layer. Continue layering, finishing with a layer of aubergine slices. Sprinkle with the Parmesan cheese and bake, uncovered, in the preheated oven for 20–30 minutes, or until the top is golden and the aubergines are tender. Serve hot, garnished with parsley sprigs.

#286 French bean casserole

Serves 4–6

Ingredients

500 g/1 lb 2 oz French beans, cut into 4-cm/1½-inch lengths

300 ml/10 fl oz canned condensed mushroom soup

225 ml/8 fl oz milk

1 tsp soy sauce

1 tbsp corn oil

15 g/½ oz butter

1 onion, sliced into rings

salt

1. Preheat the oven to 180°C/350°F/Gas Mark 4. Bring a saucepan of lightly salted water to the boil , add the beans. Bring back to the boil and cook for 5 minutes. Drain well.

2. Put the soup, milk and soy sauce into a bowl and mix together, then stir in the beans. Tip into a 1.4-litre/2½-pint casserole and distribute evenly. Bake in the preheated oven for 25-30 minutes, until bubbling and golden.

3. Meanwhile, heat the oil and butter in a frying pan, add the onion rings and fry over a fairly high heat, stirring frequently, until golden brown and crisp. Remove and drain on absorbent kitchen paper.

4. Arrange the onion rings on top of the casserole and bake for a further 5 minutes. Serve hot.

#287 Squash, kale & farro stew

Serves 6

Ingredients

1 large dense-fleshed squash

2 tbsp vegetable oil

1 onion, finely chopped

2 tsp dried oregano

2 garlic cloves, finely sliced

400 g/14 oz canned chopped tomatoes

700 ml/1¼ pints vegetable stock

125 g/4½ oz quick-cook farro, rinsed

250 g/9 oz kale, sliced into ribbons

400 g/14 oz canned chickpeas

6 tbsp chopped fresh coriander

juice of 1 lime

salt and pepper

1. Cut the squash into quarters, peel and deseed. Cut the flesh into large cubes (you will need about 650 g/1 lb 7 oz).

2. Heat the oil in a flameproof casserole or heavy-based saucepan. Add the onion and fry over a medium heat for 5 minutes, until translucent. Add the oregano and garlic and fry for 2 minutes. Add the squash and cook, covered, for 10 minutes.

3. Add the tomatoes, stock and farro, cover and bring to the boil. Reduce the heat to a gentle simmer and cook for 20 minutes, stirring occasionally. Add the kale and chickpeas. Cook for a further 15 minutes, or until the kale is just tender.

4. Season to taste with salt and pepper. Stir in the coriander and lime juice just before serving.

#288 Courgette Flatbread Pizza

Serves 4

Ingredients

50 g/1¾ oz crème fraîche

150 g/5½ oz courgettes, shredded into ribbons using a carrot peeler

55 g/2 oz cherry tomatoes, quartered

50 g/1¾ oz ricotta

1 garlic clove, crushed

2 tbsp olive oil

Pizza bases

100 g/3½ oz wholemeal plain flour, plus extra to dust

50 g/1¾ oz quinoa flour

¾ tsp bicarbonate of soda

1 tbsp olive oil

2 tbsp warm water

sea salt

1. Preheat the oven to 200°C/400°F/Gas Mark 6. To make the pizza bases, put the flours and bicarbonate of soda in a mixing bowl, season with salt and stir. Add the oil, then gradually mix in enough of the warm water to make a soft but not sticky dough.

2. Lightly dust a work surface with flour. Knead the dough on the surface for 2 minutes, or until smooth and slightly elastic.

3. Put a large, flat baking sheet in the oven to get hot.

4. Divide the dough into two pieces. Roll out the first piece to a rough 5-mm/⅕-inch thick circle. Remove the hot baking sheet from the oven and, working quickly, lay the dough on top. Spread half the crème fraîche over the dough, then scatter with half the courgettes and tomatoes. Add half the ricotta in small dollops on top and return the pizza to the oven.

5. Bake for 7–10 minutes, or until the crust is crispy and slightly puffed up, and the ricotta is tinged golden.

186

6. Meanwhile, quickly repeat to construct and cook the second pizza. Mix the garlic and oil together in a jug, and drizzle over the pizzas. Serve immediately.

#289 Chilli bean stew

Ingredients

2 tbsp olive oil

1 onion, chopped

2–4 garlic cloves, chopped

2 fresh red chillies, deseeded and sliced

225 g/8 oz canned kidney beans

225 g/8 oz canned cannellini beans

225 g/8 oz canned chickpeas

1 tbsp tomato purée

850 ml/1½ pints vegetable stock

1 red pepper, deseeded and chopped

4 tomatoes, chopped

175 g/6 oz shelled fresh broad beans

1 tbsp chopped fresh coriander, plus extra to garnish

paprika, to garnish

soured cream, to serve

1. Heat the oil in a large, heavy-based saucepan with a tight-fitting lid. Add the onion, garlic and chillies and cook, stirring frequently, for 5 minutes until soft.

2. Drain and rinse the kidney beans, cannellini beans and chickpeas and add to the pan. Blend the tomato purée with a little of the stock and pour over the bean mixture, then add the remaining stock.

3. Bring to the boil, then reduce the heat and simmer for 10–15 minutes. Add the red pepper, tomatoes and broad beans.

4. Simmer for a further 15–20 minutes or until all the vegetables are tender. Stir in most of the chopped coriander.

5. Garnish with the remaining coriander and a pinch of paprika and serve topped with spoonfuls of soured cream.

#290 Tofu moussaka

Ingredients

140 g/5 oz baking potatoes, scrubbed

4 tbsp lemon juice

1 tsp rapeseed or vegetable oil

1 tsp sugar

2 tsp crushed garlic

1 tsp ground cumin

2 tbsp dried oregano

250 g/9 oz aubergine, diced

100 g/3½ oz onion, sliced

175 g/6 oz mixed peppers, diced

200 g/7 oz canned tomatoes, chopped

400 ml/14 fl oz natural yogurt

30 ml/2 tbsp cornflour

2 tbsp English mustard powder

200 g/7 oz silken tofu, sliced

85 g/3 oz beef tomato, sliced

1. Preheat the oven to 190°C/375°F/Gas Mark 5. Bake the potatoes in their skins in the oven for 45 minutes, then remove and cut into 1-cm/½-inch slices.

2. Mix the lemon juice, oil, sugar, garlic, cumin and oregano together in a small bowl, then lightly brush over the diced aubergine, reserving the remaining mixture. Spread out on a non-stick baking tray and bake in the oven for 15 minutes. Heat the reserved lemon juice mixture in a small saucepan over a high heat, add the onion and peppers and cook, stirring occasionally, until lightly browned. Add the canned tomatoes, reduce the heat and simmer for 4 minutes.

3. In a separate saucepan, whisk the yogurt and cornflour together, then bring to the boil, whisking constantly until the yogurt boils and thickens. Remove from the heat and whisk in the mustard powder.

4. Layer the ingredients in an oven-proof dish, starting with the tofu and ensuring there's a ladle of tomato sauce between each layer. Finish with a layer of beef tomatoes, topped with the yogurt sauce. Bake in the preheated oven for 25 minutes, or until golden brown.

Rice & lentil curry

Ingredients

2.5-cm/1-inch piece fresh ginger

2 garlic cloves

1 onion

2 carrots

225 g/8 oz cauliflower

225 g/8 oz kale

2 tbsp olive oil

2 tbsp curry powder

1 tsp salt

90 g/3¼ oz basmati rice

90 g/3¼ oz small green lentils or red lentils

700 ml/1¼ pints vegetable stock or water

125 ml/4 fl oz coconut milk

1 lime

natural yogurt and sriracha sauce, to serve

1. Peel and finely chop the ginger and garlic. Dice the onion and carrots. Chop the cauliflower into small pieces. Trim the thick stems and centre ribs from the kale leaves and cut the leaves into ribbons.

2. Heat the oil in a large frying pan over a medium–high heat. Add the ginger, garlic and onion and cook, stirring, for about 2 minutes until the onion begins to soften. Stir in the curry powder and salt. Add the vegetables, rice, lentils, stock and coconut milk and bring to the boil.

3. Reduce the heat to low, cover and simmer for 15–20 minutes until the lentils and rice are tender. Juice the lime and stir in. Serve immediately topped with yogurt and sriracha sauce.

Serves
9

Chard & ricotta filo pie

Ingredients

900 g/2 lb rainbow chard

55 g/2 oz butter

2 leeks, sliced

2 garlic cloves, thinly sliced

3 tbsp chopped mixed fresh herbs, such as thyme, marjoram and flat-leaf parsley

400 g/14 oz ricotta cheese

55 g/2 oz freshly grated Parmesan cheese

freshly grated nutmeg, to taste

2 eggs, beaten

12 large sheets filo pastry

olive oil, for brushing

55 g/2 oz pine nuts

sea salt and pepper

1. Chop the chard stems into chunks. Slice the leaves into thin ribbons. Heat the butter in a large frying pan over a medium heat. Add the leeks and chard stalks, cover and fry for 5–7 minutes, until soft. Add the chard leaves, garlic and herbs. Cover and gently fry until the leaves are tender. Tip the vegetables into a colander and drain.

2. Beat together the ricotta cheese, Parmesan cheese, nutmeg and eggs in a large bowl. Mix in the drained vegetables. Season with salt and pepper.

3. Preheat the oven to 190°C/375°F/Gas Mark 5. Place 1 sheet of filo pastry in a greased 23 x 30-cm/9 x 12-inch roasting tin, trimming to fit as necessary. Brush with oil and sprinkle with a few pine nuts. Add 5 more sheets, lightly brushing each one with oil and sprinkling with pine nuts. Pour in the filling and level the surface. Cover with 5 more sheets of filo pastry, brushing each sheet with oil and sprinkling with pine nuts. Add the final sheet and brush with oil. Using a sharp knife, cut through all the pastry and filling layers to make 7.5-cm/3-inch squares. Bake in the preheated oven for 35–40 minutes, until golden and crisp. Cut into squares and serve hot or at room temperature.

293 Baked aubergine with courgette & tomato

Serves
6–8

Ingredients

2 large aubergines

olive oil, for brushing

2 large courgettes, sliced

4 tomatoes, sliced

1 garlic clove, finely chopped

15 g/½ oz dry breadcrumbs

15 g/½ oz grated Parmesan cheese

salt and pepper

freshly torn basil leaves, to garnish

1. Preheat the slow cooker, if necessary, or according to the manufacturer's instructions.

2. Cut the aubergines into fairly thin slices and brush with oil. Heat a large griddle pan or heavy-based frying pan over a high heat, then add the aubergines and cook in batches for 6–8 minutes, turning once, until soft and brown.

3. Layer the aubergines in the slow cooker with the courgettes, tomatoes and garlic, seasoning with salt and pepper between the layers.

4. Mix the breadcrumbs with the cheese and sprinkle over the vegetables. Cover and cook on low for 4 hours. Serve hot, garnished with basil.

#294 Spinach & squash casserole

Serves 2

Ingredients

2 small red onions

250 g/9 oz butternut squash, peeled deseeded and cubed

2 tsp vegetable oil

pepper

250 ml/9 fl oz skimmed milk

20 g/¾ oz cornflour

1 tsp mustard powder

1 small white onion

2 bay leaves

4 tsp grated Parmesan cheese

125 g/4½ oz baby spinach leaves

1 tbsp water

2 tbsp wholemeal breadcrumbs

1. Preheat the oven to 200°C/400°F/Gas Mark 6 and heat an ovenproof serving dish. Cut each of the red onions into 8 pieces. Arrange the squash and red onions on a baking sheet and coat with the oil and plenty of pepper. Bake in the preheated oven for 20 minutes, turning once.

2. Put the milk into a small saucepan with the cornflour, mustard powder, white onion and bay leaves. Whisk over a medium heat until thick. Remove from the heat, discard the onion and bay leaves and stir in the cheese. Set aside, stirring occasionally to prevent a skin forming.

3. Put the spinach in a large saucepan with the water and stir over a medium heat for 2–3 minutes, or until just wilted. Put half the squash mixture in the prepared dish and top with half the spinach. Repeat the layers. Pour over the sauce and sprinkle over the breadcrumbs. Transfer to the preheated oven and bake for 15–20 minutes, or until golden. Serve immediately.

#295 Harvester's pie

Serves 4

Ingredients

400 g/14 oz ready-made rich shortcrust pastry

1 small onion, finely chopped

1 parsnip, finely chopped

1 small turnip, finely chopped

115 g/4 oz mushrooms, chopped

115 g/4 oz drained canned haricot beans

175 g/6 oz Cheddar cheese, grated

1 tsp chopped fresh thyme

2 tbsp plain flour

4 tbsp vegetable stock

salt and pepper

1. Cut off and reserve a quarter of the pastry and roll out the remainder. Use the larger piece to line an 850-ml/1½-pint pudding basin, easing it gently into place. Roll out the smaller piece of pastry to make a lid.

2. Half fill a large saucepan with water and bring to the boil. Cut out a round of greaseproof paper and a round of foil 5 cm/2 inches larger than the top of the basin. Place them together and make a pleat in the centre.

3. Mix the onion, parsnip, turnip, mushrooms, beans and cheese together in a bowl. Sprinkle with the thyme and flour, season with salt and pepper and mix well. Spoon the mixture into the lined basin, pressing it down gently. Add the stock and cover with the pastry lid. Put the greaseproof paper and foil rounds over the basin and tie securely with kitchen string.

4. Carefully put the basin into the boiling water, which should come about half-way up the side. Cover the pan with a tight-fitting lid and steam for 3 hours.

5. Lift the basin out of the pan. Discard the cover and turn out the pie. Serve immediately.

Serves
6

Kale & butter bean casserole with chilli & lime

Ingredients

350 g/12 oz canned butter beans

1 tbsp cumin seeds

2 tsp dried oregano

3 tbsp groundnut oil

2 onions, chopped

2 garlic cloves, thinly sliced

1–3 fresh red or green chillies, and sliced

400 g/14 oz canned chopped tomatoes

450 ml/16 fl oz vegetable stock

175 g/6 oz shredded kale

5 tbsp chopped fresh coriander

juice of 1 lime

sea salt and pepper

2 avocados, cubed and tossed with lime juice, and red onion slivers, to garnish

1. Drain and rinse the beans and set aside. Put the cumin seeds into a small dry frying pan over a medium heat and fry until fragrant. Add the oregano, fry for a few seconds, then immediately remove the mixture from the pan and lightly crush with a mortar and pestle.

2. Heat the oil in a large, flameproof casserole over a medium heat. Add the onions and the spice and herb mixture. Fry for 5 minutes, until the chopped onions are translucent. Add the garlic and chillies and fry for a further 2 minutes.

3. Stir in the tomatoes, beans and stock. Season with salt and pepper and bring to the boil. Reduce the heat, cover and simmer for 30 minutes, stirring occasionally.

4. Increase the heat and stir in the kale. Simmer, uncovered, for 7 minutes, or until tender but still brightly coloured. Stir in the coriander and lime juice. Ladle into warmed bowls, garnish with the avocado and red onion and serve immediately.

Nutty Stilton roast

Serves
4

Ingredients

2 tbsp virgin olive oil, plus extra for oiling

2 onions, one finely chopped and one cut into thin wedges

3–5 garlic cloves, crushed

2 celery stalks, finely sliced

175 g/6 oz cooked chestnuts, peeled

175 g/6 oz mixed chopped nuts

55 g/2 oz ground almonds

55 g/2 oz fresh wholemeal breadcrumbs

225 g/8 oz Stilton cheese, crumbled

1 tbsp chopped fresh basil

1 egg, beaten

1 red pepper, peeled, deseeded and cut into thin wedges

1 courgette, cut into wedges

salt and pepper

1. Preheat the oven to 180°C/350°F/Gas Mark 4. Lightly oil a 900-g/2-lb loaf tin. Heat 1 tablespoon of the oil in a frying pan over medium heat, add the chopped onion, 1–2 of the garlic cloves, and the celery and cook for 5 minutes, stirring occasionally. Remove from the pan, drain through a sieve and transfer to a food processor with the nuts, breadcrumbs, half the cheese and the basil. Using the pulse button, blend the ingredients together, then slowly blend in the egg to form a stiff mixture. Season.

2. Heat the remaining oil in a frying pan over medium heat, add the onion wedges, remaining garlic, red pepper and courgette and cook for 5 minutes, stirring frequently. Remove from the pan, add salt and pepper and drain through a sieve.

3. Place half the nut mixture in the prepared tin and smooth the surface. Cover with the onion and red pepper mixture and crumble over the remaining cheese. Top with the remaining nut mixture and press down firmly. Cover with foil. Bake in the preheated oven, for 45 minutes. Remove the foil and bake for a further 25–35 minutes, or until cooked and firm to the touch.

#298 Vegetable & hazelnut loaf

Serves 4

Ingredients

2 tbsp sunflower oil, plus extra for oiling

1 onion, chopped

1 garlic clove, finely chopped

2 celery sticks, chopped

1 tbsp plain flour

200 ml/7 fl oz canned tomatoes, strained

115 g/4 oz fresh wholemeal breadcrumbs

2 carrots, peeled and grated

115 g/4 oz ground toasted hazelnuts

1 tbsp dark soy sauce

2 tbsp chopped fresh coriander

1 egg, lightly beaten

salt and pepper

lettuce leaves, to serve

1. Preheat the oven to 180°C/350°F/Gas Mark 4. Oil and line a 450-g/1-lb loaf pan. Heat the oil in a heavy-based frying pan. Add the onion and cook over medium heat, stirring frequently, for 5 minutes, or until soft. Add the garlic and celery and cook, stirring frequently, for 5 minutes. Add the flour and cook, stirring, for 1 minute. Gradually stir in the canned tomatoes and cook, stirring constantly, until thickened. Remove from the heat.

2. Place the breadcrumbs, carrots, hazelnuts, soy sauce and coriander in a bowl. Add the tomato mixture and stir well. Leave to cool slightly, then beat in the egg and season with salt and pepper.

3. Spoon into the prepared tin and smooth the surface. Cover with foil and bake in the preheated oven for 1 hour. If serving hot, turn the loaf out onto a warmed serving dish and serve with lettuce. Alternatively, cool the loaf in the tin before turning out.

#299 Vegetable toad in the hole

Serves 4–6

Ingredients

100 g/3½ oz plain flour

pinch of salt

2 eggs, beaten

200 ml/7 fl oz milk

2 tbsp wholegrain mustard

2 tbsp vegetable oil

25 g/1 oz butter

2 garlic cloves, crushed

1 onion, cut into 8 wedges

75 g/2¾ oz baby carrots, halved lengthways

50 g/1¾ oz French beans

50 g/1¾ oz canned sweetcorn, drained

2 tomatoes, deseeded and cut into chunks

1 tsp wholegrain mustard

1 tbsp chopped fresh mixed herbs

salt and pepper

1. Preheat the oven to 200°C/400°F/Gas Mark 6. To make the batter, sift the flour and salt into a bowl. Beat in the eggs and milk to make a batter. Stir in the mustard and leave to stand.

2. Pour the oil into a shallow ovenproof dish and place in the preheated oven for 10 minutes.

3. To make the filling, melt the butter in a frying pan, add the garlic and onion and sauté, stirring constantly, for 2 minutes. Bring a saucepan of water to the boil, add the carrots and beans, bring back to the boil and cook for 7 minutes, or until tender. Drain well.

4. Add the sweetcorn and tomatoes to the frying pan with the mustard and chopped mixed herbs. Season to taste with salt and pepper and add the carrots and beans.

5. Remove the preheated dish from the oven and pour in the batter over the hot oil. Spoon the vegetables into the centre, return to the oven and cook for 30–35 minutes, or until the batter has risen and set. Serve immediately.

#300 Nut roast

Serves 6

Ingredients

2 tbsp olive oil, plus extra
for brushing

1 large onion, finely chopped

100 g/3½ oz ground almonds

100 g/3½ oz cashew nuts,
finely chopped

55 g/2 oz fresh wholemeal
breadcrumbs

100 ml/3½ fl oz vegetable stock

finely grated rind and juice of
1 small lemon

1 tbsp finely chopped
rosemary leaves

salt and pepper

fresh rosemary sprigs and lemon
slices, to garnish

1. Preheat the oven to 200°C/400°F/Gas Mark 6.
Brush a 700-ml/1¼-pint loaf tin with oil and line with
baking paper.

2. Heat the oil in a large saucepan, add the onion and fry
over a medium heat, stirring, for 3–4 minutes until soft.

3. Stir in the almonds, cashew nuts, breadcrumbs, stock, lemon rind and juice and rosemary.
Season to taste with salt and pepper and stir well to mix.

4. Press the mixture into the prepared tin, brush with oil and bake in the preheated oven for
30–35 minutes, until golden brown and firm.

5. Turn out and serve hot, garnished with rosemary sprigs, lemon slices and black pepper.

#301 Roast butternut squash

Serves 4

Ingredients

1 butternut squash, about 450 g/1 lb

1 onion, chopped

2–3 garlic cloves, crushed

4 small tomatoes, chopped

85 g/3 oz chestnut mushrooms,
chopped

85 g/3 oz canned butter beans, drained,
rinsed and roughly chopped

1 courgette, trimmed and grated

1 tbsp chopped fresh oregano,
plus extra to garnish

2 tbsp tomato purée

300 ml/10 fl oz water

4 spring onions, trimmed and chopped

1 tbsp Worcestershire sauce,
or to taste

pepper

1. Preheat the oven to 190°C/375°F/Gas Mark 5. Prick
the squash all over with a metal skewer then roast for
40 minutes, or until tender. Remove from the oven and
leave to rest until cool enough to handle.

2. Cut the squash in half, scoop out and discard the seeds, then scoop out some of the flesh,
making hollows in both halves. Chop the scooped-out flesh and put in a bowl. Place the two
squash halves side by side in a large roasting tin.

3. Add the onion, garlic, tomatoes and mushrooms to the squash flesh in the bowl. Add the
butter beans, courgette, oregano and pepper to taste and mix well. Spoon the filling into the
two halves of the squash, packing it down as firmly as possible.

4. Mix the tomato purée with the water, spring onions and Worcestershire sauce in a small
bowl and pour around the squash. Cover loosely with a large sheet of foil and bake for
30 minutes, or until piping hot. Serve in bowls, garnished with some chopped oregano.

Fish & seafood

#302 Breton fish soup

Ingredients

2 tsp butter

1 large leek, thinly sliced

2 shallots, finely chopped

125 ml/4 fl oz dry cider

300 ml/10 fl oz fish stock

250 g/9 oz potatoes, diced

1 bay leaf

4 tbsp plain flour

200 ml/7 fl oz milk

200 ml/7 fl oz double cream

55 g/2 oz fresh sorrel leaves, chopped

350 g/12 oz skinless monkfish or cod fillet, cut into 2.5-cm/1-inch pieces

salt and pepper

1. Melt the butter in a large saucepan over a medium–low heat. Add the leek and shallots and cook for about 5 minutes, stirring frequently, or until they start to soften.

2. Add the cider and bring to the boil. Stir in the stock, potatoes and bay leaf with a pinch of salt and bring back to the boil. Reduce the heat, cover and cook gently for 10 minutes. Put the flour in a small bowl and very slowly whisk in a few tablespoons of the milk to make a thick paste. Stir in a little more milk to make a smooth liquid. Adjust the heat so the soup bubbles gently. Stir in the flour mixture and cook, stirring frequently, for 5 minutes. Add the remaining milk and half of the cream. Cook for a further 10 minutes, or until the potatoes are tender.

3. Combine the sorrel with the remaining cream. Stir into the soup and add the fish. Continue cooking, stirring occasionally, for about 3 minutes, or until the fish is cooked through. Taste the soup and adjust the seasoning, if necessary. Remove the bay leaf and serve immediately.

#303 Prawn laksa

Ingredients

20–24 large raw unpeeled prawns

450 ml/16 fl oz fish stock

pinch of salt

2.5-cm/1-inch piece fresh ginger

3 large garlic cloves, crushed

1 fresh red chilli, chopped

1 lemon grass stalk, chopped

1½ tbsp shrimp paste

½ tsp turmeric

2½ tbsp groundnut oil

450 ml/16 fl oz coconut milk

2 tsp nam pla (fish sauce)

½ tbsp lime juice

115 g/4 oz dried medium rice noodles

55 g/2 oz beansprouts

fresh coriander sprigs, to garnish

1. Peel and devein the prawns. Put the fish stock, salt and the prawn heads, peels and tails in a saucepan over a high heat and slowly bring to the boil. Reduce the heat and simmer for 10 minutes.

2. Peel and chop the ginger, put into a food processor with the garlic, chilli, lemon grass, shrimp paste and turmeric and process. With the motor running, slowly add up to 2 tablespoons of the oil, just until a paste forms. Set aside.

3. Heat the remaining oil in a large saucepan over a high heat. Add the paste and stir-fry until fragrant. Strain the stock through a muslin-lined sieve. Stir into the paste with the coconut milk, nam pla and lime juice. Bring to the boil, then reduce the heat, cover and simmer for 30 minutes.

4. Meanwhile, cook the noodles according to the packet instructions. Drain and set aside. Add the prawns and beansprouts to the stew and simmer until the prawns turn opaque and curl. Divide the noodles between warmed bowls and ladle the stew over. Garnish with the coriander and serve immediately.

#304 New England clam chowder

Ingredients

900 g/2 lb clams, scrubbed
4 bacon rashers, chopped
25 g/1 oz butter
1 onion, chopped
1 tbsp chopped fresh thyme
1 large potato, diced
300 ml/10 fl oz milk
1 bay leaf
375 ml/13 fl oz double cream
1 tbsp chopped fresh parsley
salt and pepper

1. Discard any clams with broken shells and any that refuse to close when tapped. Put the remainder into a large saucepan with a splash of water. Cook over a high heat for 3–4 minutes, until they open. Discard any that remain closed. Strain, reserving the cooking liquid. Leave until cool enough to handle. Reserve some clams in their shells for the garnish, then remove the remainder from their shells, chopping them roughly if large, and set aside.

2. Dry-fry the bacon in a saucepan until brown and crisp. Drain on kitchen paper. Add the butter to the pan and, when it has melted, add the onion. Cook for 4–5 minutes, until soft but not coloured. Add the thyme and cook briefly before adding the potato, reserved cooking liquid, milk and bay leaf. Bring to the boil, then reduce the heat and simmer for 10 minutes, or until the potato is just tender. Remove from the heat and leave to cool slightly. Remove and discard the bay leaf, then transfer the soup to a food processor and process to a purée. Return the soup to the rinsed-out pan and add the clams, bacon and cream. Simmer for a further 2–3 minutes, until heated through. Season to taste with salt and pepper. Stir in the parsley and ladle the soup into warmed bowls. Garnish with the reserved clams in their shells and serve immediately.

#305 Bouillabaisse

Serves 8

Ingredients

1 kg/2 lb 4 oz selection of firm white fish fillets, scaled and cleaned, but not skinned
500 g/1 lb 2 oz live mussels
100 ml/3½ fl oz olive oil
2 onions, finely chopped
1 fennel bulb, finely chopped
4 garlic cloves, crushed
1.2 kg/2 lb 10 oz canned chopped tomatoes
1.5 litres/2¾ pints fish stock
pinch of saffron strands
grated rind of 1 orange
1 bouquet garni
500 g/1 lb 2 oz cooked prawns, shell-on
salt and pepper
rouille and baguettes, to serve

1. Carefully pin-bone the fish, then cut the fillets into bite-sized pieces. Scrub and debeard the mussels, discarding any with broken shells and any that refuse to close when tapped. Set aside.

2. Heat the oil in a very large frying pan or wide saucepan with a lid and gently fry the onion and fennel for about 15 minutes, until soft. Add the garlic and fry for 2 minutes, then add the tomatoes and simmer for 2 minutes. Stir in the stock, saffron, orange rind and bouquet garni and bring to the boil. Simmer, uncovered, for 15 minutes.

3. Add the fish pieces, mussels and prawns, and cover the pan. Simmer for a further 5–10 minutes, until the mussels have opened. Discard any that remain closed. Taste and adjust the seasoning, adding salt and pepper if needed.

4. Remove the soup from the heat and ladle into warmed bowls. Serve immediately with rouille and baguettes.

#306 Prawn & vegetable bisque

Serves 4

Ingredients

3 tbsp butter

1 garlic clove, chopped

1 onion, sliced

1 carrot, peeled and chopped

1 celery stick, trimmed and sliced

1.2 litres/2 pints fish stock

4 tbsp red wine

1 tbsp tomato purée

1 bay leaf

600 g/1 lb 5 oz prawns, peeled

100 ml/3½ fl oz double cream

salt and pepper

single cream and whole cooked prawns, to garnish

1. Melt the butter in a large saucepan over a medium heat. Add the garlic and onion and cook, stirring, for 3 minutes, until just soft. Add the carrot and celery and cook for a further 3 minutes, stirring constantly. Pour in the stock and wine, then add the tomato purée and bay leaf. Season to taste with salt and pepper. Bring to the boil, then reduce the heat and simmer for 20 minutes. Remove from the heat and leave to cool for 10 minutes, then remove and discard the bay leaf.

2. Transfer half the soup into a food processor or blender and blend until smooth. Return to the pan with the rest of the soup. Add the prawns and cook over a low heat for 5–6 minutes.

3. Stir in the cream and cook for a further 2 minutes, then remove from the heat and ladle into four warmed bowls. Garnish with swirls of single cream and whole cooked prawns. Serve immediately.

#307 Tuna chowder

Serves 4

Ingredients

2 tbsp butter

1 large garlic clove, chopped

1 large onion, sliced

1 carrot, peeled and chopped

400 g/14 oz potatoes

400 g/14 oz canned cannellini beans

600 ml/1 pint fish stock

400 g/14 oz canned chopped tomatoes

1 tbsp tomato purée

1 courgette, trimmed and chopped

225 g/8 oz canned tuna in brine, drained

1 tbsp chopped fresh basil

1 tbsp chopped fresh parsley

100 ml/3½ fl oz double cream

salt and pepper

fresh basil sprigs, to garnish

1. Melt the butter in a large saucepan over a low heat. Add the garlic and onion and cook, stirring, for 3 minutes, until slightly softened. Add the carrot and cook for a further 5 minutes, stirring.

2. Meanwhile, peel the potatoes and cut them into chunks and drain the beans. Pour the stock into the pan, then add the potatoes, beans, tomatoes and tomato purée. Season to taste with salt and pepper. Bring to the boil, then reduce the heat, cover the pan and simmer for 20 minutes.

3. Add the courgette, tuna, chopped basil and parsley and cook for a further 15 minutes. Stir in the cream and cook very gently for a further 2 minutes.

4. Remove from the heat and ladle into warmed bowls. Garnish with sprigs of fresh basil and serve immediately.

#308 Traditional Catalan salt cod salad

Ingredients

400 g/14 oz dried salt cod in 1 piece

6 spring onions, thinly sliced diagonally

6 tbsp extra virgin olive oil

1 tbsp sherry vinegar

1 tbsp lemon juice

2 large red peppers, grilled, peeled, deseeded and very finely diced

12 large black olives, stoned and sliced

2 large, juicy tomatoes, thinly sliced

salt and pepper

2 tbsp chopped fresh flat-leaf parsley

1. Place the dried salt cod in a large bowl, then cover with cold water and soak for 48 hours, changing the water 3 times a day.

2. Pat the salt cod very dry with kitchen paper and remove the skin and bones, then use your fingers to tear into fine shreds. Place in a large, non-metallic bowl with the spring onions, oil, vinegar and lemon juice and toss together. Season with pepper, then cover and marinate in the refrigerator for 3 hours.

3. Stir in the red peppers and olives. Taste and adjust the seasoning, if necessary, remembering that the cod and olives might be salty. Arrange the tomato slices on a large serving platter or individual serving plates and spoon the salad on top. Sprinkle with chopped parsley and serve.

#309 Prawn & white bean salad

Serves 4

Ingredients

400 g/14 oz canned haricot beans, drained and rinsed

½ red onion, finely chopped

1 celery stick, finely diced

300 g/10½ oz large cooked peeled prawns, tails intact

1 garlic clove, finely chopped

juice of 1 lemon

5 tbsp extra virgin olive oil

2 tbsp chopped fresh flat-leaf parsley

4 thick slices country bread

85 g/3 oz baby plum tomatoes, halved

handful of fresh flat-leaf parsley leaves

salt and pepper

1. Place the beans, onion, celery, prawns and garlic in a large shallow bowl. Add the lemon juice, 2 tablespoons of the oil and the chopped parsley. Lightly season with salt and pepper. Stir well, then cover and set aside.

2. Brush the slices of bread with some of the remaining oil. Preheat a griddle pan, add the bread and cook for 2–3 minutes on each side until golden. Place on 4 serving plates.

3. Gently stir the tomatoes and parsley leaves into the salad. Pile the salad onto the hot toasts. Drizzle over the remaining oil, season with a little more pepper and serve.

New potato & salmon salad

Ingredients

650 g/1 lb 7 oz baby new
potatoes, halved or thickly
sliced if large

450 g/1 lb salmon fillet

1 red onion, thinly sliced

½ iceberg lettuce, torn into
bite-sized pieces

115 g/4 oz kale, shredded

85 g/3 oz pea shoots

salt and pepper

Dressing

4 tbsp olive oil

juice of 1 lemon

2 tsp clear honey

1 tbsp capers, drained and chopped

1. Put cold water in the base of a steamer, bring to the boil, then add the potatoes and bring back to the boil. Put the salmon in the top of the steamer in a single layer, season with salt and pepper, then put it on the steamer base, cover and steam for 10 minutes, or until the salmon is cooked. Remove the steamer top and cook the potatoes for 4—5 minutes more, or until tender.

2. Meanwhile, to make the dressing, put the oil, lemon juice and honey in a salad bowl, mix well together, then stir in the capers and season to taste with salt and pepper.

3. Add the onion to the dressing, then add the hot potatoes and gently toss together.

4. Divide the lettuce and kale between four bowls and spoon over the potato mixture. Flake the salmon into large pieces, discarding any skin and bones, sprinkle over the salad, then top with the pea shoots and serve immediately.

#311 Smoked trout salad

Serves 4

Ingredients

1 red pepper, halved and deseeded

4 smoked trout fillets, skinned, any small bones removed, and flaked

4 spring onions, trimmed and finely chopped

2 large chicory heads, halved, cored and shredded

1½ tbsp Chinese rice vinegar

½ tbsp sunflower oil

2 tbsp chopped fresh flat-leaf parsley

mixed salad leaves

salt and pepper

1. Run a swivel-bladed vegetable peeler along the length of the cut edges of the pepper to make very thin slices. Chop the slices and put them in a bowl.

2. Add the trout, spring onions and chicory to the bowl, tossing to mix together.

3. In a small bowl, whisk together 1 tablespoon of the vinegar, the oil, parsley and salt and pepper. Pour over the trout salad and toss again, then taste and add extra vinegar as required.

4. Cover and chill until ready to serve. Arrange the mixed salad leaves on 4 serving plates. Toss the salad again and adjust the seasoning, if necessary. Serve the trout on top of the mixed salad leaves.

#312 Tuna Niçoise salad

Serves 4

Ingredients

350 g/12 oz dried conchiglie

115 g/4 oz French beans

50 g/1¾ oz canned anchovy fillets, drained

2 tbsp milk

2 small crisp lettuces

3 large beef tomatoes

4 hard-boiled eggs

225 g/8 oz canned tuna, drained

115 g/4 oz stoned black olives

3 tbsp extra virgin olive oil

2 tbsp white wine vinegar

1 tsp wholegrain mustard

salt and pepper

1. Bring a large saucepan of lightly salted water to the boil. Add the pasta, bring back to the boil and cook for 8–10 minutes, until tender but still firm to the bite. Drain and refresh in cold water.

2. Bring a small saucepan of lightly salted water to the boil. Add the beans and cook for 10–12 minutes, or until tender but still firm to the bite. Drain, refresh in cold water, drain again and reserve. Put the anchovies in a shallow bowl, pour over the milk and leave to stand for 10 minutes. Meanwhile, tear the lettuces into large pieces. Blanch the tomatoes in boiling water for 1–2 minutes, then drain, peel and roughly chop the flesh. Shell the eggs and cut into quarters. Flake the tuna into large chunks. Drain the anchovies and the pasta. Put all the salad ingredients, along with the olives, into a large bowl and gently mix together.

3. Beat together the oil, vinegar and mustard and season to taste with salt and pepper. Chill in the refrigerator until required. Just before serving, pour the dressing over the salad.

#313 Fish goujons with chilli mayonnaise

Serves 4

Ingredients

200 g/7 oz plain flour

3 eggs

140 g/5 oz matzo meal

450 g/1 lb firm white fish fillets, cut into strips

sunflower oil or groundnut oil, for frying

2 tbsp sweet chilli sauce

4–5 tbsp mayonnaise

salt and pepper

1. Mix the flour with plenty of salt and pepper on a large flat plate. Beat the eggs in a bowl. Spread out the matzo meal on a separate flat plate.

2. Dip the fish pieces into the seasoned flour, then into the beaten egg, then into the matzo meal, ensuring a generous coating.

3. Pour the oil into a non-stick frying pan to a depth of 1 cm/½ inch and heat. Cook the fish pieces in batches for a few minutes, turning once, until golden and cooked through.

4. Put the chilli sauce and mayonnaise in a bowl and beat together until combined.

5. Transfer the fish to serving plates and serve with the chilli mayonnaise on the side.

#314 Prawn & scallop kebabs

Serves 4

Ingredients

24 raw tiger prawns

12 large scallops, corals attached

4–5 tbsp olive oil, plus extra for greasing

juice of 1 lime

salt and pepper

chopped fresh coriander and lime wedges, to garnish

1. Using a sharp knife, remove and discard the heads from the prawns, then remove the shells but leave the tails attached. Cut along the back of the prawns and remove the dark intestinal vein. Remove the tough muscle from the side of the scallops. Slice in half lengthways through the coral.

2. Combine the oil and lime juice in a shallow dish. Season to taste with salt and pepper. Add the scallops and prawns, and leave to marinate for 15 minutes.

3. Preheat the grill to medium high. Drain the prawns and scallops, reserving the marinade. Thread the prawns and scallops alternately onto 8 metal or pre-soaked wooden skewers.

4. Cook the kebabs under the grill, turning frequently and brushing with the reserved marinade, for 4–6 minutes, or until cooked through and the prawns have changed colour. Arrange on a serving dish and garnish with the coriander and lime wedges.

Makes
6

Crab cakes with tartare sauce

Ingredients

1 large egg, beaten
250 ml/9 fl oz mayonnaise
½ tsp Dijon mustard
½ tsp Worcestershire sauce
½ tsp celery salt
40 g/1½ oz cream crackers, crushed
450 g/1 lb fresh crabmeat
4 tbsp sweet pickle relish
1 tbsp very finely chopped onion
1 tbsp chopped capers
1½ tbsp freshly squeezed lemon juice
85–140 g/3–5 oz fresh breadcrumbs
25 g/1 oz unsalted butter
1 tbsp vegetable oil
salt and pepper
salad leaves and lemon wedges, to serve

1. Whisk together the egg, 2 tablespoons of the mayonnaise, the mustard, half the Worcestershire sauce, the celery salt and a little salt in a large bowl until combined. Stir in the cracker crumbs with a spatula, then leave to stand for 5 minutes. Pick over the crabmeat to remove any pieces of shell or cartilage, then gently fold into the mixture, trying to avoid breaking it up too much. Cover with clingfilm and chill in the refrigerator for at least 1 hour.

2. Meanwhile, mix the remaining mayonnaise and Worcestershire sauce, relish, onion, capers and lemon juice together and season to taste with salt and pepper. Cover and chill in the refrigerator for at least 1 hour before serving.

3. Sprinkle the breadcrumbs over a large plate until lightly covered. Shape the crab mixture into 6 even-sized cakes, about 2.5 cm/1 inch thick and place on the plate. Lightly dust the tops with more breadcrumbs. Melt the butter with the oil in a large frying pan over a medium–high heat. Add the crab cakes and cook for 4 minutes on each side, until golden brown. Remove from the pan and drain on kitchen paper. Serve with the tartare sauce, salad leaves and lemon wedges.

Serves
4

Tuna & tomato pitta pockets

Ingredients

4 pittas
1 Little Gem lettuce, roughly shredded
8 cherry tomatoes, halved
375 g/13 oz canned tuna in oil, drained and flaked
125 ml/4 fl oz mayonnaise
1 tsp finely grated lemon rind
2 tbsp lemon juice
3 tbsp snipped fresh chives
salt and pepper

1. Lightly toast the pitta breads under a preheated grill or toaster, then leave to cool slightly. Cut the pitta breads in half and open them out to make a pocket.

2. Divide the lettuce between the pittas, then add the tomatoes and tuna.

3. Put the mayonnaise, lemon rind, lemon juice and chives into a bowl and mix together. Season to taste with salt and pepper and spoon over the pitta filling to serve.

Scallops in vermouth

Serves 4

Ingredients

1 kg/2 lb 4 oz shelled fresh scallops
55 g/2 oz unsalted butter
4 tbsp dry vermouth
3 tbsp chopped fresh flat-leaf parsley
salt and pepper

1. If necessary, rinse the scallops and pat dry with kitchen paper. Season with salt and pepper.

2. Melt 15 g/½ oz of the butter in a large frying pan until just beginning to colour. Add half the scallops and cook, turning occasionally, for 4–5 minutes until light golden brown on both sides. Remove from the pan and keep warm. Melt another 15 g/½ oz of the butter in the pan and cook the remaining scallops in the same way, then remove them from the pan and keep warm.

3. Add the vermouth to the pan and stir in the remaining butter. When it has melted, stir in the parsley and pour the sauce over the scallops. Serve immediately, seasoned with pepper.

Salmon fingers with potato wedges

Serves 2–3

Ingredients

140 g/5 oz fine cornmeal or polenta
1 tsp paprika
400 g/14 oz salmon fillet, skinned and sliced into 12 chunky fingers
1 egg, beaten
sunflower oil, for frying

Potato wedges

500 g/1 lb 2 oz potatoes, scrubbed and cut into thick wedges
1–2 tbsp olive oil
½ tsp paprika
salt

1. Preheat the oven to 200°C/400°F/Gas Mark 6. To make the potato wedges, dry the potatoes on a clean tea towel. Spoon the oil into a roasting tin and put into the preheated oven to heat. Toss the potatoes in the warm oil until well coated. Sprinkle with the paprika, and salt to taste and roast for 30 minutes, turning half-way through, until crisp and golden.

2. Meanwhile, mix the cornmeal and paprika together on a plate. Dip each salmon finger into the beaten egg, then roll in the cornmeal mixture until evenly coated. Preheat the oven to low.

3. Heat enough oil to cover the base of a large heavy-based frying pan over a medium heat. Carefully arrange half the salmon fingers in the pan and cook for 6 minutes, turning half-way through, until golden. Drain on kitchen paper and keep warm in the preheated oven while you cook the remaining salmon fingers. Serve immediately with the potato wedges.

#319 Fish finger burritos

Serves 2

Ingredients

4 frozen chunky cod fish fingers

2 soft tortillas

4 tbsp ready-made salsa, plus extra to serve

1 Little Gem lettuce, shredded

1 ripe avocado, halved and stone removed

sea salt

1. Preheat the grill to medium and cook the frozen fish fingers for 15–18 minutes, turning once or twice, or until golden and cooked through. Meanwhile, warm the tortillas according to the packet instructions.

2. Spread the surface of each warmed tortilla with the salsa and top with the shredded lettuce. Slice the avocado and arrange over the top. Sprinkle with a little sea salt. Place two fish fingers on each tortilla and roll up, tucking in the edges to form a parcel. Cut each burrito in half and serve with extra salsa.

#320 Prawn & garlic butter pancakes

Serves 4

Ingredients

150 g/5½ oz plain white flour

1½ tsp baking powder

250 ml/9 fl oz milk

1 large egg

2 tbsp melted butter

sunflower oil, for greasing

pinch of salt

Prawn & garlic butter

100 g/3½ oz butter

2 garlic cloves, crushed

400 g/14 oz raw peeled tiger prawns

1 tbsp lemon juice

2 tbsp chopped parsley

salt and pepper

1. Sift the flour, baking powder and a pinch of salt into a bowl. Add the milk, egg and butter and whisk to a smooth batter. Leave to stand for 5 minutes.

2. Preheat the oven to low. Lightly grease a griddle pan or frying pan and heat over a medium heat. Spoon tablespoons of batter onto the pan and cook until bubbles appear on the surface.

3. Turn over with a palette knife and cook the other side until golden brown. Repeat this process using the remaining batter, while keeping the cooked pancakes warm in the preheated oven.

4. To make the prawn and garlic butter, heat the butter in a medium-sized saucepan until melted, add the garlic and prawns and stir for 2–3 minutes, until the prawns turn evenly pink. Add the lemon juice and parsley and season to taste with salt and pepper. Spoon the prawn and garlic butter over the pancakes and serve immediately.

Prawn po' boys

Ingredients

175 ml/6 fl oz milk

2 eggs

450 g/1 lb raw prawns, peeled and deveined

100 g/3½ oz finely ground cornmeal

100 g/3½ oz plain flour

1 tsp salt

¾ tsp garlic powder

½ tsp onion powder

½ tsp cayenne pepper

½ tsp sweet paprika

¼ tsp freshly ground black pepper

vegetable oil, for frying

4 large bread rolls

115 g/4 oz cos lettuce, shredded

1 large tomato, cut into 5-mm/¼-inch thick slices

½ lemon

Remoulade sauce

125 ml/4 fl oz mayonnaise

1 tbsp hot pepper sauce

1 tbsp prepared horseradish

1 tbsp Dijon mustard

1 tbsp sweet pickle relish

1. Put the milk and eggs into a large bowl and whisk together. Add the prawns and toss together to coat.

2. Put the cornmeal, flour, salt, garlic powder, onion powder, cayenne pepper, paprika and black pepper into a separate wide, shallow bowl and mix to combine.

3. Pour about 2.5 cm/1 inch of the oil into a wide saucepan and heat over a medium-high heat until very hot.

4. Remove several prawns at a time from the milk mixture and dredge them in the cornmeal mixture until well coated. Drop them into the hot oil and cook, turning once, for 5–6 minutes, until golden brown all over. Transfer to a plate lined with kitchen paper and repeat with the remaining prawns.

5. To make the sauce, put all the ingredients into a small bowl and stir to combine.

6. To make the sandwiches, spread some of the sauce onto the top and bottom halves of the rolls. Pile some shredded lettuce and 1–2 tomato slices on the bottom half of each roll. Top with a quarter of the prawns and a squeeze of lemon. Replace the roll lid and serve immediately.

#322 Crabmeat & dill tart

Serves 4–6

Ingredients

200 g/7 oz plain flour, plus extra for dusting

1 tbsp chopped fresh dill

100 g/3½ oz butter

2–3 tbsp cold water

1 bunch spring onions, chopped

175 g/6 oz crabmeat, light and dark meat

2 tbsp chopped fresh dill

1 large egg, beaten

175 ml/6 fl oz single cream

25 g/1 oz Parmesan cheese, finely grated

salt and pepper

1. Sift the flour into a bowl, add the dill and rub in the butter with your fingertips until the mixture resembles fine breadcrumbs. Stir in just enough water to make a soft dough. Turn out onto a lightly floured surface and roll out until it is big enough to line a 23-cm/9-inch flan tin. Press the pastry into the edge of the tin, trim the excess and prick the base with a fork. Chill in the refrigerator for 15 minutes. Preheat the oven to 200°C/400°F/Gas Mark 6. Line the pastry case with a piece of baking paper and fill with baking beans, then bake in the preheated oven for 10 minutes. Remove from the oven, take out the paper and beans and bake for a further 10 minutes.

2. To make the filling, put the onions, crabmeat and dill into a bowl and mix together. Stir in the egg and cream. Season with salt and pepper, then spoon into the pastry case and sprinkle with the cheese. Reduce the oven temperature to 190°C/375°F/Gas Mark 5. Bake the tart in the oven for 25–30 minutes, until the filling is just set. Serve warm or cold.

#323 Spicy salmon fish cakes

Serves 4

Ingredients

400 g/14 oz potatoes, cut into medium-sized chunks

400 g/14 oz skinless salmon fillet

2 tbsp mayonnaise

1 egg, beaten

dash of milk, if needed

2 fresh jalapeño chillies, deseeded and finely chopped

1 small bunch fresh coriander leaves

plain flour, for dusting

1 tbsp olive oil

salt and pepper

1. Bring a large saucepan of lightly salted water to the boil, add the potatoes, bring back to the boil and cook for 15 minutes, or until tender.

2. Meanwhile, lightly poach the salmon fillet in a saucepan of gently simmering water for 5–6 minutes (if in one piece), or until just cooked but still moist. Using a fork, flake the flesh into a bowl.

3. Drain the potatoes, return to the pan and, while still warm, roughly mash with a fork, adding the mayonnaise, egg and milk, if needed – the mixture must remain firm, so only add the milk if necessary. Stir in the chillies, coriander leaves, and salt and pepper to taste, then lightly mix in the salmon flakes.

4. With floured hands, form the mixture into 8 small patties. Heat the oil in a large non-stick frying pan over a medium–high heat, add the patties and cook for 5 minutes on each side, or until golden brown. Carefully remove with a fish slice and serve.

#324 Chilli-prawn tacos

Ingredients

1 tbsp olive oil

1 onion, finely chopped

1 green pepper, deseeded and diced

1–2 hot green chillies, finely chopped

3 garlic cloves, crushed

1 tsp ground cumin

1 tsp ground coriander

1 tsp brown sugar

450 g/1 lb ripe tomatoes, chopped

juice of ½ lemon

600 g/1 lb 5 oz raw prawns, shelled and deveined

2 tbsp chopped fresh flat-leaf parsley

12 tortilla shells

chopped spring onions, to garnish

salt and pepper

soured cream and lettuce, to serve

1. Heat the oil in a deep frying pan over medium heat. Add the onion and cook for 5 minutes, or until softened. Add the pepper and chillies and cook for 5 minutes. Add the garlic, cumin, coriander and sugar and cook the sauce for a further 2 minutes, stirring.

2. Add the tomatoes, lemon juice and salt and pepper to taste. Bring to the boil, then reduce the heat and simmer for 10 minutes.

3. Preheat the oven to 180°C/350°F/Gas Mark 4. Stir the prawns and parsley into the taco sauce, cover and cook gently for 5–8 minutes, or until the prawns are pink and tender.

4. Place the tortilla shells, open-side down, on a baking sheet and warm in the preheated oven, for 2–3 minutes.

5. Spoon the prawn mixture into the tortilla shells, garnish with the spring onions and serve with the soured cream and lettuce.

#325 Tuna & cheese quiche

Ingredients

450 g/1 lb floury potatoes, diced

2 tbsp butter

6 tbsp plain flour, plus extra for dusting

1 tbsp vegetable oil

1 shallot, chopped

1 garlic clove, crushed

1 red pepper, deseeded and diced

175 g/6 oz canned tuna, drained

50 g/1¾ oz canned sweetcorn, drained

150 ml/5 fl oz skimmed milk

3 eggs, beaten

1 tbsp chopped fresh dill

50 g/1¾ oz Cheddar cheese, grated

salt and pepper

1. Preheat the oven to 200°C/400°F/Gas Mark 6. Cook the potatoes in a saucepan of lightly salted boiling water for 10 minutes, or until tender. Drain and mash the potatoes. Add the butter and flour and mix to a dough.

2. Knead the dough on a lightly floured surface and press the mixture into a 20-cm/8-inch tart tin. Prick the base with a fork, cover with a piece of baking paper and fill with baking beans, then bake in the preheated oven for 20–30 minutes until lightly browned. Remove from the oven and take out the paper and beans.

3. Heat the oil in a frying pan. Add the shallot, garlic and red pepper and cook for 5 minutes. Spoon the mixture into the flan case. Flake the tuna and arrange it on top with the sweetcorn.

4. Combine the milk, eggs and dill and season to taste with salt and pepper. Pour the mixture into the flan case and sprinkle the grated cheese on top. Bake in the preheated oven for 20 minutes, until the filling has set. Serve.

Linguine with sardines

Ingredients

8 sardines, filleted, washed and dried

4 tbsp olive oil

3 garlic cloves, sliced

1 tsp chilli flakes

1 fennel bulb, trimmed and thinly sliced

350 g/12 oz dried linguine

½ tsp finely grated lemon rind

1 tbsp lemon juice

2 tbsp toasted pine kernels

2 tbsp chopped fresh parsley

salt and pepper

1. Roughly chop the sardines into large pieces and reserve.

2. Heat 2 tablespoons of the oil in a large frying pan over a medium-high heat and add the garlic and chilli flakes. Cook for 1 minute, then add the fennel. Cook, stirring occasionally, for 4–5 minutes, or until soft. Reduce the heat, add the sardine pieces and cook for a further 3–4 minutes.

3. Meanwhile, bring a large saucepan of lightly salted water to the boil. Add the pasta, bring back to the boil and cook for 8–10 minutes, until tender but still firm to the bite. Drain thoroughly and return to the pan.

4. Add the lemon rind, lemon juice, pine kernels and parsley to the sardine mixture and toss. Season to taste with salt and pepper. Add to the pasta with the remaining oil and toss. Transfer to a warmed serving dish and serve immediately.

327

Garlic & herb Dublin Bay prawns

Serves 2

Ingredients

juice of ½ lemon

2 garlic cloves, crushed

3 tbsp chopped fresh parsley

1 tbsp chopped fresh dill

40 g/1½ oz butter, softened

12 raw Dublin Bay prawns or langoustines

salt and pepper

lemon wedges and fresh crusty bread, to serve

1. Mix the lemon juice with the garlic, herbs and butter to form a paste. Season well with salt and pepper. Spread the paste over the prawns and leave to marinate for 30 minutes.

2. Preheat the grill to medium. Cook the prawns under the preheated grill for 5–6 minutes. Alternatively, heat a frying pan and fry the prawns in the paste until cooked through and pink.

3. Turn out onto warmed plates and pour over the pan juices. Serve immediately with lemon wedges for squeezing over and crusty bread for mopping up the juices.

#328 Roast cod with parsley couscous

Serves 2

Ingredients

2 cod fillets, about 200 g/7 oz each

1–2 tbsp black olive tapenade

2 tbsp olive oil, plus extra for greasing

50 ml/2 fl oz white wine or water

225 g/8 oz cherry tomatoes on the vine

85 g/3 oz couscous

100 ml/3½ fl oz vegetable stock

1 tbsp chopped parsley

1 tsp lemon zest

1 garlic clove, finely chopped

salt and pepper

1. Preheat the oven to 200°C/400°F/Gas Mark 6. Lightly grease a baking dish. Season the fish with salt and pepper and place in the prepared dish. Spread the tapenade over the top of the fish and drizzle with 1 tablespoon of the oil. Pour the wine around the fish and add the branches of cherry tomatoes. Bake in the preheated oven for 15 minutes.

2. Put the couscous in a bowl and pour over the stock. Cover and leave to stand for 3 minutes. Mix the parsley, lemon zest and garlic together with the remaining tablespoon of oil.

3. Transfer the fish fillets to serving plates and arrange the branches of tomatoes over the top. Spoon any juices in the dish around the fish. Fluff the couscous with a fork, stir in the parsley mixture and serve with the fish.

#329 Speedy tuna pizza

Serves 2–4

Ingredients

3 tbsp red pesto

1 x 30-cm/12-inch ready-made pizza base

200 g/7 oz canned tuna in sunflower oil, drained

175 g/6 oz cherry tomatoes, halved

100 g/3½ oz mozzarella cheese, diced

2 tbsp capers

8 small black olives, stoned

1 tbsp olive oil

salt and pepper

1. Preheat the oven to 220°C/425°F/Gas Mark 7. Spread the pesto evenly over the pizza base.

2. Roughly flake the tuna and arrange over the pizza.

3. Scatter over the tomatoes, mozzarella, capers and olives. Season to taste with salt and pepper.

4. Drizzle the oil over the pizza and bake in the preheated oven for about 15 minutes, or until golden and bubbling.

5. Serve the pizza hot or cold.

Grilled stuffed trout

Ingredients

2 whole trout, each about 350 g/12 oz,
gutted and fins removed

1 tbsp vegetable oil

salt and pepper

Stuffing

25 g/1 oz butter

2 shallots, finely chopped

55 g/2 oz mushrooms, finely chopped

55 g/2 oz baby spinach

1 tbsp chopped fresh parsley or tarragon

grated rind of 1 lemon

whole nutmeg, for grating

Tomato salsa

2 tomatoes, peeled, deseeded and finely
diced

10-cm/4-inch piece cucumber, finely
diced

2 spring onions, finely chopped

1 tbsp olive oil

salt and pepper

1. Rinse the trout inside and out under cold running water and pat dry with kitchen paper. Leave the head and tail on and slash the skin of each fish on both sides about 5 times. Brush with the oil and season well with salt and pepper inside and out.

2. To make the stuffing, melt the butter in a small saucepan, add the shallots and gently soften for 2–3 minutes. Add the mushrooms and cook for a further 2 minutes. Add the spinach and heat until it is just wilted. Remove from the heat and add the parsley, lemon rind and a good grating of nutmeg. Leave to cool.

3. Preheat the grill to medium. Fill the cavities of the trout with the mushroom and spinach stuffing, then reshape them as neatly as you can.

4. Cook the trout under the preheated grill for 10–12 minutes, turning once, until cooked through.

5. To make the tomato salsa, mix all the ingredients together and season well with salt and pepper. Serve the trout hot with the tomato salsa spooned over.

#331 Spiced mackerel with tomato salad

Ingredients

4 garlic cloves, well crushed

finely grated zest and juice of 1 lemon

1 heaped tsp ground cumin

1 heaped tsp smoked paprika

2–3 tbsp olive oil

4 large mackerel fillets

Tomato salad

300 g/10½ oz juicy ripe tomatoes

1 small red onion, thinly sliced

1 heaped tbsp chopped fresh herbs

2 tbsp olive oil

1 tbsp white wine vinegar

pinch of caster sugar

salt and pepper

1. Mix the garlic, lemon zest and juice, cumin, paprika and oil together in a small bowl. Put the mackerel fillets in a shallow, non-metallic dish and thoroughly rub both sides with the spice mixture. Cover and leave to marinate in a cool place for 30 minutes, if possible.

2. Preheat the grill to high. Lay the mackerel fillets in the grill pan and cook under the preheated grill for 3 minutes on one side, then turn over, drizzle with any remaining marinade and cook for a further 2–3 minutes, or until the mackerel is cooked through.

3. Meanwhile, prepare the salad. Slice the tomatoes and arrange with the onion on a serving platter. Put the herbs, oil, vinegar, sugar and a little salt and pepper to taste in a screw-top jar and shake well to combine.

4. Drizzle the dressing over the salad and serve with the hot mackerel fillets.

#332 Classic fish burger

Ingredients

4 x 115–175-g/4–6-oz mahi mahi or other white fish fillets

2 tsp vegetable oil or rapeseed oil

½ tsp sea salt

¼ tsp pepper

4 soft burger buns, split

4 tbsp ready-made tartare sauce

To serve

onion slices

lettuce leaves

tomato slices

1. Rinse the fish and pat dry. Rub the fillets on both sides with the oil and sprinkle with the salt and pepper. Place on a large baking sheet.

2. Preheat the grill to high and place the rack about 8 cm/3¼ inches below the heat.

3. Place the fish on the rack and cook under the preheated grill for 4 minutes, then turn and cook for a further 3 minutes, or until the edges start to brown and the fish is just cooked through (the centre of the fish should flake easily when cut into).

4. Spread both halves of each bun with the tartare sauce. Place a fish fillet on each bun base and top with the onion slices, lettuce leaves and tomato slices. Add the bun lids and serve immediately.

#333 Tuna & pasta casserole

Serves
4–6

Ingredients

200 g/7 oz dried ribbon egg pasta

25 g/1 oz butter, plus extra for greasing

55 g/2 oz fine fresh breadcrumbs

400 ml/14 fl oz canned condensed cream of mushroom soup

125 ml/4 fl oz milk

2 celery sticks, chopped

1 red pepper, chopped

1 green pepper, chopped

140 g/5 oz Cheddar cheese, grated

2 tbsp chopped fresh parsley

200 g/7 oz canned tuna in oil, drained and flaked

salt and pepper

1. Preheat the oven to 200°C/400°F/Gas Mark 6. Grease an ovenproof dish. Bring a large saucepan of salted water to the boil. Add the pasta, bring back to the boil and cook for 2 minutes less than specified on the packet. Drain the pasta well and set aside.

2. Meanwhile, melt the butter in a small saucepan. Stir in the breadcrumbs, remove from the heat and set aside. Pour the soup into the pasta pan over a medium heat, then stir in the milk, celery, red and green peppers, half the cheese and the parsley. Add the tuna and gently stir in. Season to taste. Heat just until small bubbles appear around the edge of the mixture – do not boil. Stir the pasta into the pan and use 2 forks to mix all the ingredients together. Spoon into the ovenproof dish and spread it out. Stir the remaining cheese into the buttered breadcrumbs, then sprinkle over the top of the pasta. Bake in the preheated oven for 20–25 minutes until golden. Leave to stand for 5 minutes before serving straight from the dish.

#334 Seared sesame salmon with pak choi

Serves
4

Ingredients

2.5-cm/1-inch piece fresh ginger

1 tbsp soy sauce

2 tsp sesame oil

4 skinless salmon fillets

2 tbsp sesame seeds

2 small pak choi

1 bunch spring onions

1 tbsp sunflower oil

salt and pepper

lime wedges, to serve

1. Peel and finely grate the ginger and mix with the soy sauce and half the sesame oil in a shallow dish. Add the salmon fillets, turning to coat evenly on both sides. Sprinkle the salmon on one side with half the sesame seeds, then turn and sprinkle the other side with the remaining sesame seeds.

2. Cut the pak choi lengthways into quarters. Cut the spring onions into thick diagonal slices.

3. Preheat a heavy-based frying pan. Add the salmon and cook for 3–4 minutes. Turn and cook for a further 3–4 minutes.

4. Meanwhile, heat the sunflower oil and the remaining sesame oil in a wok, add the pak choi and spring onions and stir-fry for 2–3 minutes. Season to taste with salt and pepper.

5. Divide the vegetables between warmed serving plates and place the salmon on top. Serve immediately with lime wedges for squeezing over.

#335 Baked fish

Ingredients

500 g/1 lb 2 oz firm, waxy potatoes, very thinly sliced

1 large garlic clove, very finely chopped

2 onions, thinly sliced

2 tbsp olive oil, plus extra for greasing

2 whole sea bass, haddock, pollack or red snapper, about 400 g/14 oz total weight, heads removed, scaled, gutted and well rinsed

4 fresh thyme sprigs

½ lemon, sliced

150 g/5½ oz black olives, stoned and sliced

salt and pepper

lemon wedges, to serve

1. Preheat the oven to 220°C/425°F/Gas Mark 7 and grease a roasting dish large enough to hold the fish and potatoes. Arrange the potatoes, garlic and onions in a layer on the bottom of the dish, drizzle over half of the oil and season with salt and pepper. Tightly cover with foil and bake in the preheated oven for 30 minutes, until the potatoes are almost tender.

2. Meanwhile, make three slashes on each side of the fish and rub salt and pepper into the slashes. Divide the thyme sprigs and lemon slices between the fish slashes, then set aside.

3. Reduce the oven temperature to 190°C/375°F/Gas Mark 5. Uncover the dish and stir the olives into the potatoes. Arrange the fish on top, drizzle over the remaining oil, return to the oven and cook for 10 minutes per 2.5 cm/1 inch of fish thickness, or until the fish is cooked through and the flesh flakes easily. Remove the dish from the oven. Fillet and skin the fish and divide the fillets between four warmed plates. Serve with the potatoes, onions and olives, and with lemon wedges for squeezing over.

#336 Ginger prawns with oyster mushrooms

Ingredients

150 ml/5 fl oz chicken stock

2 tsp sesame seeds

1 tbsp grated fresh ginger

1 tbsp soy sauce

¼ tsp hot pepper sauce

1 tsp cornflour

3 tbsp vegetable oil

3 carrots, thinly sliced

350 g/12 oz oyster mushrooms, sliced

1 large red pepper, deseeded and thinly sliced

450 g/1 lb raw king prawns, peeled and deveined

2 garlic cloves, crushed

freshly cooked rice, to serve

fresh coriander sprigs, to garnish

1. In a small bowl, stir together the stock, sesame seeds, ginger, soy sauce, hot pepper sauce and cornflour until well blended. Set aside.

2. Add 2 tablespoons of the oil to a large wok and heat. Add the carrots and stir-fry for 3 minutes, remove from the wok and set aside. Add the remaining oil to the wok, add the mushrooms and stir-fry for 2 minutes. Remove from the wok and set aside. Add the red pepper, prawns and garlic to the wok and stir-fry for 3 minutes, until the prawns turn pink and start to curl.

3. Stir the sauce again and pour it into the wok. Cook until the mixture bubbles, then return the carrots and mushrooms to the wok. Cover and cook for a further 2 minutes.

4. Serve over cooked rice and garnished with coriander sprigs.

#337 Steamed salmon

Serves
4

Ingredients

40 g/1½ oz butter, melted

4 salmon fillets, about 140 g/5 oz each

finely grated rind and juice of 1 lemon

1 tbsp snipped chives

1 tbsp chopped parsley

salt and pepper

salad and crusty bread, to serve

1. Preheat the oven to 200°/400°F/Gas Mark 6. Cut 4 x 30-cm/12-inch squares of double thickness foil and brush with the melted butter.

2. Place a piece of salmon on each square and spoon over the lemon rind and juice. Sprinkle with the chives, parsley, and salt and pepper.

3. Wrap the foil over loosely and seal firmly with the join on top.

4. Place the parcels in a baking tin and bake for 20 minutes, or until the fish flakes easily.

5. Transfer the salmon and juices to warmed serving plates and serve immediately with salad and crusty bread.

#338 Baked lemon cod

Serves
4

Ingredients

4 thick cod fillets

olive oil, for brushing

8 thin lemon slices

salt and pepper

Sauce

4 tbsp olive oil

1 garlic clove, crushed

4 tbsp chopped fresh parsley

2 tbsp chopped fresh mint

juice of ½ lemon

salt and pepper

1. Preheat the oven to 200°C/400°F/Gas Mark 6. Rinse the cod fillets and pat dry with kitchen paper, then brush with oil. Place each fillet on a piece of greaseproof paper that is large enough to encase the fish in a parcel. Top each fillet with 2 lemon slices and season to taste with salt and pepper. Fold over the paper to encase the fish and bake in the preheated oven for 20 minutes, or until just cooked through.

2. Meanwhile, to make the sauce, put all the ingredients into a food processor and process until finely chopped. Season to taste with salt and pepper.

3. Carefully unfold each parcel and transfer the cod to serving plates. Drizzle a spoonful of herb sauce around each piece of fish before serving.

#339 Fish baked in tomato sauce

Ingredients

25 g/1 oz butter

2 tbsp olive oil

2 shallots, finely chopped

2 garlic cloves, finely chopped

1 celery stick, finely chopped

400 g/14 oz canned chopped tomatoes

2 tbsp tomato purée

brown sugar, to taste

2 tbsp chopped fresh parsley

100 ml/3½ fl oz dry white wine

butter, for greasing

4 white fish steaks

2 tbsp dry breadcrumbs

salt and pepper

1. Melt the butter with the oil in a saucepan. Add the shallots, garlic and celery and cook over a low heat, stirring occasionally, for 5 minutes, until softened. Stir in the tomatoes, tomato purée, sugar to taste, parsley and wine and season to taste with salt and pepper. Increase the heat to medium and bring to the boil, then reduce the heat and simmer, stirring occasionally, for 15-20 minutes, until thickened.

2. Meanwhile, preheat the oven to 190°C/375°F/Gas Mark 5. Grease an ovenproof dish with butter. Put the fish into the prepared dish in a single layer. Spoon the sauce over the fish steaks and sprinkle with the breadcrumbs.

3. Bake in the preheated oven, spooning the cooking juices over the fish 2-3 times, for 20-30 minutes, until the topping is crisp and golden brown. Serve.

#340 Fusilli with Cajun seafood sauce

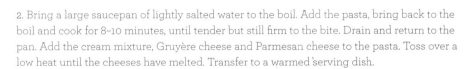

Ingredients

500 ml/18 fl oz whipping cream

8 spring onions, thinly sliced

55 g/2 oz chopped fresh parsley

1 tbsp chopped fresh thyme

½ tbsp pepper

½-1 tsp dried chilli flakes

1 tsp salt

450 g/1 lb dried fusilli

40 g/1½ oz Gruyère cheese, grated

20 g/¾ oz freshly grated Parmesan cheese

2 tbsp olive oil

225 g/8 oz raw prawns, peeled and deveined

225 g/8 oz scallops, sliced

1 tbsp shredded fresh basil, to garnish

1. Heat the cream in a large saucepan over a medium heat, stirring constantly. When almost boiling, reduce the heat and add the spring onions, parsley, thyme, pepper, chilli flakes and salt. Simmer for 7-8 minutes, stirring, until thickened. Remove from the heat.

2. Bring a large saucepan of lightly salted water to the boil. Add the pasta, bring back to the boil and cook for 8-10 minutes, until tender but still firm to the bite. Drain and return to the pan. Add the cream mixture, Gruyère cheese and Parmesan cheese to the pasta. Toss over a low heat until the cheeses have melted. Transfer to a warmed serving dish.

3. Heat the oil in a large frying pan over a medium-high heat. Add the prawns and scallops. Cook for 2-3 minutes, until the prawns have turned opaque and are firm to the touch.

4. Pour the seafood over the pasta and toss to mix. Sprinkle with the basil and serve.

Cajun catfish

Serves 4

Ingredients

cooking spray, for greasing
125 ml/4 fl oz low-fat buttermilk
40 g/1½ oz pecan nuts, chopped
50 g/1¾ oz polenta
1½ tsp finely chopped fresh thyme
1 tsp salt
1 tsp cayenne pepper
1 tsp garlic powder
1 tsp sweet paprika
½ tsp onion powder
½ tsp freshly ground black pepper
4 catfish fillets, about 175 g/6 oz each
2 tbsp finely chopped fresh flat-leaf
parsley and 4 lemon wedges, to garnish

1. Preheat the grill to high, place a wire rack on top of a large baking sheet and lightly spray the rack with cooking spray.

2. Put the buttermilk into a shallow bowl.

3. Put the nuts into a food processor and pulse until coarsely ground.

4. Put the ground nuts, polenta, thyme, salt, cayenne pepper, garlic powder, paprika, onion powder and black pepper into a shallow bowl and stir to combine.

5. Dip each fish fillet in the buttermilk and then in the spiced polenta mixture, turning to coat completely with both the milk and the spices.

6. Arrange the fish on the prepared rack in a single layer and cook under the preheated grill for 3 minutes. Turn and cook for a further 3 minutes, or until the fish is cooked through.

7. Serve the fish immediately with lemon wedges for squeezing over and garnished with parsley.

#342 Honey salmon with couscous

Serves 2

Ingredients

4 tbsp clear honey

2 tbsp Dijon mustard

2 tbsp warm water

2 tsp soy sauce

1 tsp olive oil, plus extra for drizzling

2 salmon fillets

115 g/4 oz couscous

200 ml/7 fl oz vegetable stock

2 spring onions, chopped

salt and pepper

steamed baby courgettes, halved, to serve

1. Heat the honey, mustard, water, soy sauce and oil in a saucepan over a low heat for 5 minutes, stirring occasionally. Place the salmon fillets on a sheet of foil and season with salt and pepper. Brush generously with some of the sauce. Preheat the grill to high.

2. Put the couscous in a heatproof bowl. Pour over the stock, cover and leave for 10 minutes. Meanwhile, cook the salmon under the preheated grill for 4 minutes then turn them over, brush with more of the sauce and cook for a further 4 minutes or until cooked through.

3. Drizzle the couscous with a little oil and run a fork through it to fluff it up. Brush the salmon with the last of the sauce and sprinkle with the chopped spring onions. Serve the salmon with the couscous and steamed baby courgettes.

#343 Tiger prawn & coriander pesto pizza

Makes 2

Ingredients

2 ready-made pizza bases

8 tbsp ready-made coriander pesto

8 spring onions, finely chopped

300 g/10½ oz cooked tiger prawns

125 g/4½ oz Parmesan cheese shavings

salt and pepper

1. Preheat the oven to 220°C/425°F/Gas Mark 7. Place the pizza bases on two baking trays.

2. Divide the coriander pesto between the two pizza bases, spreading almost to the edges. Scatter over the spring onions, prawns and cheese, then season to taste with salt and pepper.

3. Bake in the preheated oven for 10–12 minutes, or until the cheese is melting and turning golden and the bases are crisp underneath. Serve immediately.

344 Prawns with coconut rice

Serves
4

Ingredients

115 g/4 oz dried Chinese mushrooms

1 tbsp vegetable oil or groundnut oil

6 spring onions, chopped

55 g/2 oz desiccated coconut

1 fresh green chilli, deseeded and chopped

225 g/8 oz jasmine rice

150 ml/5 fl oz fish stock

400 ml/14 fl oz coconut milk

350 g/12 oz cooked peeled prawns

6 sprigs fresh Thai basil

1. Place the mushrooms in a small bowl, cover with hot water and set aside to soak for 30 minutes. Drain, then cut off and discard the stalks and slice the caps.

2. Heat the oil in a wok, add the spring onions, coconut and chilli and stir-fry for 2–3 minutes, until lightly browned. Add the mushrooms and stir-fry for 3–4 minutes.

3. Add the rice and stir-fry for 2–3 minutes, then add the stock and bring to the boil. Reduce the heat and add the coconut milk. Simmer for 10–15 minutes, until the rice is tender. Stir in the prawns and basil, heat through and serve.

345 Baked sea bass

Serves
4

Ingredients

1.3 kg/3 lb fresh sea bass, gutted

2–4 fresh rosemary sprigs

½ lemon, thinly sliced

4 tbsp olive oil, plus extra for brushing

2 tsp coarse sea salt

2 tsp capers

2 garlic cloves, crushed

4 tbsp water

2 fresh bay leaves, plus extra to garnish

1 tsp lemon juice or wine vinegar

pepper

lemon wedges, to serve

1. Preheat the oven to 190°C/375°F/Gas Mark 5. Scrape off the scales from the fish and cut off the sharp fins. Make diagonal cuts along both sides. Wash and dry thoroughly. Place a sprig of rosemary in the cavity of each of the smaller fish with half the lemon slices, or put two sprigs and all the lemon slices in the large fish. Brush a roasting tin with oil then brush the fish with 2 tablespoons of the oil. Cook in the preheated oven for 30 minutes for the small fish or 45–50 minutes for the large fish, until the thickest part of the fish is opaque.

2. Crush the salt, capers and garlic in a mortar with a pestle, then work in the water. Bruise the bay leaves and the remaining rosemary and put into a bowl. Add the garlic mixture, lemon juice and the remaining oil and pound together until the flavours are released. Season with pepper.

3. Place the fish on a serving dish and spoon some of the sauce over the fish. Remove the bruised bay leaves, garnish with fresh bay leaves and serve with lemon wedges and sauce.

#346 Cod steaks with caper sauce

Ingredients

oil, for brushing

4 cod steaks, about 175 g/6 oz each

½ lemon

85 g/3 oz butter

2 tbsp pickled capers, plus 1 tbsp vinegar from the jar

1 tbsp chopped fresh parsley

salt and pepper

1. Brush the grill with oil and preheat. Season the fish with salt and pepper and squeeze over the lemon.

2. Put the butter in a saucepan and melt over a low heat. Continue to cook until it turns brown, but do not let it become black.

3. When the grill is hot, add the cod steaks and cook for 6–8 minutes until the flesh is opaque and flakes easily with a fork.

4. Stir the capers and vinegar into the butter, then stir in the chopped parsley and remove from the heat. Place the fish on warmed serving plates, spoon over the caper sauce and serve immediately.

#347 Poached salmon

Serves 6–8

Ingredients

1 whole salmon (head on), about 2.7–3.6 kg/6–8 lb prepared weight

3 tbsp salt

3 bay leaves

10 black peppercorns

1 onion, peeled and sliced

1 lemon, sliced

lemon wedges, to serve

1. Wipe the salmon thoroughly inside and out with kitchen paper, then use the back of a cook's knife to remove any scales that might still be on the skin. Remove the fins with a pair of scissors and trim the tail. Some people prefer to cut off the head but it is traditionally served with it on.

2. Place the salmon on the two-handled rack that comes with a fish kettle, then place it in the kettle. Fill the kettle with enough cold water to cover the salmon adequately. Sprinkle over the salt, bay leaves and peppercorns and scatter in the onion and lemon slices.

3. Place the kettle over a low heat, over two burners, and very slowly bring just to the boil.

4. Cover and simmer very gently. To serve cold, simmer for 2 minutes only, remove from the heat and leave to cool in the water for about 2 hours with the lid on. To serve hot, simmer for 6–8 minutes and leave to stand in the hot water for 15 minutes before removing. Serve with lemon wedges for squeezing over.

#348 Breaded swordfish with tomato & courgette sauce

Ingredients

85 g/3 oz butter

2 tbsp olive oil

1 Spanish onion, finely chopped

2 garlic cloves, finely chopped

1 celery stick, finely chopped

3 courgettes, thickly sliced

400 g/14 oz canned chopped tomatoes

2 tbsp tomato purée

1 tbsp drained capers

pinch of cayenne pepper

100 ml/3½ fl oz water

4 swordfish steaks

85 g/3 oz dry breadcrumbs

1 tsp dried oregano

2 eggs

salt and pepper

1. Melt two thirds of the butter with the oil in a large saucepan. Add the onion, garlic, celery and courgettes and cook over a low heat, stirring occasionally, for 8–10 minutes, until lightly browned. Stir in the tomatoes, tomato purée, capers, cayenne pepper and water and season to taste with salt and pepper. Increase the heat to medium and bring to the boil, then reduce the heat and simmer, stirring occasionally, for 15 minutes, until thickened.

2. Meanwhile, cut the fish steaks in half. Mix the breadcrumbs and oregano together in a shallow dish and lightly beat the eggs in a separate shallow dish. Dip the fish first into the eggs and then into the breadcrumb mixture to coat.

3. Melt the remaining butter in a large frying pan. Add the fish and cook over a medium heat, turning occasionally, for 6–8 minutes, until lightly browned. Transfer to the saucepan and spoon the sauce over. Simmer, gently stirring occasionally, for 15 minutes, until the fish flakes easily. Transfer to a warmed serving dish and serve immediately.

#349 Peppered tuna steaks

Ingredients

4 tuna steaks, about 175 g/6 oz each

4 tsp sunflower oil or olive oil

1 tsp salt

2 tbsp pink, green and black peppercorns, roughly crushed

handful of fresh rocket leaves, to garnish

lemon wedges, to serve

1. Brush the tuna steaks on each side with oil and sprinkle with the salt.

2. Scatter the peppercorns on a large flat dish and press each steak into the peppercorns, ensuring they are evenly coated.

3. Heat a ridged griddle pan over a medium heat. Add the tuna and cook for 2–3 minutes on each side.

4. Transfer the fish to warmed plates, garnish with rocket leaves and serve with lemon wedges for squeezing over.

#350 Beer-battered fish & chips

Serves 4

Ingredients

Batter

225 g/8 oz self-raising flour, plus extra for dusting

½ tsp salt

300 ml/10 fl oz cold lager

Mushy peas

350 g/12 oz frozen peas

30 g/1 oz butter

2 tbsp single cream

vegetable oil, for deep-frying

6 large floury potatoes, such as King Edward, Maris Piper or Desirée, cut into chips

4 thick cod fillets, about 175 g/6 oz each

salt and pepper

lemon wedges, to serve

1. Sift the flour into a bowl with a little salt and whisk in most of the lager. Check the consistency and add the remaining lager; it should be thick, like double cream. Chill in the refrigerator for half an hour. Meanwhile, bring a saucepan of lightly salted water to the boil, add the peas, bring back to the boil and cook for 3 minutes. Drain and mash to a thick purée, add the butter and cream and season to taste. Set aside and keep warm.

2. Heat the oil to 120°C/250°F in a large saucepan using a thermometer. Preheat the oven to 150°C/300°F/Gas Mark 2. Fry the chips for about 8–10 minutes until soft but not coloured. Remove from the oil, drain on kitchen paper and place in a dish in the warm oven. Increase the temperature of the oil to 180–190°C/350°–375°F. Season the fish with salt and pepper to taste and dust lightly with a little flour. Dip one fillet in the batter and coat thickly. Carefully place in the hot oil and repeat with the remaining fillets. Cook for 8–10 minutes, turning them over halfway through. Remove from the oil, drain and keep warm.

3. Reheat the oil to 180–190°C/350–375°F and recook the chips for a further 2–3 minutes until golden brown. Drain and season with salt and pepper to taste. Serve the chips immediately with the fish, mushy peas and lemon wedges for squeezing over.

224

Serves
4

Fish with white wine, chilli & tapenade

Ingredients

1 tbsp olive oil

4 white fish fillets

4 tbsp tapenade

1 small red finger chilli, finely diced

4 tbsp freshly grated Parmesan cheese

4 tbsp dry white wine

salt and pepper

cooked rice, to serve

1. Preheat the oven to 220°C/425°F/Gas Mark 7. Brush a wide, ovenproof dish with the oil.

2. Season the fish with salt and pepper to taste and place in the prepared dish in a single layer.

3. Mix the tapenade and chilli together and spread the mixture over the fish, then sprinkle with the cheese.

4. Pour the wine around the fish and bake in the preheated oven for about 15 minutes, or until the flesh flakes easily. Serve with rice.

352 Thai fish curry

Serves
4

Ingredients

1 tbsp oil

2 spring onions, sliced

1 tsp cumin seeds, ground

2 fresh green chillies, chopped

1 tsp coriander seeds, ground

4 tbsp chopped fresh coriander

1 tsp chopped fresh mint

1 tbsp snipped fresh chives

150 ml/5 fl oz light coconut milk

4 white fish fillets, about 225 g/8 oz each

salt and pepper

1 tsp chopped fresh mint, to garnish

cooked basmati rice, to serve

1. Heat the oil in a large frying pan or shallow saucepan and add the spring onions. Fry the spring onions over a medium heat until they are softened but not coloured.

2. Stir in the cumin, chillies and ground coriander seeds, and cook until fragrant. Add the fresh coriander, mint, chives and coconut milk and season to taste with salt and pepper.

3. Carefully place the fish fillets in the pan and poach for 10–15 minutes, or until the flesh flakes when tested with a fork.

4. Garnish the curry with the chopped mint and serve immediately, with the basmati rice on the side.

#353 Sea bass with olive gremolata

Serves 4

Ingredients

900 g/2 lb small new potatoes

grated rind of 1 lemon

1 garlic clove, chopped

55 g/2 oz fresh flat-leaf parsley

70 g/2½ oz stoned black olives

2 tbsp capers

3 tbsp olive oil

4 sea bass fillets, about 175 g/6 oz each

4 tbsp dry white wine

salt and pepper

1. Cook the potatoes in a saucepan of lightly salted boiling water for 15–20 minutes, or until tender.

2. Place the lemon rind, garlic, parsley, olives, capers and 2 tablespoons of the oil in a food processor and process briefly to a rough paste.

3. Brush the fish with the remaining oil and season to taste with salt and pepper. Heat a heavy-based frying pan and fry the sea bass for 5–6 minutes, turning once. Remove the fish from the pan and keep warm. Stir the wine into the pan and boil for 1 minute, stirring. Add the gremolata to the pan and stir for a few seconds to heat gently.

4. Drain the potatoes when tender and crush lightly with a wooden spoon or potato masher.

5. Serve the sea bass and crushed potatoes topped with the gremolata.

#354 Tuna with ginger & chilli sauce

Serves 4

Ingredients

4 tuna steaks, 2 cm/¾ inch thick, about 175 g/6 oz each

2 tbsp olive oil

salt

lime wedges, to garnish

Sauce

100 g/3½ oz soft light brown sugar

125 ml/4 fl oz water

2.5-cm/1-inch piece fresh ginger, shredded

1 green chilli, deseeded and finely chopped

1 large garlic clove, crushed

juice of ½ lime

1. Put the tuna steaks in a shallow dish in which they sit snugly in a single layer. Rub with salt and the olive oil.

2. To make the sauce, put the sugar and water in a small saucepan and bring to the boil. Boil for 7–8 minutes until syrupy. Add the ginger, chilli, garlic and lime juice, and boil for another minute. Pour into a bowl and leave until completely cold.

3. Pour the cold sauce over the tuna steaks, turning to coat. Cover with clingfilm and leave to marinate in the refrigerator for 30–60 minutes, turning occasionally.

4. When ready to cook, preheat the grill to medium–high. Reserve the marinade and cook the tuna steaks for 6–8 minutes, turning once, until just cooked.

5. Pour the reserved marinade into a small saucepan. Bring to the boil and boil for 2 minutes. Pour into a small jug. Arrange the steaks on plates, garnish with lime wedges and serve immediately with the hot marinade.

#355 Monkfish with onions & coriander

Serves 4

Ingredients

1 kg/2 lb 4 oz monkfish tail
4 tbsp lime juice
1 garlic clove, finely chopped
1 tsp ground cumin
1 tsp paprika
1 Spanish onion, sliced into rings
2 fresh red chillies, deseeded and finely chopped
1 tbsp chopped fresh coriander
2 tbsp olive oil
salt and pepper

1. Remove the grey membrane that covers the monkfish tail with a sharp knife, then cut along one side of the central bone to remove the fillet of flesh. Repeat on the other side to remove the other fillet from the bone, then tie the fillets together with string. Transfer to a shallow, non-metallic, ovenproof dish.

2. Place the lime juice, garlic, cumin and paprika in a bowl, stir to mix, and season to taste with salt and pepper. Spoon the marinade over the monkfish, cover and leave to marinate in the refrigerator for 1 hour.

3. Preheat the oven to 220°C/425°F/Gas Mark 7. Sprinkle the onion rings, chillies and the chopped coriander over the fish and drizzle with the oil. Roast in the preheated oven for 20 minutes, or until the fish is cooked through and the flesh flakes easily. Cut the fish into slices and serve.

#356 Calamari with prawns & broad beans

Serves 4–6

Ingredients

2 tbsp olive oil
4 spring onions, thinly sliced
2 garlic cloves, finely chopped
500 g/1 lb 2 oz cleaned squid bodies, thickly sliced
100 ml/3½ fl oz dry white wine
225 g/8 oz fresh or frozen baby broad beans
250 g/9 oz raw king prawns, peeled and deveined
4 tbsp chopped fresh flat-leaf parsley
salt and pepper
fresh crusty bread, to serve

1. Heat the oil in a large frying pan with a lid, add the spring onions and cook over a medium heat, stirring occasionally, for 4–5 minutes, until soft. Add the garlic and cook, stirring, for 30 seconds, until soft.

2. Add the squid and cook over a high heat, stirring occasionally, for 2 minutes, or until golden brown. Stir in the wine and bring to the boil. Add the beans, reduce the heat, cover and simmer for 5–8 minutes, if using fresh beans, or 4–5 minutes, if using frozen beans, until tender.

3. Add the prawns, re-cover and simmer for a further 2–3 minutes, until the prawns turn pink and start to curl. Stir in the parsley and season to taste with salt and pepper.

4. Serve immediately with crusty bread.

227

#357 Scallops with breadcrumbs

Serves 4

Ingredients

20 large fresh scallops, removed from their shells and deveined

200 g/7 oz butter, plus extra, if needed

85 g/3 oz day-old French bread, made into fine breadcrumbs

4 garlic cloves, finely chopped

5 tbsp finely chopped fresh flat-leaf parsley

salt and pepper

lemon wedges, to serve

1. Preheat the oven to 110°C/225°F/Gas Mark ¼. Season the scallops with salt and pepper to taste and set aside.

2. Melt half the butter in a large frying pan over a high heat. Add the breadcrumbs and garlic, reduce the heat to medium and fry, stirring, for 5–6 minutes, or until golden brown. Remove the breadcrumbs from the pan and drain on kitchen paper, then keep warm in the preheated oven. Wipe out the pan, add the remaining butter and heat over a high heat until melted. Reduce the heat to medium, add the scallops in a single layer and fry for 2 minutes.

3. Turn the scallops over and cook for a further 2–3 minutes, or until they are golden and cooked through if you cut one with a knife. Add more butter to the pan if needed. Divide the scallops between four warmed plates and sprinkle with the breadcrumbs and parsley. Serve with lemon wedges for squeezing over.

#358 Nut-crusted halibut

Serves 4

Ingredients

3 tbsp butter, melted

750 g/1 lb 10 oz halibut fillet

55 g/2 oz pistachio nuts, shelled and very finely chopped

lemon wedges, to garnish

mixed salad, to serve

1. Brush the melted butter over the halibut fillet.

2. Spread out the nuts on a large, flat plate. Roll the fish in the nuts, pressing down gently.

3. Preheat a griddle pan over a medium heat. Add the halibut to the pan, turning once, and cook for 10 minutes, or until firm but tender – the exact cooking time will depend on the thickness of the fillet.

4. Lift out the fish and any loose nuts from the pan and serve immediately, garnished with lemon wedges and accompanied by the salad.

#359 Baked salmon with wild rice

Serves 4

Ingredients

70 g/2½ oz butter

1 tbsp olive oil, plus extra for greasing

400 g/14 oz button mushrooms, wiped and thinly sliced

1 tbsp chopped fresh tarragon, or ½ tbsp dried tarragon

300 g/10½ oz leeks, trimmed and thinly sliced

12 thin lemon slices

4 salmon fillets, any small bones removed

4 tbsp dry white vermouth

125 g/4½ oz crème fraîche

salt and pepper

250 g/9 oz wild rice, cooked, to serve

1. Preheat the oven to 220°C/425°F/Gas Mark 7. Cut out four rounds of greaseproof paper large enough to hold a salmon fillet with some mushrooms and leeks spooned on top. Fold the rounds in half and brush the bottom halves with oil.

2. Melt 30 g/1 oz of the butter with the oil in a large frying pan over a high heat. Add the mushrooms and cook, stirring, for 6 minutes or until they start to give off their liquid. Add the tarragon, and salt and pepper to taste and stir. Remove from the pan and set aside. Melt the remaining butter in the pan, add the leeks, season to taste and cook, stirring, for 6 minutes, or until tender.

3. Arrange 3 lemon slices in a row along the fold on each of the paper rounds. Place a salmon fillet on top, top with one quarter of the mushrooms and the leeks and add a tablespoon of vermouth, 2 tablespoons of crème fraîche and salt and pepper. Fold over and crimp the edges to seal. Transfer to a baking tray, place in the preheated oven and bake for 12 minutes, or until the flesh flakes. Place the salmon on a bed of wild rice and serve.

#360 Ravioli with crabmeat & ricotta

Serves 4

Ingredients

300 g/10½ oz type 00 pasta flour or strong white flour

1 tsp salt

3 eggs, beaten

70 g/2½ oz butter, melted

Filling

175 g/6 oz white crabmeat

175 g/6 oz ricotta cheese

finely grated rind of 1 lemon

pinch of dried chilli flakes

2 tbsp chopped fresh flat-leaf parsley

salt and pepper

1. Sift the flour and salt onto a board, make a well in the centre and add the eggs. Stir with a fork to gradually incorporate the flour into the liquid to form a dough. Knead for about 5 minutes, until the dough is smooth. Wrap in clingfilm and leave to rest for 20 minutes.

2. To make the filling, stir together the crabmeat, ricotta cheese, lemon rind, chilli flakes and parsley. Season to taste with salt and pepper.

3. Roll out the dough to a thickness of about 3 mm/⅛ inch and cut into 32 x 6-cm/2½-inch squares. Place a spoonful of the filling in the centre of half the squares. Brush the edges with water and place the remaining squares on top, pressing to seal.

4. Bring a saucepan of lightly salted water to the boil. Add the ravioli, bring back to the boil and cook for 3 minutes, or until tender but still firm to the bite. Drain well. Drizzle the melted butter over the ravioli, sprinkle with pepper and serve immediately.

Blackened salmon

Ingredients

1 tsp salt

1 tsp cayenne pepper

1 tsp garlic powder

1 tsp sweet paprika

1½ tsp finely chopped fresh thyme

1½ tsp finely chopped fresh oregano

½ tsp freshly ground black pepper

4 x 175-g/6-oz salmon fillets

2 tbsp vegetable oil

zest and juice of 1 lemon and 2 tbsp finely chopped fresh flat-leaf parsley, to garnish

1. Put the salt, cayenne pepper, garlic powder, paprika, thyme, oregano and black pepper into a shallow bowl and mix well to combine.

2. Generously coat the flesh side of each salmon fillet with the spice mixture.

3. Heat the oil in a large frying pan over a medium-high heat until very hot and beginning to smoke. Reduce the heat to medium and place the fish fillets, flesh side down, in the hot oil. Cook for 3–4 minutes, until well browned, then carefully turn the fish over and cook for a further 5–6 minutes, until the skin is brown and very crisp.

4. Serve immediately, garnished with the lemon zest and juice and parsley.

#362 Grilled monkfish with herb polenta slices

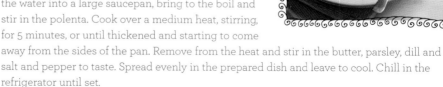

Ingredients

1 litre/1¾ pints boiling water

200 g/7 oz medium-grain polenta

25 g/1 oz butter

2 tbsp finely chopped fresh parsley

2 tsp chopped fresh dill

4 x 175 g/6 oz pieces monkfish fillet

1 tbsp olive oil, plus extra for greasing

salt and pepper

lemon wedges, to serve

1. Lightly grease a rectangular baking dish or tin. Pour the water into a large saucepan, bring to the boil and stir in the polenta. Cook over a medium heat, stirring, for 5 minutes, or until thickened and starting to come away from the sides of the pan. Remove from the heat and stir in the butter, parsley, dill and salt and pepper to taste. Spread evenly in the prepared dish and leave to cool. Chill in the refrigerator until set.

2. Preheat the grill to high. Brush the monkfish with oil and sprinkle with salt and pepper. Arrange on the grill rack and cook for 6–8 minutes, turning once, until cooked through.

3. Meanwhile, turn out the polenta and cut into slices. Add to the grill about halfway through the fish cooking time and cook until golden, turning once. Slice the monkfish and arrange on the polenta slices. Serve hot, with lemon wedges for squeezing over.

#363 Monkfish with a lemon & parsley crust

Ingredients

4 tbsp sunflower oil

4 tbsp fresh breadcrumbs

4 tbsp chopped fresh parsley, plus extra sprigs to garnish

finely grated rind of 1 large lemon

4 monkfish fillets, about 140–175 g/5–6 oz each

salt and pepper

1. Preheat the oven to 180°C/350°F/Gas Mark 4. Mix the oil, breadcrumbs, parsley and lemon rind together in a bowl until well combined. Season to taste with salt and pepper.

2. Place the fish fillets in a large roasting tin.

3. Divide the breadcrumb mixture between the fish and press it down with your fingers to ensure it covers the fillets.

4. Bake in the preheated oven for 7–8 minutes, or until the fish is cooked through.

5. Garnish with parsley sprigs and serve.

#364 Fish & potato stew

Ingredients

1½ tbsp olive oil, plus extra for brushing

1 onion, finely chopped

3 large garlic cloves, 2 chopped and 1 halved

1 tbsp fennel seeds

½ tsp dried chilli flakes, or to taste

pinch of saffron threads

400 g/14 oz canned chopped tomatoes

125 ml/4 fl oz fish stock or water

2 bay leaves

500 g/1 lb 2 oz floury potatoes, sliced

900 g/2 lb mixed fish, boned, skinned and trimmed

2 red peppers, deseeded and sliced

2 tbsp chopped fresh parsley

salt and pepper

1. Preheat the oven to 180°C/350°F/Gas Mark 4. Heat the oil in a saucepan over a medium heat. Add the onion and fry, stirring, for 2 minutes. Add the chopped garlic, fennel seeds, chilli flakes and saffron and fry for a further minute, or until the onion is soft. Add the tomatoes, stock and bay leaves and season to taste with salt and pepper. Cover and bring to the boil, then reduce the heat to very low and simmer for 10 minutes. Discard the bay leaves.

2. Meanwhile, rub the garlic halves all over a 1.5-litre/2¾-pint ovenproof baking dish. Bring a large saucepan of lightly salted water to the boil, add the potatoes, bring back to the boil and cook for 8–10 minutes, or until starting to soften. Drain well, pat dry and set aside.

3. Place the prepared dish on a baking sheet and arrange half the potatoes in a layer at the bottom of the dish. Place the fish and red peppers on top. Spoon over the tomato sauce, sprinkle with the parsley and shake the dish slightly. Arrange the remaining potatoes on top to cover all the other ingredients and lightly brush with oil. Bake in the preheated oven for 20–25 minutes, or until the fish and potatoes are tender when pierced with a skewer. Serve.

#365 Seafood risotto

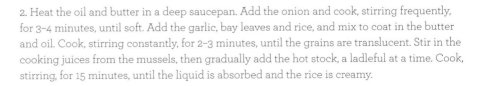

Ingredients

150 ml/5 fl oz dry white wine

4 baby squid, cleaned and sliced

250 g/9 oz raw prawns, peeled and deveined

250 g/9 oz live mussels, scrubbed and debearded

2 tbsp olive oil

55 g/2 oz butter

1 onion, finely chopped

2 garlic cloves, finely chopped

2 bay leaves

350 g/12 oz risotto rice

about 1.5 litres/2¾ pints hot fish stock

salt and pepper

chopped fresh flat-leaf parsley, to garnish

1. Heat the wine in a saucepan until boiling. Add the squid and prawns, cover and cook for 2 minutes. Remove with a slotted spoon and set aside. Discard any mussels with broken shells and any that refuse to close when tapped. Add to the pan, cover and cook for 2–3 minutes, until they have opened. Discard any that remain closed. Drain, reserving the juices and remove from their shells.

2. Heat the oil and butter in a deep saucepan. Add the onion and cook, stirring frequently, for 3–4 minutes, until soft. Add the garlic, bay leaves and rice, and mix to coat in the butter and oil. Cook, stirring constantly, for 2–3 minutes, until the grains are translucent. Stir in the cooking juices from the mussels, then gradually add the hot stock, a ladleful at a time. Cook, stirring, for 15 minutes, until the liquid is absorbed and the rice is creamy.

3. Stir in the cooked seafood, cover and cook for a further 2 minutes to heat through. Season to taste with salt and pepper. Garnish with parsley and serve immediately.

#366 Spicy grilled salmon

Serves
4

Ingredients

4 garlic cloves, finely chopped

2 tbsp extra virgin olive oil

pinch of ground allspice

pinch of ground cinnamon

juice of 2 limes

1–2 tsp marinade from canned chipotle chillies

¼ tsp ground cumin

pinch of sugar

4 x 175-g/6-oz salmon steaks

salt and pepper

lime slices, to garnish

mixed salad, to serve

1. Place the garlic in a non-metallic bowl with the oil, allspice, cinnamon, lime juice, chipotle marinade, cumin and sugar. Season to taste with salt and pepper and stir to combine.

2. Coat the salmon with the marinade, then transfer to a large non-metallic dish. Cover with clingfilm and leave to marinate in the refrigerator for 1 hour.

3. Preheat the grill to medium. Transfer the salmon to the grill rack and cook under the preheated grill for 3–4 minutes on each side, or until cooked through.

4. Place the salmon on serving plates, garnish with lime slices and serve immediately with a mixed salad.

#367 Mediterranean swordfish

Serves
4

Ingredients

2 tbsp olive oil

1 onion, finely chopped

1 celery stick, finely chopped

115 g/4 oz stoned green olives

450 g/1 lb tomatoes, chopped

3 tbsp capers

4 x 140-g/5-oz swordfish steaks

salt and pepper

fresh flat-leaf parsley sprigs, to garnish

1. Heat the oil in a large, heavy-based frying pan. Add the onion and celery and cook over a low heat, stirring occasionally, for 5 minutes, or until soft.

2. Meanwhile, roughly chop half the olives. Stir the chopped and whole olives into the pan with the tomatoes and capers and season to taste with salt and pepper.

3. Bring to the boil, then reduce the heat, cover and simmer gently, stirring occasionally, for 15 minutes.

4. Add the swordfish steaks to the pan and return to the boil. Cover and simmer, turning once during cooking, for 20 minutes, until the fish is just cooked through and the flesh flakes easily.

5. Transfer the swordfish steaks to serving plates and spoon the sauce over them. Garnish with parsley sprigs and serve immediately.

#368 Prawn & mussel paella

Serves 6–8

Ingredients

16 live mussels

½ tsp saffron threads

6 tbsp olive oil

6-8 boned chicken thighs

140 g/5 oz chorizo sausage, sliced

2 large onions, chopped

4 large garlic cloves, crushed

1 tsp mild or hot Spanish paprika

350 g/12 oz paella rice, rinsed

100 g/3½ oz French beans, chopped

125 g/4½ oz frozen peas

1.3 litres/2¼ pints fish stock

16 raw prawns, peeled and deveined

2 grilled red peppers, peeled and sliced

salt and pepper

chopped fresh parsley, to garnish

1. Soak the mussels in lightly salted water for 10 minutes. Put the saffron threads into a small bowl with a little hot water and leave to infuse for a few minutes. Discard any mussels that remain closed.

2. Heat 3 tablespoons of the oil in a 30-cm/12-inch paella pan or flameproof casserole. Add the chicken and cook over a medium–high heat, turning frequently, for 5 minutes, or until golden and crisp. Using a slotted spoon, transfer to a bowl. Add the chorizo to the pan and cook, stirring, for 1 minute, or until beginning to crisp. Add to the chicken. Heat the remaining oil in the pan, add the onions and cook, stirring frequently, for 2 minutes. Add the garlic and paprika and cook for a further 3 minutes, or until the onions are soft but not brow. Add the rice, beans and peas and stir until coated in oil. Return the chicken and chorizo and any accumulated juices to the pan. Stir in the stock, saffron and its soaking liquid, and salt and pepper to taste and bring to the boil, stirring constantly. Reduce the heat to low and simmer, uncovered, for 15 minutes, or until the rice is almost tender.

3. Arrange the mussels, prawns and red peppers on top, then cover and simmer, without stirring, for a further 5 minutes. Discard any mussels that remain closed. Sprinkle with parsley and serve.

#369 Linguini with clams

Serves 2–4

Ingredients

200 g/7 oz dried linguini pasta

3 tbsp extra virgin olive oil

4 garlic cloves, finely chopped

2 shallots, finely chopped

½ fresh red chilli, finely chopped

125 ml/4 fl oz white wine

1 kg/2 lb 4 oz fresh clams, tellines or cockles, cleaned

handful of parsley, chopped

zest of 1 lemon

salt and pepper

1. Cook the linguini according to the packet instructions, drain and toss with a splash of oil. Cover and keep warm.

2. Add half the remaining oil to a large saucepan with a lid and place over a high heat. Add the garlic, shallots and chilli and cook gently for 8–10 minutes until soft. Add the wine, bring to the boil and cook for 2 minutes.

3. Add the clams, cover and cook for a further 2–5 minutes, or until all the clams have opened. Discard any clams that remain closed. Add the drained linguini, parsley, lemon zest, the remaining oil and some salt and pepper and mix thoroughly.

4. Serve in warmed bowls, with a separate bowl for discarded shells.

Jambalaya

Serves 4

Ingredients

2 tbsp vegetable oil

2 onions, chopped roughly

1 green pepper, deseeded and roughly chopped

2 celery sticks, chopped roughly

3 garlic cloves, chopped finely

2 tsp paprika

300 g/10½ oz skinless, boneless chicken breasts, chopped

100 g/3½ oz kabanos sausages, chopped

3 tomatoes, peeled and chopped

450 g/1 lb long-grain rice

850 ml/1½ pints hot chicken or fish stock

1 tsp dried oregano

2 bay leaves

12 large raw prawns, peeled and deveined

4 spring onions, chopped finely

2 tbsp chopped fresh parsley

salt and pepper

chopped fresh herbs, to garnish

1. Heat the vegetable oil in a large frying pan over a low heat. Add the onions, pepper, celery and garlic and cook for 8–10 minutes until all the vegetables are soft. Add the paprika and cook for a further 30 seconds. Add the chicken and sausages and cook for 8–10 minutes until lightly browned. Add the tomatoes and cook for 2–3 minutes until they have collapsed.

2. Add the rice to the pan and stir well. Pour in the hot stock, oregano and bay leaves and stir well. Cover and simmer for 10 minutes.

3. Add the prawns and stir. Cover again and cook for a further 6–8 minutes until the rice is tender and the prawns are cooked through. Remove the bay leaves.

4. Stir in the spring onions and parsley and season to taste with salt and pepper. Transfer to serving dishes, garnish with chopped fresh herbs and serve immediately.

#371 Fisherman's pie

Serves 6

Ingredients

900 g/2 lb white fish fillets, such as plaice, skinned

150 ml/5 fl oz dry white wine

1 tbsp chopped fresh parsley, tarragon or dill

175 g/6 oz small mushrooms, sliced

70 g/2½ oz butter, plus extra for greasing

175 g/6 oz cooked peeled prawns

40 g/1½ oz plain flour

125 ml/4 fl oz double cream

creamy mashed potatoes, for topping

salt and pepper

1. Preheat the oven to 180°C/350°F/Gas Mark 4. Grease a 1.7-litre/3-pint baking dish with butter. Fold the fish fillets in half and place in the prepared dish. Season well with salt and pepper, pour over the wine and scatter over the herbs. Cover with foil and bake in the preheated oven for 15 minutes until the fish starts to flake. Strain off the liquid and reserve. Increase the oven temperature to 220°C/425°F/Gas Mark 7.

2. Sauté the mushrooms in a frying pan with 15 g/½ oz of the butter and spoon over the fish. Scatter over the prawns.

3. Heat the remaining butter in a saucepan and stir in the flour. Cook for a few minutes without browning, remove from the heat, then add the reserved cooking liquid gradually, stirring well between each addition. Return to the heat and gently bring to the boil, still stirring to ensure a smooth sauce. Add the cream and season to taste with salt and pepper. Pour over the fish in the dish and smooth over the surface. Pile or pipe the potatoes onto the fish and sauce, return to the oven and bake for 10–15 minutes until golden brown.

#372 Monkfish parcels

Serves 4

Ingredients

4 tsp olive oil

2 courgettes, sliced

1 large red pepper, peeled, deseeded and cut into strips

2 monkfish fillets, about 125 g/4½ oz each, skin and membrane removed

6 smoked streaky bacon rashers

salt and pepper

slices of olive bread, to serve

1. Preheat the oven to 190°C/375°F/Gas Mark 5. Cut out four large pieces of foil, each about 23 cm/9 inches square. Lightly brush them with a little oil, then divide the courgettes and red pepper between them.

2. Rinse the fish fillets under cold running water and pat dry with kitchen paper. Cut them in half, then put 1 piece on top of each pile of courgettes and red pepper. Cut the bacon rashers in half and lay 3 pieces across each piece of fish. Season to taste with salt and pepper, drizzle over the remaining oil and close up the parcels. Seal tightly, transfer to an ovenproof dish and bake in the preheated oven for 25 minutes.

3. Remove from the oven, open each foil parcel slightly and serve with slices of olive bread.

#373 Fennel-roasted tilapia

Ingredients

1 large tilapia, about 2 kg/4 lb 8 oz, cleaned

4 garlic cloves, coarsely chopped

4 bay leaves

2 fresh thyme sprigs

handful of fresh parsley

2 lemons, sliced

1 large fennel bulb, sliced and fronds reserved

70 g/2½ oz butter, thinly sliced, plus extra for greasing

100 ml/3½ fl oz white wine

salt and pepper

1. Preheat the oven to 190°C/375°F/Gas Mark 5. Rinse the fish and pat dry inside and out. Season with salt and pepper and put 2 garlic cloves, 2 bay leaves, one third of the herbs and 6 lemon slices inside the cavity.

2. Lay two large sheets of foil on top of each other (they should be wide enough to double wrap the whole fish) and grease with butter to prevent the fish sticking to it. Pull the sides up a little so the ingredients don't spill. Place half of the remaining herbs, lemon slices, fennel slices and butter slices on the foil and lay the fish on top. Scatter the remaining herbs, lemon, fennel and butter on top, pour over the wine and season with salt and pepper.

3. Loosely wrap the fish, folding over the ends of the foil. Put the parcel in a roasting tin, place in the preheated oven and bake for 30–40 minutes. Carefully open the parcel and serve immediately.

#374 Tuna steaks with courgettes

Ingredients

3 tbsp extra virgin olive oil

finely grated rind and juice 1 lemon

2 tbsp chopped fresh oregano, or 2 tsp dried oregano

4 tuna steaks

4 courgettes

salt and pepper

fresh oregano sprigs, to garnish

cooked new potatoes, to serve

1. Lightly whisk together the oil, lemon rind and juice and oregano. Lay the tuna steaks in a wide dish in a single layer and pour over half the dressing. Cover and chill in the refrigerator for about 1 hour.

2. Top and tail the courgettes and cut lengthways into 5-mm/¼-inch thick slices. Place in a bowl with the remaining dressing and stir to coat evenly.

3. Preheat the grill to high. Lift the tuna out of the dressing and arrange with the courgettes on a large baking sheet with a rim. Season well with salt and pepper.

4. Cook under the preheated grill for 6–8 minutes, turning once, until the fish is just cooked and the courgettes are tender. Brush over any spare dressing during cooking.

5. Serve the tuna and courgettes immediately with new potatoes, garnished with oregano.

#375 Mussels in cider

Ingredients

2 kg/4 lb 8 oz live mussels, scrubbed and debearded

300 ml/10 fl oz dry cider

6 shallots, finely chopped

6 tbsp double cream

pepper

baguettes, to serve

1. Discard any mussels with broken shells or any that refuse to close when tapped.

2. Pour the cider into a large casserole, add the shallots and season with pepper. Bring to the boil and cook for 2 minutes.

3. Add the mussels, cover with a tight-fitting lid and cook over a high heat, shaking the casserole dish occasionally, for about 5 minutes, or until the shells have opened. Remove the mussels with a slotted spoon, discarding any that remain closed, and keep warm.

4. Strain the cooking liquid through a muslin-lined sieve into a saucepan. Bring to the boil and cook for 8–10 minutes, or until reduced by about half. Stir in the cream and add the mussels. Cook for 1 minute to reheat the shellfish, then serve immediately with baguettes.

#376 Swordfish steaks with lemon

Serves 4

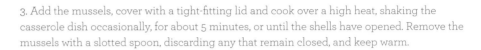

Ingredients

5 tbsp olive oil, plus extra for brushing

juice of ½ large or 1 small lemon

2 garlic cloves, well crushed

2 tsp finely chopped fresh oregano

2 tbsp chopped fresh parsley

4 x 175-g/6-oz swordfish steaks

salt and pepper

lemon wedges, to garnish

freshly cooked asparagus, to serve

1. Put all the ingredients, except the swordfish, in a screw-top jar with salt and pepper to taste and shake well to combine.

2. Preheat a ridged griddle pan over a high heat. Pat the swordfish steaks dry with kitchen paper and lightly brush with oil on both sides. When the pan is very hot, add the swordfish steaks and cook for 2 minutes on each side, or until cooked through but still moist inside.

3. Serve immediately with the asparagus and the lemon dressing drizzled over. Garnish with the lemon wedges.

#377 Super surf & turf

Ingredients

500 g/1 lb 2 oz new potatoes, cut into large slices

8 tbsp olive oil

1 garlic bulb, broken into cloves

3 fresh rosemary sprigs

2 rib-eye steaks, about 350 g/12 oz each, seasoned

25 g/1 oz butter

500 g/1 lb 2 oz large raw prawns, shell on

3 garlic cloves, sliced

juice of ½ lemon

salt and pepper

1. Preheat the oven to 200°C/400°F/Gas Mark 6. In a large bowl mix together the potatoes, 4 tablespoons of the oil, the garlic and rosemary, and season to taste with salt and pepper. Tip onto a large, non-stick baking tray and cook in the preheated oven, turning at least once, for 25 minutes, or until golden and soft.

2. When the potatoes have been in the oven for 15 minutes, heat a large non-stick frying pan and add the remaining oil. When it starts to smoke, add the steaks and butter. Cook the steaks on each side for 2–3 minutes or until cooked to your liking. Remove from the pan and leave to rest in a warm place.

3. Add the prawns and garlic to the pan. Cook the prawns on each side for 2 minutes, or until pink. Add the lemon juice and season to taste with salt and pepper. Remove from the heat. Serve the steaks immediately with the prawns and potatoes.

#378 Layered fish & potato pie

Ingredients

900 g/2 lb waxy potatoes, sliced

70 g/2½ oz butter

1 red onion, halved and sliced

5 tbsp plain flour

450 ml/16 fl oz milk

150 ml/5 fl oz double cream

225 g/8 oz smoked haddock fillet, skinned and diced

225 g/8 oz cod fillet, skinned and diced

1 red pepper, deseeded and diced

125 g/4½ oz broccoli florets

salt and pepper

50 g/1¾ oz freshly grated Parmesan cheese

1. Cook the sliced potatoes in a saucepan of boiling water for 10 minutes. Drain well and set aside.

2. Meanwhile, melt the butter in a saucepan over a low heat, add the onion and cook for 3–4 minutes. Add the flour and cook for 1 minute. Blend in the milk and cream and bring to the boil, stirring until the sauce has thickened.

3. Arrange about half of the potato slices in the base of a shallow baking dish. Add the fish, red pepper and broccoli to the sauce and cook over low heat for 10 minutes. Season to taste, then spoon the mixture over the potatoes in the dish.

4. Preheat the oven to 180°C/350°F/Gas Mark 4. Arrange the remaining potato slices in a layer over the fish mixture. Sprinkle the cheese over the top. Bake in the preheated oven for 30 minutes, until golden brown. Serve immediately.

#379 Sole meunière

Ingredients

4 sole fillets, each about 175 g/6 oz, all dark skin and bones removed

100 ml/3½ fl oz milk

4 tbsp plain flour

85 g/3 oz butter

juice of ½ lemon

salt and pepper

chopped fresh flat-leaf parsley, to garnish

cooked asparagus and lemon wedges, to serve

1. Rinse the fish under cold running water and pat dry with kitchen paper. Pour the milk into a flat dish at least as large as the fillets and put the flour on a plate. Season each fillet on both sides with salt and pepper to taste. Working with one fillet at a time, pull it very quickly through the milk, then put it in the flour, turn once to coat all over and shake off any excess flour. Continue until all the fillets are prepared.

2. Melt half the butter in a frying pan large enough to hold the fillets in a single layer, over a medium-high heat. Add the fillets to the pan, skinned-side down, and fry for 2 minutes. Turn over the fillets and fry for 2–3 minutes, or until the flesh flakes easily. Transfer to warmed serving plates, skinned-side up, and reserve.

3. Reduce the heat to medium and melt the remaining butter in the pan. When it stops foaming, add the lemon juice and stir, scraping the sediment from the base of the pan. Spoon the butter mixture over the fish and sprinkle with parsley. Serve with asparagus and lemon wedges.

#380 Moroccan fish tagine

Ingredients

2 tbsp olive oil

1 large onion, finely chopped

pinch of saffron threads

½ tsp ground cinnamon

1 tsp ground coriander

½ tsp ground cumin

½ tsp ground turmeric

200 g/7 oz canned chopped tomatoes

300 ml/10 fl oz fish stock

4 small red mullet, cleaned, boned and heads and tails removed

55 g/2 oz stoned green olives

1 tbsp chopped preserved lemon

3 tbsp chopped fresh coriander

salt and pepper

couscous, to serve (optional)

1. Heat the oil in a flameproof casserole. Add the onion and cook over a very low heat, stirring occasionally, for 10 minutes, until soft, but not coloured. Add the saffron, cinnamon, ground coriander, cumin and turmeric and cook for a further 30 seconds, stirring constantly.

2. Add the tomatoes and fish stock and stir well. Bring to the boil, reduce the heat, cover and simmer for 15 minutes. Uncover and simmer for 20–35 minutes, or until thickened.

3. Cut each red mullet in half, then add the fish pieces to the casserole, pushing them down into the liquid. Simmer the stew for a further 5–6 minutes, or until the fish is just cooked.

4. Carefully stir in the olives, preserved lemon and chopped coriander. Season to taste with salt and pepper and serve with couscous, if using.

Oven-roasted smoked haddock with French beans

Ingredients

4 pieces smoked haddock fillet,
about 175 g/6 oz each

1 tbsp butter

400 g/14 oz French beans,
topped and tailed

1 tbsp olive oil

salt and pepper

2 tbsp flaked almonds, lightly toasted,
and 2 tbsp snipped chives, to garnish

lemon wedges, to serve

1. Preheat the oven to 200°C/400°F/Gas Mark 6. Arrange the fish fillets in a baking tray, skin side down, in a single layer.

2. Dot the fish with butter and sprinkle with pepper. Cover the tray with foil and cook in the preheated oven for about 15 minutes, or until the fish flakes easily.

3. Meanwhile, place the beans in a bowl and drizzle with the oil. Season with salt and pepper and toss well to coat evenly. Spread in a baking tray in a single layer. Place in the oven 5 minutes after the fish goes in, and roast for 8–10 minutes, turning once, until the beans are tender and just starting to brown.

4. Remove the fish and beans from the oven. Spoon the beans onto warmed serving plates, add the fish and scatter over the almonds and chives. Spoon over the juices from the tray and serve with lemon wedges on the side.

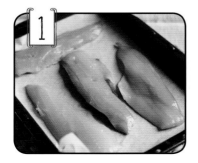

#382 Chunky monkfish hotpot

Serves 4

Ingredients

2 tbsp olive oil

1 onion, thinly sliced

1 yellow pepper, deseeded and sliced

1 celery stick, sliced

300 ml/10 fl oz fish stock

400 g/14 oz canned chopped tomatoes

200 g/7 oz fresh or canned sweetcorn

500 g/1 lb 2 oz monkfish fillet

8 raw tiger prawns, peeled and deveined

finely grated rind of 1 lemon

2 tbsp chopped fresh flat-leaf parsley

1 garlic clove, finely chopped

salt and pepper

1. Heat the oil in a large, flameproof casserole over a medium heat and fry the onion, pepper and celery, stirring occasionally, for about 10 minutes, or until soft but not brown.

2. Add the fish stock and tomatoes and bring to the boil. Stir in the sweetcorn, season to taste with salt and pepper, cut the monkfish into chunks, add to the casserole and bring back to the boil. Place the prawns on top. Reduce the heat to low and leave to simmer gently for about 10 minutes, or until the fish is firm and the prawns have turned pink.

3. Meanwhile, mix the lemon rind, parsley and garlic together in a small bowl. Sprinkle over the hotpot and serve immediately.

#383 Mussels fried rice

Serves 4

Ingredients

2 tsp groundnut oil or corn oil

1 large onion, chopped

1 garlic clove, finely chopped

8 large tomatoes, peeled, deseeded and chopped

225 g/8 oz paella or risotto rice

850 ml/1½ pints fish stock, plus extra if needed

450 g/1 lb live mussels, scrubbed and debearded

400 g/14 oz frozen mixed seafood, thawed

175 g/6 oz petits pois, cooked

2 tsp chopped fresh parsley, plus extra to garnish

salt and pepper

1. Preheat a wok or large frying pan, then add the oil and heat. Add the onion and fry until just soft. Add the garlic and half the tomatoes and stir together well.

2. Add the rice and stir-fry for 2–3 minutes before adding half the stock and bringing to the boil. Simmer for 12–15 minutes, adding more stock, if needed.

3. Discard any mussels with broken shells and any that refuse to close when tapped. Add the mussels to the wok with the mixed seafood and the petits pois. Season to taste with salt and pepper and cook for a further 3-4 minutes until the mussels have opened and most of the liquid has been absorbed. Discard any mussels that remain closed.

4. Stir in the remaining tomatoes and the parsley. Adjust the seasoning, if needed, and serve immediately, garnished with parsley.

#384 Fish stew with cider

Serves 4

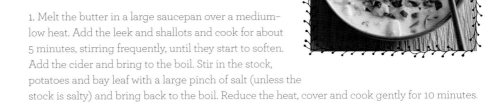

Ingredients

2 tsp butter

1 large leek, thinly sliced

2 shallots, finely chopped

125 ml/4 fl oz dry cider

300 ml/10 fl oz fish stock

250 g/9 oz potatoes, diced

1 bay leaf

4 tbsp plain flour

200 ml/7 fl oz milk

200 ml/7 fl oz double cream

55 g/2 oz fresh sorrel leaves, chopped

350 g/12 oz skinless monkfish or cod fillet, cut into 2.5-cm/1-inch pieces

salt and pepper

1. Melt the butter in a large saucepan over a medium-low heat. Add the leek and shallots and cook for about 5 minutes, stirring frequently, until they start to soften. Add the cider and bring to the boil. Stir in the stock, potatoes and bay leaf with a large pinch of salt (unless the stock is salty) and bring back to the boil. Reduce the heat, cover and cook gently for 10 minutes.

2. Put the flour in a small bowl and very slowly whisk in a few tablespoons of the milk to make a thick paste. Stir in a little more milk to make a smooth liquid. Adjust the heat so the stew bubbles gently. Stir in the flour mixture and cook, stirring frequently, for 5 minutes. Add the remaining milk and half the cream. Continue cooking for about 10 minutes until the potatoes are tender. Remove and discard the bay leaf.

3. Combine the sorrel with the remaining cream. Stir into the stew and add the fish. Continue cooking, stirring occasionally, for about 3 minutes, until the monkfish stiffens. Taste the stew and adjust the seasoning, if needed. Ladle into warmed bowls and serve.

#385 Clams with spaghetti

Serves 4

Ingredients

1 kg/2 lb 4 oz small live clams, scrubbed

350 g/12 oz dried spaghetti

125 ml/4 fl oz olive oil

4 garlic cloves, chopped

125 ml/4 fl oz dry white wine

4 tbsp chopped fresh flat-leaf parsley

salt and pepper

1. Discard any clams with broken shells and any that refuse to close when tapped. Set the remainder aside.

2. Bring a large saucepan of heavily salted water to the boil. Add the spaghetti, bring back to the boil and cook for 2 minutes less than specified in the packet instructions. Set aside in the cooking water.

3. Meanwhile, heat the oil in a large, deep frying pan over a medium heat. Add the garlic and stir for 1 minute, until golden but not brown. Increase the heat to high, add the wine and leave it to bubble for 2 minutes, or until reduced by half. Add the clams and stir for 2–3 minutes, until they open. Discard any clams that remain closed.

4. Add 250 ml/9 fl oz of the pasta cooking water to the clam pan. Strain and add the pasta to the pan and cook, stirring, for a further 2 minutes, until the pasta is tender but still firm to the bite. Season to taste with salt and pepper. Stir in the parsley and serve immediately.

#386 Ginger-steamed halibut with tomatoes & beans

Serves 4

Ingredients

1 tbsp finely chopped fresh ginger

2 garlic cloves, finely chopped

1–2 hot red chillies, diced

2 tbsp Thai fish sauce

2 tbsp mirin or sweet white wine

1 tsp sugar

4 halibut fillets

vegetable oil, for oiling

350 g/12 oz French beans, topped and tailed

450 g/1 lb cherry tomatoes, halved

4 spring onions, thinly sliced, finely chopped fresh coriander and fresh basil leaves, shredded, to garnish

1. Put the ginger, garlic, chillies, fish sauce, mirin and sugar into a baking dish large enough to hold the fish and stir to combine. Add the fish and turn to coat in the mixture. Cover and place in the refrigerator to marinate for 30 minutes. Meanwhile, brush four large squares of baking paper with oil.

2. Divide the beans evenly between the prepared squares of paper, piling them in the middle. Scatter the tomatoes evenly over them. Top each pile of vegetables with a fish fillet and some of the marinade. Fold up the packets securely, leaving a little room for the steam to circulate, and place them in a slow cooker. Cover and cook on high for about 2 hours, until the halibut is flaky and cooked through.

3. To serve, carefully remove the packets from the slow cooker, open them and slide the contents onto warmed plates, then garnish with spring onions, coriander and basil.

#387 Squid with potatoes, lemon & parsley

Serves 4–6

Ingredients

675 g/1 lb 8 oz prepared squid

3 tbsp olive oil

1 onion, finely chopped

3 garlic cloves, finely chopped

½ tsp thyme leaves

7 tbsp chopped flat-leaf parsley

125 ml/4 fl oz white wine

250 g/9 oz canned chopped tomatoes

450 g/1 lb potatoes, cut into bite-sized chunks

grated zest of 1 lemon

salt and pepper

1. Slice the body of the squid crossways into thin rings. Cut the rings in half if large. Slice the tentacles and wings into bite-sized pieces.

2. Heat a heavy-based casserole over a medium heat, add the oil, then add the onion and gently fry for about 10 minutes until golden. Stir in the garlic, thyme and 3 tablespoons of the parsley. Add the squid and cook for 2–3 minutes, stirring, until opaque. Pour in the wine and simmer for 2 minutes, then add the tomatoes and ¼ teaspoon of pepper. Bring to the boil, then cover and simmer for 1–1½ hours until the squid is tender. Stir occasionally to prevent sticking, adding a little water if necessary.

3. Add the potatoes to the casserole, and season to taste with salt and pepper. Cover and simmer for 20–30 minutes, or until the potatoes are tender but not breaking up.

4. Combine the lemon zest with the remaining parsley and add to the casserole just before serving.

#388 Pan-cooked tuna with radish relish

Serves 4

Ingredients

4 tuna steaks, about 150 g/5½ oz each

1 tbsp sesame seeds

cooked rice, to serve (optional)

Marinade

2 tbsp dark soy sauce

2 tbsp sunflower oil

1 tbsp sesame oil

1 tbsp rice vinegar

1 tsp grated fresh ginger

Relish

½ cucumber, peeled

1 bunch red radishes, trimmed

1. Place the tuna steaks in a dish and sprinkle over the sesame seeds, pressing them in with the back of a spoon so they stick to the fish.

2. To make the marinade, whisk together all the ingredients. Transfer 3 tablespoons of the marinade to a medium-sized bowl. Pour the remaining marinade over the fish, turning each steak to coat lightly. Cover and chill in the refrigerator for 1 hour.

3. Very thinly slice the cucumber and radishes and add to the marinade in the bowl. Toss the vegetables to coat, then cover and chill.

4. Heat a large, heavy-based frying pan over a high heat. Add the steaks and cook for 3–4 minutes on each side depending on the thickness of the fish. Serve immediately with the radish relish and rice (if using).

#389 Turbot steaks with garlic & lemon

Serves 4

Ingredients

2 tbsp olive oil, for brushing

4 turbot steaks

juice and finely grated rind of 1 lemon

2 garlic cloves, finely chopped

4 tbsp finely chopped fresh flat-leaf parsley

40 g/1½ oz pine nuts, toasted

salt and pepper

cooked seasonal vegetables, to serve

1. Preheat the oven to 220°C/425°F/Gas Mark 7. Brush a wide, ovenproof dish with oil.

2. Place the turbot steaks in the dish, brush with oil, season to taste with salt and pepper and pour over the lemon juice.

3. Mix together the lemon rind, garlic, parsley and pine nuts and spoon over the fish. Drizzle with the remaining oil.

4. Bake in the preheated oven for 15–20 minutes until the fish flakes easily with a fork.

5. Serve hot with vegetables.

Shellfish in saffron sauce

Ingredients

24 large raw prawns, peeled and deveined, heads and shells reserved

400 ml/14 fl oz water

200 ml/7 fl oz dry white vermouth

1 fennel bulb, sliced

1 leek, chopped

2 garlic cloves, crushed

large pinch of saffron threads

900 g/2 lb live mussels, scrubbed and debearded

900 g/2 lb live clams, scrubbed

30 g/1 oz butter

1 shallot, finely chopped

250 ml/9 fl oz crème fraîche

salt and white pepper

chopped fresh flat-leaf parsley, to garnish

1. Put the prawn shells, water, vermouth, fennel, leek, garlic, saffron and a pinch of salt into a saucepan. Cover and bring to the boil, then reduce the heat and simmer for 15 minutes to concentrate the flavours. Strain the stock and set aside. Meanwhile, discard any mussels or clams with broken shells and any that refuse to close when tapped.

2. Melt the butter in a large frying pan. Add the shallot and fry, stirring, for 2–3 minutes, or until soft. Stir in 250 ml/9 fl oz of the reserved stock and bring to the boil. Reduce the heat to low, add the prawns and simmer for 2–3 minutes, or until pink. Using a slotted spoon, remove the prawns from the liquid and keep warm. Add the mussels and clams to the pan, cover and cook, shaking the pan, for 2–5 minutes, or until all the mussels and clams open. Use tongs to remove the open mussels and clams, discarding any that remain closed. When the mussels and clams are cool enough to handle, remove the top shells and discard, then set the mussels and clams aside with the prawns and keep warm.

3. Stir the crème fraîche and the remaining stock into the pan. Return the liquid to the boil and boil for 5–8 minutes, or until reduced to about 350 ml/12 fl oz. Taste and adjust the seasoning, if necessary. Divide the prawns, mussels and clams between four warmed bowls and ladle over the saffron sauce. Garnish with parsley and serve immediately.

#391 Wine steamed mussels

Ingredients

115 g/4 oz butter

1 shallot, chopped

3 garlic cloves, finely chopped

2 kg/4 lb 8 oz live mussels, scrubbed and debearded

225 ml/8 fl oz dry white wine

½ tsp salt

4 tbsp chopped fresh parsley

pepper

fresh crusty bread, to serve

1. Place half the butter in a large saucepan over a low heat and heat until melted. Add the shallot and garlic and cook for 2 minutes.

2. Discard any mussels with broken shells and any that refuse to close when tapped. Add the mussels and wine to the pan with the salt, and pepper to taste. Cover and bring to the boil, then cook for 3 minutes, shaking the pan from time to time.

3. Remove the mussels from the pan with a slotted spoon and place in individual serving bowls. Discard any mussels that remain closed.

4. Stir the remaining butter and the parsley into the cooking juices in the pan. Bring to the boil, then pour over the mussels.

5. Serve immediately with fresh crusty bread for mopping up the juices.

#392 Italian fish stew

Ingredients

2 tbsp olive oil

2 red onions, finely chopped

1 garlic clove, crushed

2 courgettes, sliced

400 g/14 oz canned chopped tomatoes

850 ml/1½ pints fish stock

100 g/3½ oz dried pasta shapes

350 g/12 oz firm white fish, such as cod, haddock or hake, skinned and boned

1 tbsp chopped fresh basil, plus extra leaves to garnish

1 tsp grated lemon rind

1 tbsp cornflour

1 tbsp water

1. Heat the oil in a large saucepan. Add the onions and garlic and cook over a low heat, stirring occasionally, for about 5 minutes until soft. Add the courgettes and cook, stirring frequently, for 2–3 minutes. Add the tomatoes and stock and bring to the boil. Add the pasta, bring back to the boil, reduce the heat, cover and simmer for 5 minutes.

2. Cut the fish into chunks and add to the pan with the basil and lemon rind. Simmer for 5 minutes until the fish is opaque and flakes easily and the pasta is tender but still firm to the bite. Take care not to overcook the fish.

3. Mix the cornflour and water to a smooth paste and stir into the stew. Cook over a low heat for 2 minutes, stirring constantly, until thickened.

4. Ladle the stew into four warmed bowls, garnish with basil and serve immediately.

#393 Potato & smoked salmon gratin

Serves 6

Ingredients

400 ml/14 fl oz milk

3 whole cloves

2 bay leaves

50 g/1¾ oz onion, sliced

85 g/3 oz leek, chopped

100 g/3½ oz smoked salmon, sliced

350 g/12 oz potatoes, sliced

2 tbsp finely chopped fresh chives

2 tbsp finely chopped fresh dill

1 tbsp finely chopped fresh tarragon

2 tsp wholegrain mustard

oil, for greasing

pepper

fresh watercress sprigs, to garnish

1. Pour the milk into a large, heavy-based saucepan, add the cloves, bay leaves, onion, leek and smoked salmon and heat over a low heat. When the milk is just about to reach simmering point, carefully remove the smoked salmon with a slotted spoon and cool on a plate.

2. Add the potatoes to the milk and stir. Return to a simmer and cook, stirring occasionally to prevent the potatoes sticking, for 12 minutes, or until the potatoes are just beginning to soften. Preheat the oven to 200°C/400°F/Gas Mark 6. Add the herbs, mustard and pepper and stir well. Pour the mixture into a greased and base-lined 19-cm/7½-inch casserole dish. Cover with a layer of greaseproof paper and then foil and bake in the preheated oven for 30 minutes.

3. Leave to cool for 20 minutes. Meanwhile, preheat the grill, then place the dish under the grill and brown the top. Serve with the smoked salmon and garnish with sprigs of watercress.

#394 Fishermen's stew

Serves 6

Ingredients

1.5 kg/3 lb 5 oz live mussels

3 tbsp olive oil

2 onions, chopped

3 garlic cloves, finely chopped

1 red pepper, deseeded and sliced

3 carrots, chopped

800 g/1 lb 12 oz canned chopped tomatoes

125 ml/4 fl oz dry white wine

2 tbsp tomato purée

1 tbsp chopped fresh dill

2 tbsp chopped fresh parsley

1 tbsp chopped fresh thyme

1 tbsp fresh basil, plus extra to garnish

900 g/2 lb white fish fillets, cut into chunks

450 g/1 lb raw prawns

350 ml/12 fl oz fish stock or water

salt and pepper

1. Clean the mussels by scrubbing or scraping the shells and pulling off any beards. Discard any with broken shells and any that refuse to close when tapped with a knife. Rinse under cold running water.

2. Heat the oil in a flameproof casserole. Add the onions, garlic, red pepper and carrots and cook over a low heat, stirring occasionally, for 5 minutes, or until soft.

3. Add the tomatoes and their can juices, the white wine, tomato purée, dill, parsley and thyme, and tear in the basil leaves. Bring to the boil, then reduce the heat and simmer for 20 minutes. Add the chunks of fish, mussels, prawns and stock and season to taste with salt and pepper. Bring back to the boil and simmer for 6–8 minutes, or until the prawns are pink and the mussel shells have opened. Discard any shells that remain closed.

4. Serve immediately, garnished with basil leaves.

#395 Rustic fish casserole

Serves 4

Ingredients

300 g/10½ oz live clams
2 tbsp olive oil
1 large onion, chopped
2 garlic cloves, crushed
2 celery sticks, sliced
350 g/12 oz firm white fish fillet
250 g/9 oz prepared squid rings
400 ml/14 fl oz fish stock
6 plum tomatoes, chopped
small bunch of fresh thyme
salt and pepper
crusty bread, to serve

1. Clean the clams under cold running water, scrubbing the shells. Discard any with broken shells and any that refuse to close when tapped.

2. Heat the oil in a large saucepan, add the onion, garlic and celery and fry for 3–4 minutes, until soft but not brown.

3. Meanwhile, cut the fish into chunks. Stir the fish and squid into the pan, then fry gently for 2 minutes. Stir in the stock, tomatoes and thyme and season to taste with salt and pepper. Cover and simmer gently for 3–4 minutes.

4. Add the clams, cover and cook over a high heat for a further 2 minutes, or until the shells open. Discard any that remain closed.

5. Serve immediately with chunks of bread.

#396 Sea bass with fennel & olives

Serves 4

Ingredients

4 sea bass, about 300 g/10½ oz each, cleaned
2 fennel bulbs
12 green olives, stoned
juice and finely grated rind of 1 lemon
3 tbsp olive oil
175 ml/6 fl oz dry white wine
3 tbsp chopped fresh thyme leaves
salt and pepper

1. Preheat the oven to 200°C/400°F/Gas Mark 6. Cut three deep slashes into one side of each fish and place in a roasting tin.

2. Trim the fennel bulbs, reserving the green fronds. Cut into 5-mm/¼-inch thick slices. Bring a saucepan of water to the boil, add the fennel and blanch for 1 minute. Drain and arrange around the fish with the olives.

3. Lightly whisk together the lemon juice, lemon rind, oil, wine and thyme with salt and pepper to taste. Spoon over the fish and fennel, then bake in the preheated oven for 30–35 minutes, until the fish comes away from the bones easily.

4. Transfer to a serving plate and garnish with the reserved fennel fronds.

#397 Garlic-crusted roast haddock

Serves
4

Ingredients

900 g/2 lb floury potatoes

125 ml/4 fl oz milk

55 g/2 oz butter

4 haddock fillets, about 225 g/8 oz each

1 tbsp sunflower oil

4 garlic cloves, finely chopped

salt and pepper

2 tbsp chopped fresh parsley, to garnish

1. Preheat the oven to 230°C/450°F/ Gas Mark 8.

2. Cut the potatoes into chunks and cook in a saucepan of lightly salted water for 15 minutes, or until tender. Drain well. Mash in the saucepan until smooth. Set over a low heat and beat in the milk, butter and salt and pepper to taste.

3. Put the haddock fillets in a roasting tin and brush the fish with the oil. Sprinkle the garlic on top, add salt and pepper to taste, then spread with the mashed potatoes. Roast in the oven for 8–10 minutes, or until the fish is just tender.

4. Meanwhile, preheat the grill. Transfer the fish to the grill and cook for about 2 minutes, or until golden brown. Sprinkle with the chopped parsley and serve immediately.

#398 One-pot clam bake

Serves
2-4

Ingredients

2 tbsp olive oil

25 g/1 oz butter

4 shallots, finely chopped

4 garlic cloves, chopped

4 celery sticks, finely chopped

1 tbsp smoked paprika

450 ml/16 fl oz apple cider

2 litres/3½ pints hot chicken stock

500 g/1 lb 2 oz new potatoes

2 corn cobs, each cut into 3 pieces

200 g/7 oz smoked sausage, sliced

1 kg/2 lb 4 oz live clams, scrubbed

1 kg/2 lb 4 oz large raw prawns, shell-on

small bunch fresh parsley, chopped

salt and pepper

fresh crusty bread, to serve

1. Add the oil, butter, shallots, garlic and celery to a large casserole with a tight-fitting lid. Cook uncovered over a medium-low heat for 10 minutes, or until the shallots are translucent.

2. Add the smoked paprika, cider and stock, bring to the boil and add the potatoes. Cover and simmer for 10 minutes, then add the corn cobs and sausage. Cook for a further 10 minutes, until the potatoes are almost soft.

3. Discard any clams with broken shells and any that refuse to close when tapped. Add the clams and prawns to the casserole, and cook for a further 2 minutes, until the clams have opened and the prawns have turned pink. Discard any clams that remain closed.

4. Remove from the heat and leave to stand for 1–2 minutes, then add the parsley and season to taste with salt and pepper. Transfer to a large serving dish and serve immediately with fresh crusty bread.

#399 Baked oregano lobster

Ingredients

4 frozen lobster tails, about 175 g/6 oz each, thawed and patted dry

4 tbsp olive oil, plus extra for drizzling

1 large shallot, very finely chopped

2 garlic cloves, very finely chopped

6 tbsp fine dry breadcrumbs

2 tsp dried oregano

finely grated rind of 2 lemons

1 tbsp very finely chopped fresh flat-leaf parsley

salt and pepper

1. Preheat the oven to 180°C/350°F/Gas Mark 4. Put a lobster tail on a board, shell down. Use scissors to cut lengthways through the shell without cutting through the tail fan. Do not crush the shell. Use a small knife to cut the tail meat in half lengthways without cutting through the shell. Cut away the cartilage on top of the shell. Use the tip of a knife to cut out the black intestinal vein. Repeat with the remaining tails. Cover and chill until required.

2. Heat the oil in a small frying pan. Add the shallot and fry for 1–2 minutes, until golden. Add the garlic and stir for a further 1 minute, or until the shallot is soft. Stir in the breadcrumbs, oregano, lemon rind and parsley and season with salt and pepper.

3. Very lightly season inside the split tails, then place them in a deep roasting tin, using balls of foil to wedge them upright, if necessary. Divide the oregano mixture between them, lightly pressing it into the splits and covering half the tails. Drizzle with oil. Add enough boiling water to come half-way up the sides of the tails. Bake in the preheated oven for 20 minutes, until the flesh at the thickest part is white. Remove from the oven and serve immediately.

#400 Roast salmon with lemon & herbs

Ingredients

6 tbsp extra virgin olive oil

1 onion, sliced

1 leek, trimmed and sliced

juice of ½ lemon

2 tbsp chopped fresh parsley

2 tbsp chopped fresh dill

500 g/1 lb 2 oz salmon fillets

salt and pepper

freshly cooked baby spinach leaves and lemon wedges, to serve

1. Preheat the oven to 200°C/400°F/Gas Mark 6. Heat 1 tablespoon of the oil in a frying pan over a medium heat. Add the onion and leek and cook, stirring, for about 4 minutes until slightly soft.

2. Meanwhile, put the remaining oil in a small bowl with the lemon juice and herbs, and season. Stir together well. Rinse the fish under cold running water, then pat dry with kitchen paper. Arrange the fish in a shallow, ovenproof baking dish.

3. Remove the pan from the heat and spread the onion and leek over the fish. Pour the oil mixture over the top, ensuring that everything is well coated. Roast in the centre of the preheated oven for about 10 minutes or until the fish is cooked through.

4. Arrange the cooked spinach on warmed serving plates. Remove the fish and vegetables from the oven and arrange on top of the spinach. Serve immediately with lemon wedges.

Super sauces, sides & sundries

#401 Home-made tomato ketchup

Ingredients

2 tbsp olive oil

1 red onion, peeled and chopped

2 garlic cloves, chopped

250 g/9 oz plum tomatoes, chopped

250 g/9 oz canned chopped tomatoes

½ tsp ground ginger

½ tsp chilli powder

40 g/1½ oz soft dark brown sugar

100 ml/3½ fl oz red wine vinegar

salt and pepper

1. Heat the oil in a large saucepan and add the onion, garlic and all the tomatoes. Add the ginger and chilli and season to taste with salt and pepper. Cook for 15 minutes, or until soft.

2. Pour the mixture into a food processor or blender and blend well. Pass through a sieve to remove all the seeds. Return the mixture to the pan and add the sugar and vinegar. Bring back to the boil and cook until it is the consistency of ketchup.

3. Bottle quickly in sterilized bottles or jars and store in a cool place or in the refrigerator until required.

#402 Home-made mustard

Ingredients

3 tbsp brown mustard seeds

3 tbsp cider vinegar

3 tbsp mustard powder

2 tsp salt

2 tsp honey

1. Put the mustard seeds into a small, non-metallic container with the vinegar and enough cold water to cover completely. Cover and set aside for 2 days at room temperature.

2. Strain the mustard seeds, reserving the liquid. Grind in a spice grinder until some seeds are still whole while some are ground. You may have to push the seeds down and grind again, but the more you grind, the spicier the mustard will be.

3. Place the mixture in a small bowl with the mustard powder, salt and honey. Add the reserved vinegar water and stir.

4. Place in a sterilized jar, seal and refrigerate for at least 2 days before serving.

#403 Tomato & red onion relish

Serves 4

Ingredients

8 ripe tomatoes

1-2 tbsp virgin olive oil

salt and pepper

Sauce

1 tbsp virgin olive oil

2 large red onions, thinly sliced

55 g/2 oz rocket or baby spinach leaves

1. Preheat the oven to 150°C/300°F/Gas Mark 2. Cut the tomatoes in half and arrange in a large roasting tin in a single layer. Drizzle with the oil and season to taste with salt and pepper. Cook in the preheated oven for 1¼–1½ hours, or until roasted but still moist.

2. To make the sauce, heat the oil in a large frying pan. Add the onions and fry over a low heat until soft and golden brown. Place 8 of the oven-dried tomato halves in a food processor or blender and process until puréed. Add to the onions in the pan.

3. Slice the remaining tomato halves and add to the pan with the rocket. Season to taste with salt and pepper and cook until the leaves have just wilted. Serve immediately.

#404 Guacamole

Serves 4

Ingredients

1 ripe tomato

2 limes

2-3 ripe avocados

¼-½ onion, finely chopped

pinch of ground cumin

pinch of mild chilli powder

½-1 fresh green chilli, such as jalapeño or serrano, deseeded and finely chopped

1 tbsp finely chopped fresh coriander leaves, plus extra to garnish

1. Place the tomato in a heatproof bowl, pour over boiling water to cover and leave to stand for 30 seconds. Drain and plunge into cold water. Peel off the skin. Cut the tomato in half, deseed and chop the flesh.

2. Squeeze the juice from the limes into a small bowl. Cut 1 avocado in half around the stone. Twist the two halves apart in opposite directions, then remove the stone with a knife. Carefully peel off the skin, dice the flesh and toss in the bowl of lime juice to prevent discoloration. Repeat with the remaining avocados. Coarsely mash the avocados with a fork.

3. Add the onion, tomato, cumin, chilli powder, chilli and coriander to the avocados and mix together. Cover and chill in the refrigerator until ready to serve, garnished with the fresh coriander.

#405 Macaroni salad

Ingredients

225 g/8 oz dried elbow macaroni

50 ml/2 fl oz mayonnaise,
plus extra if needed

50 ml/2 fl oz natural yogurt

1 tbsp fresh lemon juice

½ tsp garlic salt

½ tsp pepper

40 g/1½ oz celery, diced

40 g/1½ oz spring onions, finely
chopped

40 g/1½ oz black olives, finely chopped

50 g/1¾ oz tomatoes, finely chopped

2 tbsp chopped fresh flat-leaf parsley

salt and pepper

1. Bring a medium-sized saucepan of lightly salted water to the boil, add the macaroni and cook according to the packet instructions. Drain.

2. Meanwhile, combine the mayonnaise, yogurt, lemon juice, garlic salt and pepper in a large bowl. Stir in the hot macaroni, then add the celery, spring onions, olives, tomatoes and parsley. Season to taste with salt and pepper and add more mayonnaise if it seems dry, then leave to cool completely.

3. Cover with clingfilm and chill for at least 2 hours until cold. Serve cold. The salad will keep in the refrigerator for up to 3 days.

#406 Coleslaw

Serves 4

Ingredients

350 g/12 oz white cabbage, thinly sliced

1 carrot, peeled and grated

4 spring onions, thinly sliced

2 tbsp finely chopped fresh parsley

Dressing

4 tbsp mayonnaise

2 tbsp soured cream or crème fraîche

1 tsp wholegrain mustard

1 tbsp lemon juice

salt and pepper

1. Combine all the vegetables in a large bowl.

2. Add the parsley and stir to mix evenly.

3. To make the dressing, stir together the mayonnaise, soured cream, mustard and lemon juice. Season to taste with salt and pepper.

4. Spoon the dressing into the vegetables. Toss well to mix evenly. Adjust the seasoning to taste. Serve.

#407 Potato salad

Serves 4–6

Ingredients

900 g/2 lb small red-skinned salad potatoes, unpeeled

16–18 cornichons, halved diagonally

2 tbsp finely chopped red onion

3 tbsp snipped fresh chives

¼ tsp pepper

salt

Vinaigrette

2 tsp Dijon mustard

1 tbsp red wine vinegar

¼ tsp pepper

4 tbsp extra virgin olive oil

sea salt flakes

1. Put the potatoes in a saucepan of lightly salted water and bring to the boil. Reduce the heat to medium and cook for 10–12 minutes until tender. Drain, then return to the pan and set aside for a few minutes.

2. To make the vinaigrette, combine the mustard, vinegar, pepper and a pinch of sea salt flakes in a bowl mixing well. Add the oil and whisk until smooth and thickened.

3. Put the potatoes in a serving bowl and pour over the dressing. Add the remaining ingredients and gently toss to mix. Leave to stand at room temperature for at least 30 minutes before serving.

#_408 Mayonnaise

Ingredients

2 large egg yolks

2 tsp Dijon mustard

¾ tsp salt, or to taste

2 tbsp lemon juice or white wine vinegar, plus extra if needed

about 300 ml/10 fl oz sunflower oil

white pepper

1. Whizz the egg yolks with the Dijon mustard, salt and white pepper to taste in a food processor, blender or by hand. Add the lemon juice and whizz again.

2. With the motor still running, add the oil, drop by drop at first. When the sauce begins to thicken, the oil can then be added in a slow, steady stream. Taste and adjust the seasoning with extra salt, pepper and lemon juice if necessary. If the sauce seems too thick, slowly add 1 tablespoon of hot water or lemon juice.

3. Use at once or store in a sterilized airtight container in the refrigerator for up to 1 week.

#_409 Aioli

Ingredients

3 large garlic cloves, finely chopped

2 egg yolks

225 ml/8 fl oz extra virgin olive oil

1 tbsp lemon juice

1 tbsp lime juice

1 tbsp Dijon mustard

1 tbsp chopped fresh tarragon

salt and pepper

fresh tarragon sprig, to garnish

1. Ensure that all the ingredients are at room temperature. Place the garlic and egg yolks in a food processor and process until well blended. With the motor running, pour in the oil teaspoon by teaspoon through the feeder tube until the mixture starts to thicken, then pour in the remaining oil in a thin stream until a thick mayonnaise forms.

2. Add the lemon juice, lime juice, mustard and tarragon and season to taste with salt and pepper. Blend until smooth, then transfer to a non-metallic bowl. Garnish with a tarragon sprig, cover with clingfilm and refrigerate until required.

#410 Tapenade

Serves 4

Ingredients

100 g/3½ oz canned anchovy fillets

350 g/12 oz black olives, stoned and roughly chopped

2 garlic cloves, roughly chopped

2 tbsp capers in brine, drained and rinsed

1 tbsp Dijon mustard

3 tbsp extra virgin olive oil

2 tbsp lemon juice

1. Drain the anchovies, reserving the oil from the can. Roughly chop the fish and place in a food processor. Add the reserved oil and all the remaining ingredients. Process to a smooth purée, stopping to scrape down the sides.

2. Transfer the tapenade to a dish, cover with clingfilm and chill in the refrigerator until required. If you are not planning to use the tapenade until the following day (or even the day after), cover the surface with a layer of olive oil to prevent it drying out.

#411 Classic pesto

Serves 4

Ingredients

40 fresh basil leaves

3 garlic cloves, crushed

25 g/1 oz pine nuts

50 g/1¾ oz freshly grated Parmesan cheese

2–3 tbsp extra virgin olive oil

salt and pepper

1. Put the basil leaves, garlic, pine nuts and cheese into a blender and blend for 30 seconds or until smooth. Alternatively, pound all of the ingredients in a mortar with a pestle.

2. Add the oil drop by drop while stirring briskly. Season to taste with salt and pepper. Use as required.

#412 Cheese-stuffed potatoes

Serves
4

Ingredients

4 large jacket potatoes,
about 400 g/14 oz each

oil, for brushing

2 tbsp milk or single cream

2 eggs, separated

100 g/3½ oz Cheddar cheese, grated

15 g/½ oz butter

4 spring onions, finely chopped

salt and pepper

1. Preheat the oven to 200°C/400°F/Gas Mark 6. Place the potatoes on a baking sheet, brush with oil and rub with salt. Bake in the preheated oven for 1–1¼ hours until tender. Do not switch off the oven.

2. Cut a slice from the top of the potatoes and scoop out the flesh, leaving a 5-mm/¼-inch thick shell. Put the flesh into a bowl. Add the milk, egg yolks and half the cheese and mash together well.

3. Melt the butter in a small saucepan, add the spring onions and stir-fry for 1–2 minutes until soft. Stir into the potato mixture and season to taste with salt and pepper.

4. Whisk the egg whites until they hold soft peaks. Lightly fold them into the potato mixture, then spoon the mixture back into the shells.

5. Place the filled potatoes on the baking sheet and sprinkle the remaining cheese on top. Bake for 15–20 minutes until golden. Serve immediately.

413 Rocket & Parmesan salad

Serves
4

Ingredients

2 handfuls rocket leaves

1 small fennel bulb

5 tbsp olive oil

2 tbsp balsamic vinegar

50 g/1¾ oz pine nuts

100 g/3½ oz Parmesan cheese shavings

salt and pepper

1. Divide the rocket between four serving plates.

2. Halve and finely slice the fennel bulb. Arrange the sliced fennel over the rocket.

3. Whisk together the oil and vinegar with salt and pepper to taste. Drizzle a little of the dressing over each serving.

4. Toast the pine nuts in a dry frying pan until golden brown.

5. Top the salad with the cheese shavings and toasted pine nuts and serve.

414 Tomato, mozzarella & basil salad

Serves
4

Ingredients

250 g/9 oz buffalo mozzarella cheese, thinly sliced

2 large beef tomatoes, cut into 5-mm/¼-inch slices

6 large fresh basil leaves

sea salt and pepper

extra virgin olive oil and aged balsamic vinegar, to serve

1. Divide the cheese and tomato slices between four plates, arranging them decoratively in a circular wheel shape. Sprinkle with salt and pepper.

2. Lay the basil leaves on top of each other, roll up in a cigar shape and thinly slice crossways to make fine shreds.

3. Sprinkle the basil shreds over the salads and serve immediately, with some oil and vinegar drizzled over the top. Place the oil and the vinegar on the table so that more can be added, if desired.

Serves
4

Roasted balsamic & honey onions

Ingredients

4 red onions, peeled and cut into chunky wedges

4 tsp clear honey

4 tbsp balsamic vinegar

1 tsp fresh thyme, finely chopped

salt and pepper

1. Preheat the grill to high. Divide the onion wedges between four squares of double-thickness foil. Bring up the sides of the foil a little.

2. Drizzle the honey and balsamic vinegar over the onions, add the thyme and season to taste with salt and pepper. Loosely seal the parcels and place under the preheated grill for 15–20 minutes, or until the onions are soft.

416 Hot roast peppers

Serves
6

Ingredients

6 red peppers, deseeded and cut into thick strips

140 g/5 oz fresh green serrano or jalapeño chillies, deseeded and sliced into thin strips

2 garlic cloves, crushed

4 tbsp extra virgin olive oil

1. Preheat the oven to 200°C/400°F/Gas Mark 6. Make alternating layers of peppers, chillies and garlic in a shallow casserole. Pour in the oil.

2. Cover and bake in the preheated oven for 50–60 minutes, or until the peppers are soft. Uncover and reduce the oven temperature to 180°C/350°F/Gas Mark 4. Return the casserole to the oven and bake for a further 45 minutes, or until the peppers are very soft and beginning to char.

3. Serve immediately if serving hot. Alternatively, leave to cool, then transfer to a large screw-top jar and store in the refrigerator for up to 3 weeks, topped up with more olive oil.

#417 Creamy corn custard

Serves 8

Ingredients

butter, for greasing

450 g/1 lb fresh or frozen corn kernels, thawed if frozen

400 ml/14 fl oz double cream

125 ml/4 fl oz milk

1¼ tsp salt

pinch of cayenne pepper

3 egg yolks

4 eggs

1. Preheat the oven to 160°C/325°F/Gas Mark 3. Generously grease eight ramekins.

2. Put the corn, cream, milk, salt and cayenne pepper into a saucepan. Bring to a simmer over a medium heat. Remove from the heat and leave to cool slightly. Carefully pour into a blender and purée until very smooth. Set aside.

3. Add the eggs and egg yolks to a mixing bowl and whisk for 30 seconds. Gradually stir in the warm corn custard mixture. When everything is combined, ladle the mixture into the prepared ramekins.

4. Pour 2.5 cm/1 inch of hot water into a roasting tin and put the filled ramekins into the tin. Bake in the preheated oven for 35 minutes, or until the custard is just set. Remove the ramekins from the tin and leave to cool for 15 minutes before serving.

#418 Mushrooms & spring onions with garlic

Serves 4

Ingredients

2 garlic bulbs

2 tbsp olive oil

350 g/12 oz assorted mushrooms, such as chestnut, open-cap and chanterelles, halved if large

1 tbsp chopped fresh parsley

8 spring onions, cut into 2.5-cm/1-inch lengths

salt and pepper

1. Preheat the oven to 180°C/350°F/Gas Mark 4. Slice off the tops of the garlic bulbs and press down to loosen the cloves. Place them in an ovenproof dish and season to taste with salt and pepper.

2. Drizzle 2 teaspoons of the oil over the bulbs and roast in the preheated oven for 30 minutes. Remove from the oven and drizzle with 1 teaspoon of the remaining oil. Return to the oven and roast for a further 45 minutes. Remove the garlic from the oven and, when cool enough to handle, peel the cloves.

3. Tip the oil from the dish into a heavy-based frying pan. Add the remaining oil and heat. Add the mushrooms and cook over a medium heat, stirring frequently, for 4 minutes. Add the garlic cloves, parsley and spring onions and cook, stirring frequently, for 5 minutes. Season with salt and pepper to taste and serve immediately.

Spanish rice

Ingredients

2 tbsp olive oil

½ small onion

275 g/9¾ oz long-grain white rice

3 garlic cloves, finely chopped

1 tsp ground cumin

1 tsp mild chilli powder

1 tsp dried oregano

600 ml/1 pint chicken stock

225 ml/8 fl oz tomato sauce

10 g/¼ oz chopped fresh coriander,
to garnish (optional)

1. Heat the oil in a large frying pan over a medium heat. Add the onion and cook, stirring frequently, for about 5 minutes until soft. Add the rice and garlic and cook, stirring occasionally, for a further 5 minutes, or until the rice is golden brown.

2. Add the cumin, chilli powder and oregano. Slowly add the stock and tomato sauce, stirring to mix. Bring to the boil, reduce the heat to low, cover and simmer for about 20 minutes until the rice is tender.

3. Remove from the heat, fluff with a fork, garnish with coriander, if using, and serve immediately.

Pilau rice
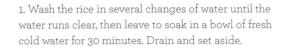

Serves
2–4

Ingredients

200 g/7 oz basmati rice

30 g/1 oz ghee

3 green cardamom pods

2 cloves

3 black peppercorns

½ tsp salt

½ tsp saffron threads

400 ml/14 fl oz cold water

1. Wash the rice in several changes of water until the water runs clear, then leave to soak in a bowl of fresh cold water for 30 minutes. Drain and set aside.

2. Melt the ghee in a heavy-based saucepan over a medium–high heat. Add the cardamom pods, cloves and peppercorns and stir-fry for 1 minute. Add the rice and stir-fry for a further 2 minutes.

3. Add the salt, saffron and water to the rice mixture. Bring to the boil, then reduce the heat to low, cover and simmer for 20 minutes, or until all the water has been absorbed.

4. Use a fork to fluff up the grains of rice. Transfer to a large serving dish and serve hot.

421 Coconut rice

Serves
4–6

Ingredients

225 g/8 oz basmati rice

450 ml/16 fl oz water

60 g/2¼ oz creamed coconut

2 tbsp mustard oil

1½ tsp salt, or to taste

1. Wash the rice in several changes of water until the water runs clear, then leave to soak in a bowl of fresh cold water for 30 minutes. Drain and set aside.

2. Bring the water to the boil in a small saucepan, stir in the creamed coconut until it dissolves and set aside.

3. Heat the mustard oil in a large saucepan over a high heat until it smokes. Remove from the heat and leave to cool completely.

4. When you are ready to cook, reheat the mustard oil over a medium–high heat. Add the reserved rice and stir until the grains are coated in oil. Add the dissolved coconut and bring to the boil. Reduce the heat to its lowest setting, stir in the salt and cover the pan tightly. Simmer for 8–10 minutes, until the rice is tender and all the liquid has been absorbed.

5. Remove from the heat and fluff up the grains of rice with a fork. Add more salt if needed. Re-cover the pan and leave the rice to stand for 5 minutes before serving.

#422 Hush puppies

Ingredients

280 g/10 oz polenta

70 g/2½ oz plain flour, sifted

1 small onion, finely chopped

1 tbsp caster sugar

2 tsp baking powder

½ tsp salt

175 ml/6 fl oz milk

1 egg, beaten

corn oil, for deep-frying

1. Put the polenta, flour, onion, sugar, baking powder and salt into a bowl, stir to combine and make a well in the centre.

2. Beat together the milk and egg in a jug, then pour into the dry ingredients and stir until a thick batter forms.

3. Heat at least 5 cm/2 inches of oil in a deep frying pan or heavy-based saucepan to 180–190°C/350–375°F, or until a cube of bread browns in 30 seconds.

4. Drop in as many teaspoons of the batter as will fit without overcrowding the pan and cook, stirring constantly, until the hush puppies puff up and turn golden.

5. Remove from the oil with a slotted spoon and drain on kitchen paper. Reheat the oil, if necessary, and cook the remaining batter. Serve hot.

#423 Onion rings

Ingredients

115 g/4 oz plain flour

pinch of salt

1 egg

150 ml/5 fl oz semi-skimmed milk

4 large onions

vegetable oil, for deep-frying

salt and pepper

1. Sift the flour and salt into a large bowl and make a well in the centre. Break the egg into the well and gently beat with a whisk. Gradually whisk in the milk, drawing the flour from the sides of the bowl into the liquid in the centre to make a smooth batter.

2. Slice the whole onions widthways into 5-mm/¼-inch slices, then separate the slices into rings. Heat the oil in a deep-fat fryer or deep, heavy-based saucepan to 180–190°C/350–375°F, or until a cube of bread browns in 30 seconds.

3. Using the tines of a fork, pick up several onions rings at a time and dip in the batter. Allow any excess batter to drip off, then add the onions to the oil and deep-fry for 1–2 minutes until they rise to the surface and become crisp and golden brown. Remove from the oil, drain on kitchen paper and keep warm while cooking the remaining onion rings in batches.

4. Season the onion rings with salt and pepper to taste, then serve immediately.

Serves 4

Asparagus with lemon butter sauce

Ingredients

800 g/1 lb 12 oz asparagus spears, trimmed

1 tbsp olive oil

salt and pepper

Sauce

juice of ½ lemon

2 tbsp water

100 g/3½ oz butter, cut into cubes

1. Preheat the oven to 200°C/400°F/Gas Mark 6.

2. Lay the asparagus spears on a large baking sheet in a single layer. Drizzle over the oil, season to taste with salt and pepper and roast in the preheated oven for 10 minutes, or until just tender.

3. Meanwhile, make the sauce. Pour the lemon juice into a saucepan and add the water. Heat for about 1 minute, then slowly add the butter, cube by cube, stirring constantly until it has all been incorporated. Season to taste with pepper and serve warm with the asparagus.

425

Serves 4

Slow-cooked peppers & onions

Ingredients

3 tbsp olive oil

1 large onion, thinly sliced

3 mixed peppers, such as red, orange and yellow, deseeded and cut into strips

2 garlic cloves, finely chopped

400 g/14 oz canned chopped tomatoes

2 tsp dried thyme

salt and pepper

1. Heat the oil in a large frying pan with a tight-fitting lid over a medium heat. Stir in the onion, cover, reduce the heat to low and simmer for 8–10 minutes, until the onion is soft but not brown.

2. Stir in the mixed peppers and garlic and season to taste with salt and pepper. Re-cover the pan and simmer for 5 minutes. Stir in the tomatoes and thyme and bring to the boil, stirring.

3. Reduce the heat to very low (use a heat diffuser if you have one), re-cover the pan and leave to simmer for 20 minutes, until the peppers are tender. If the sauce is too runny, uncover and boil until it reaches the desired consistency. Adjust the seasoning, if necessary.

4. Spoon into a serving dish and serve hot or at room temperature.

#426 Roasted beetroot with horseradish butter

Serves 4

Ingredients

8 small beetroot, peeled and halved lengthways

olive oil, for coating

4 fresh thyme sprigs

115 g/4 oz unsalted butter, at room temperature

125 g/4½ oz prepared horseradish

sea salt flakes and pepper

1. Preheat the oven to 190°/375°F/Gas Mark 5. Put the beetroot in a bowl and toss with enough oil to coat.

2. Cut out four squares of foil. Place 4 beetroot halves and a thyme sprig on each square. Season with salt and pepper. Loosely wrap the contents of each foil square, sealing the edges well.

3. Cook in the preheated oven for about 1 hour, or until the beetroot is soft.

4. Meanwhile, mash the butter with the horseradish and salt and pepper to taste, mixing well. Scrape the mixture onto a piece of clingfilm and shape into a log. Chill in the refrigerator.

5. Open the foil packages and add a slice of horseradish butter to each. Serve immediately, still in the packages.

#427 Hot garlic-stuffed mushrooms

Serves 4

Ingredients

4 large field mushrooms

4 sprays olive oil

2–3 garlic cloves, crushed

2 shallots

25 g/1 oz fresh wholemeal breadcrumbs

few fresh basil sprigs, plus extra to garnish

25 g/1 oz ready-to-eat dried apricots, chopped

1 tbsp pine kernels

55 g/2 oz feta cheese

pepper

1. Preheat the oven to 180°C/350°F/Gas Mark 4. Remove the stalks from the mushrooms and set aside. Spray the bases of the mushrooms with the oil and place underside up in a roasting tin.

2. Put the mushroom stalks in a food processor with the garlic, shallots and breadcrumbs. Reserve a few basil sprigs for the garnish then place the remainder in the food processor with the apricots, pine kernels and feta cheese. Add pepper to taste.

3. Process for 1–2 minutes, or until a stuffing consistency is formed, then divide among the mushroom caps.

4. Bake for 10–12 minutes, or until the mushrooms are tender and the stuffing is crisp on the top. Serve garnished with basil sprigs.

Roman-style artichokes

Serves
4

Ingredients

1 tbsp lemon juice

4 globe artichokes

6 tbsp finely chopped fresh
flat-leaf parsley

leaves from 8 fresh mint sprigs,
finely chopped

4 large garlic cloves, 2 finely chopped,
2 sliced

200 ml/7 fl oz olive oil

300 ml/10 fl oz dry white wine

salt and pepper

1. Preheat the oven to 160°C/325°F/Gas Mark 3. Put the lemon juice in a bowl of cold water large enough to hold the artichokes and set aside. To prepare the artichokes, remove all the outer leaves and trim the stalks. Cut off the tops and remove and discard the hairy chokes. Drop each artichoke in the bowl of lemon water to prevent discoloration.

2. Mix together the parsley, mint, chopped garlic and 3 tablespoons of the oil and season well. Remove the artichokes from the water and drain on kitchen paper. Divide the mint mixture between the artichokes, pressing the filling into each hole left by the chokes. Transfer the artichokes to a deep baking dish that will hold them upright. Mix the remaining oil and the wine together and pour around the artichokes. Scatter over the sliced garlic and cover with foil. Bake in the preheated oven for 40–50 minutes, until the artichokes are tender. Remove the artichokes from the dish and leave to cool.

3. Transfer the cooking liquid to a small saucepan and boil until reduced by half. Remove the garlic slices, adjust the seasoning and set aside to cool. When both the juices and artichokes are cool, return the artichokes to the sauce, standing upright, and chill for up to 2 days. Remove the artichokes from the refrigerator 15 minutes before serving to bring to room temperature. Serve with the juices spooned over the artichokes.

#429 Sticky carrots with whisky & ginger glaze

Serves 2–3

Ingredients

1 tsp sugar

½ tsp pepper

good pinch of sea salt flakes

4 tbsp groundnut oil

3 tbsp lightly salted butter

4 large carrots, sliced diagonally into 1-cm/½-inch rounds

2-cm/¾-inch piece fresh ginger, cut into batons

2 tbsp whisky

125 ml/4 fl oz chicken stock

1. Mix the sugar, pepper and salt together in a bowl and set aside.

2. Heat the oil with half the butter in a large frying pan. Add the carrots in a single layer and sprinkle with the sugar mixture. Cook over a medium-high heat for 3 minutes, then start turning the slices with tongs and reduce the heat if necessary. When brown on both sides and starting to blacken at the edges, transfer to a plate.

3. Wipe out the pan with kitchen paper. Add the ginger and cook over a medium–high heat for 1–2 minutes, until golden. Add to the carrots.

4. Add the remaining butter, the whisky and stock. Bring to the boil, then reduce the heat and simmer for 3 minutes or until syrupy. Return the carrots and ginger to the pan and swirl with the syrup for 1 minute. Serve immediately.

#430 Peas with baby onions

Serves 4

Ingredients

15 g/½ oz unsalted butter

175 g/6 oz whole baby onions

900 g/2 lb frozen peas

125 ml/4 fl oz water

2 tbsp plain flour

150 ml/5 fl oz double cream

1 tbsp chopped fresh parsley

1 tbsp lemon juice

salt and pepper

1. Melt the butter in a large, heavy-based saucepan. Add the onions and cook, stirring occasionally, for 5 minutes. Add the peas and cook, stirring constantly, for a further 3 minutes, then add the water and bring to the boil.

2. Reduce the heat to low, partially cover and simmer for 10 minutes. Beat the flour into the cream. Remove the pan from the heat, stir in the cream mixture and parsley and season to taste with salt and pepper.

3. Return the pan to the heat and cook, stirring gently but constantly, for about 3 minutes, until thickened. Stir the lemon juice into the sauce and serve the peas immediately.

New potatoes with garlic & chilli butter

Ingredients

700 g/1 lb 9 oz baby new potatoes

40 g/1½ oz butter

1 garlic clove, finely chopped

1 red chilli, deseeded and finely chopped

salt and pepper

chopped fresh coriander leaves, to garnish

1. Bring a large saucepan of lightly salted water to the boil, add the potatoes, bring back to the boil and cook for 15 minutes, or until tender. Drain well.

2. Melt the butter in a large saucepan, add the garlic and chilli and gently stir-fry for 30 seconds, without browning.

3. Add the potatoes and stir to coat in the butter, then season to taste with salt and pepper. Sprinkle with the coriander and serve hot.

Grilled polenta with fennel seeds

Ingredients

1 litre/1¾ pints water

200 g/7 oz instant polenta

25 g/1 oz butter

1 tbsp fennel seeds

2 tbsp finely chopped fresh flat-leaf parsley

olive oil, for brushing

salt and pepper

1. Place the water in a saucepan, add salt to taste and bring to the boil. Sprinkle in the polenta and stir over a medium heat for 5 minutes, or until the polenta thickens and comes away from the sides of the pan. Remove from the heat and stir in the butter, fennel seeds and parsley. Season to taste with pepper.

2. Brush a rectangular ovenproof dish with oil. Spoon the polenta mixture into the prepared dish, spread the surface level and leave to set. Turn out and cut into slices.

3. Preheat the grill to high. Brush the polenta slices with oil and place under the preheated grill until brown and crisp. Serve immediately.

#433 Hot & sour courgettes

Serves 4

Ingredients

2 large courgettes, thinly sliced

1 tsp salt

2 tbsp groundnut oil

1 tsp Sichuan peppercorns, crushed

½–1 red chilli, deseeded and sliced into thin strips

1 large garlic clove, thinly sliced

½ tsp finely chopped fresh ginger

1 tbsp rice vinegar

1 tbsp light soy sauce

2 tsp sugar

1 spring onion, green part included, thinly sliced

a few drops of sesame oil and 1 tsp sesame seeds, to garnish

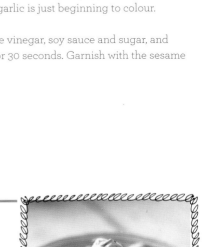

1. Put the courgette slices in a large colander and toss with the salt. Cover with a plate and put a weight on top. Leave to drain for 20 minutes. Rinse off the salt and spread out the slices on kitchen paper to dry.

2. Preheat a wok over a high heat and add the groundnut oil. Add the peppercorns, chilli, garlic and ginger. Fry for about 20 seconds until the garlic is just beginning to colour.

3. Add the courgette slices and toss in the oil. Add the vinegar, soy sauce and sugar, and stir-fry for 2 minutes. Add the spring onion and fry for 30 seconds. Garnish with the sesame oil and sesame seeds and serve immediately.

#434 Broad beans with feta

Serves 4–6

Ingredients

500 g/1 lb 2 oz shelled broad beans

4 tbsp extra virgin olive oil

1 tbsp lemon juice

1 tbsp finely chopped fresh dill, plus extra to garnish

55 g/2 oz feta cheese, diced

salt and pepper

1. Bring a large saucepan of lightly salted water to the boil. Add the beans and cook for 2–3 minutes, until tender. Drain thoroughly and set aside.

2. When the beans are cool enough to handle, remove and discard the grey skins. Put the peeled beans in a serving bowl.

3. Combine the oil and lemon juice in a small bowl, then season to taste with salt and pepper. Pour the dressing over the warm beans, add the dill and stir gently. Adjust the seasoning, adding salt and pepper if needed.

4. If serving hot, add the cheese, gently toss and sprinkle with dill, then serve immediately. Alternatively, set aside the beans in their dressing to cool and then chill until required. To serve cold, remove from the refrigerator 10 minutes before serving to bring to room temperature. Taste and adjust the seasoning, then sprinkle with the cheese and dill and serve.

#435 Buttered kale with chives & lemon

Serves 4–6

Ingredients

225 g/8 oz kale

grated zest of 1 lemon

handful of snipped fresh chives

lightly salted butter, for tossing

sea salt flakes and white pepper

1. Remove the tough stems from the kale, then stack the leaves and slice into wide ribbons. Steam for 10–12 minutes until tender but still bright green.

2. Transfer the kale to a warmed serving dish, add the lemon zest, chives, and butter to taste, and toss together. Season with salt and pepper. Serve immediately.

#436 Steamed vegetable parcels

Serves 4

Ingredients

115 g/4 oz French beans

55 g/2 oz mangetout

12 baby carrots

8 baby onions or shallots

12 baby turnips

8 radishes

55 g/2 oz unsalted butter or margarine

4 thinly pared strips of lemon rind

4 tsp finely chopped fresh chervil

4 tbsp dry white wine

salt and pepper

1. Cut out four double thickness 30-cm/12-inch rounds of greaseproof paper.

2. Divide the French beans, mangetout, carrots, onions, turnips and radishes between the rounds, placing them on one half. Season to taste with salt and pepper and dot with the butter. Add a strip of lemon rind to each. Sprinkle with the chervil and drizzle with the wine. Fold over the double layer of paper, twisting the edges together to seal.

3. Bring a large saucepan of water to the boil and place a steamer on top. Put the parcels in the steamer, cover tightly and steam for 8–10 minutes. Serve the parcels immediately, to be unwrapped at the table.

#437 Red cabbage with nuts, mushrooms & bacon

Serves 4

Ingredients

½ head of red cabbage

2 tablespoons rapeseed oil

6 thin bacon rashers, chopped

1 onion, chopped

2 tsp thyme leaves

150 g/5½ oz chestnut mushrooms, roughly chopped

55 g/2 oz toasted hazelnuts, chopped

grated zest of 1 lemon

1 tsp sea salt flakes

½ tsp pepper

½ tsp sugar

2 tbsp cider vinegar

225 ml/8 fl oz beef stock

15 g/½ oz fresh parsley, chopped

lightly salted butter, to serve

1. Cut the cabbage in quarters lengthways, discarding the tough central core. Slice the leaves widthways into ribbons.

2. Heat the oil in a flameproof casserole dish over a medium-high heat. Add the bacon and cook for about 5 minutes until crisp.

3. Reduce the heat to medium, add the onion and thyme and cook for 5 minutes, until the onion is translucent. Add the mushrooms and cabbage and cook for a further 5 minutes, until starting to soften.

4. Stir in the nuts, lemon zest, salt, pepper and sugar, and cook for a further 3 minutes. Pour in the vinegar and stock, cover and bring to the boil, then reduce the heat and simmer for 15 minutes until the cabbage is tender.

5. Transfer to a warmed serving dish. Stir in the parsley and a little butter and serve immediately.

#438 Lemon beans

Serves 4

Ingredients

900 g/2 lb mixed green beans, such as shelled broad beans, French beans and runner beans

70 g/2½ oz butter or margarine

4 tsp plain flour

300 ml/10 fl oz vegetable stock

5 tbsp dry white wine

6 tbsp single cream

3 tbsp chopped fresh mixed herbs

grated rind of 1 lemon

2 tbsp lemon juice

salt and pepper

strips of lemon zest, to garnish

1. Bring a saucepan of lightly salted water to the boil, add the beans, bring back to the boil and cook for 10 minutes, or until tender. Drain and place in a warmed serving dish.

2. Meanwhile, melt the butter in a saucepan. Add the flour and cook, stirring constantly, for 1 minute. Remove from the heat and gradually stir in the stock and wine. Return to the heat and bring to the boil, stirring.

3. Remove from the heat once again and stir in the cream, herbs and lemon rind and juice. Season to taste with salt and pepper. Pour the sauce over the beans, mixing well to coat thoroughly. Serve immediately, garnished with strips of lemon zest.

Honey-roasted red potatoes

Ingredients

cooking spray, for greasing

2 tbsp olive oil

2 tbsp honey

1 tbsp Dijon mustard

½ tsp salt

⅛ tsp cayenne pepper

675 g/1 lb 8 oz small red potatoes,
halved or quartered

1 shallot, diced

1 garlic clove, finely chopped

1. Preheat the oven to 200°C/400° F/Gas Mark 6 and spray a large baking dish with cooking spray.

2. Put the oil, honey, mustard, salt and cayenne pepper into a small bowl and stir to mix.

3. Put the potatoes, shallot and garlic into the prepared dish and toss together. Drizzle the honey mixture over the top and toss to coat well. Bake in the preheated oven, stirring occasionally, for 45–60 minutes until brown and crisp. Serve hot.

#440 Mushrooms in red wine

Serves 3–4

Ingredients

25 g/1 oz butter

4 finely chopped shallots

2 finely chopped garlic cloves

100 g/3½ oz shiitake mushrooms

100 g/3½ oz chestnut mushrooms

175 ml/6 fl oz beef stock or vegetable stock

175 ml/6 fl oz red wine

1 tablespoon chopped fresh thyme

1. Melt the butter in a frying pan over a medium heat, add the shallots and garlic and cook for 1–2 minutes until the shallots are soft.

2. Add the shiitake mushrooms and chestnut mushrooms to the pan and stir well. Add the stock and wine with the thyme and simmer until the sauce has reduced by half and the mushrooms are soft. Serve immediately.

#441 Baked mushrooms

Serves 2

Ingredients

4 large flat mushrooms, stalks removed

2 garlic cloves, finely chopped

1 tbsp finely chopped fresh thyme

4 tbsp melted butter

juice of 1 lemon

2 tbsp olive oil

1. Preheat the oven to 200°C/400°F/Gas Mark 6.

2. Place the mushrooms in a baking dish and sprinkle over the garlic and thyme. Add the butter and lemon juice.

3. Drizzle over the oil and bake in the preheated oven for 20–25 minutes, basting from time to time.

#442 Hand-cut chips

Serves 4

Ingredients

900 g/2 lb potatoes

500 ml/18 fl oz vegetable oil

500 ml/18 fl oz beef suet

sea salt

1. Peel the potatoes, if desired, and cut into 5 x 5-mm/¼ x ¼-inch sticks. Soak in a bowl of cold water for 5 minutes, then drain, rinse and wrap in a clean tea towel to dry.

2. Place the oil and suet in a large, heavy-based saucepan or a deep-fryer and heat to 180–190°C/350–375°F, or until a cube of bread browns in 30 seconds. Carefully add the cut potatoes, in batches, if necessary, to avoid overcrowding. Cook for about 3–4 minutes, until beginning to brown. Remove using tongs and drain on a plate lined with kitchen paper.

3. Reheat the oil to 180–190°C/350–375°F, then add the potatoes and fry for 3–5 minutes, until golden brown and crisp. Remove from the oil and drain on a plate lined with kitchen paper. Season generously with sea salt and serve immediately.

#443 Sweet potato chips

Serves 4

Ingredients

1 litre/1¾ pints vegetable oil

60 g/2¼ oz plain flour, plus extra if needed

1 tsp salt

225 ml/8 fl oz water, plus extra if needed

900 g/2 lb orange-fleshed sweet potatoes, peeled and cut into 5-mm/¼-inch sticks

sea salt

1. Place the oil in a large, heavy-based saucepan or a deep-fryer and heat to 180–190°C/350–375°F, or until a cube of bread browns in 30 seconds.

2. Meanwhile, combine the flour and salt in a medium-sized bowl. Whisk in the water until well combined. The batter should be the consistency of a very thin pancake batter. If it is too thick, add more water, 1 tablespoon at a time. If it is too thin, add more flour, 1 tablespoon at a time.

3. Add a handful of the sweet potatoes to the batter and stir to coat. Remove from the batter using tongs, allowing the excess to drip back into the bowl. Transfer the battered potatoes to the hot oil and cook for 3–4 minutes, until golden brown and crisp. Remove using tongs and drain on a plate lined with kitchen paper. Continue cooking in batches until all of the potatoes are cooked. Season generously with salt and serve immediately.

#444 Spiced lentils with spinach

Ingredients

2 tbsp olive oil

1 large onion, finely chopped

1 large garlic clove, crushed

½ tbsp ground cumin

½ tsp ground ginger

250 g/9 oz Puy lentils

about 600 ml/1 pint vegetable stock

100 g/3½ oz baby spinach leaves

2 tbsp fresh mint leaves

1 tbsp fresh coriander leaves

1 tbsp fresh flat-leaf parsley

lemon juice

salt and pepper

strips of lemon rind, to garnish

1. Heat the oil in a large frying pan over a medium heat. Add the onion and cook, stirring occasionally, for about 6 minutes. Stir in the garlic, cumin and ginger and cook, stirring occasionally, until the onion is just brown.

2. Stir in the lentils. Pour in enough stock to cover the lentils by 2.5 cm/1 inch and bring to the boil. Reduce the heat and simmer for 20–30 minutes until the lentils are tender.

3. Meanwhile, rinse the spinach leaves in several changes of cold water and shake dry. Finely chop the mint, coriander leaves and parsley.

4. Add the spinach to the pan and stir through until it just wilts. Stir in the mint, coriander and parsley. Adjust the seasoning, adding lemon juice and salt and pepper. Transfer to a serving bowl and serve, garnished with lemon rind.

#445 Honey-glazed sautéed squash

Ingredients

40 g/1½ oz butter

3 tbsp clear honey

500 g/1 lb 2 oz prepared winter squash flesh, cut into 2-cm/¾-inch cubes

1 tsp finely chopped fresh thyme

salt and pepper

fresh thyme sprigs, to garnish

1. Put the butter and honey in a non-stick frying pan over a low heat and heat until melted.

2. Add the squash, chopped thyme and seasoning and mix well. Sauté over a medium heat for 8–10 minutes, turning and tossing regularly, until the squash cubes are tender and glazed all over (the glaze will gradually thicken and coat the squash cubes).

3. Garnish with thyme sprigs and serve.

#446 Okra stir-fried with onions

Ingredients

2 tbsp vegetable oil or groundnut oil

1 tsp black or brown mustard seeds

½ tsp cumin seeds

3 large garlic cloves, lightly crushed and chopped

280 g/10 oz okra, trimmed and halved diagonally

1 small red pepper, cored, deseeded and cut into 4-cm/1½-inch strips

1 onion, halved lengthways and cut into 5-mm/¼-inch slices

½ tsp chilli powder

½ tsp garam masala

salt

1. Heat the oil in a heavy-based frying pan or wok over a medium heat. When hot, but not smoking, add the mustard seeds, followed by the cumin seeds. Remove from the heat and add the garlic.

2. Return to a low heat and cook the garlic, stirring, for 1 minute, or until lightly browned.

3. Add the okra, red pepper and onion, increase the heat to medium–high and stir-fry for 2 minutes. Add the chilli powder, and salt to taste and stir-fry for a further 3 minutes. Add the garam masala and stir-fry for 1 minute. Remove from the heat and serve immediately.

#447 Spicy chickpeas

Serves 4

Ingredients

400 g/14 oz canned chickpeas, drained

2 potatoes, diced

2 tbsp tamarind paste

6 tbsp water

1 tsp chilli powder

2 tsp sugar

1 onion, chopped

1 tsp salt

To garnish

1 tomato, sliced

2 fresh green chillies, chopped

2–3 tbsp chopped fresh coriander

1. Place the drained chickpeas in a large bowl.

2. Place the potatoes in a saucepan of lightly salted water, bring to the boil and cook for 10–12 minutes or until cooked through. Drain and set aside.

3. Mix the tamarind paste and water together in a small bowl.

4. Add the chilli powder, sugar and 1 teaspoon of salt to the tamarind paste mixture and mix together. Pour the mixture over the chickpeas.

5. Add the onion and the diced potatoes, and stir to mix.

6. Transfer to a serving bowl, garnish with tomato, chillies and chopped coriander and serve immediately.

#448 Sweet & sour red cabbage

Ingredients

1 head of red cabbage, about
750 g/1 lb 10 oz

2 tbsp olive oil

2 onions, finely sliced

1 garlic clove, chopped

2 small cooking apples, peeled, cored
and sliced

2 tbsp muscovado sugar

½ tsp ground cinnamon

1 tsp crushed juniper berries

whole nutmeg, for grating

2 tbsp red wine vinegar

grated rind and juice of 1 orange

2 tbsp redcurrant jelly

salt and pepper

1. Cut the cabbage into quarters, remove the centre stalk and finely shred the leaves.

2. Heat the oil in a large saucepan over a medium heat and add the cabbage, onions, garlic and apples. Stir in the sugar, cinnamon and juniper berries and grate in a quarter of the nutmeg. Pour over the vinegar and orange juice and add the orange rind.

3. Stir well and season to taste with salt and pepper. The pan will be quite full but the volume of the cabbage will reduce during cooking.

4. Cook over a medium heat, stirring occasionally, for 10–15 minutes until the cabbage is just tender but still firm to the bite.

5. Stir in the redcurrant jelly, then taste and adjust the seasoning. Serve immediately.

449 Champ

Serves 4

Ingredients

900 g/2 lb potatoes

2 bunches of spring onions

55 g/2 oz butter, plus extra for serving

200 ml/7 fl oz milk or single cream

salt and pepper

2 tbsp chopped chives and 2 tbsp chopped parsley, to garnish

1. Peel the potatoes and cut them into large chunks. Bring a large saucepan of water to the boil, add the potatoes and cook for 15–20 minutes until tender.

2. Cut the spring onions into 1-cm/½-inch slices.

3. Drain the potatoes well and mash with a potato masher. If you want very smooth champ you could press them through a sieve. Keep warm.

4. Melt the butter in a medium-sized saucepan and add the spring onions. Sweat for 3–4 minutes until soft. Add the milk and bring to a simmer, season well and continue to simmer until slightly thickened.

5. Stir the onion mixture into the warm potatoes and adjust the seasoning, if necessary. Scatter over the chopped herbs and serve immediately, with extra butter on the side.

450 Pan haggerty

Serves 4–5

Ingredients

450 g/1 lb firm potatoes, such as Desirée or waxy salad potatoes

4 tbsp olive oil

55 g/2 oz butter

225 g/8 oz onions, halved and thinly sliced

115 g/4 oz Cheddar cheese, grated

salt and pepper

1. Thinly slice the potatoes using a mandolin or food processor. Rinse the slices quickly in cold water and dry thoroughly using a tea towel or kitchen paper.

2. Heat half the oil and half the butter in a 23-cm/9-inch frying pan. Remove the pan from the heat and arrange some of the sliced potatoes in the base. Build up layers of potato, onion and cheese, seasoning well with salt and pepper between each layer. Finish with a layer of potato and dot the remaining butter over the top.

3. Return the pan to a medium heat and cook for 15–20 minutes. The base should become brown but not burn. Place a large plate over the pan and invert the potato onto it by tilting the pan. Add the remaining oil to the pan, slip the potato back in and cook the other side for a further 15 minutes until the base is crusty. Remove from the heat and serve immediately on warmed plates.

Serves
4

New potatoes in cream sauce

Ingredients

12 small new potatoes, washed and scraped

3 tbsp unsalted butter or margarine

3 tbsp plain flour

½ tsp salt

¼ tsp white pepper

225 ml/8 fl oz milk

125 ml/4 fl oz light cream

1 tbsp chopped fresh chives

1. Put the potatoes in a large saucepan, cover with water and bring to the boil over a medium heat. Cover, reduce the heat and simmer for 15–20 minutes, or until the potatoes are tender. Remove from the heat and drain well.

2. Melt the butter in a heavy-based saucepan over a low heat. Add the flour, salt and pepper, stirring until smooth. Cook for 1 minute, stirring constantly. Gradually stir in the milk and cream and cook over a medium heat, stirring constantly, until thickened and bubbling. Pour over the potatoes, sprinkle with the chives and serve.

Serves
4

Summer succotash

Ingredients

4 bacon rashers

4 fresh corn cobs

1 onion, chopped

35 g/1¼ oz green pepper, chopped

450 g/1 lb fresh butter beans, shelled

2 tbsp butter or margarine

⅛ tsp pepper

1. Cook the bacon in a large frying pan until crisp, then remove from the pan and set aside leaving the fat in the pan.

2. Meanwhile, remove and discard the husks and silks from the corn cobs, then cut off the kernels using a sharp knife. Add the onion and green pepper to the pan and sauté until soft. Add the beans, corn, butter and pepper, cover and cook over a low heat for 30 minutes or until soft. Crumble the bacon, sprinkle over the vegetable mixture and serve.

#453 Fried courgettes

Serves 4

Ingredients

2 tbsp olive oil, plus extra
for drizzling

1 onion, finely chopped

2 large garlic cloves, finely chopped

400 g/14 oz courgettes, halved
lengthways and thinly sliced

½ tsp dried oregano

150 ml/5 fl oz passata

salt and pepper

crusty white bread, to serve (optional)

1. Heat the oil in a large frying pan over a medium heat. Add the onion, reduce the heat to low and fry, stirring, for 5–8 minutes, until it is just starting to turn a pale golden colour. Stir in the garlic.

2. Add the courgettes and oregano and season to taste with salt and pepper. Increase the heat to medium-high and fry, turning over the courgette slices occasionally, for 5–8 minutes, until just starting to become tender.

3. Add the passata, bring to the boil and cook, without stirring, until the courgettes are tender but not mushy. Adjust the seasoning, if necessary.

4. Transfer the courgettes to a warmed serving dish and drizzle with a little oil. Set aside to cool and serve with slices of bread (if using).

#454 Almond French beans

Serves 4

Ingredients

300 g/10½ oz French beans, topped
and tailed

1 tbsp sunflower oil

55 g/2 oz flaked almonds

30 g/1 oz butter

2 tsp lemon juice

2 tbsp finely chopped fresh
flat-leaf parsley

salt and pepper

1. Bring a saucepan of lightly salted water to the boil. Add the beans, bring back to the boil and cook for 3–5 minutes, or until tender. Drain well.

2. Meanwhile, heat the oil in a large frying pan over a high heat. Add the almonds and fry, stirring, until golden brown, taking care that they do not burn. Set aside. Use a slotted spoon to transfer the beans to a plate lined with kitchen paper and drain well. Wipe out the frying pan with kitchen paper.

3. Melt the butter in the pan. Add the beans and stir. Add the lemon juice, and salt and pepper to taste, then stir in the parsley. Transfer the beans to a serving dish and sprinkle with the almonds to serve.

#455 Garlic mash

Ingredients

900 g/2 lb floury potatoes, peeled
and cut into chunks

8 garlic cloves, crushed

150 ml/5 fl oz milk

85 g/3 oz butter

pinch of freshly grated nutmeg

salt and pepper

1. Place the potatoes in a large saucepan with enough water to cover and a pinch of salt. Bring to the boil and cook for 10 minutes. Add the garlic and cook for a further 10–15 minutes, or until the potatoes are tender.

2. Drain the potatoes and garlic, reserving 3 tablespoons of the cooking liquid. Return the reserved cooking liquid to the saucepan, then add the milk and bring to a simmer. Add the butter, return the potatoes and garlic to the pan and remove from the heat. Mash thoroughly with a potato masher.

3. Season the potato mixture to taste with nutmeg, salt and pepper and beat thoroughly with a wooden spoon until light and fluffy. Serve immediately.

#456 Baked beans

Ingredients

oil, for greasing

900 g/2 lb tinned baked beans with
pork sausages

170 g/6 oz soft light brown sugar

60 g/2¼ oz onion, chopped

115 g/4 oz tomato ketchup

35 g/1¼ oz green pepper, chopped

2 tsp American mustard

4 bacon rashers

1 green pepper, sliced into thin rings

1. Preheat the oven to 180°C/350°F/Gas Mark 4. Grease a large baking dish.

2. Put all the ingredients, except the bacon and green pepper rings, into a bowl and stir well to combine.

3. Spoon the mixture into the prepared dish. Arrange the bacon and green pepper rings on top and bake in the preheated oven for 1 hour.

Serves
4

Brussels sprouts with chestnuts

Ingredients

350 g/12 oz Brussels sprouts

3 tbsp butter

100 g/3½ oz canned whole chestnuts

pinch of nutmeg

salt and pepper

50 g/1¾ oz flaked almonds, to garnish

1. Bring a large saucepan of water to the boil. Add the sprouts, bring back to the boil and cook for 5 minutes. Drain thoroughly.

2. Melt the butter in a large saucepan over a medium heat. Add the sprouts and cook, stirring, for 3 minutes.

3. Add the chestnuts and nutmeg to the pan. Season with salt and pepper and stir well. Cook for a further 2 minutes, stirring constantly, then remove from the heat.

4. Transfer to a serving dish, scatter over the almonds and serve.

458 Baked celery with cream

Serves
4

Ingredients

1 head of celery

½ tsp ground cumin

½ tsp ground coriander

1 garlic clove, crushed

1 red onion, thinly sliced

50 g/1¾ oz pecan nuts, halved

150 ml/5 fl oz vegetable stock

150 ml/5 fl oz single cream

50 g/1¾ oz fresh wholemeal breadcrumbs

25 g/1 oz Parmesan cheese, grated

salt and pepper

1. Preheat the oven to 200°C/400°F/Gas Mark 6. Trim the celery and cut into matchsticks. Place in an ovenproof dish with the cumin, coriander, garlic, onion and nuts.

2. Mix the stock and cream together in a jug and pour over the vegetables. Season to taste with salt and pepper. Mix the breadcrumbs and cheese together in a small bowl and sprinkle over the top to cover the vegetables.

3. Cook in the preheated oven for 40 minutes, or until the vegetables are tender and the top is crispy. Serve immediately.

#459 Fried cabbage & bacon

Serves 4

Ingredients

1 tbsp olive oil

15 g/½ oz butter

1 large onion, sliced

200 g/7 oz lean smoked bacon lardons

1 garlic clove, crushed

1 tsp fennel seeds

500 g/1 lb 2 oz firm green cabbage, such as Savoy, shredded

salt and pepper

jacket potatoes or creamy mashed potatoes, to serve

1. Heat the oil and butter in a large saucepan over a medium-high heat, add the onion and bacon and fry for 4–5 minutes, stirring, until lightly browned.

2. Stir in the garlic and fennel seeds, then add the cabbage and stir to combine. Reduce the heat to medium, season to taste with salt and pepper and cook, stirring frequently, for 5–6 minutes, until the cabbage is just tender.

3. Season again with salt and pepper and serve immediately with potatoes.

#460 Cauliflower with lemon & mustard

Serves 4

Ingredients

1 head of cauliflower, about 450 g/1 lb, cut into florets

1 tbsp olive oil

1 tbsp wholegrain mustard

finely grated rind of 1 lemon

salt and pepper

1. Place the cauliflower florets in a steamer over a saucepan of gently boiling water. Cover and steam for 6–8 minutes, or until almost tender. Drain well.

2. Whisk together the oil, mustard and lemon rind with a fork in a small bowl until combined. Stir the dressing into the cauliflower, gently turning to coat evenly. Season to taste with salt and pepper.

3. Tip the cauliflower into a warmed serving dish and serve immediately.

#461 Honeyed parsnips

Serves 4

Ingredients

8 parsnips, quartered

4 tbsp vegetable oil

1 tbsp honey

1. Preheat the oven to 180°C/350°F/Gas Mark 4.

2. Bring a large saucepan of water to the boil. Reduce the heat, add the parsnips and cook for 5 minutes. Drain well.

3. Pour 2 tablespoons of the oil into a shallow ovenproof dish and add the parsnips. Mix the remaining oil with the honey and drizzle over the parsnips. Roast in the preheated oven for 45 minutes, until golden brown and tender. Remove from the oven and serve.

#462 Braised peas with lettuce & tarragon

Serves 4

Ingredients

15 g/½ oz butter
1 tbsp olive oil
1 leek, thinly sliced
2 tsp plain flour
250 ml/9 fl oz vegetable stock
375 g/13 oz fresh or frozen peas
2 large Little Gem lettuces, sliced
3 tbsp chopped fresh tarragon
1 tbsp lemon juice
salt and pepper

1. Heat the butter and oil in a large saucepan. Add the leek, cover and cook over a low heat for 5 minutes until soft. Stir in the flour, then gradually stir in the stock.

2. Add the peas, increase the heat, cover and simmer for 4 minutes. Add the lettuce without stirring it in, cover and simmer for a further 2 minutes until the vegetables are tender.

3. Stir the lettuce, tarragon and lemon juice into the peas. Season with salt and pepper and serve immediately.

#463 Parsley butter & sweet potato mash

Serves 4

Ingredients

70 g/2½ oz butter, softened
2 tbsp chopped fresh parsley
900 g/2 lb sweet potatoes, scrubbed
salt

1. Put two thirds of the butter into a bowl with the parsley and beat together. Turn out onto a square of foil or clingfilm, shape into a block and chill in the refrigerator until required.

2. Cut the sweet potatoes into even-sized chunks. Bring a large saucepan of lightly salted water to the boil, add the sweet potatoes, bring back to the boil and cook, covered, for 15–20 minutes until tender.

3. Drain well, then cover the pan with a clean tea towel and leave to stand for 2 minutes. Remove the skins and mash with a potato masher until fluffy.

4. Add the remaining butter to the potatoes and stir in evenly. Spoon the mash into a serving dish and serve hot, topped with chunks of parsley butter.

293

#464 Hash browns

Ingredients

8 potatoes
2 tbsp olive oil
1 large onion, sliced
1 egg, beaten
70 g/2½ oz instant mashed potato
vegetable oil, for deep-frying
salt and pepper

1. Place the potatoes in a large saucepan of lightly salted water. Bring to the boil, then remove from the heat and leave to cool. Heat the olive oil in a frying pan over a low heat. Add the onion and sauté until translucent but not brown.

2. Drain the potatoes and coarsely shred into a large bowl. Add the onion, egg and instant mashed potato. Mix together well and season to taste with salt and pepper.

3. Heat enough vegetable oil for deep-frying in a large saucepan or deep-fryer to 180–190°C/350—375°F, or until a cube of bread browns in 30 seconds.

4. Meanwhile, roll the potato mixture into walnut-sized balls and flatten each ball to make a patty. Add the patties to the oil, in batches, and cook until golden. Drain on kitchen paper and serve hot.

#465 Creamed spinach

Serves 4

Ingredients

1 tbsp butter

1 kg/2 lb 4 oz fresh young spinach leaves, rinsed and drained

4 tbsp single cream

½ tsp freshly grated nutmeg

salt and pepper

1. Melt the butter in a large frying pan over a medium heat, add the spinach and cook, stirring constantly, until wilted. Continue to cook over a medium heat, stirring occasionally, until most of the liquid has evaporated.

2. Stir in the cream and nutmeg, then season to taste with salt and pepper and serve immediately.

#466 Roasted vegetables

Serves 4–6

Ingredients

3 parsnips, cut into 5-cm/2-inch chunks

4 baby turnips, cut into quarters

3 carrots, cut into 5-cm/2-inch chunks

450 g/1 lb butternut squash, cut into 5-cm/2-inch chunks

450 g/1 lb sweet potatoes, cut into 5-cm/2-inch chunks

2 garlic cloves, finely chopped

2 tbsp chopped fresh rosemary, plus extra to garnish

2 tbsp chopped fresh thyme, plus extra to garnish

2 tsp chopped fresh sage, plus extra to garnish

3 tbsp olive oil

salt and pepper

1. Preheat the oven to 220°C/425°F/Gas Mark 7. Arrange all the vegetables in a single layer in a large roasting tin. Scatter over the garlic and the herbs. Pour over the oil and season well with salt and pepper.

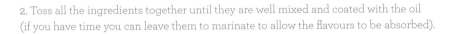

2. Toss all the ingredients together until they are well mixed and coated with the oil (if you have time you can leave them to marinate to allow the flavours to be absorbed).

3. Roast the vegetables at the top of the preheated oven for 50–60 minutes until they are cooked and nicely browned. Turn over half-way through the cooking time.

4. Serve with a good handful of fresh herbs scattered on top and a final sprinkling of salt and pepper to taste.

#467 Roasted shallots with breadcrumbs & cheese

Serves 4–6

Ingredients

8 shallots

2 tbsp apple juice concentrate

6 tbsp olive oil

½ tbsp finely chopped fresh thyme or rosemary

¼ tsp black pepper

70 g/2½ oz coarse dried breadcrumbs

115 g/4 oz mild Cheddar cheese, grated

sea salt flakes

1 tbsp chopped fresh parsley, to garnish

1. Preheat the oven to 220°C/425°F/Gas Mark 7. Halve the shallots lengthways and place in a shallow bowl.

2. Whisk together the apple juice concentrate, 4 tablespoons of the oil and the thyme. Pour the mixture over the shallots, turning to coat well.

3. Transfer the contents of the bowl into a small non-stick roasting tin in which the shallots fit in a single layer. Turn the shallots cut-side up and season with the pepper and a good pinch of salt. Sprinkle with the breadcrumbs and the remaining oil.

4. Roast in the preheated oven for 25–30 minutes, or until the shallots are soft and the edges are beginning to blacken. Scatter the cheese over the top, and roast for an a further 3 minutes, or until the cheese is melted and bubbling.

5. Garnish with the parsley and serve immediately.

#468 Perfect roast potatoes

Serves 6

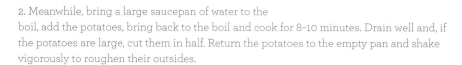

Ingredients

70 g/2½ oz goose fat or duck fat or 5 tbsp olive oil

1 kg/2 lb 4 oz even-sized potatoes

coarse sea salt

1. Preheat the oven to 230°C/450°F/Gas Mark 8. Put the fat in a large roasting tin, sprinkle generously with sea salt and place in the oven.

2. Meanwhile, bring a large saucepan of water to the boil, add the potatoes, bring back to the boil and cook for 8–10 minutes. Drain well and, if the potatoes are large, cut them in half. Return the potatoes to the empty pan and shake vigorously to roughen their outsides.

3. Arrange the potatoes in a single layer in the roasting tin and roast for 45 minutes. If they look as if they are beginning to char around the edges, reduce the oven temperature to 200°C/400°F/Gas Mark 6. Turn the potatoes over and roast for a further 30 minutes until crisp. Serve immediately.

#469 Dauphinoise potatoes

Serves 8

Ingredients

1 tbsp butter, plus extra for greasing

1 tbsp plain flour

225 ml/8 fl oz double cream

450 ml/16 fl oz milk

1 tsp salt

pinch of freshly grated nutmeg

pinch of freshly ground white pepper

4 fresh thyme sprigs

2 garlic cloves, finely chopped

2 kg/4 lb 8 oz baking potatoes, thinly sliced

115 g/4 oz Gruyère cheese or white Cheddar cheese, grated

salt and black pepper

1. Preheat the oven to 190°C/375°F/Gas Mark 5. Grease a 38 x 25-cm/15 x 10-inch ovenproof dish.

2. Melt the butter in a saucepan over a medium heat. Stir in the flour and cook, stirring constantly, for 2 minutes. Gradually whisk in the cream and milk and bring to simmering point. Add the salt, the nutmeg, white pepper, thyme and garlic, reduce the heat to low and simmer for 5 minutes. Remove the thyme sprigs.

3. Make a layer of half the potatoes in the prepared dish and season generously with salt and pepper. Top with half the sauce and cover with half the cheese. Repeat the layers with the remaining potatoes, sauce and cheese.

4. Bake in the preheated oven for about 1 hour, or until the top is browned and the potatoes are tender. Remove from the oven and leave to rest for 15 minutes before serving.

#470 Italian herb roast potatoes

Serves 4

Ingredients

3 fresh rosemary sprigs, plus extra to garnish

800 g/1 lb 12 oz small potatoes, cubed

3 garlic cloves, roughly chopped

5 tbsp olive oil, plus extra for brushing

salt and pepper

1. Preheat the oven to 200°C/400°F/Gas Mark 6. Brush a large baking dish with oil.

2. Remove the leaves from the rosemary sprigs, discarding the stems, and chop the leaves roughly. Set aside.

3. Place a layer of potatoes in the prepared baking dish, then sprinkle over a little of the garlic and rosemary and season to taste with salt and pepper. Repeat the layers until all the potatoes, garlic and rosemary have been used up.

4. Drizzle over the oil, then transfer the dish to the preheated oven and cook, stirring frequently, for 45 minutes, or until the potatoes are tender and lightly browned.

5. Garnish with a rosemary sprig and serve the potatoes immediately, straight from the baking dish.

Rosemary & basil mash

Ingredients

4 fresh rosemary sprigs

600 g/1 lb 5 oz floury potatoes, cut into small pieces

small handful of fresh basil leaves

125 ml/4 fl oz extra virgin olive oil, plus extra to taste

salt and pepper

1. Place the rosemary in a large saucepan of lightly salted water and bring to the boil. Bring a smaller saucepan of unsalted water to the boil. Set aside a small bowl of iced water. Add the potatoes to the salted water, bring back to the boil and cook, partially covered, for 20–25 minutes, until very tender but not falling apart. Remove from the heat and leave to cool, without draining.

2. Meanwhile, drop the basil leaves into the unsalted water, push them down with a wooden spoon and boil for just a few seconds until they wilt. Drain and place in the iced water to cool. Remove and pat completely dry with kitchen paper, then finely chop and set aside.

3. Drain the cooled potatoes and rosemary, reserving about 4 tablespoons of the cooking water and all the rosemary. Return the potatoes to the pan with the reserved water and season with salt and pepper. Break them up using an electric hand-held mixer.

4. When they begin to mash, slowly beat in the oil and then stir in the reserved rosemary and the basil. Adjust the seasoning, if necessary, and serve immediately.

#472 Spinach in Gorgonzola sauce

Serves 4

Ingredients

1 kg/2 lb 4 oz spinach
60 g/2¼ oz butter
½ tsp freshly grated nutmeg
125 ml/4 fl oz dry white wine
125 ml/4 fl oz milk
125 g/4½ oz Gorgonzola cheese, crumbled
2 egg yolks
salt and pepper

1. Remove and discard any tough stems from the spinach, then place the leaves in a colander and wash under cold running water. Leave to drain.

2. Melt half of the butter in a large saucepan over a medium heat. Stir in the spinach, with the water still clinging to its leaves, cover and cook for 3–4 minutes, until wilted. Stir in the nutmeg and season to taste with salt and pepper, then reduce the heat to low to keep the spinach warm while you prepare the sauce.

3. Pour the wine and milk into a separate saucepan, bring to the boil, then simmer until reduced slightly. Add the Gorgonzola and stir until melted. Remove from the heat.

4. Beat the egg yolks in a small bowl, stir in a little of the hot sauce, then tip back into the pan with the remaining butter and the spinach. Stir thoroughly and place over a medium heat to warm through. Taste and adjust the seasoning and serve immediately.

#473 Roast fennel with cherry tomatoes & rosemary

Serves 4

Ingredients

4 fennel bulbs, cut into slim wedges
2 tbsp olive oil
6 tbsp dry white wine
2 garlic cloves, crushed
2 tsp chopped fresh rosemary
200 g/7 oz cherry tomatoes
16 stoned black olives
2 tbsp chopped fresh parsley
salt and pepper

1. Preheat the oven to 200°C/400°F/Gas Mark 6. Place the fennel in a roasting tin large enough to hold it in a single layer. Mix the oil, 2 tablespoons of the wine, the garlic and rosemary together. Pour the mixture over the fennel, season with salt and pepper and toss together.

2. Roast in the preheated oven for 15–20 minutes until almost tender and lightly browned. Scatter the tomatoes and olives over the fennel. Pour over the remaining wine, then return to the oven for 8–10 minutes until the tomatoes are soft and the skins have burst. Toss with the parsley and serve warm or cold.

#474 Roasted potato wedges with shallots & rosemary

Serves 4

Ingredients

1 kg/2 lb 4 oz potatoes
6 tbsp olive oil
2 fresh rosemary sprigs
150 g/5½ oz baby shallots
2 garlic cloves, sliced
salt and pepper

1. Preheat the oven to 200°C/400°F/Gas Mark 6. Peel and cut each potato into 8 thick wedges. Put the potatoes in a large saucepan of lightly salted water and bring to the boil. Reduce the heat and simmer for 5 minutes.

2. Heat the oil in a large roasting tin. Drain the potatoes well and add to the tin. Strip the leaves from the rosemary sprigs, finely chop and sprinkle over the potatoes.

3. Roast the potatoes in the preheated oven for 35 minutes, turning twice during cooking. Add the shallots and garlic and roast for a further 15 minutes until golden brown. Season to taste with salt and pepper.

4. Transfer to a warmed serving dish and serve hot.

#475 Spring cabbage with bacon

Serves 8

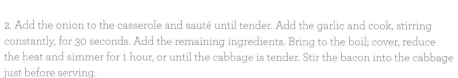

Ingredients

8 bacon rashers
250 g/9 oz onions, chopped
2 tsp finely chopped garlic
450 g/1 lb spring cabbage, chopped
400 ml/14 fl oz canned chicken soup
1 tsp salt
½ tsp pepper
¼ tsp dried crushed red pepper

1. Put the bacon into a casserole and cook over a medium-high heat for 8–10 minutes or until crisp. Remove from the casserole, drain on kitchen paper, crumble and set aside.

2. Add the onion to the casserole and sauté until tender. Add the garlic and cook, stirring constantly, for 30 seconds. Add the remaining ingredients. Bring to the boil; cover, reduce the heat and simmer for 1 hour, or until the cabbage is tender. Stir the bacon into the cabbage just before serving.

#476 Whole artichokes

Ingredients

2 lemons

4 large globe artichokes

250 g/9 oz butter

2 tbsp fresh thyme leaves

zest and juice of 1 lemon

salt and pepper

1. Half fill a large saucepan with cold water. Halve the lemons, squeeze the juice into the water and drop the skins in too. Cut the stalks off the artichokes near the base, then chop off the top 2.5 cm/1 inch of the leaves. Add them to the water, cover and bring to the boil. Once boiling, the artichokes will take 20–30 minutes to cook, depending on their tenderness and size. They are ready when the outer leaves can be pulled off without any effort.

2. Drain the artichokes, turn them upside down and leave to cool for 15 minutes while you make the lemon and thyme-flavoured butter. Gently melt the butter in a small saucepan, and mix in the thyme, lemon zest and juice, and salt and pepper to taste.

3. Place the artichokes in four shallow bowls and season to taste with salt and pepper. Serve the butter with the artichokes, in four small bowls or in the removed outer leaves of the artichoke. Place a large bowl in the middle of the table for discarded bits and leaves.

#477 Pecan-glazed Brussels sprouts

Ingredients

650 g/1 lb 7 oz Brussels sprouts

125 ml/4 fl oz water

55 g/2 oz unsalted butter

70 g/2½ oz soft light brown sugar

3 tbsp soy sauce

¼ tsp salt

60 g/2¼ oz finely chopped pecan nuts, toasted

1. Cut off the stem ends of the sprouts and slash the base of each sprout with a shallow 'X'. Bring the water to the boil in a large saucepan; add the sprouts, cover, then reduce the heat and simmer for 8–10 minutes, or until the sprouts are slightly softened, then drain and set aside.

2. Melt the butter in a frying pan and stir in the sugar, soy sauce and salt. Bring to the boil, stirring constantly. Add the nuts, reduce the heat and simmer, uncovered, for 5 minutes, stirring occasionally. Add the sprouts and cook over a medium heat for 5 minutes. Stir well before serving.

Thanksgiving stuffing

Ingredients

cooking spray, for greasing

110 g/3¾ oz raisins

225 ml/8 fl oz hot water

450 g/1 lb sourdough bread,
cut into 2.5-cm/1-inch cubes

55 g/2 oz unsalted butter

4 celery sticks, diced

1 onion, diced

2 tbsp finely chopped fresh
thyme leaves

3 tbsp finely chopped fresh
flat-leaf parsley

1 tbsp finely chopped fresh sage

½ tsp salt

½ tsp pepper

850 ml/1½ pints chicken stock

1. Preheat the oven to 180°C/350°F/Gas Mark 4 and spray a large baking dish with cooking spray.

2. Place the raisins in a small bowl, cover with the hot water and leave to soak for about 20 minutes.

3. Meanwhile, spread the bread cubes in a single layer on two large baking sheets and toast them in the preheated oven for about 20 minutes, until they are very dry and beginning to brown. Transfer to a large bowl. Do not switch off the oven.

4. Melt the butter in a large frying pan over a medium–high heat. Add the celery, onion and thyme and cook, stirring frequently, for about 5 minutes, until the vegetables are soft. Stir in the parsley, sage, salt and pepper. Drain the raisins and add them to the pan with the stock.

5. Pour the vegetable mixture over the bread cubes and toss until the bread has absorbed all the liquid. Transfer the mixture to the prepared baking dish and bake for 45 minutes, or until the top is golden brown. Leave to cool for about 15 minutes before serving.

#479 Glazed yams

Ingredients

juice of 1 lemon

1.2 kg/2 lb 8 oz orange-fleshed yams

2 tbsp unsalted butter, plus extra
for greasing

55 g/2 oz soft light brown sugar

½ tsp salt, or to taste

⅛ tsp cayenne pepper

1. Preheat the oven to 180°C/350°F/Gas Mark 4. Lightly grease a baking dish.

2. Add the lemon juice to a large mixing bowl. Peel the yams, cut into 2.5-cm/1-inch cubes and toss with the lemon juice.

3. Melt the butter in a large frying pan over a medium–high heat. Add the yams, lemon juice, sugar, salt and cayenne pepper. Cook, stirring, for 5–7 minutes, until a sticky syrup forms and the edges of the yams begin to caramelize.

4. Remove from heat and transfer into the prepared dish. Bake in the preheated oven for 20–25 minutes, or until soft. Serve hot.

#480 Cauliflower cheese

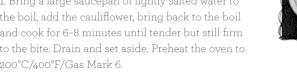

Ingredients

600 g/1 lb 5 oz cauliflower florets

150 ml/5 fl oz dry white wine

1 bay leaf

450 ml/16 fl oz milk

25 g/1 oz butter, cut into pieces

25 g/1 oz plain flour

70 g/2½ oz mature Cheddar cheese, grated

40 g/1½ oz freshly grated Parmesan cheese

1 tsp English mustard

1 tbsp snipped fresh chives

1 tbsp chopped fresh parsley

salt

1. Bring a large saucepan of lightly salted water to the boil, add the cauliflower, bring back to the boil and cook for 6–8 minutes until tender but still firm to the bite. Drain and set aside. Preheat the oven to 200°C/400°F/Gas Mark 6.

2. Place the wine and bay leaf in a saucepan, bring to the boil and boil rapidly until the wine is reduced by half. Add the milk, butter and flour and whisk until the butter has melted and the sauce boils and thickens. Simmer for 1 minute.

3. Remove from the heat. Mix the Cheddar cheese and Parmesan cheese together, add two thirds of the mixture to the sauce, stirring until smooth, then stir in the mustard, chives and parsley. Remove and discard the bay leaf.

4. Spoon a little of the sauce into the base of a shallow baking dish. Tip the cauliflower into the dish and spread out in an even layer. Spoon the remaining sauce over the top and sprinkle with the remaining cheese. Bake in the preheated oven for 20 minutes until lightly browned and bubbling. Serve immediately.

481 Baked acorn squash

Ingredients

2 acorn squash

2 tbsp freshly squeezed orange juice

1 tbsp soft light brown sugar

2 tbsp unsalted butter

2 tbsp maple syrup

salt and pepper

1. Preheat the oven to 200°C/400°F/Gas Mark 6. Cut the squash in half lengthwise, and scoop the seeds and strings out of the cavity. Carefully score the inside of each squash with a sharp knife, making shallow cuts about 1 cm/½ inch apart. Use a brush to coat each half with the orange juice. Generously sprinkle with salt and bake in the preheated oven for 30 minutes.

2. Put the sugar, butter, maple syrup and some pepper into a small saucepan over a medium heat. Bring to the boil, stir, and cook for 1 minute. Set aside.

3. Take the squash out of the oven and spoon off any liquid that has accumulated in the cavities. Brush the glaze evenly over each half, return to the oven and bake for a further 40 minutes, or until tender and caramelized at the edges. Leave to rest for 15 minutes, then sprinkle with salt and serve.

482 Mini Yorkshire puddings

Ingredients

30 g/1 oz beef dripping or 2 tbsp sunflower oil

140 g/5 oz plain flour

½ tsp salt

2 eggs

225 ml/8 fl oz milk

1. Grease six metal pudding moulds with the dripping, then divide the remaining dripping between the moulds. Preheat the oven to 220°C/425°F/Gas Mark 7, placing the moulds in the oven so the dripping can melt while the oven heats.

2. Sift the flour and salt together into a large mixing bowl and make a well in the centre. Break the eggs into the well, add the milk and beat, gradually drawing in the flour from the side to make a smooth batter. Remove the moulds from the oven and spoon in the batter until they are about half full.

3. Bake in the preheated oven for 30–35 minutes, without opening the door, until the puddings are well risen, puffed and golden brown. Serve immediately, as they will collapse if left to stand.

#483 Mango & macadamia nut stuffing

Ingredients

25 g/1 oz butter, plus extra
for greasing

1 small onion, finely chopped

1 celery stick, diced

175 g/6 oz fresh white breadcrumbs

1 egg, beaten

1 tbsp Dijon mustard

1 small mango, peeled,
stoned and diced

85 g/3 oz macadamia nuts, chopped

salt and pepper

1. Preheat the oven to 200°C/400°F/Gas Mark 6. Grease a 700-ml/1¼-pint ovenproof dish.

2. Melt the butter in a saucepan, add the onion and fry, stirring constantly, for 3-4 minutes until soft. Add the celery and cook for a further 2 minutes.

3. Remove from the heat and stir in the breadcrumbs, egg and mustard. Add the mango and nuts, then season to taste with salt and pepper.

4. Spread the mixture into the prepared dish and bake in the preheated oven for 20-25 minutes until golden and bubbling.

#484 Chestnut & sausage stuffing

Ingredients

225 g/8 oz pork sausage meat

225 g/8 oz unsweetened chestnut
purée

85 g/3 oz walnuts, chopped

115 g/4 oz ready-to-eat dried apricots,
chopped

2 tbsp chopped fresh parsley

2 tbsp snipped fresh chives

2 tsp chopped fresh sage

4-5 tbsp double cream

salt and pepper

1. Preheat the oven to 190°C/375°F/Gas Mark 5. Combine the sausage meat and chestnut purée in a bowl, then stir in the walnuts, apricots, parsley, chives and sage. Stir in enough cream to make a firm, but not dry, mixture. Season to taste with salt and pepper.

2. If you are planning to stuff a turkey or goose, fill the neck cavity only to ensure the bird cooks all the way through. It is safer and more reliable to cook the stuffing separately, either rolled into small balls and placed on a baking sheet or spooned into an ovenproof dish.

3. Cook the separate stuffing in a preheated oven for 30-40 minutes at 190°C/375°F/Gas Mark 5. It should be allowed a longer time to cook if you are roasting a bird at a lower temperature in the same oven.

485 Gravy

Serves 6

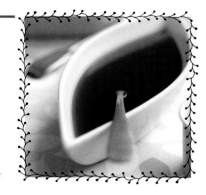

Ingredients

900 g/2 lb meat bones, raw or cooked

1 large onion, chopped

1 large carrot, chopped

2 celery sticks, chopped

1 bouquet garni

1.7 litres/3 pints water

1. Preheat the oven to 200°C/400°F/Gas Mark 6. Put the bones in a roasting tin and roast in the preheated oven for 20 minutes, or until brown. Remove from the oven and leave to cool.

2. Chop the bones into small pieces and put them into a large saucepan with all the remaining ingredients. Bring to the boil, then reduce the heat, cover and simmer for 2 hours.

3. Strain and leave until cold, then remove all traces of fat. Store, covered, in the refrigerator for up to 4 days. Boil vigorously for 5 minutes before using. The gravy can be frozen in ice-cube trays for up to 1 month.

486 Bread sauce

Serves 6–9

Ingredients

1 onion

12 cloves

1 bay leaf

6 black peppercorns

600 ml/1 pint milk

115 g/4 oz fresh white breadcrumbs

2 tbsp butter

whole nutmeg, for grating

2 tbsp double cream (optional)

salt and pepper

1. Make small holes in the onion with a skewer, then stick a clove in each hole.

2. Put the onion, bay leaf and peppercorns in a saucepan and pour in the milk. Bring to the boil over a medium heat, then remove from the heat, cover and leave to infuse for 1 hour.

3. Discard the onion and bay leaf and strain the milk to remove the peppercorns. Return the milk to the rinsed-out pan and add the breadcrumbs. Cook over a very low heat for 4–5 minutes, until the breadcrumbs have swollen and the sauce is thick.

4. Beat in the butter and season well with salt and pepper and a good grating of nutmeg. Stir in the cream just before serving, if using.

#487 Roasted garlic & herb sauce

Ingredients

1 garlic bulb

1 tbsp olive oil

2 handfuls of mixed herbs, such as
flat-leaf parsley, basil, thyme and sage,
coarse stalks removed

3–4 tbsp soured cream

salt and pepper

1. Preheat the oven to 200°C/400°F/Gas Mark 6. Peel the outer papery layers from the garlic bulb but leave the individual cloves intact. Using a sharp knife, cut a 5-10-mm/¼–½-inch slice off the top of the garlic to expose the cloves.

2. Put the bulb into a small ovenproof container, such as a ramekin, and drizzle with the oil. Cover with foil and roast in the preheated oven for 35–40 minutes until the cloves feel soft.

3. Remove from the oven and leave until cool enough to handle, then squeeze out the pulp from each clove into a food processor or blender. Add the herbs and soured cream and process until combined. Reheat the sauce gently over a low heat without boiling, if required. Season to taste with salt and pepper and use as required.

#488 Apple sauce

Serves
4

Ingredients

5 large cooking apples, about
900 g/2 lb total weight

85 g/3 oz caster sugar

2–3 tbsp water

25 g/1 oz unsalted butter

1. Peel, core and chop the apples. Put them in a heavy-based saucepan with the sugar and water. Bring to the boil, then reduce the heat, cover and simmer, stirring occasionally, for 10–12 minutes, or until the apples have collapsed and are fluffy.

2. Add the butter and stir until melted. Beat with a wooden spoon until smooth. Serve warm or cold.

#489 Cranberry sauce

Serves
4

Ingredients

450 g/1 lb fresh or frozen cranberries,
thawed if frozen

1 tbsp grated orange rind,
preferably unwaxed

150 ml/5 fl oz freshly squeezed
orange juice

115 g/4 oz soft light brown sugar

150 ml/5 fl oz water

1–2 tbsp triple sec (optional)

1. Put the cranberries in a heavy-based saucepan with the orange rind and juice, most of the sugar and the water. Bring to the boil, then reduce the heat and simmer for 12–15 minutes until the cranberries have burst.

2. Remove from the heat, taste and add the remaining sugar, if liked, with the triple sec, if using. Serve warm or cold.

#490 Tartare sauce

Ingredients

2 small gherkins

1 spring onion

1 tbsp capers

handful of fresh
flat-leaf parsley

175 ml/6 fl oz mayonnaise

1 tbsp lemon juice

salt and pepper

1. Finely chop the gherkins, spring onion, capers and parsley. Put them into a small bowl and stir in the mayonnaise.

2. Add the lemon juice and stir, then season to taste with salt and pepper. Cover and chill in the refrigerator for at least 30 minutes or up to 2 days before serving.

#491 Horseradish sauce

Ingredients

6 tbsp ready-made creamed
horseradish sauce

6 tbsp crème fraîche

1. In a small serving bowl, mix the horseradish sauce and crème fraîche together. Serve the sauce with roast beef, or with smoked fish such as trout or mackerel.

#492 Red wine sauce

Serves 6

Ingredients

150 ml/5 fl oz Gravy (see page 307)

4 tbsp red wine

1 tbsp redcurrant jelly

1. Blend the gravy with the wine and pour into a small, heavy-based saucepan. Add the redcurrant jelly and warm over a gentle heat, stirring, until blended.

2. Bring to the boil, then reduce the heat and simmer for 2 minutes. Serve hot.

#493 Mint sauce

Serves 4

Ingredients

3 tbsp chopped fresh mint

2–3 tsp caster sugar, or to taste

2 tbsp just-boiled water

3–4 tbsp white wine vinegar or malt vinegar

1. Put the mint in a small heatproof bowl and add 2 teaspoons of the sugar. Leave the boiled water to cool for about 1 minute, then pour it over the mint. Stir until the sugar has dissolved, then leave to infuse for 10 minutes.

2. Add the vinegar to taste, cover and leave to stand for 1 hour. Stir and serve.

#494 Refrigerator rolls

Makes
36

Ingredients

225 ml/8 fl oz cold water

55 g/2 oz unsalted butter or margarine,
plus extra for greasing

115 g/4 oz white vegetable fat

55 g/2 oz sugar

1½ tsp salt

2 sachets easy-blend dried yeast

225 ml/8 fl oz lukewarm water

2 eggs, beaten

750 g/1 lb 10 oz plain flour, plus extra for
dusting

1. Put the cold water, butter, vegetable fat, sugar and salt in a small saucepan and mix to combine. Place over a low heat until the butter and fat have melted. Remove from the heat and leave to cool until the temperature registers 70–76°C/158–169°F on a sugar thermometer.

2. Dissolve the yeast in the lukewarm water in a large mixing bowl and leave to stand for 5 minutes. Stir in the cooled butter mixture and the eggs. Gradually add one third of the flour, beating until smooth. Stir in enough of the remaining flour to form a thick dough. Turn out the dough onto a floured surface and knead for 5–8 minutes, or until smooth and elastic. Place in a well-greased bowl, cover and chill in the refrigerator for 1½–2 hours.

3. Preheat the oven to 200°C/400°F/Gas Mark 6. Grease two baking sheets. Knock back the dough and turn out onto a lightly floured surface. Roll out to a thickness of 5 mm/¼ inch. Cut out rounds with a 6-cm/2½-inch cutter. Use the blunt edge of a knife, to make a crease just off centre on each round. Fold over so that the top overlaps slightly, then gently press the edges together. Place on the prepared baking sheets. Cover and leave to rise in a warm place for 1 hour, or until doubled in size. Bake in the preheated oven for 12–15 minutes, or until golden. Serve warm.

#495 Mixed seed bread

Makes 1 loaf

Ingredients

375 g/13 oz strong white flour, plus extra for dusting

125 g/4½ oz rye flour

1½ tbsp skimmed milk powder

1½ tsp salt

1 tbsp soft light brown sugar

1 tsp easy-blend dried yeast

1½ tbsp sunflower oil, plus extra for greasing and brushing

2 tsp lemon juice

300 ml/10 fl oz lukewarm water

1 tsp caraway seeds

½ tsp poppy seeds

½ tsp sesame seeds

1 egg beaten with 1 tbsp water

1 tbsp sunflower seeds

1. Place the white flour, rye flour, milk powder, salt, sugar and yeast in a large bowl. Pour in the oil and add the lemon juice and water. Stir in the caraway, poppy and sesame seeds and mix well to make a smooth dough. Turn out onto a lightly floured surface and knead well for about 10 minutes until smooth.

2. Brush a bowl with oil. Shape the dough into a ball, place in the bowl and cover with a damp tea towel. Leave to rise in a warm place for 1 hour, until the dough has doubled in volume. Oil a 900-g/2-lb loaf tin. Turn out the dough onto a lightly floured surface and knead for 1 minute until smooth. Shape into a loaf the length of the tin and three times the width. Fold the dough in three lengthways and place in the tin with the join underneath. Cover and leave in a warm place for 30 minutes until it has risen above the tin.

3. Preheat the oven to 220°C/425°F/Gas Mark 7. Brush the egg glaze over the loaf, then gently press the sunflower seeds all over the top. Bake in the preheated oven for 30 minutes, or until golden brown and hollow on the base when tapped. Transfer to a wire rack to cool.

#496 Crusty white bread

Makes 1 loaf

Ingredients

1 egg

1 egg yolk

lukewarm water, as required

500 g/1 lb 2 oz strong white bread flour, plus extra for dusting

1½ tsp salt

2 tsp sugar

1 tsp easy-blend dried yeast

25 g/1 oz butter, diced

sunflower oil, for greasing

1. Place the egg and egg yolk in a jug and lightly mix. Add enough water to make up to 300 ml/10 fl oz. Stir well. Place the flour, salt, sugar and yeast in a large bowl. Add the butter and rub it in with your fingertips until the mixture resembles breadcrumbs. Make a well in the centre, add the egg mixture and work to a smooth dough. Turn out onto a lightly floured surface and knead well for about 10 minutes, until smooth. Brush a bowl with oil. Shape the dough into a ball, place in the bowl and cover with a damp tea towel. Leave to rise in a warm place for 1 hour, until the dough has doubled in volume.

2. Oil a loaf tin. Turn out the dough onto a lightly floured surface and knead for 1 minute until smooth. Shape the dough the length of the tin and three times the width. Fold in three lengthways and place it in the tin with the join underneath. Cover and leave in a warm place for 30 minutes until it has risen above the tin. Preheat the oven to 220°C/425°F/Gas Mark 7. Bake the loaf in the preheated oven for 30 minutes, or until firm and golden brown and sounds hollow on the base when tapped. Transfer to a wire rack to cool.

#497 Poppy seed knots

Makes
16 rolls

Ingredients

2 tsp salt

500 g/1 lb 2 oz strong white flour

1½ tsp easy-blend dried yeast

2 tbsp olive oil, plus extra
for greasing

300 ml/10 fl oz lukewarm water

1 tsp poppy seeds

1. Place the salt in a mixing bowl and sift in the flour. Add the yeast and make a small well in the top. Pour the oil and water into the dry ingredients and mix to form a dough. Knead the dough on a lightly oiled surface for about 10 minutes, or until you have a smooth, elastic texture.

2. Transfer the dough to an oiled bowl, cover and set aside to rise in a warm place for about 45 minutes, or until the dough has doubled in size. Grease a baking tray with oil. Knead the dough until it has returned to its original volume, then divide into 16 pieces and roll each into a 20-cm/8-inch-long sausage shape. Tie each sausage into a knot. Transfer the rolls to the prepared baking tray, cover and set aside to rise in a warm place for about 30 minutes.

3. Meanwhile, preheat the oven to 200°C/400°F/Gas Mark 6 and lightly grease a baking tray. Scatter the poppy seed over the rolls and bake in the preheated oven for 18–20 minutes, until golden. Transfer to a wire rack to cool.

#498 Southern spoon bread

Serves
6–8

Ingredients

3 tbsp unsalted butter or margarine, plus extra for greasing

450 ml/16 fl oz milk

½ tsp salt

135 g/4¾ oz cornmeal

175 ml/6 fl oz water

3 eggs, separated

1. Preheat the oven to 190°C/375°F/Gas Mark 5. Grease a large, ovenproof casserole. Combine the milk, butter and salt in a medium-sized saucepan over a medium heat and bring to the boil. Gradually add the cornmeal, stirring constantly with a wire whisk. Remove from the heat. Gradually add the water, stirring well. Pour into a mixing bowl.

2. Beat the egg yolks until thick and lemon-coloured. Stir one quarter of the hot mixture into the yolks, then return to the bowl with the remaining hot mixture, stirring constantly.

3. Whisk the egg whites until they hold stiff peaks, then gently fold into the cornmeal mixture with a wire whisk. Pour the mixture into the prepared casserole and bake in the preheated oven, uncovered, for 30 minutes, or until a knife inserted in the centre comes out clean. Serve immediately.

#499 Roasted pepper & garlic focaccia

Serves 6–8

Ingredients

500 g/1 lb 2 oz strong white flour, plus extra for dusting

1½ tsp salt

1 sachet easy-blend dried yeast

350 ml/12 fl oz lukewarm water

4 tbsp olive oil, plus extra for greasing

1 red pepper, halved and deseeded

3 garlic cloves, unpeeled

1. Preheat the oven to 240°C/475°F/Gas Mark 9. Grease a baking sheet. Put the flour and salt into a mixing bowl and stir in the yeast. Add the water and 3 tablespoons of the oil and mix to a soft dough. Turn out the dough onto a lightly floured surface and knead until smooth. Return to the bowl, cover and leave in a warm place for 30 minutes.

2. Meanwhile, place the red pepper cut side down on a baking sheet, add the garlic and roast in the preheated oven for 20 minutes, until the skins are charred. Remove from the oven. Do not switch off the oven. Peel the pepper and cut it into strips. Squeeze out the garlic flesh and chop.

3. Turn out the dough onto a lightly floured surface and lightly knead until smooth. Roll out to a rectangle and press into the prepared sheet with your knuckles. Scatter the dough with the red peppers and garlic, pressing them into the dough. Cover and leave to rise in a warm place for about 1 hour, until doubled in size. Drizzle the remaining oil over the dough and bake for 20–25 minutes, until golden brown and firm. Turn out and leave to cool on a wire rack.

#500 Soda bread

Makes 1 loaf

Ingredients

2 tbsp each fennel, poppy, sunflower and pumpkin seeds

125 g/4½ oz wholemeal bread flour

250 g/9 oz strong white bread flour

40 g/1½ oz butter, plus extra for greasing

½ tsp caster sugar

1 tsp bicarbonate of soda

330 ml/11 fl oz buttermilk

1 tsp salt

1. Preheat the oven to 200°C/400°F/Gas Mark 6 and grease a baking tray. Mix all the seeds together in a small dish.

2. Place the wholemeal flour, white flour and butter in a mixing bowl. Rub in the butter until it resembles fine breadcrumbs. Add the remaining ingredients and two thirds of the seeds and mix to a dough.

3. Place the dough on the prepared tray, cover and leave to rest for 15 minutes. Use a sharp knife to score a cross in the top of the dough and scatter over the remaining seeds.

4. Bake in the preheated oven for 20–25 minutes, until golden. Transfer to a wire rack to cool.

Index